THE 1984
GUINNESS BOOK OF
OLYMPIC RECORDS

- Viewer's Guide to 1984's Winter and Summer Games
- New Photos of Winners in Action
- Dramatic and Fascinating Facts, Information and History
- 1984 Schedule of Events

Inside are more answers than you have questions!
Track and Field, Skiing, Hockey, Skating,
Basketball, Judo, Weightlifting, Boxing,
Wrestling, Swimming, Fencing, Cycling,
Yachting, and many, many more!

—PLUS—

A COMPLETE ROLL OF OLYMPIC MEDAL
WINNERS FROM 1896 THROUGH 1980!

Bantam Books in the Guinness Series

GUINNESS BOOK OF WORLD RECORDS
GUINNESS BOOK OF OLYMPIC RECORDS 1984

GUINNESS BOOK OF OLYMPIC RECORDS

COMPLETE ROLL OF
OLYMPIC MEDAL WINNERS (1896–1980,
including 1906) FOR THE 28 SPORTS (7 WINTER
and 21 SUMMER) CONTESTED IN THE
1980 CELEBRATIONS AND OTHER
USEFUL INFORMATION

Editors and Compilers

NORRIS McWHIRTER
(ROSS McWHIRTER 1964–1975)

Associate Editors
STAN GREENBERG
PETER MATTHEWS
STEPHEN TOPPING

BANTAM BOOKS
TORONTO · NEW YORK · LONDON · SYDNEY · AUCKLAND

PICTURE CREDITS

The editors and publisher wish to thank the following for pictures used in this book: Aitken Ltd.; Allsport Photographic; Associated Press; Canoeing Magazine; Central Press; Gerry Cranham; Tony Duffy; European Picture Union; Mary Evans; International News Photo; Keystone Press Agency; E.D. Lacey; London & Wide World Photos; Don Morley; Planet News; Radio Times Hulton Picture Library; Popperfoto; Sports and General Press Agency; United Press International; World Sports.

*This low-priced Bantam Book
has been completely reset in a type face
designed for easy reading, and was printed
from new plates. It contains the complete
text of the original hard-cover edition.*
NOT ONE WORD HAS BEEN OMITTED.

GUINNESS BOOK OF OLYMPIC RECORDS

*A Bantam Book / published by arrangement with
Sterling Publishing Co., Inc.*

PRINTING HISTORY

*Original Sterling edition published May 1964
2nd printing . . . August 1964
Revised edition / October 1975
Revised Bantam edition / June 1967
New Revised Bantam edition / December 1971
New Revised Bantam edition / February 1976
New Revised Bantam edition / November 1979
New Revised Bantam edition / December 1983*

Back cover photographs courtesy of Sports Illustrated

PRINTED IN THE UNITED STATES OF AMERICA

O   0 9 8 7 6 5 4

TABLE OF SUPERLATIVES

Most gold medals (men)	10	Ray Ewry (USA)	1900–1908
Most gold medals (women)	9	Larissa Latynina (URS)	1956–1964
Most medals (men)	15	Nikolai Andrianov (URS)	1972–1980
Most medals (women)	18	Larissa Latynina (URS)	1956–1964
Oldest gold medalist (men)	64 yr 258 days	Oscar Swahn (SWE)	1912
Oldest gold medalist (women)	45 yr 13 days	Liselott Linsenhoff (GER)	1972
Oldest medalist (men)	72 yr 280 days	Oscar Swahn (SWE)	1920
Oldest medalist (women)	45 yr 71 days	Ilona Elek (HUN)	1952
Youngest gold medalist (men)	7–10 yr	Unknown French boy	1900
Youngest gold medalist (women)	13 yr 267 days	Marjorie Gestring (USA)	1936
Youngest medalist (men)	7–10 yr	Unknown French boy	1900
Youngest medalist (women)	12 yr 24 days	Inge Sörensen (DEN)	1936
Most gold medals in one Games (men)	7	Mark Spitz (USA)	1972
Most gold medals in one Games (women)	4	Seven women	
Most medals in one Games (men)	8	Alexandr Dityatin (URS)	1980
Most medals in one Games (women)	7	Maria Gorochowskaya (URS)	1952
Most Games attended (men)	8	Raimondo d'Inzeo (ITA)	1948–1976
Most Games attended (women)	6	Janice York-Romary (USA)	1948–1968
	6	Lia Manoliu (ROM)	1952–1972
Longest span (men)	40 yr	Ivan Osiier (DEN)	1908–1948
	40 yr	Magnus Konow (NOR)	1908–1948
Longest span (women)	24 yr	Ellen Müller-Preis (AUT)	1932–1956
Oldest competitor (men)	72 yr 280 days	Oscar Swahn (SWE)	1920
Oldest competitor (women)	70 yr 5 days	Lorna Johnstone (GBR)	1972
Youngest competitor (men)	1–10 yr	Unknown French boy	1920
Youngest competitor (women)	11 yr 78 days	Cecilia Colledge (GBR)	1932

TABLE OF CONTENTS

TABLE OF MEDAL WINNERS
BY NATIONS 1896 TO 1980

Note: These totals include all first, second and third places including those in events no longer on the current schedule. (Not included are medals for the official Olympic art competitions of 1912 to 1948.) The 1906 Games which were officially staged by the International Olympic Committee have been included.

OLYMPIC GAMES (Summer)

		GOLD	SILVER	BRONZE	TOTAL
1.	U.S.A.	625	468	418	1,511
2.	U.S.S.R.	340	292	258	885
3.	Great Britain	163	201	176	540
4.	France	142	155	155	452
5.	Germany[1]	129	174	169	472
6.	Sweden	128	125	156	409
7.	Italy	127	111	108	346
8.	East Germany[2]	116	94	97	307
9.	Hungary	113	106	130	349
10.	Finland	92	72	102	266
11.	Japan	73	64	61	198
12.	Australia	64	53	70	187
13.	Czechoslovakia	42	45	47	134
14.	Switzerland	40	59	52	151
15.	Norway	39	30	31	100
16.	Poland	38	51	86	175
17.	Netherlands	36	43	52	134
18.	Belgium	34	47	38	119
19.	Denmark	31	54	49	134
20.	Rumania	28	37	59	124

1. Germany 1896–1964, West Germany from 1968
2. East Germany (GDR) from 1968

Development of the Olympic Games

These figures relate to the Summer Games and exclude Demonstration Sports.

	Countries Represented	Number of Sports	Number of Competitors Male	Female
1896	13	9	311	0
1900	22	17	1,319	11
1904	12	14	617	8
1906	20	11	877	7
1908	22	21	1,999	36
1912	28	14	2,490	57
1920	29	22	2,543	64
1924	44	18	2,956	136
1928	46	15	2,724	290
1932	37	15	1,281	127
1936	49	20	3,738	328
1948	59	18	3,714	385
1952	69	17	4,407	518
1956	71	17	2,958	384
1960	83	17	4,738	610
1964	93	19	4,457	683
1968	112	18	4,750	781
1972	122	21	6,077	1,070
1976	92	21	4,834	1,251
1980	81	21	4,265	1,088

For the Winter Olympics see tables on page 220

AUTHOR'S PREFACE

Students of the modern Olympic Games movement seem to be offered in existing books either a bare Roll of Champions since 1896, or else a highly detailed and expensive (and in the case of the earlier Games, very rare) report of a single celebration. We have attempted, in an inexpensive form and in as much detail as space permits, to set out *all* the medal winners of all time—that is, the holders of the gold, silver, and bronze awards for every event on the 1980 program.

The Olympics have many fascinations to those who follow them round the world for television, radio, or the press, but there are two peculiarities perhaps above all others.

First, the competitors themselves make friendships that will last for the rest of their lives. This happens despite the tendencies of some commentators to overemphasize any disagreement that inevitably occurs in such a highly charged competitive atmosphere. Occasionally there are even Olympic marriages. Olympic friendships, particularly notable since the custom started in 1932 of lodging the participants in an Olympic village, transcend the mere difficulties of conflicting language, race and creed. The Olympic spirit of common interest in the techniques of sport makes rather light of nationalistic differences, which so often leave professional diplomats in deadlock.

Secondly, especially in those sports that enjoy a dependence on absolute measurement of either time, distance, or weight to determine their results—such as track and field athletics, swimming, and weightlifting—the continuous urge to improve on previous high-water marks is most evident. It is practically a law of the Olympics that every record set in previous Games will be in great jeopardy when the next celebration takes place four years later.

This work has been again revised in the light of continuing research, including attention to the earlier Games. The leading authority is Erich Kamper whose *Enzyklopädie der Olympischen Spiele* (Römer, 1972) and *Lexikon der Olympischen Winter Spiele* (Union Verlag Stuttgart, 1964) should be recognized as the most complete text of Olympic results yet compiled of the first 18 Games.

NORRIS McWHIRTER

Celebrations of the
Modern Olympic Games

I	1896	Athens	April 6–15
II	1900	Paris	May 20–Oct. 28
III	1904	St. Louis	July 1–Nov. 23
*	1906	Athens	April 22–May 2
IV	1908	London	April 27–Oct. 31
V	1912	Stockholm	May 5–July 22
VI	1916	Berlin	not celebrated owing to war
VII	1920	Antwerp	April 20–Sept. 12
VIII	1924	Paris	May 4–July 27
IX	1928	Amsterdam	May 17–Aug. 12
X	1932	Los Angeles	July 30–Aug. 14
XI	1936	Berlin	Aug. 1–16
XII	1940	Tokyo, then Helsinki	not celebrated owing to war
XIII	1944	London	not celebrated owing to war
XIV	1948	London	July 29–Aug. 14
XV	1952	Helsinki	July 19–Aug. 3
XVI	1956	Melbourne[1]	Nov. 22–Dec. 8
XVII	1960	Rome	Aug. 25–Sept. 11
XVIII	1964	Tokyo	Oct. 10–24
XIX	1968	Mexico	Oct. 12–27
XX	1972	Munich	Aug. 26–Sept. 10
XXI	1976	Montreal	July 17–Aug. 1
XXII	1980	Moscow	July 19–Aug. 3
XXIII	1984	Los Angeles	July 28–Aug. 12
XXIV	1988	Seoul	Sept. 20–Oct. 5 (prov.)

* *This celebration (to mark the 10th anniversary of the modern Games) was officially intercalated but is not numbered.*
[1] *The equestrian events were held in Stockholm June 10–17, 1956.*

The Winter Olympic Games

I	1924	Chamonix, France	Jan. 25–Feb. 4
II	1928	St. Moritz, Switzerland	Feb. 11–19
III	1932	Lake Placid, U.S.A.	Feb. 4–15
IV	1936	Garmisch-Partenkirchen, Germany	Feb. 6–16
V	1948	St. Moritz, Switzerland	Jan. 30–Feb. 8
VI	1952	Oslo, Norway	Feb. 14–25
VII	1956	Cortina d'Ampezzo, Italy	Jan. 26–Feb. 5
VIII	1960	Squaw Valley, California	Feb. 18–28
IX	1964	Innsbrück, Austria	Jan. 29–Feb. 9
X	1968	Grenoble, France	Feb. 6–18
XI	1972	Sapporo, Japan	Feb. 3–13
XII	1976	Innsbrück, Austria[2]	Feb. 4–15
XIII	1980	Lake Placid, U.S.A.	Feb. 14–23
XIV	1984	Sarajevo, Yugoslavia	Feb. 8–19
XV	1988	Calgary, Canada	Feb. 23–March 6

[2] *Originally awarded to Denver, U.S.A.*

HISTORY OF THE OLYMPIC GAMES

1. THE ANCIENT GAMES

Few human institutions can even remotely approach the antiquity of the Olympic Games. Though precise records of the Ancient Games began only in 776 B.C., there is abundant evidence of their occasional celebration up to six centuries earlier. A date conservatively attributed to the Games at Olympia sponsored by Pelops is 1370 B.C. This date is, of course, subject to adjustment in the light of evidence of new archeological techniques. All the signs are, however, that Olympic history spans some thirty-three centuries.

The Olympic Games faded away about the middle of the 9th Century B.C., but were reputedly revived by King Iphitos of Elis. During this period came the idea of a temporary truce among all the warring factions in Greece: the Olympic peace or *ekecheiria* was proclaimed to last for about three months before the Games (which themselves lasted for five days) and long enough after them for the competitors to enjoy a safe passage back to their homes.

The Games of 776 B.C.—the first of which there is an actual record of the name of a champion—seem to have consisted of merely one event: the stadium race (about 170 meters or 186 yd.), won by Coroibos of Elis. But the Games rapidly expanded in scope—with longer races, plus a penthathlon of running, discus throwing (about 9lb *4kg* in weight), long jump with weights, javelin throwing with a lever, and wrestling; as well as boxing and wrestling. Moreover, the Greeks had to compete soon against the challenge of both Sicilians and Cretans.

Even in those days each celebration had its hero. There were winners of what would now be called the sprint double, there were heats for the shorter events, and eventually women had their own Games.

A famous champion, Chionis, in the middle of the 7th century B.C. is credited by modern researchers to have long jumped, almost certainly with the aid of dumb-bell weights, *7 m 05 cm* or 23 feet 1½ in.

From this time onwards, the names and feats of many champions are recorded and competitions in the fine arts were added.

The original prizes were only olive wreaths, but gradually the champions began to acquire valuable rewards and the Games became corrupted. The long Roll of Champions ends in A.D. 369, and in 393 the Emperor Theodosius decreed from Milan the end of the Olympic Games. So the Olympic torch went out for 1,503 summers.

2. THE MODERN (OR REVIVED) GAMES

The germ of the idea of reviving the Ancient Olympic Games was born in Germany. J. C. F. Guts-Muths (1759–1839), the founder of

Pierre, Baron de Coubertin (1863–1937), the founder of the Olympic movement, stated the ideals of the Modern Olympic Games that have inspired succeeding generations.

the notable German gymnastics movement, put forward the idea. Ernst Curtius (1814–96) gave a lecture on the Ancient Games in Berlin on January 10, 1852. His researches aroused interest in Greece where the wealthy Major Euangelis Zappas organized the first "Pan-Hellenic Games," in 1859 watched by 20,000 spectators. These games—a purely national affair—were repeated in 1870, 1875, 1888 and 1889. They at least kindled a spark of interest in other countries.

It is Baron Pierre de Coubertin (1863–1937) of France who is, however, rightly styled the "Founder of the Modern Olympic Games." This wealthy young nobleman was commissioned by the French Government in 1889 to study physical culture throughout the civilized world. His inquiries produced a disquieting picture of feuding and dissension between sport and sport, nation and nation, and the already apparent commercial spirit in sport.

On November 25, 1892, de Coubertin in a lecture at the Sorbonne in Paris for the first time publicly advanced his conviction that there should be a modern revival of the Ancient Games. His lecture was received with an ovation. In 1893, de Coubertin convened an international conference at the Hall of Sciences at the Sorbonne from June 16–23, 1894. Thirteen countries sent representatives and 21 others sent messages of support. On the last day a resolution was passed that "sport competitions should be held every fourth year on the lines of the Greek Olympic Games and every nation should be invited to participate."

De Coubertin envisaged the first Games being in Paris at the beginning of the century, but a Greek motion was passed giving the Greeks the privilege of holding the First Celebration at Athens in 1896. Accordingly, the International Olympic Committee (IOC)—then 12 strong—was formed.

1896—The Ist Games at Athens

On April 6, after a gap of 1,503 years 80,000 Athenians witnessed the revival of the Olympics.

Despite the support of 34 nations at the Paris Conference only 13 sent representatives to Athens. The white marble stadium was a splendid sight, but too long and narrow for track events. The small American team won 9 out of the 12 track and field events, while the Germans dominated the gymnastics, and the French the cycling. The Greeks became depressed as the titles, even those which they regarded as their national specialties, such as the discus throw, were won by foreigners. Happily, the last event—the Marathon—(24 miles 1503 yd *40 km*) was dramatically won by Spyridon Louis, a post office messenger from Marusi near Athens, one of 21 Greek starters.

1900—The IInd Games at Paris

It was feared that the Second Games would rival the World Exhibition in Paris in the same year, so de Coubertin was subdued and the Games were allowed to be nothing more than a sideshow. Another factor that reduced interest was that the Games in the Bois de Boulogne, Paris, were spread over more than five months. Despite these drawbacks, the standards shot up and quite a few world best performances were set. The hero of the Games was Alvin Kraenzlein (U.S.A.) who won the 60 meters, 100 meters hurdles, 200 meters hurdles, and long jump.

1904—The IIIrd Games at St. Louis

Again the Olympics were organized as a mere sideshow to a World's Fair. Because of the distance and expense of travel, only seven European and five other countries were represented. Interest in the 85 Olympic events was minimal: the record crowd was 2,000.

Despite the rather crude facilities, mostly at Washington University, the competitive spirit and advancing skill of the contestants—the golden thread of the whole Olympic tapestry—was undiminished. There was a major scandal in the Marathon when an American (Lorz) got a clandestine 10 mile lift in a car in the middle section of the race and naturally arrived in the Stadium first. When the truth dawned, wild applause soon thinned to vituperative abuse and immediate expulsion.

1906—The Intercalated Games at Athens

These Games were to mark the tenth anniversary of the Ist Games at Athens in 1896.

They were in no sense unofficial—the International Olympic Committee sanctioned them—but they were unnumbered because they did not conform to the regular Olympic four-year cycle.

The Games were far more successful than the Exhibition sideshow type of Games in 1900 or 1904. Twenty nations were represented by 884 competitors. Great crowds, including a galaxy of royalty, thronged to the marble stadium.

There were 11 sports including 22 track and field, 16 shooting and 8 fencing events.

The individual hero was Paul H. Pilgrim (U.S.A.) who financed his own journey to Athens and won the 400 and 800 meters double.

Reginald Walker turned in a time under 11 seconds in the 100 meters event at the 1908 Games.

1908—The IVth Games at London

Italy was originally awarded the IVth Games but resigned them and London took on the job. With the White City Stadium that could hold 100,000, full royal patronage, a vast schedule, good publicity, and 2,035 competitors from 22 nations, the Olympics at last broke through as a world event.

The two most memorable incidents were in the track and field athletics, and both sadly involved disqualification. There was an unfortunate rumpus over the 400 meters final in which the U.S. runner Carpenter was disqualified for obstruction. His compatriots Robbin and Taylor then scratched in protest, so the only remaining competitor, Lt. Wyndham Halswell (G.B.), had a 50.0 sec. walk-over for the gold medal.

The marathon from Windsor to the Stadium was watched by the then world's largest recorded sports crowd—an estimated 250,000 people. The leader, a frail looking little Italian, Dorando Pietri, tottered into the Stadium in the last stages of exhaustion. Harassed officials aided him when he fell for a second time, so he had to be disqualified for receiving aid, and the race went to the U.S. runner Johnny Hayes, who took the gold medal while Pietri got a gold cup from a sympathetic Queen Alexandra.

1912—The Vth Games at Stockholm

Following the success of the London Games, this celebration at Stockholm confirmed and cemented worldwide interest in the Olympics. The number of participants rose to 2,547, drawn from 28 countries. The hero of the Games was the American Indian, Jim Thorpe, who won both the pentathlon and the decathlon. Thorpe was later discovered by the A.A.U. to have rather thoughtlessly transgressed their amateur rules by earlier acceptance of payment for some minor baseball appearances. Inevitably he was struck off the Roll of Champions and his two gold medals were re-awarded to his runners-up. But he was reinstated as an amateur in 1973 by the A.A.U. twenty years after his death.

1916—The VIth Games, awarded to Berlin
Owing to the World War which developed following Germany's invasion of Belgium and part of France, in August, 1914, the Games inevitably had to be cancelled.

1920—The VIIth Games at Antwerp
The Olympics were resumed at Antwerp but were without any representation from the defeated central European countries or the Russians, who remained absent until 1952. The Games were highly successful, with the Finns challenging even the Americans in the track events.

Forty years elapsed between the appearance of Czarist Russia's last Olympic team in 1912, shown above, and the first Soviet team in 1952.

1924—The VIIIth Games at Paris
The Olympic Games again leapt forward in growth—44 countries entered 3,092 competitors. The Finn, Paavo Nurmi, won 5 gold medals—for the 1,500 meters, 5,000 meters, 10,000 meters cross-country race (both team and individual), and the 3,000 meters team event. The American, Johnny Weissmuller, later to be the most famous of Hollywood's dynasty of Tarzans, won 3 gold medals for sprint swimming.

1928—The IXth Games at Amsterdam
At Amsterdam the Germans reappeared. Olympic medals tended to be more widely distributed among the nations. The Finns were again dominant in distance running, but this time Nurmi won only

the 10,000 meters. Weissmuller won two more swimming gold medals. Women's events were successfully introduced in track and field with world records being set in all five events.

1932—The Xth Games at Los Angeles

Under the famous sunny California climatic conditions a profusion of Olympic and world records were set. Every single track and field Olympic record, except the long jump, was improved. America's black sprinters and jumpers excelled while the Japanese collected five gold medals in the men's swimming events. It was wrongly predicted that records made under these "freak California conditions" would remain unbroken for years.

1936—The XIth Games at Berlin

At Berlin the Nazi government of Germany disgracefully attempted to turn the Olympic movement into a propaganda vehicle for the glorification of their creed. The strong internationalism of the Games prevented complete subversion. The levels of performance in most events left many of the 1932 "super-records" well behind, against all prediction. The hero of the Games was the modest American Jesse Owens, who won the 100 meters, 200 meters, 4 × 100 meters relay, and the long jump. The Japanese marathon runners (gold and bronze medals) and the Dutch women swimmers made a strong impression.

Paavo Nurmi, the Flying Finn, is the most successful medal winner in Olympic track and field history, with 9 gold and 3 silver medals in the 1920, 1924, and 1928 Games.

The Olympic flame was lit in Berlin's opening ceremony in 1936—the first
time the torch relay was part of the Olympic rites.

1940–44—The XIIth Games, awarded to Tokyo and then Helsinki; the XIIIth Games awarded to London

Neither of these two celebrations could be held because of the
World War. The 1940 Games were originally awarded to Tokyo but
when the Japanese became involved in war with China, they were
re-awarded to Helsinki. The 1944 Games were hopefully given to
London but the war still had a year to run.

1948—The XIVth Games at London

London and the Wembley Stadium attracted 4,099 competitors
from 59 countries. For the first time a woman became the Victrix
Ludorum and Mvr. Fanny Blankers-Koen, the mother of two children,
won the 100 meters, 200 meters, 80 meter hurdles, and the 4 × 100
meters relay for the Netherlands. Other athletes who attracted great
interest were Harrison Dillard (U.S.) in the 100 meters and 4 × 100
meters relay; Emil Zatopek (Czechoslovakia) in the 10,000 meters;
Bob Mathias (U.S.) in the decathlon; and Willi Grut (Sweden) in
the modern pentathlon.

1952—The XVth Games at Helsinki

Sixty-nine nations and 4,925 competitors came to the Finnish capi-
tal city, Helsinki (population 350,000) in 1952. The Games were
notable for the reappearance of the Russians after an absence of 40
years. The undoubted heroes of the Games were the Zatopeks of
Czechoslovakia. Emil won the unprecedented triple—the 5,000 meters,
10,000 meters, and the marathon—all in Olympic record time. On
the day he won the 5,000 meters, his wife, Dana, won the women's
javelin throwing title, also with an Olympic record.

1956—The XVIth Games at Melbourne

The Games were celebrated in the Southern Hemisphere for the
first and so far only time. Inevitably, the difficulties of season,

distances, and expense reduced the entries, but only slightly. The equestrian events had to be held separately in Stockholm because of rigid horse quarantine laws in Australia. Outstanding on the track was Vladimir Kuts (U.S.S.R.) with a great 5,000 meters and 10,000 meters double victory; and the sprinters Bobby-Joe Morrow (U.S.) and Miss Betty Cuthbert of Australia, each of whom won three gold medals in the 100 meters, 200 meters and 4 × 100 meters relay. The Australians dominated the swimming, winning 8 out of 13 events.

1960—The XVIIth Games at Rome

Rome, which missed its opportunity of staging the Games in 1908, made a magnificent setting for the XVIIth Games. Eighty-three nations contributed 5,348 competitors to a fortnight of the most intense competition, for the most part in exceptionally hot conditions. Awards were widely spread with 23 countries gaining at least one gold medal. Outstanding achievements were the 1,500 meters world record by the Australian, Herbert Elliott, and the unexpected marathon success of the Ethiopian, Abebe Bikila. In the women's events, Miss Wilma Rudolph, a black American runner, dominated the sprints and won three gold medals. The Australians in equestrianism and the Russian girl gymnasts left a great impression.

1964—The XVIIIth Games at Tokyo

The first celebration in Asia was the organizational high-water mark of the Games, thanks to meticulous attention to detail by the Japanese. A conservative estimate is that the cost of all the public works and other expenses with a direct bearing on the Games was $560,000,000.

Vast crowds, undeterred by frequent rain, added atmosphere to a celebration in which Olympic records again fell wholesale, though, perhaps significantly, the number of world records set was fewer than in past Games. The highlights included the unique marathon double by Abebe Bikila (Ethiopia); a blazing finish in the 10,000 meters by Billy Mills (U.S.) with less than 1½ seconds between the three medalists; the four swimming gold medals won by Don Schollander (U.S.); and the third successive win in the 100 meters free-style by Dawn Fraser (Australia).

1968—XIXth Games at Mexico City

A record 5,531 competitors from one hundred and twelve nations did battle at nearly seven and a half thousand feet above sea level: these are the two salient figures to remember for the first Games in Latin America—the size and the height.

The technical organization in Mexico was excellent, while the brilliantly colorful fiesta atmosphere excused the few flaws in the ancillary arrangements for programs, information to the public, and transport.

Because nobody dropped dead it did not mean that the altitude problem was insignificant. Just as predicted the performances in the "explosive" events—memorably Bob Beamon's incredible long jump of 29 ft 2½ in (8,90 m)—were records, while those involving more than three minutes' continuous effort were in some cases back to standards achieved as long ago as 1948.

Bob Mathias (U.S.A) won the decathlon title in 1948 when he was only 17 years old. He successfully defended his crown at Helsinki in 1952—the only man ever to retain this championship.

Up 90 steps to the Olympic flame cauldron in 1968 in Mexico City ran the first woman to take the final pass of the torch and to light the Olympic flame.

Olga Korbut was the darling of the spectators at the Munich Games in 1972. The elfin Russian gymnast won a silver and 3 gold medals.

The opening ceremonies for the 1976 Games in Montreal, in which 6,189 athletes from 88 countries participated.

1972—XXth Games at Munich

West Germany's massive effort to provide perfect and efficient Olympic conditions was cruelly marred by the callous murder of 11 members of the Israeli team by Palestinian terrorists on September 5th.

The great show stumbled, some commentators mistakenly predicted the death of the whole Olympic movement. After a stunned 24-hour pause the Games started off again and the entire program was fulfilled.

The Olympics, which attracted over 4,000 "media men" and an estimated 1,000,000,000 world television viewership, had become an irresistible stage for murderous protesters. Obviously the Olympics were becoming too large but the IOC was finding it very difficult to hold the program to its present size.

The heroine of the Games was the diminutive Russian gymnast, Olga Korbut, who was the darling of the crowds and the despair of the judges. The male hero was the swimmer Mark Spitz (U.S.A) who won 7 gold medals each in a world record time.

In the stadium there were two sprint doubles by Valeriy Borzov (U.S.S.R.) and East Germany's Renate Stecher, but the greatest acclaim went rightly to Finland's Lasse Viren who won the 5,000 and 10,000 meters double. The almost traditional United States dominance suffered a partial eclipse and the termination of its famous pole-vault monopoly.

The Soviet team won ten more medals than the United States including 17 more golds than their traditional rivals. The efficiency of the U.S.S.R.'s deployment of their strength over the entire Olympic program certainly produced handsome dividends.

1976—XXIst Games at Montreal

The 1976 Games, the first in Canada, saw some substantial changes in the program but all attempts to reduce the number of events from the 1972 record of 195 were frustrated and in fact there were 198 Olympic titles open for competition.

The program changes included the elimination of the 50 kilometer walk, the tandem event, the slalom canoeing events, the free rifle event and three swimming events.

But the pruning was more than cancelled by the introduction of women's basketball, four canoeing events over 500 meters, women's handball and no less than seven new rowing events, six of them for women.

The run-up to the Games was beset by financial, constructional and political disputes. The excessive costs of the facilities, the industrial problems, and then the withdrawal of 22 Third World countries, mainly African, seemed destined to diminish the Games. However, once they were underway, the quality of performance was exceptionally high and provided, in the petite form of gymnast Nadia Comaneci of Romania, and the powerful Cuban runner, Alberto Juantorena, two athletes whose deeds will far outlive a single Olympiad.

1980—XXIInd Games at Moscow

There had been only a little dissent in 1974 when the IOC voted by a substantial majority to award the 1980 Games to Moscow. Tsarist

Russia had competed in 1900 and from 1906 to 1912. Athletes from Estonia and Latvia, which had been provinces of Russia prior to 1918 and were taken over by the Soviet Union in 1940, had competed independently from 1920 to 1936. The Soviet Union had entered the Games in force in 1952 and was now the second highest medal scorer of all time.

In December 1979 the Soviet Union invaded Afghanistan, and much of the non-Communist world, led by the United States, tried to impose a boycott on the Games—but not, it should be noted, on trade and other economic activity. Not all countries supported the boycott, although sports within those countries sometimes did. It is difficult to finalize a list of those who did not go to Moscow in support of the boycott, as a number of those previously included were unlikely to attend anyway for other, usually financial, reasons. The most reliable estimate is 45–50, of which the most important in sporting terms were the United States, the Federal Republic of (West) Germany, and Japan. When the Games were officially opened by Leonid Brezhnev, President of the U.S.S.R., there were eight first time entries to the Games, not including Zimbabwe which had previously been at the Olympics as Rhodesia.

Facilities, including the 103,000 capacity Lenin Stadium, were excellent and large crowds attended most sports. New competitions such as women's hockey, two extra judo classes, one extra weightlifting class, and reintroduced events brought the total of gold medals available to a record 203 (barring ties).

The heroine of Montreal, Nadia Comaneci (ROM) returned but was not the force she had been, and the star of the gymnastics was a male, Alexandr Ditiatin (URS). By winning three golds, four silvers and one bronze he set a record for the most medals ever won by a competitor, of any sport, in a single Games. He also was awarded a maximum 10.00 in the horse vault, the first such score ever to a man in the Olympics. His teammate Nikolai Andrianov brought his total of medals to a men's record 15, comprising seven golds, five silvers and three bronze, in three Games. This total has only ever been exceeded in Olympic history by Larissa Latynina (URS), also a gymnast.

1984—XXIIIrd Games at Los Angeles

The IOC awarded the Games of 1984 to Los Angeles only after involved negotiations about the financial guarantees usually required from the city hosting the Olympics. Various innovations to protect Los Angeles from a Montreal-like deficit have been tried, including widespread sponsorship by private corporations.

The Los Angeles Memorial Coliseum, the site of the 1932 Games, will again be the main venue, but many new facilities are being built, including a velodrome for cycling and a swimming and diving stadium. Halls and stadia in the many major universities in the Los Angeles area will be used for most other sports. Yachting will be at Long Beach, and rowing and canoeing on Lake Casitas. The Coliseum, which has not been used for track and field meetings since 1974, will be fully refurbished and a new synthetic surface will be laid on the track and jump areas. Seating capacity is currently 92,604.

A number of new events have been added to the 1984 program. Women's cycling will make its debut with a road race, and rhythmic gymnastics will be represented by a single event. In the swimming pool three events, comprising the 200m medley for men and women, and the men's 4 × 100m freestyle, will be reinstated, and a synchronized swimming (duet) competition will be added. Three shooting events (pistol, air rifle, and standard rifle) for women make their debut, and board sailing (commonly but incorrectly called windsurfing) has been added to the yachting program. Track and field has been extended by the inclusion of 3000m, 400m hurdles, and marathon races for women. In total there will be record 215 official events plus a demonstration of baseball. It has been estimated that there will be a television audience of 2½ billion for these Games.

Official Olympic International Abbreviations of Names of Countries

AFG — Afghanistan
AHO — Netherlands Antilles
ALB — Albania
ALG — Algeria
AND — Andorra
ANG — Angola
ANT — Antigua
ARG — Argentina
ARS — Saudi Arabia
AUS — Australia
AUT — Austria
BAH — Bahamas
BAN — Bangladesh
BAR — Barbados
BEL — Belgium
BEN — Benin
BER — Bermuda
BIR — Burma
BIZ — Belize
BOH — Bohemia
BOL — Bolivia
BOT — Botswana
BRA — Brazil
BRN — Bahrain
BUL — Bulgaria
BWI — British West Indies
CAF — Central Africa
CAN — Canada
CAY — Cayman Islands
CEY — Ceylon (now Sri Lanka)
CGO — Congo
CHA — Chad
CHI — Chile
CHN — China
CIV — Ivory Coast
CMR — Cameroun
COL — Columbia
CRC — Costa Rica
CUB — Cuba
CYP — Cyprus
DAH — Dahomey
DEN — Denmark
DOM — Dominican Republic
ECU — Ecuador
EGY — Egypt
ESA — El Salvador
ESP — Spain
EST — Estonia
ETH — Ethiopia
FIJ — Fiji Islands
FIN — Finland
FRA — France
GAB — Gabon
GBR — United Kingdom
GDR — German Democratic Republic
GER — Germany (but West Germany only from 1968)
GHA — Ghana
GRE — Greece
GUA — Guatemala
GUI — Guinea
GUY — Guyana
HAI — Haiti

HBR — British Honduras
HKG — Hong Kong
HOL — Netherlands
HON — Honduras
HUN — Hungary
INA — Indonesia
IND — India
IRL — Ireland
IRN — Iran
IRQ — Iraq
ISL — Iceland
ISR — Israel
ISV — Virgin Islands
ITA — Italy
JAM — Jamaica
JOR — Jordan
JPN — Japan
KEN — Kenya
KHM — Cambodia
KOR — Korea
KUW — Kuwait
LAO — Laos
LAT — Latvia
LBA — Libya
LBR — Liberia
LES — Lesotho
LIB — Lebanon
LIE — Liechtenstein
LIT — Lithuania
LUX — Luxembourg
MAD — Madagascar
MAL — Malaysia
MAR — Morocco
MAW — Malawi
MEX — Mexico
MGL — Mongolia
MLI — Mali
MLT — Malta
MON — Monaco
MOZ — Mozambique
MRI — Mauritius
MTN — Mauritania
NCA — Nicaragua
NEP — Nepal
NGR — Nigeria
NGU — Papua New Guinea
NIG — Niger
NOR — Norway
NZL — New Zealand
PAK — Pakistan
PAN — Panama
PAR — Paraguay
PER — Peru
PHI — Philippines
POL — Poland
POR — Portugal
PRK — Dem. People's Rep. of Korea
PUR — Puerto Rico
QAT — Qatar
RHO — Rhodesia (now Zimbabwe)
ROC — Republic of China
ROM — Rumania
SAF — South Africa

SAU	— Saudi Arabia	TOG	— Togo
SEN	— Senegal	TPE	— Taiwan
SEY	— Seychelles	TRI	— Trinidad and Tobago
SIN	— Singapore	TUN	— Tunisia
SLE	— Sierra Leone	TUR	— Turkey
SMR	— San Marino	UAE	— United Arab Emirates
SOM	— Somali Republic	UGA	— Uganda
SRI	— Sri Lanka	URS	— U.S.S.R.
SUD	— Sudan	URU	— Uruguay
SUI	— Switzerland	USA	— United States of America
SUR	— Surinam	VEN	— Venezuela
SWE	— Sweden	VIE	— Vietnam
SWZ	— Swaziland	VOL	— Upper Volta
SYR	— Syria	YUG	— Yugoslavia
TAN	— Tanzania	ZAM	— Zambia
TCH	— Czechoslovakia	ZAI	— Zaire
THA	— Thailand	ZIM	— Zimbabwe

ROLL OF OLYMPIC MEDAL WINNERS SINCE 1896 IN THE 21 CURRENT SPORTS

*throughout indicates an Olympic record or best performance.
d.n.a. indicates data not available.

1. Archery

MEN'S DOUBLE F.I.T.A. ROUND

(2 × 36 arrows at 90, 70, 50 and 30 meters. Possible is 2,880 points.)

	GOLD	SILVER	BRONZE
1972	John C. Williams (USA) 2,528	Gunnar Jarvil (SWE) 2,481	Kyoesti Laasonen (FIN) 2,467
1976	Darrell Place (USA) 2,571*	Hiroshi Michinaga (JPN) 2,502	Giancarlo Ferrari (ITA) 2,495
1980	Tomi Polkolainen (FIN) 2,455	Boris Isachenko (URS) 2,452	Giancarlo Ferrari (ITA) 2,449

WOMEN'S DOUBLE F.I.T.A. ROUND

(2 × 36 arrows at 70, 60, 50 and 30 meters. Possible is 2,880 points)

1972	Doreen Wilbur (USA) 2,424	Irena Szydlwska (POL) 2,407	Emma Gapchenko (URS) 2,403
1976	Luann Ryon (USA) 2,499*	Valentina Kovpan (URS) 2,460	Zebiniso Rustamova (URS) 2,407
1980	Keto Losaberidze (URS) 2,491	Natalya Butuzova (URS) 2,477	Paivi Meriluoto (FIN) 2,449

(Archery was included in the Games of 1900, 1904, 1908 and 1920. But none of the events in those celebrations compare with the championship events of 1972–80.)

Action in the 1948 basketball finals between the United States (in white) and France. From the introduction of the sport in the Olympic program in 1936 to the disputed title of 1972, the U.S.A. never lost a single Olympic match.

2. Basketball (Men)

GOLD	SILVER	BRONZE
1896–1932 Event not held[1]		
1936 UNITED STATES	CANADA	MEXICO
Francis Johnson	James Stewart	Carlos Borja Morco
Carl S. Knowles	Jan Allison	Victor H. Borja Morco
Joe Fortenberry	Charles Chapman	Luis I. de la Vega Leija
William Wheatly	Malcolm Wiseman	José Pamplona
Jack W. Ragland	Gordon Aitchison	Lecuanda
Ralph Bishop	Douglas Peden	Rodolfo Choperanna
Carl Shy	Arthur Chapman	Irizarri
Duane A. Swanson	Irving Meretsky	Jesus Olmos Moreno
Samuel Balter	Edward J. Dawson	Raul Fernández Robert
John H. Gibbons		Greer Skousen
Frank J. Lubin		Spilsbury
Arthur O. Mollner		Francisco Martinez
Donald A. Piper		Cordero
Willard Schmidt		Silvio Hernandez del
		Valle
		Andrés Gómez
		Domingues

---

[1] There were basketball competitions in the 1904 and 1928 Games, but they were only demonstration events.

	GOLD	SILVER	BRONZE
1948	**UNITED STATES** Clifford Barker Donald Barksdale Ralph Beard Louis Beck Vincent Boryla Gordon Carpenter Alexander Groza Wallace Jones Robert Kurland Raymond Lumpp Robert C. Pitts Jesse Renick R. Jackie Robinson Kenneth Rollins	**FRANCE** André Barrais Michel Bonnevie André Buffière René Chocat René Dérency Maurice Desaymonnet André Even Fernand Guillou Maurice Girardot Raymond Offner Jacques Perrier Yvan Quénin Lucien Rebuffic Pierre Thiolon	**BRAZIL** Zenny de Azevedo João F. Braz Marcus V. Dias Alfonso A. Evora Ruy de Freitas Alexandre Gemignani Alberto Marson Alfredo R. da Mota Nilton P. de Oliveira Massinet Sorcinelli
1952	**UNITED STATES** Charles Hoag William Hougland John Keller M. Dean Kelley Robert Kenney William Lienhard Clyde Lovelette Marcus Frieberger V. Wayne Glasgow Frank McCabe Daniel Pippin Howard Williams Ronald Bontemps Robert Kurland	**U.S.S.R.** Viktor Vlassov Styapas Butautas Yvan Lysov Kazis Petkyavitschus Nodar Dzhordzhikiya Anatoliy Konyev Otar Korkiya Ilmar Kullam Yuriy Ozerov Aleksandr Moiseyev Heino Kruus Yustinas Lagunavichus Maigonis Valdmanis Stassis Stonkus	**URUGUAY** Martin Acosta y Lara Enrique Boliño Victorio Cieslinkas Héctor Costa Nelson Demarco Héctor Garcia Otero Tabaré Larre Borges Adesio Lombardo Roberto Lovera Sergio Matto Wilfredo Pelaez Carlos Roselló
1956	**UNITED STATES** Carl C. Cain William Hougland K. C. Jones William Russell James P. Walsh William Evans Burdette Haldorson Ronald Tomsic Richard J. Boushka Gilbert Ford Robert E. Jeangerard Charles F. Darling	**U.S.S.R.** Valdis Muizhnieks Maigonis Valdmanis Vladimir Torban Stassis Stonkus Kazis Petkyavitschus Arkhadiy Bochkaryev Yanis Kruminsch Mikhail Semyonov Alguirdas Lauritenas Yuriy Ozerov Viktor Zoubkov Mikhail Studenetskiy	**URUGUAY** Carlos Blixen Ramiro Cortes Héctor Costa Nelson Chelle Nelson Demarco Héctor Garcia Otero Carlos Gonzalez Sergio Matto Oscar Moglia Raúl Mera Ariel Olascoaga Milton Scarón

1960	**UNITED STATES**
	Jerry West
	Walter Bellamy
	Robert Boozer
	Terry Dischinger
	Burdette Haldorson
	Darrall Imhoff
	Allen Kelley
	Lester Lane
	Jerry Lucas
	Adrian Smith
	Jay Arnette
	Oscar Robertson
		U.S.S.R.
		Valdis Muizhnieks
		Maigonis Valdmanis
		Tsezars Ozers
		Guram Minashvili
		Viktor Zoubkov
		Vladimir Ugrekhelidze
		Yanis Kruminsch
		Mikhail Semyonov
		Yuriy Korneyev
		Aleksandr Petrov
		Albert Valtin
		Gennady Volnov
			BRAZIL
			Zenny de Azevedo
			Amaury A. Pasos
			Wlamir Marques
			Moyses Blas
			Carlos Domingos
			       Massoni
			Fernando Pereira
			      de Freitas
			Carmo de Souza
			Jatyr E. Schall
			Edson Bispo dos Santos
			Antônio Salvador Sucar
			Waldyr Geraldo
			      Boccardo
			Waldemar Blatkauskas

GOLD	SILVER	BRONZE
1964 UNITED STATES	**U.S.S.R.**	**BRAZIL**
Jim Barnes	Valdis Muizhnieks	Amaury A. Pasos
William Bradley	Nikolay Bagley	Wlamir Marques
Lawrence Brown	Armenak Alachachian	Ubiratan P. Maciel
Joe Caldwell	Aleksandr Travin	Carlos Domingos
Mel Counts	Vyacheslav Khrynin	Massoni
Richard Davies	Yanis Kruminsch	Friedrich Wilhelm Brauñ
Walter Hazzard	Levan Mosheshvili	Carmo de Souza
Lucius Jackson	Yuriy Korneyev	Jatyr E. Schall
John McCaffrey	Aleksandr Petrov	Edson Bispo dos Santos
Jeffrey Mullins	Gennady Volnov	Antônio Salvador Sucar
Jerry Shipp	Yaak Lipso	Victor Mirshawka
George Wilson	Yuris Kalninsh	Sergio de Toledo
		Machado
		José Edvar Simões
1968 UNITED STATES	**YUGOSLAVIA**	**U.S.S.R.**
Michael Barrett	Dragutin Čermac	Vladimir Andreyev
John Clawson	Krešimir Cosic	Sergei Belov
Donald Dee	Vladimir Cvetkovič	Vadim Kapranov
Calvin Fowler	Ivo Daneu	Sergei Kovalenko
Spencer Haywood	Radivoje Korač	Anatoly Krikun
William Hoskett	Zoran Maroevič	Yaak Lipso
James King	Nikola Plečas	Anatoly Polivoda
Glynn Saulters	Trajko Rajkovič	Modestas Paulauskas
Charles Scott	Dragoslav Raznatovič	Zurab Sakandelidze
Michael Silliman	Petar Skansi	Yuri Selikhov
Kenneth Spain	Damir Šolman	Priit Tomson
Joseph White	Aljoša Zorga	Gennady Volnov
1972 U.S.S.R.	**UNITED STATES**	**CUBA**
Anatoli Polivoda	Kenneth Davis	Juan Domecq
Modestas Paulauskas	Douglas Collins	Ruperto Herrera
Zurab Sakandelidze	Thomas Henderson	Juan Roca
Alshan	Michael Bantom	Pedro Chappe
Sharmukhamedov	Robert Jones	José M. Alvarez
Aleksander Boloshev	Dwight Jones	Rafael Camizares
Ivan Edeshko	James Forbes	Conrado Perez
Sergei Belov	James Brewer	Miguel Calderon
Mishako Korkia	Tommy Burleson	Tomas Herrera
Yvan Dvorni	Thomas McMillen	Oscar Varona
Gennadi Volnov	Kevin Joyce	Alejandro Urgelles
Aleksander Belov	Ed Ratleff	Franklin Standard
Sergei Kovalenko	Henry Iba	Juan C. Ortega
Vladimir Kondrashin		
1976 UNITED STATES	**YUGOSLAVIA**	**U.S.S.R.**
Phil Ford	Blagoye Georgijevski	Vladimir Arzamaskov
Steve Sheppard	Dragan Kicanovic	Alexandr Salnikov
Adrian Dantley	Vinko Jelovac	Valeriy Miloserdov
Walter Davis	Rajko Zizic	Alshan Shamukhamedov
William Buckner	Zeljko Jerkov	Andrei Makeyev
Ernie Grunfeld	Andro Knego	Ivan Edeshko
Kenneth Carr	Zoran Slavnic	Sergei Belov
Scott May	Kresimir Cosic	Vladimir Tkachenko
Michel Armstrong	Damir Solman	Anatoli Mychkin
Thomas La Garde	Zarko Varajic	Mikhail Korkiya
Philip Hubbard	Drazen Dalipagic	Aleksander Belov
Mitchell Kupchak	Mirza Delibasic	Vladimir Zhigiliy

The 1972 U.S. basketball squad (dark uniforms), seen here against Brazil, lost to the U.S.S.R. in a highly controversial final match.

	GOLD	SILVER	BRONZE
1980	**YUGOSLAVIA**	**ITALY**	**U.S.S.R.**
	Andro Knego	Romeo Sacchetti	Stanislav Yeremin
	Dragan Kicanovic	Roberto Brunamonti	Valeriy Miloserdov
	Rajko Zizic	Michael Sylvester	Sergey Tarakanov
	Minovil Nakic	Enrico Gilardi	Aleksandr Salnikov
	Zeljko Jerkov	Fabizio Della Fiori	Andrei Lopatov
	Branko Skroce	Marco Solfrini	Nikolai Deryugin
	Zoran Slavnic	Marco Bonamico	Sergei Belov
	Kresimir Cosic	Dino Meneghin	Vladimir Tkachenko
	Ratko Radovanovic	Renato Villalta	Anatoliy Mishkin
	Duje Krstulovic	Renzo Vecchaito	Sergey Yovaysha
	Drazen Dalipagic	Pier Luigi Marzorati	Aleksandr Belostenny
	Mirza Delibasic	Pietro Generali	Vladimir Shigili

Basketball (Women)

1896–1972	Event not held		
1976	**U.S.S.R.**	**UNITED STATES**	**BULGARIA**
	Angele Rupshene	Cindy Brogdon	Nadka Goltcheva
	Tatyana Zakharova	Susan Rojcewicz	Penka Methodieva
	Raisa Kurvyakova	Ann Meyers	Petkana Makaveyeva
	Olga Barisheva	Lusia Harris	Snejana Mikhailova
	Tatyana Ovetchkina	Nancy Dunkle	Krassim Guiourova
	Nadyezhda Shuvayeva	Charlotte Lewis	Krassim Bogdanova
	Iuliyana Semenova	Nancy Lieberman	Todorka Yardanova
	Nadyezhda Zakharova	Gail Marquis	Diana Dilova
	Nelli Feryabnikova	Patricia Roberts	Margari Shtarkelova
	Olga Sukharnova	Mary Anne O'Connor	Maria Stoyanova
	Tamara Daunene	Patricia Head	Guirgui Skerlatova
	Natalia Klimova	Juliene Simpson	Penka Stoyanova

GOLD	SILVER	BRONZE
1980 U.S.S.R.	BULGARIA	YUGOSLAVIA
Angele Rupshene	Nadka Goltcheva	Vera Djuraskovic
Lubov Sharmay	Penka Methodieva	Mersada Berhirspahic
Vida Besselene	Petkana Makaveyeva	Jelica Komnenovic
Olga Korosteleva	Snejana Mikhailova	Mir Bjedov
Tatiana Ovechkina	Vania Dermenoyieva	Vukica Mitic
Nadezda Olkhova	Krassim Bogdanova	Sanja Ozegovic
Iuliana Semenova	Angelina Mikhailova	Sofija Pekic
Ludmila Rogozina	Diana Brainova	Marija Tonkovic
Nelly Feriabnikova	Evladia Slavcheva	Zorica Djurkovic
Olga Sukharnova	Kostadinka Radkova	Vesna Despotovic
Tatiana Nadyrova	Silvia Ghermanova	Biljana Majstorovic
Tatiana Ivinskaya	Penka Stoyanova	Jasmina Perazic

---

3. Boxing

From 1952 each losing semi-finalist was awarded a bronze medal.

LIGHT FLYWEIGHT
Weight up to *48 kg* 105.8 lb

1896–1964 Event not held		
1968 Francisco Rodriguez (VEN)	Yong-ju jee (KOR)	Harlan Marbley (USA)
		Hubert Skrzypczak (POL)
1972 Gyoergy Gedo (HUN)	U. Gil Kim (PRK)	Ralph Evans (GBR)
		Enrique Rodriguez (ESP)
1976 Jorge Hernandez (CUB)	Byong Uk Li (PRK)	Payao Pooltarat (THA)
1980 Shamil Sabyrov (URS)	Hipolito Ramos (CUB)	Byong Uk Li (PRK)
		Ismail Moustafov (BUL)

FLYWEIGHT

From 1948 the weight limit has been *51 kg* 112½ lb. In 1904 it was 105 lb *47,6 kg*. From 1920–1936 it was 112 lb *50,8 kg*.

1896–1900 Event not held		
1904 George Finnegan (USA)	Miles Burke (USA)	d.n.a.
1906–1912 Event not held		
1920 Frank De Genaro (USA)	Anders Petersen (DEN)	William Cuthbertson (GBR)
1924 Fidel LaBarba (USA)	James McKenzie (GBR)	Raymond Fee (USA)
1928 Antal Kocsis (HUN)	Armand Appel (FRA)	Carlo Cavagnoli (ITA)
1932 István Énekes (HUN)	Francisco Cabañas (MEX)	Louis Salica (USA)

GOLD	SILVER	BRONZE
1936 Willi Kaiser (GER)	Gavino Matta (ITA)	Louis D. Lauric (USA)
1948 Pascual Perez (ARG)	Spartaco Bandinelli (ITA)	Soo-Ann Han (KOR)
1952 Nathan Brooks (USA)	Edgar Basel (GER)	Anatoliy Bulakov (URS) William Toweel (SAF)
1956 Terence Spinks (GBR)	Mircea Dobrescu (ROM)	John Caldwell (IRL) René Libeer (FRA)
1960 Gyula Török (HUN)	Sergey Sivko (URS)	Kiyoshi Tanabe (JPN) Abdelmoneim Elguindi (EGY)
1964 Fernando Atzori (ITA)	Artur Olech (POL)	Robert Carmody (USA) Stanislav Sorokin (URS)
1968 Ricardo Delgado (MEX)	Artur Olech (POL)	Servilio Oliveira (BRA) Leo Rwabwogo (UGA)
1972 Gheorghi Kostadinov (BUL)	Leo Rwabwogo (UGA)	Leszek Blazynski (POL) Douglas Rodriguez (CUB)
1976 Leo Randolph (USA)	Ramon Duvalon (CUB)	Leszek Blazynski (POL) David Torosyan (URS)
1980 Petar Lessov (BUL)	Viktor Miroshnickenko (URS)	Hugh Russell (IRL) Janos Varadi (HUN)

Willi Kaiser (GER), the winner of the flyweight championship at the Berlin Games in 1936, rests in his corner between rounds.

BANTAMWEIGHT

From 1948 the weight limit has been *54 kg* 119 lb. In 1904 it was 115 lb *52,16 kg*. In 1908 it was 116 lb *52,62 kg*. From 1920 to 1936 118 lb *53,52 kg*.

	GOLD	SILVER	BRONZE
1896–1900	Event not held		
1904	Oliver L. Kirk (USA)	George Finnegan (USA)	d.n.a.
1906	Event not held		
1908	A. H. Thomas (GBR)	John Condon (GBR)	W. Webb (GBR)
1912	Event not held		
1920	Clarence Walker (SAF)	Christopher J. Graham (CAN)	James McKenzie (GBR)
1924	William Smith (SAF)	Salvatore Tripoli (USA)	Jean Ces (FRA)
1928	Vittorio Tamagnini (ITA)	John Daley (USA)	Harry Isaacs (SAF)
1932	Horace Gwynne (CAN)	Hans Ziglarski (GER)	José Villanueva (PHI)
1936	Ulderico Sergo (ITA)	Jack Wilson (USA)	Fidel Ortiz (MEX)
1948	Tibor Csik (HUN)	Giovanni B. Zuddas (ITA)	Juan Venegas (PUR)
1952	Pentti Hämäläinen (FIN)	John McNally (IRL)	Gennadiy Garbuzov (URS) Joon-Ho Kang (KOR)
1956	Wolfgang Behrendt (GER)	Soon-Chun Song (KOR)	Frederick Gilroy (IRL) Claudio Barrientos (CHI)
1960	Olyeg Grigoryev (URS)	Primo Zamparini (ITA)	Brunoh Bendig (POL) Oliver Taylor (AUS)
1964	Takao Sakurai (JPN)	Shin Cho Chung (KOR)	Juan Fabila Mendoza (MEX) Washington Rodriguez (URU)
1968	Valeriy Sokolov (URS)	Eridadi Mukwanga (UGA)	Eiji Morioka (JPN) Kyou-Chull Chang (KOR)
1972	Orlando Martinez (CUB)	Alfonso Zamora (MEX)	George Turpin (GBR) Ricardo Carreras (USA)
1976	Yong Jo Gu (PRK)	Charles Mooney (USA)	Patrick Cowdell (GBR) Chulsoon Hwang (KOR)
1980	Juan Hernandez (CUB)	Bernardo Pinango (VEN)	Michael Anthony (GUY) Dumitru Cipere (ROM)

FEATHERWEIGHT

From 1952 the weight limit has been *57 kg* 126 lb. In 1904 it was 125 lb *56,70 kg*. From 1908 to 1936 it was 126 lb *57,15 kg*. In 1948 it was *58 kg* 127¾ lb.

	GOLD	SILVER	BRONZE
1896–1900	Event not held		
1904	Oliver L. Kirk (USA)	Frank Haller (USA)	d.n.a.
1906	Event not held		
1908	Richard Gunn (GBR)	C. W. Morris (GBR)	Hugh Roddin (GBR)
1912	Event not held		
1920	Paul Fritsch (FRA)	Jean Gachet (FRA)	Edoardo Garzena (ITA)
1924	John Fields (USA)	Joseph Salas (USA)	Pedro Quartucci (ARG)
1928	Lambertus van Klaveren (HOL)	Victor Peralta (ARG)	Harold Devine (USA)
1932	Carmelo Robledo (ARG)	Josef Schleinkofer (GER)	Carl Carlsson (SWE)
1936	Oscar Casanovas (ARG)	Charles Catterall (SAF)	Josef Miner (GER)
1948	Ernesto Formenti (ITA)	Denis Shepherd (SAF)	Aleksey Antkiewicz (POL)
1952	Jan Zachara (TCH)	Sergio Caprari (ITA)	Joseph Ventaja (FRA) Leonard Leisching (SAF)
1956	Vladimir Safronov (URS)	Thomas Nicholls (GBR)	Henryk Niedzwiedzki (POL) Pentti Hämäläinen (FIN)
1960	Francesco Musso (ITA)	Jerzy Adamski (POL)	William Meyers (SAF) Jorma Limmonen (FIN)
1964	Stanislav Stepashkin (URS)	Antony Villaneuva (PHI)	Charles Brown (USA) Heinz Schultz (GER)
1968	Antonio Roldan (MEX)	Albert Robinson (USA)	Philip Waruinge (KEN) Ivan Michailov (BUL)
1972	Boris Kousnetsov (URS)	Philip Waruinge (KEN)	Clemente Rojas (COL) András Botos (HUN)
1976	Angel Herrera (CUB)	Richard Nowakowski (GDR)	Juan Paredes (MEX) Leszek Kosedowski (POL)
1980	Rudi Fink (GDR)	Adolfo Horta (CUB)	Viktor Rybakov (URS) Krzysztof Kosedowski (POL)

LIGHTWEIGHT

From 1952 the weight has been *60 kg* 132 lb. In 1904 and from 1920 to 1936 it was 135 lb *61,24 kg*. In 1908 it was 140 lb *63,50 kg*. In 1948 it was *62 kg*. 136½ lb.

	GOLD	SILVER	BRONZE
1896–1900	Event not held		
1904	Harry J. Spanger (USA)	James Eagan (USA)	Russel Van Horn (USA)
1906	Event not held		
1908	Frederick Grace (GBR)	Frederick Spiller (GBR)	H. H. Johnson (GBR)
1912	Event not held		
1920	Samuel Mosberg (USA)	Gotfred Johansen (DEN)	Clarence Newton (CAN)
1924	Hans Nielsen (DEN)	Alfredo Coppello (ARG)	Frederick Boylstein (USA)
1928	Carlo Orlandi (ITA)	Stephen M. Halaiko (USA)	Gunnar Berggren (SWE)
1932	Lawrence Stevens (SAF)	Thure Ahlqvist (SWE)	Nathan Bor (USA)
1936	Imre Harangi (HUN)	Nikolai Stepulov (EST)	Erik Agren (SWE)
1948	Gerald Dreyer (SAF)	Joseph Vissers (BEL)	Svend Wad (DEN)
1952	Aureliano Bolognesi (ITA)	Aleksey Antkiewicz (POL)	Gheorghe Fiat (ROM) Erkki Pakkanen (FIN)
1956	Richard McTaggart (GBR)	Harry Kurschat (GER)	Anthony Byrne (IRL) Anatoliy Lagetko (URS)
1960	Kazimierz Pazdzior (POL)	Sandro Lopopoli (ITA)	Richard McTaggart (GBR) Abel Laudonio (ARG)
1964	Józef Grudzien (POL)	Vellikton Barannikov (URS)	Ronald Harris (USA) James McCourt (IRL)
1968	Ronald Harris (USA)	Józef Grudzien (POL)	Calistrat Cutov (ROM) Zvonimir Vujin (YUG)
1972	Jan Szczepanski (POL)	László Orban (HUN)	Samuel Mbugua (KEN) Alfonso Perez (COL)
1976	Howard Davis (USA)	Simion Cutov (ROM)	Ace Rusevski (YUG) Vasiliy Solomin (URS)
1980	Angel Herrera (CUB)	Viktor Demianenko (URS)	Kazimierz Adach (POL) Richard Nowakowski (GDR)

LIGHT-WELTERWEIGHT
Weight up to 63,5 kg 140 lb

	GOLD	SILVER	BRONZE
1896–1948	Event not held		
1952	Charles Adkins (USA)	Viktor Mednov (URS)	Erkki Mallenius (FIN) Bruno Visintin (ITA)
1956	Vladimir Yengibaryan (URS)	Franco Nenci (ITA)	Henry Loubscher (SAF) Constantin Dumitrescu (ROM)
1960	Bohumil Nemeček (TCH)	Clement Quartey (GHA)	Quincy Daniels (USA) Marian Kasprzyk (POL)
1964	Jerzy Kulej (POL)	Yvgeniy Frolov (URS)	Eddie Blay (GHA) Habib Galhia (TUN)
1968	Jerzy Kulej (POL)	Enrique Regueiferos (CUB)	Arto Nilsson (FIN) James Wallington (USA)
1972	Ray Seales (USA)	Anghel Anghelov (BUL)	Zvonimir Vujin (YUG) Issaaka Daborg (NIG)
1976	Ray Leonard (USA)	Andres Aldama (CUB)	Vladimir Kolev (BUL) Kazimier Szczerba (POL)
1980	Patrizio Oliva (ITA)	Serik Konakbaev (URS)	Anthony Willis (GBR) Jose Aguilar (CUB)

WELTERWEIGHT

From 1948 the weight limit has been 67 kg 148 lb. In 1904 it was 143¾ lb 65,27 kg. From 1920 to 1936 it was 147 lb 66,68 kg.

1896–1900	Event not held		
1904	Albert Young (USA)	Harry J. Spanger (USA)	Joseph Lydon (USA)
1906–1912	Event not held		
1920	Albert Schneider (CAN)	Alexander Ireland (GBR)	Frederick Colberg (USA)
1924	Jean Delarge (BEL)	Héctor Mendez (ARG)	Douglas Lewis (CAN)
1928	Edward Morgan (NZL)	Raul Landini (ARG)	Raymond Smillie (CAN)
1932	Edward Flynn (USA)	Erich Campe (GER)	Bruno Ahlberg (FIN)
1936	Sten Suvio (FIN)	Michael Murach (GER)	Gerhard Petersen (DEN)
1948	Julius Torma (TCH)	Horace Herring (USA)	Alessandro D'Ottavio (ITA)
1952	Zygmunt Chychla (POL)	Sergey Schtscherbakov (URS)	Victor Jörgensen (DEN) Günther Heidemann (GER)
1956	Nicholae Linca (ROM)	Frederick Tiedt (IRL)	Kevin J. Hogarth (AUS) Nicholas Gargano (GBR)

	GOLD	SILVER	BRONZE
1960	Giovanni Benvenuti (ITA)	Yuriy Radonyak (URS)	Leszek Drogosz (POL) James Lloyd (GBR)
1964	Marian Kasprzyk (POL)	Ritschardas Tamulis (URS)	Pertti Purhonen (FIN) Silvano Bertini (ITA)
1968	Manfred Wolke (GDR)	Joseph Bessala (CMR)	Vladimir Musalinov (URS) Mario Guilloti (ARG)
1972	Emilio Correa (CUB)	Janos Kajdi (HUN)	Dick T. Murunga (KEN) Jesse Valdez (USA)
1976	Jochen Bachfeld (GDR)	Pedro J. Gamarro (VEN)	Reinhard Skricek (GER) Victor Zilberman (ROM)
1980	Andres Aldama (CUB)	John Mugabi (UGA)	Karl-Heinz Kruger (GDR) Kazimierz Szcezerba (POL)

LIGHT-MIDDLEWEIGHT
Weight up to *71 kg* 157 lb

	GOLD	SILVER	BRONZE
1896–1948	Event not held		
1952	László Papp (HUN)	Theunis van Schalkwyk (SAF)	Boris Tishin (URS) Eladio Herrera (ARG)
1956	László Papp (HUN)	José Torres (USA)	John McCormack (GBR) Zbigniew Pietrzykowski (POL)
1960	Wilbert McClure (USA)	Carmelo Bossi (ITA)	Boris Lagutin (URS) William Fisher (GBR)
1964	Boris Lagutin (URS)	Josef Gonzales (FRA)	Nojim Maiyegun (NGR) Jozef Grzesiak (POL)
1968	Boris Lagutin (URS)	Rolando Garbey (CUB)	John Baldwin (USA) Günther Meier (GER)
1972	Dieter Kottysch (GER)	Wieslaw Rudkowski (POL)	Alan Minter (GBR) Peter Tiepold (GDR)
1976	Jerzy Rybicki (POL)	Tadija Kacar (YUG)	Rolando Garbey (CUB) Victor Savchenko (URS)
1980	Armando Martinez (CUB)	Aleksandr Koshkin (URS)	Jan Franek (TCH) Detlef Kastner (GDR)

MIDDLEWEIGHT

From 1952 the weight limit has been *75 kg* 165 lb. From 1904 to 1908 it was 158 lb *71,68 kg*. From 1920 to 1936 it was 160 lb *72,57 kg*. In 1948 it was *73 kg* 161 lb.

GOLD	SILVER	BRONZE
1896–1900 Event not held		
1904 Charles Mayer (USA)	Benjamin Spradley (USA)	d.n.a.
1906 Event not held		
1908 John Douglas (GBR)	Reginald Baker (AUS/NZL)	W. Philo (GBR)
1912 Event not held		
1920 Harry W. Mallin (GBR)	Georges A. Prud'homme (CAN)	Moe H. Herscovitch (CAN)
1924 Harry W. Mallin (GBR)	John Elliott (GBR)	Joseph Beecken (BEL)
1928 Piero Toscani (ITA)	Jan Hermánek (TCH)	Léonard Steyaert (BEL)
1932 Carmen Barth (USA)	Amado Azar (ARG)	Ernest Pierce (SAF)
1936 Jean Despeaux (FRA)	Henry Tiller (NOR)	Raúl Villareal (ARG)
1948 László Papp (HUN)	John Wright (GBR)	Ivano Fontana (ITA)
1952 Floyd Patterson (USA)	Vasile Tita (ROM)	Boris Nikolov (BUL) Stig Sjolin (SWE)
1956 Genadiy Schatkov (URS)	Ramón Tapia (CHI)	Gilbert Chapron (FRA) Victor Zalazar (ARG)

Laszlo Papp (HUN), a southpaw, is the first of two boxers to win three gold medals. He took the middleweight title in 1948, and the light-middleweight title in 1952 and 1956.

	GOLD	SILVER	BRONZE
1960	Edward Crook (USA)	Tadeusz Walasek (POL)	Iona Monea (ROM) Evgeniy Feofanov (URS)
1964	Valeriy Popentschenko (URS)	Emil Schultz (GER)	Franco Valle (ITA) Tadeusz Walasek (POL)
1968	Christopher Finnegan (GBR)	Aleksey Kisselyov (URS)	Agustin Zaragoza (MEX) Alfred Jones (USA)
1972	Viatcheslav Lemechev (URS)	Reima Virtanen (FIN)	Prince Amartey (GHA) Marvin Johnson (USA)
1976	Michael Spinks (USA)	Rufat Riskiev (URS)	Alec Nastac (ROM) Luis Martinez (CUB)
1980	Jose Gomez (CUB)	Viktor Savchenko (URS)	Valentin Silaghi (ROM) Jerzy Rybicki (POL)

The future professional champion Floyd Patterson (USA) captured the middle-weight title at Helsinki in 1952.

LIGHT-HEAVYWEIGHT

From 1952 the weight limit has been *81 kg* 178½ lb. From 1920 to 1936 it was 175 lb. *79,38 kg*. In 1948 it was *80 kg* 176¼ lb.

GOLD	SILVER	BRONZE
1896–1912 Event not held		
1920 Edward Eagen (USA)	Sverre Sörsdal (NOR)	H. Franks (GBR)
1924 Harry Mitchell (GBR)	Thyge Petersen (DEN)	Sverre Sörsdal (NOR)
1928 Victor Avendaño (ARG)	Ernst Pistulla (GER)	Karel L. Miljon (HOL)
1932 David Carstens (SAF)	Gino Rossi (ITA)	Peter Jörgensen (DEN)
1936 Roger Michelot (FRA)	Richard Vogt (GER)	Francisco Risiglione (ARG)
1948 George Hunter (SAF)	Donald Scott (GBR)	Maurio Cia (ARG)
1952 Norvel Lee (USA)	Antonio Pacenza (ARG)	Anotiliy Perov (URS) Harri Siljander (FIN)
1956 James F. Boyd (USA)	Gheorghe Negrea (ROM)	Carlos Lucas (CHI) Romualdas Murauskas (URS)
1960 Cassius Clay (USA)	Zbigniew Pietrzykowski (POL)	Anthony Madigan (AUS) Giulio Saraudi (ITA)
1964 Cosimo Pinto (ITA)	Aleksey Kisselyov (URS)	Aleksandar Nikolov (BUL) Zbigniew Pietrzykowski (POL)

Cassius M. Clay (USA), then an 18-year-old schoolboy, and later three-time heavyweight champion of the world, is shown on the way to his 1960 Olympic light-heavyweight gold medal, bouncing a right off the head of Tony Madigan (AUS), the bronze-medal winner.

	GOLD	SILVER	BRONZE
1968	Dan Poznyak (URS)	Ion Monea (ROM)	Georgy Stankov (BUL) Stanislav Dragan (POL)
1972	Mate Parlov (YUG)	Gilberto Carrillo (CUB)	Isaac Ikhouria (NGR) Janusz Gortat (POL)
1976	Leon Spinks (USA)	Sixto Soria (CUB)	Costica Dafinoiu (ROM) Janusz Gortat (POL)
1980	Slobodan Kacar (YUG)	Pawel Skrzecz (POL)	Herbert Bauch (GDR) Ricardo Rojas (CUB)

HEAVYWEIGHT

From 1952 the class has been for those over *81 kg* 178½ lb. From 1904 to 1908 it was over 158 lb *71,67 kg*. From 1920 to 1936 it was over 175 lb *79,38 kg*. In 1948 it was over *80 kg* 176¼ lb.

	GOLD	SILVER	BRONZE
1896–1900	Event not held		
1904	Samuel Berger (USA)	Charles Mayer (USA)	d.n.a.
1906	Event not held		
1908	A. L. Oldhan (GBR)	S. C. H. Evans (GBR)	Frederick Parks (GBR)
1912	Event not held		
1920	Ronald Rawson (GBR)	Sören Petersen (DEN)	Xavier Eluère (FRA)
1924	Otto von Porat (NOR)	Sören Petersen (DEN)	Alfredo Porzio (ARG)
1928	Arturo Rodriguez Jurado (ARG)	Nils Ramm (SWE)	M. Jacob Michaelsen (DEN)
1932	Santiago Lovell (ARG)	Luigi Rovati (ITA)	Frederick Feary (USA)
1936	Herbert Runge (GER)	Guillermo Lovell (ARG)	Erling Nilsen (NOR)
1948	Rafael Iglesias (ARG)	Gunnar Nilsson (SWE)	John Arthur (SAF)
1952	Hayes Edward Sanders (USA)	Ingemar Johansson (SWE)*	Andries Nieman (SAF) Ilkka Koski (FIN)
1956	T. Peter Rademacher (USA)	Lev Mukhin (URS)	Daniel Bekker (SAF) Giacomo Bozzano (ITA)
1960	Franco de Piccoli (ITA)	Daniel Bekker (SAF)	Josef Nemec (TCH) Günter Siegmund (GER)
1964	Joe Frazier (USA)	Hans Huber (GER)	Giuseppe Ros (ITA) Vadim Yemelyanov (URS)

---

*Medal awarded in October 1981 after initial disqualification

GOLD	SILVER	BRONZE
1968 George Foreman (USA)	Ionas Tschepulis (URS)	Giorgio Bambini (ITA) Joaquin Rocha (MEX)
1972 Teofilo Stevenson (CUB)	Ion Alexe (ROM)	Peter Hussing (GER) Hasse Thomsen (SWE)
1976 Teofilo Stevenson (CUB)	Mircea Simon (ROM)	Johnny Tate (USA) Clarence Hill (BER)
1980 Teofilo Stevenson (CUB)	Pyotr Zaev (URS)	Istvan Levai (HUN) Jurgen Fanghanel (GDR)

Teofilo Stevenson (CUB) won the heavyweight title three times. No other heavyweight ever successfully defended the title even once.

Nine canoes run head-to-head during one of the 1,000 meters K-2 preliminary heats at Munich in 1972.

---

4. Canoeing (Men)

500 METERS KAYAK SINGLES (K-1)

GOLD	SILVER	BRONZE
1896–1972 Event not held		
1976 Vasile Diba (ROM) 1:46.41	Zoltan Szytanity (HUN) 1:46.95	Rudiger Helm (GDR) 1:48.30
1980 Vladimir Parfenovich (URS) 1:43.43	John Sumcgi (AUS) 1:44.12	Vasile Diba (ROM) 1:44.90

1,000 METERS KAYAK SINGLES (K-1)

1896–1932 Event not held		
1936 Gregor Hradetzky (AUT) 4:22.9	Helmut Cämmerer (GER) 4:25.6	Jacob Kraaier (HOL) 4:35.1
1948 Gert Fredriksson (SWE) 4:33.2	Johan F. Kobberup (DEN) 4:39.9	Henri Eberhardt (FRA) 4:41.4
1952 Gert Fredriksson (SWE) 4:07.9	Thorvald Strömberg (FIN) 4:09.7	Louis Gantois (FRA) 4:20.1
1956 Gert Fredriksson (SWE) 4:12.8	Igor Pissaryev (URS) 4:15.3	Lajos Kiss (HUN) 4:16.2
1960 Erik Hansen (DEN) 3:53.00	Imre Szöllösi (HUN) 3:54.02	Gert Fredriksson (SWE) 3:55.89
1964 Rolf Peterson (SWE) 3:57.13	Mihály Hesz (HUN) 3:57.28	Aurel Vernescu (ROM) 4:00.77

GOLD	SILVER	BRONZE
1968 Mihály Hesz (HUN) 4:02.63	Aleksandr Shaparenko (URS) 4:03.58	Erik Hansen (DEN) 4:04.39
1972 Aleksandr Shaparenko (URS) 3:48.06	Rolf Peterson (SWE) 3:48.35	Geza Csapo (HUN) 3:49.38
1976 Rudiger Helm (GDR) 3:48.20	Geza Csapo (HUN) 3:48.84	Vassile Diba (ROM) 3:49.65
1980 Rudiger Helm (GDR) 3:48.77	Alain Lebas (FRA) 3:50.20	Ion Birladeanu (ROM) 3:50.49

500 METERS KAYAK PAIRS (K-2)

1896–1972 Event not held

1976 **EAST GERMANY** 1:35.87	**U.S.S.R.** 1:36.81	**RUMANIA** 1:37.43
Joachim Mattern	Sergei Nagorny	Larion Serghei
Bernd Olbricht	Vladimir Romanovski	Policarp Malihin
1980 **U.S.S.R.** 1:32.38	**SPAIN** 1:33.65	**EAST GERMANY** 1:34.00
Vladimir Parfenovich	Herminio Menendez	Bernd Olbricht
Sergey Chukhrai	Guillermo Del Riego	Rudiger Helm

1,000 METERS KAYAK PAIRS (K-2)

1896–1932 Event not held

1936 **AUSTRIA** 4:03.8	**GERMANY** 4:08.9	**NETHERLANDS** 4:12.2
Adolf Kainz	Ewald Tilker	Nicolaas Tates
Alfons Dorfner	Fritz Bondroit	Willem van der Kroft
1948 **SWEDEN** 4:07.3	**DENMARK** 4:07.5	**FINLAND** 4:08.7
Hans Berglund	Ejvind Hansen	Thor Axelsson
Lennart Klingström	Bernhard Jensen	Nils Björklöf
1952 **FINLAND** 3:51.1	**SWEDEN** 3:51.1	**AUSTRIA** 3:51.4
Kurt Wires	Lars Glassér	Max Raub
Yrjö Hietanen	Ingemar Hedberg	Herbert Wiedermann
1956 **GERMANY** 3:49.6	**U.S.S.R.** 3:51.4	**AUSTRIA** 3:55.8
Michael Scheuer	Mikhail Kaaleste	Max Raub
Meinrad Miltenberger	Antoliy Demitkov	Herbert Wiedermann
1960 **SWEDEN** 3:34.7	**HUNGARY** 3:34.91	**POLAND** 3:37.34
Gert Fredriksson	András Szente	Stefan Kaplaniak
Sven-Olov Sjödelius	György Mészáros	Wladyslaw Zielinski
1964 **SWEDEN** 3:38.4	**NETHERLANDS** 3:39.30	**GERMANY** 3:40.69
Sven-Olov Sjödelius	Antonius Geurts	Heinz Buker
Nils Utterberg	Paul Hoekstra	Holger Zander
1968 **U.S.S.R.** 3:37.54	**HUNGARY** 3:38.44	**AUSTRIA** 3:40.71
Aleksandr Shaparenko	Csaba Giczi	Gerhard Seibold
Vladimir Morozov	István Tímár	Gunther Pfaff
1972 **U.S.S.R.** 3:31.23	**HUNGARY** 3:32.00	**POLAND** 3:33.83
Nikolai Gorbachev	Jozsef Deme	Wladyslaw Szuszkiewicz
Viktor Kratassyuk	Janos Ratkai	Rafal Piszez
1976 **U.S.S.R.** 3:29.01	**EAST GERMANY** 3:29.33	**HUNGARY** 3:30.56
Sergei Nagorny	Joachim Mattern	Zoltan Bako
Vladimir Romanovski	Bernd Olbricht	Istvan Szabo
1980 **U.S.S.R.** 3:26.72	**HUNGARY** 3:28.49	**SPAIN** 3:28.66
Vladimir Perfenovich	Istvan Szabo	Luis Ramos-Misione
Sergey Chukhrai	Istvan Joos	Herminio Menendez

1,000 METERS KAYAK FOURS (K-4)

GOLD	SILVER	BRONZE
1896–1960 Event not held		
1964 U.S.S.R. 3:14.67	GERMANY 3:15.39	RUMANIA 3:15.51
Nikolay Chuzhikov	Günther Perleberg	Simion Cuciuc
Anatoly Grishin	Bernhard Schulze	Atanase Sciotnic
Vyatscheslav Ionov	Friedhelm Wentzke	Mihai Turcas
Vladimir Morozov	Holger Zander	Aurel Vernescu
1968 NORWAY 3:14.38	RUMANIA 3:14.81	HUNGARY 3:15.10
Steinar Amundsen	Anton Calenic	Csaba Giczi
Egil W. Söby	Dimitrie Ivanov	István Timár
Tore Berger	Haralambie Ivanov	Imre Szöllösi
Jan Johansen	Mihai Turcas	István Csizmadia
1972 U.S.S.R. 3:14.02	RUMANIA 3:15.07	NORWAY 3:15.27
Yuri Filatov	Aurel Vernescu	Egil W. Söby
Yuri Stezenko	Mihai Zafiu	Steinar Amundsen
Vladimir Morozov	Roman Vartolomeu	Tore Berger
Valeri Didenko	Atanase Sciotnic	Jan Johansen
1976 U.S.S.R. 3:08.69	SPAIN 3:08.95	EAST GERMANY 3:10.76
Sergei Chuhray	Jose Celorrio	Peter Bischof
Aleksandr Degtiarev	Jose Diaz-Flor	Bernd Duvigneau
Yuri Filatov	Herminio Menendez	Rudiger Helm
Vladimir Morozov	Luis Misone	Jurgen Lehnert
1980 EAST GERMANY 3:13.76	RUMANIA 3:15.35	BULGARIA 3:15.46
Bernd Olbricht	Mihai Zafiu	Boleslaw Borissov
Bernd Duvigneau	Vasile Diba	Boshidar Milenkov
Rudiger Helm	Ion Geanta	Lazar Christov
Harald Marg	Esanu Nicusor	Ivan Manev

500 METERS CANADIAN SINGLES (C-1)

GOLD	SILVER	BRONZE
1896–1972 Event not held		
1976 Aleksandr Rogov	John Wood	Matija Ljubek
(URS) 1:59.23	(CAN) 1:59.58	(YUG) 1:59.60
1980 Sergei Postrekhin	Lubomir Lubenov	Olaf Heukrodt
(URS) 1:53.37	(BUL) 1:53.49	(GDR) 1:54.38

1,000 METERS CANADIAN SINGLES (C-1)

GOLD	SILVER	BRONZE
1896–1932 Event not held		
1936 Francis Amyot	Bohuslav Karlik	Erich Koschik
(CAN) 5:32.1	(TCH) 5:36.9	(GER) 5:39.0
1948 Josef Holeček	Douglas Bennett	Robert Boutigny
(TCH) 5:42.0	(CAN) 5:53.3	(FRA) 5:55.9
1952 Josef Holeček	János Parti	Olavi Ojanperä
(TCH) 4:56.3	(HUN) 5:03.6	(FIN) 5:08.5
1956 Leon Rotman	István Hernek	Gennadiy Bukharin
(ROM) 5:05.3	(HUN) 5:06.2	(URS) 5:12.7
1960 János Parti	Aleksandr Silayev	Leon Rotman
(HUN) 4:33.93	(URS) 4:34.41	(ROM) 4:35.87
1964 Jürgen Eschert	Andrei Igorov	Yevgeny Penyayev
(GER) 4:35.14	(ROM) 4:37.89	(URS) 4:38.31
1968 Tibor Tatai	Detlef Lewe	Vitaly Galkov
(HUN) 4:36.14	(GER) 4:38.31	(URS) 4:40.42
1972 Ivan Patzaichin	Tamas Wichmann	Detlef Lewe
(ROM) 4:08.94	(HUN) 4:12.42	(GER) 4:13.63
1976 Matija Ljubek	Vasily Urchenko	Tamas Wichmann
(YUG) 4:09.51	(URS) 4:12.57	(HUN) 4:14.11
1980 Lubomir Lubenov	Sergei Postrekhin	Eckhard Leue
(BUL) 4:12.38	(URS) 4:13.53	(GDR) 4:15.02

The Rumanian pair, Patzaichin and Covaliov, winning the 1968 Canadian Pairs event on the artificial lake, Canal de Quemanco, which was also used for rowing.

500 METERS CANADIAN PAIRS (C-2)

GOLD	SILVER	BRONZE
1896–1972 Event not held		
1976 U.S.S.R. 1:45.81	POLAND 1:47.77	HUNGARY 1:48.35
Sergei Petrenko	Jerzy Opara	Tamas Buday
Aleksandr Vinogradov	Andrzej Gronowicz	Oszkar Frey
1980 HUNGARY 1:43.39	RUMANIA 1:44.12	BULGARIA 1:44.83
Laszlo Foltan	Ivan Patzaichin	Borislaw Ananiev
Istvan Vaskuti	Istvan Capusta	Nikolai Ilkov

1,000 METERS CANADIAN PAIRS (C-2)

GOLD	SILVER	BRONZE
1896–1932 Event not held		
1936 CZECHOSLOVAKIA 4:50.1	AUSTRIA 4:53.8	CANADA 4:56.7
Vladimír Syrovátka	Rupert Weinstabl	Frank Saker
Jan-Felix Brzák	Karl Proisl	Harvey Charters
1948 CZECHOSLOVAKIA 5:07.1	U.S.A. 5:08.2	FRANCE 5:15.2
Jan-Felix Brzák	Stephen Lysak	Georges Dransart
Bohumil Kudrna	Stephan Macknowski	Georges Gandil
1952 DENMARK 4:38.3	CZECHOSLOVAKIA 4:42.9	GERMANY 4:48.3
Bent Peder Rasch	Jan-Felix Brzák	Egon Drews
Finn Haunstoft	Bohumil Kudrna	Wilfried Soltau
1956 RUMANIA 4:47.4	U.S.S.R. 4:48.6	HUNGARY 4:54.3
Alexe Dumitru	Pavel Kharin	Károly Wieland
Simion Ismailciuc	Gratsian Botev	Ferenc Mohácsi

	GOLD	SILVER	BRONZE
1960	U.S.S.R. 4:17.94	ITALY 4:20.77	HUNGARY 4:20.89
	Leonid Geyshtor	Aldo Dezi	Imre Farkas
	Sergey Makarenko	Francesco La Macchia	András Törö
1964	U.S.S.R. 4:04.64	FRANCE 4:06.52	DENMARK 4:07.48
	Andrey Khimich	Jean Boudehen	Peer N. Nielsen
	Stepan Oschepkov	Michel Chapuis	John Sorenson
1968	RUMANIA 4:07.18	HUNGARY 4:08.77	U.S.S.R. 4:11.30
	Ivan Patzaichin	Tamás Wichmann	Naum Prokupets
	Serghei Covaliov	Gyula Petrikovics	Mikhail Zamotin
1972	U.S.S.R. 3:52.60	RUMANIA 3:52.63	BULGARIA 3:58.10
	Vlados Chessyunas	Ivan Patzaichin	Fedia Damianov
	Yuri Lobanov	Serghei Covaliov	Ivan Bourtchine
1976	U.S.S.R. 3:52.76	RUMANIA 3:54.28	HUNGARY 3:55.66
	Sergei Petrenko	Gheorghe Danielov	Tamas Buday
	Aleksandr Vinogradov	Gheorghe Simionov	Oszkar Frey
1980	RUMANIA 3:47.65	EAST GERMANY 3:49.93	U.S.S.R. 3:51.28
	Ivan Patzaichin	Olaf Heukrodt	Vasiliy Yurchenko
	Toma Simionov	Uwe Madeja	Yuriy Lobanov

Nina Gopova and Galina Kreft (URS) won the 500 meters Kayak Pairs event at the 1976 Games.

Canoeing (Women)

500 METERS KAYAK SINGLES (K-1)

GOLD	SILVER	BRONZE
1896–1936 Event not held		
1948 Karen Hoff (DEN) 2:31.9	Alide Van de Anker-Doedans (HOL) 2:32.8	Fritzi Schwingl (AUT) 2:32.9
1952 Sylvi Saimo (FIN) 2:18.4	Gertrude Liebhart (AUT) 2:18.8	Nina Savina (URS) 2:21.6
1956 Elisaveta Dementyeva (URS) 2:18.9	Therese Zenz (GER) 2:19.6	Tove Söby (DEN) 2:22.3
1960 Antonina Seredina (URS) 2:08.08	Therese Zenz (GER) 2:08.22	Daniela Walkowiak (POL) 2:10.46
1964 Ludmila Khvedosyuk (URS) 2:12.87	Hilde Lauer (ROM) 2:15.35	Marcia Jones (USA) 2:15.68
1968 Ludmila Pinayeva-Khvedosyuk (URS) 2:11.09	Renate Breuer (GER) 2:12.71	Viorica Dumitru (ROM) 2:13.22
1972 Yulia Ryabchlinskaya (URS) 2:03.17	Mieke Jaapies (HOL) 2:04.03	Anna Pfeffer (HUN) 2:05.50
1976 Carola Zirzow (GDR) 2:01.05	Tatyana Korshunova (URS) 2:03.07	Klara Rajnai (HUN) 2:05.01
1980 Birgit Fischer (GDR) 1:57.96	Vania Checheva (BUL) 1:59.48	Antonina Melnikova 1:59.66

500 METERS KAYAK PAIRS (K-2)

GOLD	SILVER	BRONZE
1896–1956 Event not held		
1960 U.S.S.R. 1:54.76	GERMANY 1:56.66	HUNGARY 1:58.22
Maria Zhubina	Therese Zenz	Vilma Egresi
Antonina Seredina	Ingrid Hartmann	Klára Fried-Bánfalvi
1964 GERMANY 1:56.95	UNITED STATES 1:59.16	RUMANIA 2:00.25
Roswitha Esser	Francine Fox	Hilde Lauer
Annemarie Zimmermann	Gloriane Perrier	Cornelia Sideri
1968 GERMANY 1:56.44	HUNGARY 1:58.60	U.S.S.R. 1:58.61
Annemarie Zimmermann	Anna Pfeffer	Ludmila Pinayeva
Roswitha Esser	Katalin Rosznyói	Antonina Seredina
1972 U.S.S.R. 1:53.50	EAST GERMANY 1:54.30	RUMANIA 1:55.01
Ludmila Pinayeva	Ilse Kaschube	Maria Nichiforov
Ekaterina Kuryshko	Petra Grabowsky	Viorica Dumitru
1976 U.S.S.R. 1:51.15	HUNGARY 1:51.69	EAST GERMANY 1:51.81
Nina Gopova	Anna Pfeffer	Barbel Koster
Galina Kreft	Klara Rajnai	Carola Zirzow
1980 EAST GERMANY 1:43.88	U.S.S.R. 1:46.91	HUNGARY 1:47.95
Carsta Genauss	Galina Alexeyeva	Eva Rakusz
Martina Bischof	Nina Trofimova	Maria Zakarias

5. Cycling

1,000 METERS SPRINT

	GOLD	SILVER	BRONZE
1896–1904	Event not held		
1906	Francesco Verri (ITA) 1:42.2	H. C. Bouffler (GBR)	Eugène Debougnie (BEL)
1980[1]–1912	Event not held		
1920	Maurice Peeters (HOL) 1:38.3	H. Thomas Johnson (GBR)	Harry Ryan (GBR)
1924[2]	Lucien Michard (FRA) 12.8	Jacob Meijer (HOL)	Jean Cugnot (FRA)
1928	René Beaufrand (FRA) 13.2	Antoine Mazairac (HOL)	Willy Falck-Hansen (DEN)
1932	Jacobus van Egmond (HOL) 12.6	Louis Chaillot (FRA)	Bruno Pellizzari (ITA)
1936	Toni Merkens (GER) 11.8	Arie Van Vliet (HOL)	Louis Chaillot (FRA)
1948	Mario Ghella (ITA) 12.0	Reginald Harris (GBR)	Axel Schandorff (DEN)
1952	Enzo Sacchi (ITA) 12.0	Lionel Cox (AUS)	Werner Potzernheim (GER)
1956	Michel Rousseau (FRA) 11.4	Guglielmo Pesenti (ITA)	Richard Ploog (AUS)
1960	Sante Gaiardoni (ITA) 11.1	Leo Sterckx (BEL)	Valentino Gasparella (ITA)
1964	Giovanni Pettenella (ITA) 13.69	Sergio Bianchetto (ITA)	Daniel Morelon (FRA)
1968	Daniel Morelon (FRA) 10.68	Giordano Turrini (ITA)	Pierre Trentin (FRA)
1972	Daniel Morelon (FRA) 11 .25	John M. Nicholson (AUS)	Omari Phakadze (URS)
1976	Anton Tkac (TCH) 10.78	Daniel Morelon (FRA)	Hans-Jurgen Geschke (GDR)
1980	Lutz Hesslich (GDR) 11.40	Yave Cahard (FRA)	Sergei Kopylov (URS)

[1] There was a 1,000 meters sprint event in the 1908 Games, but it was declared void because "the riders exceeded the time limit, in spite of repeated warnings."
[2] Since 1924 only times over the last 200 meters of the event have been recorded.

1,000 METERS TIME-TRIAL

	GOLD	SILVER	BRONZE
1896–1924	Event not held		
1928	Willy Falck-Hansen (DEN) 1:14.4*	Gerard D. H. Bosch van Drakestein (HOL) 1:15.2	Edgar Gray (AUS) 1:15.6
1932	Edgar Gray (AUS) 1:13.0*	Jacobus van Egmond (HOL) 1:13.3	Charles Rampelberg (FRA) 1:13.4
1936	Arie van Vliet (HOL) 1:12.0*	Pierre Georget (FRA) 1:12.8	Rudolf Karsch (GER) 1:13.2
1948	Jacques Dupont (FRA) 1:13.5	Pierre Nihant (BEL) 1:14.5	Thomas Godwin (GBR) 1:15.0
1952	Russell Mockridge (AUS) 1:11.1*	Marino Morettini (ITA) 1:12.7	Raymond Robinson (SAF) 1:13.0
1956	Leandro Faggin (ITA) 1:09.8*	Ladislav Foucek (TCH) 1:11.4	J. Alfred Swift (SAF) 1:11.6
1960	Sante Gaiardoni (ITA) 1:07.27*	Dieter Gieseler (GER) 1:08.75	Rotislav Vargashkin (URS) 1:08.86
1964	Patrick Sercu (BEL) 1:09.59	Giovanni Pettenella (ITA) 1:10.09	Pierre Trentin (FRA) 1:10.42
1968	Pierre Trentin (FRA) 1:03.91*	Niels-Christian Fredborg (DEN) 1:04.61	Janusz Kierzkowski (POL) 1:04.63

GOLD	SILVER	BRONZE
1972 Niels-Christian Fredborg (DEN) 1:06.44	Daniel Clark (AUS) 1:06.87	Juergen Schuetze (GDR) 1:07.02
1976 Klaus-Jurgen Grunke (GDR) 1:05.93	Michel Vaarten (BEL) 1:07.52	Niels Fredborg (DEN) 1:07.62
1980 Lothar Thoms (GDR) 1:02.955	Alexandr Panfilov (URS) 1:04.845	David Weller (JAM) 1:05.241

4,000 METERS INDIVIDUAL PURSUIT

Note: Bronze medal times are set in a third place race, so can be faster than those set in the race for first and second place.

1896–1960 Event not held		
1964 Jiři Daler (TCH) 5:04.75	Giorgio Ursi (ITA) 5:05.96	Preben Isaksson (DEN) 5:01.90
1968 Daniel Rebillard (FRA) 4:41.71	Mogens Frey Jensen (DEN) 4:42.43	Xaver Kurmann (SUI) 4:39.42
1972 Knut Knudsen (NOR) 4:45.74	Xaver Kurmann (SUI) 4:51.96	Hans Lutz (GER) 4:50.80
1976 Gregor Braun (GDR) 4:47.61	Herman Ponsteen (HOL) 4:49.72	Thomas Huschke (GDR) 4:52.71
1980 Robert Dill-Bundi (SUI) 4:35.66	Alain Bondue (FRA) 4:42.96	Hans-Henrik Orsted (DEN) 4:36.54

4,000 METERS TEAM PURSUIT

Note: Bronze medal times are set in a third place race, so can be faster than those set in the race for first and second place.

1896–1912 Event not held		
1920 **ITALY 5:20.0**	**GREAT BRITAIN**	**SOUTH AFRICA**
Franco Giorgetti	Albert White	James R. Walker
Ruggero Ferrario	H. Thomas Johnson	William R. Smith
Arnaldo Carli	William Stewart	Henry J. Kaltenbrun
Primo Magnani	C. Albert Alden	Harry W. Goosen
1924 **ITALY 5:15.0**	**POLAND**	**BELGIUM**
Alfredo Dinale	Jósef Lange	Léon Dahelinczky
Francesco Zucchetti	Franciszek Szymeczyk	Henry Hoevenaers
Angelo de Martino	Jan Lazarski	Fernand Saive
Aleardo Menegazzi	Tomas Sztankiewicz	Jean van den Bosch
1928 **ITALY 5:01.8**	**NETHERLANDS** 5:06.2	**GREAT BRITAIN**
Luigi Tasselli	Adriann Braspenninx	Frank Wyld
Giacomo Gaioni	Jan Maas	Leonard Wyld
Cesare Facciani	Johannes B. N. Pijnenburg	Percy Wyld
Mario Lusiani	Piet van der Horst	M. George Southall
1932 **ITALY 4:53.0**	**FRANCE 4:55.7**	**GREAT BRITAIN** 4:56.0
Marco Cimatti	Amédé Fournier	Ernest A. Johnson
Paolo Pedretti	René Legrèves	William Harvell
Alberto Ghilardi	Henri Mouillefarine	Frank W. Southall
Nino Borsari	Paul Chocque	Charles Holland
1936 **FRANCE 4:45.0**	**ITALY 4:51.0**	**GREAT BRITAIN** 4.52.6
Robert Charpentier	Bianco Bianchi	Harry H. Hill
Jean Goujon	Mario Gentili	Ernest A. Johnson
Guy Lapébie	Armando Latini	Charles T. King
Roger Le Nizerhy	Severino Rigoni	Ernest V. Mills
1948 **FRANCE 4:57.8**	**ITALY 5:36.7**	**GREAT BRITAIN** 4:55.8
Pierre Adam	Arnaldo Benefenati	Alan Geldard
Serge Blusson	Guido Bernardi	Thomas Godwin
Charles Coste	Anselmo Citterio	David Ricketts
Ferdinand Decanali	Rino Pucci	Wilfred Waters

	GOLD	SILVER	BRONZE

	GOLD	SILVER	BRONZE
1952	**ITALY 4:46.1**	**S. AFRICA 4:53.6**	**GREAT BRITAIN** 4:51.5
	Marino Morettini	Thomas F. Shardelow	Ronald C. Stretton
	Guido Messina	Alfred J. Swift	Alan Newton
	Mino de Rossi	Robert G. Fowler	George A. Newberry
	Loris Campana	George Estman	Donald C. Burgess
1956	**ITALY 4:37.4**	**FRANCE 4:39.4**	**GREAT BRITAIN** 4:42.2
	Leandro Faggin	René Bianchi	Thomas Simpson
	Valentino Gasparella	Jean Graczyk	Donald Burgess
	Franco Gandini	Jean-Claude Lecante	John Geddes
	Tonino Domenicali	Michel Vermeulin	Michael Gambrill
1960	**ITALY 4:30.90**	**GERMANY 4:35.78**	**U.S.S.R. 4:34.05**
	Luigi Arienti	Peter Gröning	Stanislav Moskvin
	Franco Testa	Manfred Klieme	Viktor Romanov
	Mario Vallotto	Siegfried Köhler	Leonid Kolumbet
	Marino Vigna	Bernd Barleben	Arnold Belgardt
1964	**GERMANY 4:35.67**	**ITALY 4:35.74**	**NETHERLANDS** 4:38.99
	Lothar Claesges	Luigi Roncaglia	Gerard Koel
	Karl-Heinz Henrichs	Vincenzo Mantovani	Hendrik Cornelisse
	Karl Link	Carlo Rancati	Jacob Oudkerk
	Ernest Streng	Franco Testa	Cornelis Schururing
1968	**DENMARK 4:22.44**	**GERMANY 4:18.94[1]**	**ITALY 4:18.35**
	Gunnar Asmussen	Udo Hempel	Lorenzo Bossio
	Per. P. Lyngemark	Karl Link	Cipirano Chemello
	Reno B. Olsen	Karl-Heinz Henrichs	Luigi Roncaglia
	Mogens Frey Jensen	Jürgen Kissner	Giorgio Morbiato
1972	**WEST GERMANY** 4:22.14	**EAST GERMANY** 4:25.25	**GREAT BRITAIN** 4:23.78
	Jurgen Colombo	Thomas Huschke	Michael Bennett
	Günter Haritz	Heinz Richter	Ian Hallam
	Udo Hempel	Herbert Richter	Ronald Keeble
	Günther Schumacher	Uwe Unterwalder	William Moore
1976	**WEST GERMANY** 4:21.06	**U.S.S.R. 4:27.15**	**GREAT BRITAIN** 4:22.41
	Gregor Braun	Vladimir Osokin	Ian Banbury
	Hans Lutz	Aleksandr Perov	Michael Bennett
	Günther Schumacher	Vitaly Petrakov	Robin Croker
	Peter Vonhof	Victor Sokolov	Ian Hallam
1980	**U.S.S.R. 4:15.70**	**EAST GERMANY** 4:19.67	**CZECHOSLOVAKIA[2]**
	Viktor Manakov	Gerald Mortag	Teodor Cerny
	Valeriy Movchan	Uwe Unterwalder	Martin Penc
	Vladimir Osokin	Matthias Wiegand	Jiri Pokorny
	Vitaliy Petrakov	Volker Winkler	Igor Slama

[1] Won final but disqualified.
[2] Italy disqualified in third place race.

INDIVIDUAL ROAD RACE

	GOLD	SILVER	BRONZE
1896	A. Konstantinidis (GRE) 3h 22:31.0	August Goedrich (GER) 3h 42:18.0	F. Battel (GBR) d.n.a.
1900–1904	Event not held		
1906	B. Vast (FRA) 2h 41:28.0	M. Bardonneau (FRA) 2h 41:28.4	Luget (FRA) 2h 41:28.6
1908	Event not held		
1912	Rudolph Lewis (SAF) 10h 42:39.0	Frederick Grubb (GBR) 10h 51:24.2	Carl Schutte (USA) 10h 52:38.8
1920	Harry Stenqvist (SWE) 4h 40:01.8	Henry J. Kaltenbrun (SAF) 4h 41:26.6	Fernand Canteloube (FRA) 4h 42:54.4
1924	Armand Blanchonnet (FRA) 6h 20:48.0	Henry Hoevenaers (BEL) 6h 30:27.0	René Hamel (FRA) 6h 40:51.6
1928	Henry Hansen (DEN) 4h 47:18.0	Frank W. Southall (GBR) 4h 55:06.0	Gösta Carlsson (SWE) 5h 00:17.0

GOLD	SILVER	BRONZE
1932	Attilio Pavesi (ITA) 2h 28:05.6	Guglielmo Segato (ITA) 2h 29:21.4	Bernhard Britz (SWE) 2h 29:45.2
1936	Robert Charpentier (FRA) 2h 33:05.0	Guy Lapébie (FRA) 2h 33:05.2	Ernst Nievergelt (SUI) 2h 33:05.8
1948	José Beyaert (FRA) 5h 18:12.6	Gerardus P.Voorting (HOL) 5h 18:16.2	Lode Wouters (BEL) 5h 18:16.2
1952	André Noyelle (BEL) 5h 06:03.4	Robert Grondelaers (BEL) 5h 06:51.2	Edi Ziegler (GER) 5h 07:47.5
1956	Ercole Baldini (ITA) 5h 21:17.0	Arnaud Geyre (FRA) 5h 23:16.0	Alan Jackson (GBR) 5h 23:16.0
1960	Viktor Kapitonov (URS) 4h 20:37.0	Livio Trapè (ITA) 4h 20:37.0	Willy van den Berghen (BEL) 4h 20:57.0
1964	Mario Zanin (ITA) 4h 39:51.63	Kjell A. Rodian (DEN) 4h 39:51.65	Walter Godefroot (BEL) 4h 39:51.74
1968	Pierfranco Vianelli (ITA) 4h 41:25.24	Leif Mortensen (DEN) 4h 42:49.71	Gösta Pettersson (SWE) 4h 43:15.24
1972	Hennie Kuiper (HOL) 4h 14:37.0	Kevin C. Sefton (AUS) 4h 15:04.0	Jaime Huelamo (ESP) 4h 15:04.0
1976	Bernt Johansson (SWE) 4h 46:52.0	Giuseppe Martinelli (ITA) 4h 47:23.0	Mieczysl Nowicki (POL) 4h 47:23.0
1980	Sergei Sukhoruchenkov (URS) 4h 48:28.9	Czeslaw Lang (POL) 4h 51:26.9	Yuri Barinov (URS) 4h 51:26.9

This event has been held over the following distances:—1896—87 km; 1906—84 km; 1912—320 km; 1920—175 km; 1924—188 km; 1928—168 km; 1932 and 1936—100 km; 1948—194,63 km; 1952—190.4 km; 1956—187,73 km; 1960—175,38 km; 1964—194,83 km; 1968—196,2 km; 1972—200 km; 1976—176 km; 1980—189 km.

ROAD TEAM TIME-TRIAL

Held over 100 km except in 1964 (109,89 km) and 1968 (104 km)

1896-1956	Event not held		
1960	ITALY 2h 14:33.53	GERMANY 2h 16:56.31	U.S.S.R. 2h 18:41.67
	Antonio Bailetti	Gustav-Adolf Schur	Viktor Kapitonov
	Ottavio Cogliati	Egon Adler	Yevgeny Klevzov
	Giacomo Fornoni	Erich Hagen	Yuriy Melikhov
	Livio Trapè	Günter Lörke	Aleksey Petrov
1964	NETHERLANDS 2h 26:31.19	ITALY 2h 26:55.39	SWEDEN 2h 27:11.52
	Gerben Karstens	Severino Andreoli	Sven Hamrin
	Evert G. Dolman	Luciano dalla Bona	Erik Pettersson
	Johannes Pieterse	Pietro Guerra	Gösta Pettersson
	Hubertus Zoet	Ferrucio Manza	Sture Pettersson
1968	NETHERLANDS 2h 07:49.06	SWEDEN 2h 09:26.60	ITALY 2h 10:18.74
	Marinus Pijnen	Gösta Pettersson	Vittorio Marcelli
	Fedor den Hertog	Sture Pettersson	Mauro Simonetti
	Jan Krekels	Erik Pettersson	Pierfranco Vianelli
	Henk Zoetemelk	Tomas Pettersson	Giovanni Bramucci
1972	U.S.S.R. 2h 11:17.8	POLAND 2h 11:47.5	NETHERLANDS 2h 12:27.1
	Boris Chouhov	Lucjan Lis	Fedor den Hertog
	Valeri Iardy	Edward Barcik	Hennie Kuiper
	Gennady Komnatov	Stanislaw Szozda	Cees Priem
	Valery Likhachev	Ryszard Szurkowski	Aad van den Hoek
1976	U.S.S.R. 2h 08:53.0	POLAND 2h 09:13.0	DENMARK 2h 12:20.0
	Anatoli Chukanov	Tadeusz Mytnik	Verner Blaudzun
	Valeriy Chaplygin	Mieczysl Nowicki	Gert Frank
	Vladimir Kaminski	Stanisla Szozda	Jorgen Hansen
	Aavo Pikkuus	Ryszard Szurkowski	Jorn Lund
1980	U.S.S.R. 2h 01:21.7	EAST GERMANY 2h 02:53.2	CZECHOSLOVAKIA 2h 02:53.9
	Yuriy Kashirin	Falk Boden	Michal Klasa
	Oleg Logwin	Bernd Drogan	Vlastibor Konecny
	Sergey Shelpakov	Olaf Ludwig	Alipi Kostadinov
	Anatoliy Yarkin	Hans-Joachin Hartnick	Jiri Skoda

6. Equestrian Sports

GRAND PRIX (JUMPING)

GOLD	SILVER	BRONZE
1896 Event not held		
1900 Aimé Haegeman	Georges van de Poele	de Champsavin
(BEL) *Benton II*	(BEL) *Windsor Squire*	(FRA) *Terpischore*
1904–1908 Event not held		
1912 Jean Cariou	Rabod W. von Kröcher	Emanuel de Blommaert
		de Soye
(FRA) 186 *Mignon*	(GER) 186 *Dohna*	(BEL) 185 *Clonmore*
Teams—SWEDEN 545 pts.	FRANCE 538	GERMANY 530
C. Gustav Lewenhaupt	Jean Cariou	Sigismund Freyer
Hans von Rosen	Michel d'Astafort	William Graf von
Gustaf Kilman	Bernard Meyer	Hohenau
		Ernst-Hubertus Deloch
1920 Tommaso Lequio	Alessandro Valerio	C. Gustaf Lewenhaupt
(ITA) 2 faults *Trebecco*	(ITA) 3 faults *Cento*	(SWE) 4 faults
		Mon Coeur
Teams—SWEDEN 14 faults	BELGIUM 16.25	ITALY 18.75
Hans von Rosen	Count Herman	Ettore Caffaratti
Claes König	d'Oultremont	Guilio Cacciandra
Daniel Norling	André Commans	Alessandro Alvisi
	Baron Herman de	
	Gaiffier d'Hestroy	
1924 Alphonse Gemuseus	Tommaso Lequio	Adam Królikiewicz
(SUI) 6 faults *Lucette*	(ITA) 8.75 *Trebecco*	(POL) 10 *Picador*
Teams—SWEDEN 42.25 pts.	SWITZERLAND 50	PORTUGAL 53
Ake Thelning	Alphonse Gemuseus	Antonio Borges
Axel Ståhle	Werner Stüber	d'Almeida
Age Lundström	Hans Bühler	Helder de Souza Martins
		José Mouzinho
		d'Albuquerque
1928 František Ventura	Pierre Bertrand	Charles Kuhn
(TCH) no faults	de Balanda	(SUI) 4 *Pepita*
Eliot	(FRA) 2 *Papillon*	
Teams—SPAIN 4 faults	POLAND 8	SWEDEN 10
Marquis José Alvarez	Kazimierz Gzowski	Karl Hansen
de los Trujillos	Kazimierz Szosland	Carl Björnstjerna
José Navarro Morenés	Michal Antoniewicz	Ernst Hallberg
Julio Garcia Fernández		
1932[1] Takeichi Nishi	Harry Chamberlin	Clarence von Rosen jr.
(JPN) 8 pts. *Uranus*	(USA) 212 *Show Girl*	(SWE) 16 *Empire*
1936 Kurt Hasse	Henri Rang	József von Platthy
(GER) 4 faults *Tora*	(ROM) 4 *Delfis*	(HUN) 8 *Sellö*
Teams—GERMANY	NETHERLANDS 51.5	PORTUGAL 56
44 faults		
Kurt Hasse	Jan A. de Bruine	Luis Mena e Silva
Marten von Barnekow	Johan J. Greter	Luis Marquéz do
Heinz Brandt	Henri L. M. van Schaik	Funchal
		José Beltrão
1948 Humberto Mariles	Rubén Uriza	Jean F. d'Orgeix
Cortés	(MEX) 8 *Harvey*	(FRA) 8
(MEX) 6.25 faults *Arete*		*Sucre de Pomme*
Teams—MEXICO	SPAIN 56.50	GREAT BRITAIN 67
34.25 faults		
Humberto Mariles	Jaime Garcia Cruz	Henry M. V. Nicoll
Cortés	Marcelino Gavilán y	Arthur Carr
Rubén Uriza	Ponce de Leon	Harry M. Llewellyn
Alberto Valdés	José Navarro Morenés	
1952 Pierre Jonquières	Oscar Cristi	Fritz Thiedemann
d'Oriola	(CHI) 4 *Bambi*	(GER) 8 *Meteor*
(FRA) no faults		
Ali Baba		

---

[1] There was also a teams competition, but there was no nation of which all three riders completed the course.

Alwin Schockemöhle (GER) won the individual Grand Prix gold medal on "Warwick Rex" in 1976. He has also won 3 team medals, in 1960, 1968 and 1976.

	GOLD	SILVER	BRONZE
	Teams—**GREAT BRITAIN** 40.75 faults	**CHILE 45.75**	**UNITED STATES** 52.25
	Douglas Stewart	Oscar Cristi	Arthur J. McCashin
	Wilfred H. White	Ricardo Echeverria	John Russell
	Harry M. Llewellyn	Cesar Mendoza	William Steinkraus
1956	Hans Günter Winkler	Raimondo d'Inzeo	Piero d'Inzeo
	(GER) 4 faults *Halla*	(ITA) 8 *Merano*	(ITA) 11 *Uruguay*
	Teams—**GERMANY 40**	**ITALY 66**	**GREAT BRITAIN 69**
	Hans Günter Winkler	Raimondo d'Inzeo	Wilfred H. White
	Fritz Thiedemann	Piero d'Inzeo	Patricia Smythe
	Alfons Lütke-Westheus	Salvatore Oppes	Peter Robeson
1960	Raimondo d'Inzeo	Piero d'Inzeo	David Broome
	(ITA) 12 faults *Posillippo*	(ITA) 16 *The Rock*	(GBR) 23 *Sunsalve*
	Teams—**GERMANY 46.50**	**UNITED STATES 66**	**ITALY 80.50**
	Alwin Schockemöhle	George Morris	Riamondo d'Inzeo
	Fritz Thiedemann	Frank Chapot	Piero d'Inzeo
	Hans Günter Winkler	William Steinkraus	Antonio Oppes
1964	Pierre Jonquières d'Oriola	Hermann Schridde	Peter Robeson
	(FRA) 9 faults *Lutteur*	(GER) 13.75 faults *Dozen*	(GBR) 16 faults *Firecrest*
	Teams—**GERMANY 68.50**	**FRANCE 77.75**	**ITALY 88.50**
	Hermann Schridde	Pierre Jonquières d'Oriola	Piero d'Inzeo
	Kurt Jarasinksi	Janou Lefebvre	Raimondo d'Inzeo
	Hans Günter Winkler	Guy Lefrant	Graziano Mancinelli
1968	William Steinkraus	Marian Coakes	David Broome
	(USA) 4 faults *Snowbound*	(GBR) 8 faults *Stroller*	(GBR) 12 faults *Mister Softee*
	Teams—**CANADA 102.75**	**FRANCE 110.50**	**GERMANY 117.25**
	Thomas Gayford	Marcel Rozier	Hermann Schridde
	James Day	Janou Lefebvre	Alwin Schockemöhle
	James Elder	Pierre Jonquières d'Oriola	Hans Günter Winkler

GOLD	SILVER	BRONZE

1972 Graziano Mancinelli   Ann Moore   Neal Shapiro
    (ITA) 8 faults   (GBR) 9 faults   (USA) 8 faults
        Ambassador   *Psalm*   *Sloopy*
    Teams—WEST GERMANY   UNITED STATES 32.25   ITALY 48
               32

      Fritz Ligges   William Steinkraus   Vittorio Orlando
      Gerhard Wiltfang   Neal Shapiro   Raimondo d'Inzeo
      Hartwig Steenken   Kathryn Kusner   Graziano Mancinelli
      Hans Günter Winkler   Frank Chapot   Piero d'Inzeo
1976 Alwin Schockemöhle   Michael Valliancourt   Francois Mathy
    (GER) No faults   (CAN) 12 faults   (BEL) 12 faults
        Warwick Rex   *Branch County*   *Gai Luron*
    Teams—FRANCE 40   WEST GERMANY 44   BELGIUM 63

      Hubert Parot   Hans Günter Winkler   Eric Wauters
      Marcel Rozier   Paul Schockemöhle   Francois Mathy
      Michel Roche   Alwin Shockemöhle   Edgar Guepper
      Marc Roguet   Soenke Soenksen   Stanny Van Paeschen
1980 Jan Kowalczyk   Nikolai Korolkov   Joaquin Perez Heras[2]
    (POL) 8 faults   (URS) 9.5 faults   (MEX) 12 faults
        Artemor   *Espadron*   *Alymony*
    Teams—U.S.S.R. 20.25   POLAND 56   MEXICO 59.75

      Vyacheslav Chukanov   Marian Kozicki   Joaquin Perez Heras
      Viktor Poganovsky   Jan Kowalczyk   Alberto Valdes Lacarra
      Viktor Asmayev   Wieslaw Hartman   Gerardo Tazzer Valencia
      Nikolai Korolkov   Janusz Bobik   Jesus Gomez Portugal

---

[2] Won jump off.

GRAND PRIX (DRESSAGE)

1896–1908 Event not held
1912 Carl Bonde   Gustaf-Adolf   Hans von Blixen-
    (SWE) 15 pts.   Boltenstern Sr.   Finecke
        Emperor   (SWE) 21   *Neptun*   (SWE) 32   *Maggie*
1920 Janne Lundblad   Bertil Sandström   Hans von Rosen
    (SWE) 27,937 pts. *Uno*   (SWE) 26,312   *Sabel*   (SWE) 25,125
                          Running Sister
1924 Ernst Linder   Bertil Sandström   Xavier Lesage
    (SWE) 276.4 pts.   (SWE) 275.8   *Sabel*   (FRA) 265.8 *Plumard*
        Piccolomini
1928 Carl F. F. von Langen   Charles Marion   Ragnar Olsson
    (GER) 237.42 pts.   (FRA) 231.00 *Limon*   (SWE) 229.78
        Draufgänger   *Günstling*
    Teams—GERMANY   SWEDEN 650.86   NETHERLANDS
        669.72 pts.   642.96

      Carl von Langen   Ragnar Olsson   Jan van Reede
      Hermann Linkenbach   Carl Bonde   Pierre Vesteegh
      Eugen von Lotzbeck   Janne Lundblad   Gérard le Heux
1932 Xavier Lesage   Charles Marion   Hiram Tuttle
    (FRA) 1,031.25 pts   (FRA) 916.25 *Linon*   (USA) 901.50 *Olympic*
        Taine
    Teams—FRANCE   SWEDEN 2,678.00   UNITED STATES
        2,818.75 pts.   2,576.75

      Xavier Lesage   Thomas Byström   Hiram Tuttle
      Charles Marion   Gustaf-Adolf   Isaac Kitts
      André Jousseaume   Boltenstern Jr.   Alvin Moore
                   Bertil Sandström
1936 Heinz Pollay   Friedrich Gerhard   Alois Podhajsky
    (GER) 1,760 *Kronos*   (GER)1,745.5 *Absinth*   (AUT) 1,721.5 *Nero*
    Teams—GERMANY   FRANCE 4,846   SWEDEN 4,660.5
        5,074 pts.

      Heinz Pollay   André Jousseaume   Gregor von Aldercreutz
      Freidrich Gerhard   Daniel Gillois   Folke Sandström
      Hermann von Oppeln   Gérard de Ballorre   Sven Colliander
        Bronikowski

Hans Winkler (GER), the only rider in Olympic history to win five gold medals, shown in action during the Grand Prix jumping in Mexico City in 1968.

Heinz Pollay (GER), shown here on "Kronos," won both the individual and team gold medals for Grand Prix Dressage at Berlin in 1936.

GOLD	SILVER	BRONZE

1948 Hans Moser André Jousseaume Gustaf-Adolf
(SUI) 492.5 pts. (FRA) 480.0 Boltenstern Jr.
Hummer *Harpagon* (SWE) 477.5 *Trumpf*
Teams—FRANCE 1,269 pts.[1] UNITED STATES 1,256 PORTUGAL 1,182
André Jousseaume Robert Borg Fernando da Silva Paes
Jean Paillard Earl Thomson Francisco Valadas
Maurice Buret Frank Henry Luis Mena e Silva
1952 Henri St. Cyr Lis Hartel André Jousseaume
(SWE) 561 pts. (DEN) 541.5 *Jubilee* (FRA) 541.0 *Harpagon*
Master Rufus
Teams—SWEDEN SWITZERLAND GERMANY 1,501.0
1,597.5 pts. 1,759.0
Gustaf-Adolf Gustav Fischer Ida von Nagel
Boltenstern Jr. Gottfried Trachsel Fritz Thiedemann
Henri St. Cyr Henri Chammartin Heinrich Pollay
Gehnäll Persson
1956 Henri St. Cyr Lis Hartel Liselott Lisenhoff
(SWE) 860 pts. *Juli* (DEN) 850 *Jubilee* (GER) 832 *Adular*
Teams—SWEDEN,2,475pts. GERMANY 2,346 SWITZERLAND 2,346
Henri St. Cyr Liselott Lisenhoff Gustav Fischer
Gehnäll Persson Hannelore Weygand Gottfried Trachsel
Gustaf-Adolf Anneliese Küppers Henri Chammartin
Boltenstern Jr.
1960 Sergey Filatov Gustav Fischer Josef Neckermann
(URS)2,144pts.*Absent* (SUI) 2,087 *Wald* (GER) 2,082 *Asbach*
Team event not held
1964 Henri Chammartin Harry Boldt Sergey Filatov
(SUI) 1,504 pts. (GER) 1,503 *Remus* (URS) 1,486 *Absent*
Woermann
Teams—GERMANY SWITZERLAND U.S.S.R. 2,311
2,558 pts. 2,526
Harry Boldt Henri Chammartin Sergey Filatov
Josef Neckermann Gustav Fischer Ivan Kizimov
Reiner Klimke Marianne Gossweiler Ivan Kalita
1968 Ivan Kizimov Josef Neckermann Reiner Klimke
(URS) 1,572 pts.*Ikhor* (GER) 1,546 *Mariano* (GER) 1,537 *Dux*
Teams—GERMANY U.S.S.R. 2,657 SWITZERLAND 2,547
2,699 pts.
Josef Neckermann Elena Petuchkova Henri Chammartin
Liselott Linsenhoff Ivan Kizimov Marianne Gossweiler
Dr. Reiner Klimke Ivan Kalita Gustav Fischer
1972 Liselott Linsenhoff Elena Petuchkova Josef Neckermann
(GER) 1,229 pts. *Piaff* (URS) 1,185 *Pepel* (GER) 1,177 *Venetia*
Teams—WEST SWITZERLAND 4,684 UNITED STATES 4,670
GERMANY 5,155 pts.
Harry Boldt Christine Stueckelberger Hilda Gurney
Reiner Klimke Ulrich Lehmann Dorothy Morkis
Gabriela Grillo Doris Ramseier Edith Master
1976 Christine Harry Boldt Reiner Klimke
Stueckelberger (GER) 1,432 (GER) 1,395
(SUI) 1,486 pts.
Teams—WEST SWITZERLAND 4,684 UNITED STATES 4,670
Germany 5,155 pts.
Harry Boldt Christine Stueckelberger Hilda Gurney
Reiner Klimke Ulrich Lehmann Dorothy Morkis
Gabriela Grillo Doris Ramseier Edith Master
1980 Elizabeth Theurer Yuri Kovshov Viktor Ugryumov
(AUT) 1,370 pts. (URS) 1,300 *Igrok* (URS) 1,234 *Shkval*
Mon Cherie
Teams—U.S.S.R. 4,383 pts. BULGARIA 3,580 RUMANIA 3,346
Yuriy Kovshov Petar Mandajiev Anghelache Donescu
Viktor Ugryumov Svetoslav Ivanov Dumitru Veliku
Vera Misevich Gheorghi Gadjev Petre Rosca

---

[1] SWEDEN was originally declared the winner with 1,366 pts., but was disqualified
subsequently—five years later.

THREE-DAY EVENT

GOLD	SILVER	BRONZE
1896–1908 Event not held		
1912 Axel Nordlander (SWE) 46.59 pts. *Lady Artist*	Friedrich von Rochow (GER) 46.42 *Idealist*	Jean Cariou (FRA) 46.32 *Cocotte*
Teams—SWEDEN 139.06 pts.	GERMANY 138.48	UNITED STATES 137.33
Nils Adlercreutz	Friedrich von Rochow	Benjamin Lear
Axel Nordlander	Eduard von Lütcken	John C. Montgomery
Ernst G. Casparsson	Richard G. von Schaesberg-Thannheim	Guy Henry
1920 Helmer Mörner (SWE) 1,775 pts. *Germania*	Age Lundström (SWE) 1,738.75 *Yrsa*	Ettore Caffaratti (ITA) 1,733.75 *Traditore*
Teams—SWEDEN 5,057.5 pts.	ITALY 4,735	BELGIUM 4,560
Helmer Mörner	Ettore Caffaratti	Roger Moremans d'Emaus
Age Lundström	Garibaldi Spighi	Oswald Lints
George von Braun	Guilio Cacciandra	Jules Bonvalet
1924 Adolph D. C. van der Voort van Zijp (HOL) 1,976 pts. *Silver Piece*	Fröde Kirkebjerg (DEN) 1,853.5 *Meteor*	Sloan Doak (USA) 1,845.5 *Pathfinder*
Teams—NETHERLANDS 5,297.5 pts.	SWEDEN 4,743.5	ITALY 4,512.5
Adolph D. C. van der Voort van Zijp	Claes König	Alberto Lombardi
Charles F. Pahud de Mortanges	Torsten Sylvan	Alessandro Alvisi
Gerard P. C. de Kruyff	Gustaf Hagelin	Emanuele di Pralormo

The first winners of the Three-Day Event team competition were this Swedish trio at Stockholm in 1912.

GOLD	SILVER	BRONZE
1928 Charles F. Pahud de Mortanges (HOL) 1,969.82 pts. *Marcoix*	Gerard P. C. de Kruyff (HOL) 1,967.26 *Va-t-en*	Bruno Neumann (GER) 1,944.42 *Ilja*
Teams—NETHERLANDS 5.865.68 pts.	NORWAY 5,395.68	POLAND 5,067.92
Charles F. Pahud de Mortanges Gerard P. C. de Kruyff Adolph D. C. van der Voort van Zijp	Arthur Quist Bjart Ording Eugen Johansen	Jósef Trenkwald Michal Antoniewicz Karol de Rómmel
1932 Charles F. Pahud de Mortanges (HOL) 1,813.83 pts. *Marcroix*	Earl Thomson (USA) 1,811 *Jenny Camp*	Clarence von Rosen Jr. (SWE) 1,809.42 *Sunnyside Maid*
Teams—UNITED STATES 5,038.08 pts.	NETHERLANDS 4,689.08	—
Earl Thomson Harry Chamberlin Edwin Argo	Charles F. Pahud de Mortanges Karel J. Schummelketel Aernout van Lennep	
1936 Ludwig Stubbendorff (GER) 37.7 faults *Nurmi*	Earl Thomson (USA) 99.9 *Jenny Camp*	Hans Mathiesen-Lunding (DEN) 102.2 *Jason*
Teams—GERMANY 676.75 pts.	POLAND 991.70	GREAT BRITAIN 9,195.50
Ludwig Stubbendorff Rudolf Lippert Konrad von Wangenheim	Severyn Kulesza Henryk Rojcewicz Zdislaw Kawecki	Edward Howard-Vyse Alec Scott Richard Fanshawe
1948 Bernard Chevallier (FRA) plus 4 pts. *Aiglonne*	Frank Henry (USA) minus 21 *Swing Low*	J. Robert Selfelt (SWE) minus 25 *Claque*
Teams—UNITED STATES 161.50 faults	SWEDEN 165.00	MEXICO 305.25
Frank Henry Charles Anderson Earl Thomson	J. Robert Selfelt Nils Olof Stahre Sigurd Svensson	Humberto Mariles Cortés Raúl Campero Joaquin Solano Chagoya
1952 Hans von Blixen-Finecke (SWE) 28.33 faults *Jubal*	Guy Lefrant (FRA) 54.50 *Verdun*	Wilhelm Büsing (GER) 55.50 *Hubertus*
Teams—SWEDEN 221.49 pts.	GERMANY 235.49	UNITED STATES 587.16
Hans von Blixen-Finecke Nils Olof Stahre Karl F. Frölén	Wilhelm Büsing Klaus Wagner Otto Rothe	Charles Hough Walter Staley Jr. John Wofford
1956 Petrus Kastenman (SWE) 66.53 faults *Iluster*	August Lütke-Westhues (GER) 84.87 *Trux von Kamax*	Francis Weldon (GBR) 85.48 *Kilbarry*
Teams—GREAT BRITAIN 355.48 pts.	GERMANY 475.61	CANADA 572.72
Albert E. Hill Francis Weldon A. Lawrence Rook	August Lütke-Westhues Klaus Wagner Otto Rothe	James Elder Brian Herbinson John Rumble
1960 Lawrence Morgan (AUS) plus 7.15 pts. *Salad Days*	Neale Lavis (AUS) minus 16.50 *Mirrabooka*	Anton Bühler (SUI) minus 51.21 *Gay Spark*
Teams—AUSTRALIA 128.18 pts.	SWITZERLAND 386.02	FRANCE 515.71
Lawrence Morgan Neale Lavis William Roycroft	Anton Bühler Hans Schwarzenbach Rudolf Günthardt	Jack L. Le Goff Jean R. Le Roy Guy Lefrant
1964 Mauro Checcoli (ITA) 64.40 pts. *Surbean*	Carlos Moratorio (ARG) 56.40 *Chalan*	Fritz Ligges (GER) 49.20 *Donkosak*

GOLD	SILVER	BRONZE
Teams—ITALY 85.80 pts.	UNITED STATES 65.86	GERMANY 56.73
Mauro Checcoli	Michael Page	Fritz Ligges
Paolo Angioni	Kevin Freeman	Horst Karsten
Giuseppe Ravano	J. Michael Plumb	Gerhard Schultz
1968 Jean-Jacques Guyon	Derek Allhusen	Michael Page
(FRA) 38.86 pts. *Pitou*	(GBR) 41.61 *Lochinvar*	(USA) 52.31 *Faster*
Teams—GREAT BRITAIN	UNITED STATES	AUSTRALIA 331.26
175.93 pts.	245.87	
Derek Allhusen	Michael Page	Wayne Roycroft
Richard H. Meade	James Wofford	Brian Cobcroft
Reuben Jones	J. Micheal Plumb	William Roycroft
1972 Richard H. Meade	Alessa Argenton	Jan Jonsson
(GBR) 57.73 pts.	(ITA) 43.33 *Woodland*	(SWE) 39.67 *Sarajevo*
Laurieston		
Teams—GREAT BRITAIN	UNITED STATES 10.81	WEST GERMANY
95.53 pts.		minus 18.00
Mary D.	Kevin Freeman	Harry Klugmann
Gordon-Watson	Bruce Davidson	Karl Schultz
Bridget Parker	J. Michael Plumb	Ludwig Goessing
Richard H. Meade		
Mark A. Phillips (non-scorer)		
1976 Edmund Coffin	John Plumb	Karl Schultz
(US) 114.99 pts.	(USA) 125.85	(GER) 129.45 *Madrigal*
Bally—Cor	*Better & Better*	
Teams—UNITED STATES	WEST GERMANY	AUSTRALIA 599.54
441.00 pts.	584.60	
Edmund Coffin	Karl Schultz	Wayne Roycroft
John Plumb	Herbert Bloecker	Mervyn Bennett
Bruce Davidson	Helmut Rethemeier	William Roycroft
Mary Tauskey	Otto Ammermann	Denis Pigott
1980 Frederico Euro Roman	Aleksandr Blinov	Yuri Salnikov
(ITA) 108.60 pts.	(URS) 120.80 *Galzun*	(URS) 151.60 *Pintset*
Rossinan		
Teams—U.S.S.R. 457.00 pts.	ITALY 656.20	MEXICO 1,172.85
Aleksandr Blinov	Frederico Euro Roman	Manuel Mendivil Yocupicio
Yuri Salnikov	Anna Casagrande	David Barcena Rios
Valeriy Volkov	Mauro Roman	Jose Luis Perez Soto
Sergey Roghozhin	Marina Sciocchetti	Fabian Vazquez Lopez

Richard Meade (GBR) won three Olympic gold medals in the Three-Day Event.

7. Fencing (Men)

FOIL (INDIVIDUAL)

Wins are assessed on both wins (2 pts.) *and* draws (1 pt.) so, as in 1928, the winner does not necessarily have most wins.

	GOLD	SILVER	BRONZE
1896	Emile Gravelotte (FRA) 4 wins	Henri Callott (FRA) 3	Perikles Mavromichalis-Pierrakos (GRE) 2
1900	E. Coste (FRA) 6 wins	Henri Masson (FRA) 5	Jacques Boulenger (FRA) 4
1904	Ramón Fonst (CUB) d.n.a.*	Albertson Van Zo Post (CUB) d.n.a.	Charles Tatham (CUB) d.n.a.
1906	Georges Dillon-Kavanagh (FRA) d.n.a.	Gustav Casmir (GER) d.n.a.	Pierre d'Hugues (FRA) d.n.a.
1908	Event not held		
1912	Nedo Nadi (ITA) 7 wins	Pietro Speciale (ITA) 5	Richard Verderber (AUT) 4
1920	Nedo Nadi (ITA) 10 wins	Phillippe Cattiau (FRA) 9	Roger Ducret (FRA) 9
1924	Roger Ducret (FRA) 6 wins	Philippe Cattiau (FRA) 5	Maurice van Damme (BEL) 4
1928	Lucien Gaudin (FRA) 9 wins	Erwin Casmir (GER) 9	Giulio Gaudini (ITA) 9
1932	Gustavo Marzi (ITA) 9 wins	Joseph Levis (USA) 6	Giulio Gaudini (ITA) 5
1936	Giulio Gaudini (ITA) 7 wins	Edouard Gardère (FRA) 6	Giorgio Bocchino (ITA) 4
1948	Jean Buhan (FRA) 7 wins	Christian d'Oriola (FRA) 5	Lajos Maszlay (HUN) 4
1952	Christian d'Oriola (FRA) 8 wins	Edoardo Mangiarotti (ITA) 6	Manlino di Rosa (ITA) 5

Jean Buhan of France (right), the winner of the individual foil event in 1948, is shown in an early bout with John Emrys Lloyd (GBR).

GOLD	SILVER	BRONZE
1956 Christian d'Oriola (FRA) 6 wins	Giancarlo Bergamini (ITA) 5	Antonio Spallino (ITA) 5
1960 Viktor Zhdanovich (URS) 7 wins	Yuriy Sissikin (URS) 4	Albert Axelrod (USA) 3
1964 Egon Franke (POL) 3 wins	Jean-Claude Magnan (FRA) 2	Daniel Revenu (FRA) 1
1968 Ion Drimba (ROM) 4 wins	Jenö Kamuti (HUN) 3	Daniel Revenu (FRA) 3
1972 Witold Woyda (POL) 5 wins	Jenö Kamuti (HUN) 4	Christian Noël (FRA) 2
1976 Fabio Dal Zotto (ITA) 4 wins	Aleksandr Romankov (URS) 4	Bernard Talvard (FRA) 3
1980 Vladimir Smirnov (URS) 5 wins	Paskal Jolyot (FRA) 5	Aleksandr Romankov (URS) 5

FOIL (TEAM)

1896–1900 Event not held

1904 **CUBA**	**INTERNATIONAL TEAM**
Ramón Fonst	Charles Tatham (CUB)
Albertson Van Zo Post	Charles Townsend (USA)
Manuel Díaz	Arthur Fox (USA)

1906–1912 Event not held

1920 **ITALY**	**FRANCE**	**UNITED STATES**
Nedo Nadi	Lionel Bony de	Francis W. Honeycutt
Aldo Nadi	Castellane	Henry Breckinridge
Abelardo Olivier	Gaston Amson	Arthur Lyon
Pietro Speciale	André Labatut	Robert V. Sears
Rodolfo Terlizzi	Georges Trombert	Harold Rayner
Tomasso Costantino	Marcel Perrot	
Baldo Baldi	Lucien Gaudin	
Oreste Puliti	Philippe Cattiau	
	Roger Ducret	

Christian d'Oriola (FRA) (left) won 2 gold medals in the individual foil event and a gold and a silver medal in the team event, in 1952 and 1956.

	GOLD	SILVER	BRONZE
1924	**FRANCE** Lucien Gaudin Roger Ducret Philippe Cattiau Henri Jobier Jacques Coutrot Guy de Luget André Labatut Joseph Peroteaux	**BELGIUM** Désiré Beaurain Charles Crahay Fernand de Montigny Maurice van Damme Marcel Berré Albert de Roocker	**HUNGARY** László Berti István Lichteneckert Sándor Posta Zoltán Schenker Ödön Tersztyánszky
1928	**ITALY** Ugo Pignotti Oreste Puliti Giulio Gaudini Giorgio Pessina Giorgio Chiavacci Gioacchino Guaragna	**FRANCE** Lucien Gaudin Philippe Cattiau Roger Ducret André Labatut Raymond Flacher André Gaboriaud	**ARGENTINA** Roberto Larraz Raúl Anganuzzi Luis Lucchetti Hector Lucchetti Carmelo Camet
1932	**FRANCE** Edouard Gardère René Lemoine René Bougnol Philippe Cattiau René Bondoux Jean Piot	**ITALY** Gustavo Marzi Ugo Pignotti Gioacchino Guaragna Giulio Gaudini Giorgio Pessina Rodolfo Terlizzi	**UNITED STATES** George C. Calnan Frank Righeimer Jr. Richard Steere Hugh Alessandroni Dernell Every Joseph Levis
1936	**ITALY** Gustavo Marzi Gioacchino Guaragna Manlio di Rosa Ciro Verratti Giulio Gaudini Giorgio Bocchino	**FRANCE** André Gardère René Bougnol René Lemoine Jacques Coutrot Edouard Gardère René Bondoux	**GERMANY** Erwin Casmir Julius Eisenecker August Heim Seigfrid Lerdon Otto Adam Stefan Rosenbauer
1948	**FRANCE** André Bonin Christian d'Oriola Jean Buhan René Bougnol Jacques Lataste Adrien Rommel	**ITALY** Renzo Nostini Manlio di Rosa Edoardo Mangiarotti Giuliano Nostini Giorgio Pellini Saverio Ragno	**BELGIUM** Georges de Bourguignon Henry Paternoster Edoardo Yves Raymond Bru André van de W. de Vorsselaer Paul Valcke
1952	**FRANCE** Jean Buhan Christian d'Oriola Adrien Rommel Claude Netter Jacques Nöel Jacques Lataste	**ITALY** Giancarlo Bergamini Antonio Spallino Manlio di Rosa Edoardo Mangiarotti Renzo Nostini Giorgio Pellini	**HUNGARY** Endre Tilli Aladár Gerevich Endre Palócz Lajos Maszlay Tibor Berczelly József Sákovics
1956	**ITALY** Edoardo Mangiarotti Giancarlo Bergamini Antonio Spallino Vittorio Lucarelli Manlio di Rosa Luigi Carpaneda	**FRANCE** Christian d'Oriola Jacques Lataste René Coicaud Claude Netter Roger Closset Bernard Baudoux	**HUNGARY** Lajos Somodi József Gyuricza Endre Tilli József Marosi Mihály Fülöp József Sákovics
1960	**U.S.S.R.** Viktor Zhadanovich Mark Midler Yuriy Sissikin Gherman Sveshnikov Yuriy Rudov	**ITALY** Alberto Pellegrino Luigi Carpaneda Mario Curletto Aldo Aureggi Edoardo Mangiarotti	**GERMANY** Jürgen Theuerkauff Tim Gerresheim Eberhard Mehl Jürgen Brecht
1964	**U.S.S.R.** Gherman Sveshnikov Yuriy Sissikin Viktor Zhadanovich Mark Midler Yury Scharov	**POLAND** Zbigniew Skrudik Witold Woyda Ryszard Parulski Egon Franke Janusz Rózycki	**FRANCE** Daniel Revenu Jacky Courtillat Pierre Rodacanachi Christian Noël Jean-Claude Magnan

GOLD	SILVER	BRONZE
1968 **FRANCE**	**U.S.S.R.**	**POLAND**
Daniel Revenu	Gherman Sveshnikov	Witold Woyda
Gilles Berolatti	Yury Scharov	Zbigniew Skrudlik
Christian Noël	Vassily Stankovich	Ryszard Parulski
Jean-Claude Magnan	Viktor Putiatin	Egon Franke
Jacques Dimont	Yuriy Sissikin	Adam Lisewski
1972 **POLAND**	**U.S.S.R.**	**FRANCE**
Witold Woyda	Vassily Stankovich	Daniel Revenu
Lech Koziejowski	Anatoly Kotescev	Christian Noël
Jerzy Kaczmarek	Vladimir Demissov	Bernard Talvard
Marek Dabrowski	Leonid Romanov	Jean-Claude Magnan
Arkadiusz Godel	Viktor Putiatin	Gilles Berolatti
1976 **WEST GERMANY**	**ITALY**	**FRANCE**
Matthias Behr	Fabio Dal Zotto	Christian Noël
Thomas Bach	Carlo Montano	Bernard Talvard
Harald Hein	Stefano Simoncelli	Didier Flament
Klaus Reichert	Giovanni B. Coletti	Frederic Pietruska
1980 **FRANCE**	**U.S.S.R.**	**POLAND**
Didier Flament	Aleksandr Romankov	Adam Robak
Paskal Jolyot	Vladimir Smirnov	Boguslaw Zych
Bruno Boscherie	Sabiryan Rusiyev	Lech Koziejowski
Philippe Bonnin	Aschot Karagyan	Marian Sypniewski

Gaston Alibert (FRA) won the individual epée gold medal in the London Games of 1908.

EPEE (INDIVIDUAL)

	GOLD	SILVER	BRONZE
1896	Event not held		
1900	Ramón Fonst (CUB)	Louis Perrée (FRA)	Léon Sée (FRA)
1904	Ramón Fonst (CUB)	Charles Tatham (CUB)	Albertson Van Zo Post (CUB)
1906	Georges de la Falaise (FRA)	Georges Dillon-Kavanagh (FRA)	Alexander van Blijenburgh (HOL)
1908	Gaston Alibert (FRA) 5 wins	Alexandre Lippmann (FRA) 4	Eugène Olivier (FRA) 4
1912	Paul Anspach (BEL) 6 wins	Ivan Osiier (DEN) 5	Philippe Le Hardy de Beaulieu (BEL) 4

GOLD	SILVER	BRONZE
1920 Armand Massard (FRA) 9 wins	Alexandre Lippmann (FRA) 7	Gustave Buchard (FRA) 6
1924 Charles Delporte (BEL) 8 wins	Roger Ducret (FRA) 7	Nils Hellsten (SWE) 7
1928 Lucien Gaudin (FRA) 8 wins	Georges Buchard (FRA) 7	George Calnan (USA) 6
1932 Giancarlo Cornaggia-Medici (ITA) 8 wins	Georges Buchard (FRA) 7	Carlo Agostoni (ITA) 7
1936 Franco Riccardi (ITA) 5 wins	Saverio Ragno (ITA) 6	Giancarlo Cornaggia-Medici (ITA) 6
1948 Luigi Cantone (ITA) 7 wins	Oswald Zappelli (SUI) 5	Edoardo Mangiarotti (ITA) 5
1952 Edoardo Mangiarotti (ITA) 7 wins	Dario Mangiarotti (ITA) 6	Oswarld Zappelli (SUI) 6
1956 Carlo Pavesi (ITA) 5 wins	Giuseppe Delfino (ITA) 5	Edoardo Mangiarotti (ITA) 5
1960 Giuseppe Delfino (ITA) 5 wins	Allan L. N. Jay (GBR) 5	Bruno Khabarov (URS) 4
1964 Grigory Kriss (URS) 2 wins	H. William F. Hoskyns (GBR) 2	Guram Kostava (URS) 1
1968 Győző Kulcsár (HUN) 4 wins	Grigory Kriss (URS) 4	Gianluigi Saccaro (ITA) 4
1972 Csaba Fenyvesi (HUN) 4 wins	Jacques la Degaillerie (FRA) 3	Győző Kulcsár (HUN) 3
1976 Alexander Pusch (GER) 3 wins	Jurgen Hehn (GER) 3	Győző Kulcsár (HUN) 3
1980 Johan Harmenberg (SWE) 4 wins	Erno Kolczonay (HUN) 3	Philippe Riboud (FRA) 3

Belgium's gold-medal epée team poses at the 1912 Games at Stockholm after their victory.

• EPEE (TEAM)

GOLD	SILVER	BRONZE
1896–1904 Event not held		
1906 FRANCE	**GREAT BRITAIN**	**BELGIUM**
Pierre d'Hugues	William H. Derborough	Constant Cloquet
George Dillon-Kavanagh	Cosmo E. Duff-Gordon	Fernand de Montigny
	Charles N. Robinson	Edmond Grahay
Mohr	Edgar Seligman	Philippe Le Hardy
Georges de la Falaise		de Beaulieu
1908 FRANCE	**GREAT BRITAIN**	**BELGIUM**
Gaston Alibert	C. Leaf Daniell	Paul Anspach
Bernard Gravier	Cecil Haig	Désiré Beaurain
Alexandre Lippmann	Martin Holt	Ferdinand Feyerick
Eugène Olivier	Robert Montgomerie	François Rom
Jean Stern	Edward Amphlett	Fernand de Montigny
Henri-Georges Berger	Edgar Seligman	Victor Willems
Charles Collignon	Sydney Martineau	Ferdnand Bosmans
1912 BELGIUM	**GREAT BRITAIN**	**NETHERLANDS**
Paul Anspach	Edgar Seligman	Adrianus E. W. de Jong
Henri Anspach	Edward Amphlett	W. P. Hubert van
Fernand de Montigny	Robert Montgomerie	Blijenburgh
Jacques Ochs	John Blake	Jetze Doorman
Gaston Salmon	Percival Davson	George van Rossem
Francois Rom	Arthur Everitt	Leo Nardus
Victor Willems	Sydney Martineau	
Robert Hennet	Martin Holt	
1920 ITALY	**BELGIUM**	**FRANCE**
Nedo Nadi	Paul Anspach	Armand Massard
Aldo Nadi	Léon Tom	Alexandre Lippmann
Abelardo Olivier	Ernest Gevers	Gustave Buchard
Giovanni Canova	Felix G. d'Alviella	Casanova
Dino Urbani	Victor Boin	Georges Trombert
Tullio Bozza	Joseph de Craecker	Gaston Amson
Andrea Marrazzi	Maurice de Wée	Moreau
Antonio Allocchio	Philippe Le Hardy	
Paolo Thaón di Revel	de Beaulieu	
1924 FRANCE	**BELGIUM**	**ITALY**
Lucien Gaudin	Fernand de Montigny	Vincenzo Cuccia
Roger Ducret	Joseph de Craecker	Giovanni Canova
Alexandre Lippmann	Paul Anspach	Giulio Basletta
Georges Buchard	Ernest Gevers	Marcello Bertinetti
André Labatut	Léon Tom	Virgilio Mantegazza
Georges Tainturier	Charles Delporte	Oreste Moricca
Lionel Lioteel		
1928 ITALY	**FRANCE**	**PORTUGAL**
Carlo Agostoni	Armand Massard	Paolo d'Eca Leal
Marcello Bartinetti	Georges Buchard	Mário de Noronha
Giancarlo Cornaggia-Medici	Gaston Amson	Jorge Paiva
	Emile Cornic	Frederico Paredes
Renzo Minoli	Bernard Schmetz	João Sassetti
Giulio Basletta	René Barbier	Henrique da Silveira
Franco Riccardi		
1932 FRANCE	**ITALY**	**UNITED STATES**
Bernard Schmetz	Carlo Agostoni	George Calnan
Philippe Cattiau	Franco Riccardi	Gustave Heiss
Georges Buchard	Saverio Ragno	Tracy Jaeckel
Jean Piot	Giancarlo Cornaggia-Medici	Frank Righeimer Jr.
Fernand Jourdant		Curtis Shears
Georges Tainturier	Renzo Minoli	Miguel de Capriles
1936 ITALY	**SWEDEN**	**FRANCE**
Giancarlo Cornaggia-Medici	Sven Thofelt	Georges Buchard
	Gustaf Dyrssen	Paul Wormser
Edoardo Mangiarotti	Gösta Almgren	Philippe Cattiau
Saverio Ragno	Hans Granfelt	Henri Dulieux
Alfredo Pezzano	Birger Cederin	Bernard Schmetz
Giancarlo Brusati	Hans van Drakenberg	Michel Pécheux
Franco Riccardi		

GOLD	SILVER	BRONZE
1948 **FRANCE**	**ITALY**	**SWEDEN**
Henri Guérin	Edoardo Mangiarotti	Carl Forssell
Henri Lepage	Carlo Agostoni	Arne Tolbom
Marcel Desprets	Fiorenzo Marini	Bengt H. Ljunquist
Michel Pécheux	Antonio Mandruzzato	Sven Thofelt
Maurice Huet	Luigi Cantone	Frank Cervell
Edouard Artigas	Dario Mangiarotti	Per H. Carleson
1952 **ITALY**	**SWEDEN**	**SWITZERLAND**
Edoardo Mangiarotti	Lennart Magnusson	Willy Fitting
Dario Mangiarotti	Carl Forssell	Otto Rüfenacht
Carlo Pavesi	Berndt-Otto Rehbinder	Oswald Zappelli
Giuseppe Delfino	Per H. Carleson	Paul Barth
Franco Bertinetti	Sven Fahlman	Marlo Valota
Roberto Battaglia	Bengt H. Ljunquist	Paul Meister
1956 **ITALY**	**HUNGARY**	**FRANCE**
Giuseppe Delfino	Béla Rerrich	Yves Dreyfus
Franco Bertinetti	Ambrus Nagy	René Queyroux
Alberto Pellegrino	Barnabás Berszenyi	Daniel Dagallier
Giorgio Anglesio	József Marosi	Claude Nigon
Carlo Pavesi	József Sákovics	Armand Mouyal
Edoardo Mangiarotti	Lajos Balthazár	
1960 **ITALY**	**GREAT BRITAIN**	**U.S.S.R.**
Alberto Pellegrino	Allan L. N. Jay	Valentin Chernikov
Carlo Pavesi	Michael Howard	Arnold Chernusevich
Giuseppe Delfino	John Pelling	Guram Kostava
Edoardo Mangiarotti	H. William F. Hoskyns	Bruno Khabarov
Gianluigi Saccaro	Michael Alexander	Aleksandr Pavlovsky
Fiorenzo Marini	Raymond Harrison	
1964 **HUNGARY**	**ITALY**	**FRANCE**
Győző Kulcsár	Gianluigi Saccaro	Jacques Brodin
Zoltán Nemere	Giovanni Battista Breda	Yves Dreyfus
Tamás Gabor	Gianfranco Paolucci	Claude Bourquard
István Kausz	Giuseppe Delfino	Jack Guittet
Arpád Bárány	Alberto Pellegrino	Claude Brodin
1968 **HUNGARY**	**U.S.S.R.**	**POLAND**
Csaba Fenyvesi	Grigory Kriss	Bogdan Andrzejewski
Zoltán Nemere	Iosif Vitebsky	Michal Butkiewicz
Pál Schmitt	Aleksey Nikanchikov	Bogdan Gonsior
Győző Kulcsár	Yury Smolyakov	Henryk Nielaba
Pál Nagy	Viktor Modzalevsky	Kazimierz Barburski
1972 **HUNGARY**	**SWITZERLAND**	**U.S.S.R.**
Sandor Erdoes	Guy Evequoz	Viktor Modzalevsky
Győző Kulcsár	Peter Lötscher	Sergei Paramonov
Csaba Fenyvesi	Daniel Giger	Igor Valetov
Pál Schmitt	Christian Kanter	Georgy Zajitsky
Istvan Osztrics	François Suchanecki	Grigory Kriss
1976 **SWEDEN**	**WEST GERMNY**	**SWITZERLAND**
Carl Von Essen	Alexander Pusch	Francois Suchanecki
Hans Jacobson	Jurgen Hehn	Michel Poffet
Leif Hogstrom	Reinhold Behr	Daniel Giger
Rolf Edling	Volker Fischer	Christian Kauter
1980 **FRANCE**	**POLAND**	**U.S.S.R.**
Philippe Riboud	Pyotr Jablowski	Aschot Karagyan
Patrick Picot	Andrzej Lis	Boris Lukomski
Hubert Gardas	Leszek Swornowski	Aleksandr Abushakhmetov
Philippe Boisse	Ludomir Chronowski	Aleksandr Moshayev

SABRE (INDIVIDUAL)

1896 Jean Georgiadis	Telemachos Karakalos	Holger Nielsen
(GRE) 4 wins	(GRE) 3	(DEN) 2
1900 Georges de la Falaise	Léon Thiébaut	Siegfried Flesch
(FRA) d.n.a.	(FRA) d.n.a.	(AUT) d.n.a.
1904 Manuel Diaz	William Grebe	Albertson Van Zo Post
(CUB) d.n.a.	(USA) d.n.a.	(CUB) d.n.a.

	GOLD	SILVER	BRONZE
1906	Jean Georgiadis (GR) d.n.a.	Gustav Casmir (GER) d.n.a.	Federico Cesarano (ITA) d.n.a.
1908	Jenö Fuchs (HUN) 6 wins	Béla Zulavsky (HUN) 6	Vilem Goppold von Lobsdorf (BOH) 4
1912	Jenö Fuchs (HUN) 6 wins	Béla Békéssy (HUN) 5	Ervin Mészáros (HUN) 5
1920	Nedo Nadi (ITA) 11 wins	Aldo Nadi (ITA) 9	Adrianus E. W. de Jong (HOL) 7
1924	Sándor Posta (HUN) 5 wins	Rogert Ducret (FRA) 5	János Garai (HUN) 5
1928	Ödön Tersztyánszky (HUN) 9 wins	Attila Petschauer (HUN) 9	Bino Bini (ITA) 8
1932	György Piller (HUN) 8 wins	Giulio Gaudini (ITA) 7	Endre Kabos (HUN) 5
1936	Endre Kabos (HUN) 7 wins	Gustavo Marzi (ITA) 6	Aladár Gerevich (HUN) 6
1948	Aladár Gerevich (HUN) 7 wins	Vincenzo Pinton (ITA) 5	Pál Kovács (HUN) 5
1952	Pál Kovács (HUN) 8 wins	Aladár Gerevich (HUN) 7	Tibor Berczelly (HUN) 5
1956	Rudolf Kárpáti (HUN) 6 wins	Jerzy Pawlowski (POL) 5	Lev Kuznyetsov (URS) 4
1960	Rudolf Kárpáti (HUN) 5 wins	Zoltán Horvath (HUN) 4	Wladimiro Calarese (ITA) 4
1964	Tibor Pézsa (HUN) 2 wins	Claude Arabo (FRA) 2	Umar Mavlikhanov (URS) 1
1968	Jerzy Powlowski (POL) 4 wins	Mark Rakita (URS) 4	Tibor Pézsa (HUN) 3
1972	Viktor Sidiak (URS) 4 wins	Peter Maroth (HUN) 3	Vladimir Nazlimov (URS) 3
1976	Viktor Krovopouskov (URS) 5 wins	Vladimir Nazlimov (URS) 4	Viktor Sidiak (URS) 3
1980	Viktor Krovopuskov (URS) 5 wins	Mikhail Burtsev (URS) 4	Imre Gedovari (HUN) 3

SABRE (TEAM)

	GOLD	SILVER	BRONZE
1896–1904	Event not held		
1906	GERMANY Gustav Casmir Jacob Erckrath de Bary August Petri Emil Schön	GREECE Jean Georgiadis Menelaos Sakorraphos C. Zorbas Triantaphylos Kordogannis	NETHERLANDS James A. H. L. Melvill van Carnbée Johannes Franciscus Osten George van Rossem Maurits Jacob van Löben Sels
1908	HUNGARY Jenö Fuchs Oszkár Gerde Péter Tóth Lajos Werkner Dezsö Földes	ITALY Riccardo Nowak Alessandro Pirzio-Biroli Abelardo Olivier Marcello Bertinetti Sante Ceccherini	BOHEMIA Vilém Goppold von Lobsdorf Jaroslav Tucek Vlastimil Lada-Sázavsky Otakar Lada Bedřich Schéjbal
1912	HUNGARY László Berti Jenö Fuchs Ervin Mészáros Zoltán Schenker Dezsö Földes Oszkár Gerde Péter Tóth Lajos Werkner	AUSTRIA Richard Verderber Otto Herschmann Rudolf Cvetko Friedrich Golling Andreas Suttner Albert Bogen Reinhold Trampler	NETHERLANDS William P. Hubert van Blijenburgh Adrianus E. W. de Jong Daik Scalongne Jetze Doorman George van Rossem Hendrik de Iongh

Rudolf Karpati (HUN) (left) won the individual sabre competition in 1956 and 1960, one of 3 men who have won the gold medal twice.

Part of Hungary's successful sabre team poses in London in 1908. Since then, Hungarian teams have amassed 8 gold medals, a silver medal, and 3 bronze medals in this event.

	GOLD	SILVER	BRONZE
1920	**ITALY**	**FRANCE**	**NETHERLANDS**
	Nedo Nadi	Marc Perrodon	Jan van der Wiele
	Aldo Nadi	Georges Trombert	Adrianus E. W. de Jong
	Oreste Puliti	J. Margraff	Jetze Doorman
	Dino Urbani	Henri de Saint Germain	William P. Hubert van
	Baldo Baldi		Blijenburgh
	Francesco Gargano		Louis A. Delaunoy
	Giorgio Santelli		Salomon Zeldenrust
			Henri J. M. Wijnoldij-
			Daniels
1924	**ITALY**	**HUNGARY**	**NETHERLANDS**
	Oreste Puliti	László Berti	Adrianus E. W. De Jong
	Giulio Sarrocchi	János Garai	Jetze Doorman
	Marcello Bertinetti	Sándor Posta	Hendrik D.
	Oreste Moricca	József Rády	Scherpenhuysen
	Renato Anselmi	Zoltán Schenker	Jan van der Wiele
	Guido Balzarini	Jeno Uhlyárik	Maarten H. van Dulm
	Bino Bini	László Széchy	
	Vincenzo Cuccia	Ödön Tersztyánszky	
1928	**HUNGARY**	**ITALY**	**POLAND**
	János Garai	Renato Anselmi	Kazimierz Laskowski
	Gyula Glykais	Bino Bini	Aleksander Malecki
	Sándor Gombos	Gustavo Marzi	Adam Papée
	József Rády	Oreste Puliti	Wladyslaw Segda
	Ödön Tersztyánszky	Emilio Salafia	Tadeusz Friedrich
	Attila Petschauer	Giulio Sarrocchi	Jerzy Zabielski
1932	**HUNGARY**	**ITALY**	**POLAND**
	Endre Kabos	Renato Anselmi	Leszek Lubicz-Nycz
	Aladár Gerevich	Gustavo Marzi	Marian Suski
	György Piller	Arturo de Vecchi	Wladyslaw Dobrowolski
	Gyula Glykais	Giulio Gaudini	Adam Papée
	Attila Petschauer	Ugo Pignotti	Tadeusz Friedrich
	Ernö Nagy	Emilio Salafia	Wladyslaw Segda
1936	**HUNGARY**	**ITALY**	**GERMANY**
	Tibor Berczelly	Giulio Gaudini	Richard Wahl
	Aladár Gerevich	Gustavo Marzi	Erwin Casmir
	Endre Kabos	Aldo Masciotta	Julius Eisenecker
	László Rajcsányi	Aldo Montano	August Heim
	Imre Rajczy	Vincenzo Pinton	Hans Jörger
	Pál Kovács	Athos Tanzini	Hans Esser
1948	**HUNGARY**	**ITALY**	**UNITED STATES**
	Aladár Gerevich	Gastone Darè	Norman Armitage
	Rudolf Kárpáti	Carlo Turcato	George Worth
	Pál Kovács	Vincenzo Pinton	Tibor Nyilas
	Tibor Berczelly	Mauro Racca	Dean V. Cetrulo
	László Rajcsányi	Renzo Nostini	Miguel de Capriles
	Bertalan Papp	Aldo Montano	James Flynn
1952	**HUNGARY**	**ITALY**	**FRANCE**
	Rudolf Kárpáti	Gastone Daré	Jean Laroyenne
	Pál Kovács	Robert Ferrari	Jacques Lefèvre
	Tibor Berczelly	Renzo Nostini	Jean Levavasseur
	Aladár Gerevich	Giorgio Pellini	Bernard Morel
	Lászlo Rajcsányi	Vincenzo Pinton	Maurice Piot
	Bertalan Papp	Mauro Racca	Jean-François Tournon
1956	**HUNGARY**	**POLAND**	**U.S.S.R.**
	Atilla Keresztes	Zygmunt Pawlas	Yakov Rylskiy
	Aladár Gerevich	Jerzy Pawlowski	David Tychler
	Rudolf Kárpáti	Wojciech Zablocki	Lev Kuznyetsov
	Jenö Hámori	Andrzej Piatkowski	Evgeniy Cherepovskiy
	Pál Kovács	Marek Kuszewski	Leonid Bogdanov
	Dániel Magai	Ryszard Zub	

GOLD	SILVER	BRONZE
1960 HUNGARY	POLAND	ITALY
Zoltán Horváth	Jerzy Pawlowski	Pierluigi Chicca
Rudolf Kápráti	Wojciech Zablocki	Wladimiro Calarese
Tamás Mendelényi	Ryszard Zub	Mario Ravagnan
Pál Kovács	Emil Ochyra	Roberto Ferrari
Gabor Delneki	Andrzej Piatkowski	Gianpaolo Calanchini
Aladár Gerevich	Marek Kuszewski	
1964 U.S.S.R.	ITALY	POLAND
Nugzar Asatiani	Wladimiro Calarese	Emil Ochyra
Yakov Rylsky	Cesare Salvadori	Jerzy Pawlowski
Mark Rakita	Gianpaolo Calanchini	Ryszard Zub
Umar Mavlikhanov	Pierluigi Chicca	Andrzej Piatowski
Boris Melnikov	Mario Ravagnan	Wojciech Zablocki

Aladár Gerevich (right), the Hungarian sabreur, won 7 gold, 1 silver, and 2 bronze medals from 1932 to 1960. This action took place in 1948.

Action during the sabre event in Rome, 1960, with Fimamizu of Japan (right), duelling with Van Celden of Israel.

GOLD	SILVER	BRONZE
1968 **U.S.S.R.**	**ITALY**	**HUNGARY**
Vladimir Nazlimov	Wladimiro Calarese	Tamás Kovács
Viktor Sidiak	Michele Maffei	János Kalamár
Eduard Vinokurov	Cesare Salvadori	Péter Bakonyi
Mark Rakita	Pierluigi Chicca	Miklós Meszéna
Umar Mavlikhanov	Rolando Rigoli	Tibor Pezsa
1972 **ITALY**	**U.S.S.R.**	**HUNGARY**
Michele Maffei	Vladimir Nazlimov	Pál Gerevich
Mario A. Montano	Eduard Vinokurov	Tamás Kovács
Rolando Rigoli	Viktor Sidiak	Peter Maroth
Mario T. Montano	Viktor Bajenov	Tibor Pezsa
Cesare Salvadori	Mark Rakita	Péter Bakonyi
1976 **U.S.S.R.**	**ITALY**	**RUMANIA**
Viktor Krovopouskov	Mario A. Montano	Dan Irimiciuc
Eduard Vinokurov	Michele Maffei	Ioan Pop
Viktor Sidiak	Angelo Arcidiacono	Marin Mustata
Vladimir Nazlimov	Tommaso Montano	Cornel Marin
1980 **U.S.S.R.**	**ITALY**	**HUNGARY**
Mikhail Burtsev	Michele Maffei	Imra Gedovari
Viktor Krovopuskov	Mario Montano	Rudolf Nebald
Viktor Sidyak	Marco Romano	Pal Gerevich
Vladimir Nazlymov	Ferdinando Meglio	Ferenc Hammang

Nedo Nadi (ITA), winner of an unprecedented 5 gold medals at the 1920 Games, poses here with Helène Mayer (GER), gold medallist in the women's fencing event at the 1928 Games.

Fencing (Women)

FOIL (INDIVIDUAL)

	GOLD	SILVER	BRONZE
1896–1920	Event not held		
1924	Ellen Osiier (DEN) 5 wins	Gladys M. Davis (GBR) 4	Grete Heckscher (DEN) 3
1928	Helène Mayer (GER) 7 wins	Muriel B. Freeman (GBR) 6	Olga Oelkers (GER) 4
1932	Ellen Preis (AUT) 9 wins	J. Heather Guinness (GBR) 8	Ena Bogen (HUN) 7
1936	Ilona Elek (HUN) 6 wins	Helène Mayer (GER) 5	Ellen Preis (AUT) 5
1948	Ilona Elek (HUN) 6 wins	Karen Lachmann (DEN) 5	Ellen Müller-Preis (AUT) 5
1952	Irene Camber (ITA) 5 wins	Ilona Elek (HUN) 5	Karen Lachmann (DEN) 4
1956	Gillian M. Sheen (GBR) 6 wins	Olga Orban (ROM) 6	Renée Garilhe (FRA) 5
1960	Heidi Schmid (GER) 6 wins	Valentina Rastvorova (URS) 5	Maria Vicol (ROM) 4
1964	Ildikó Ujlaki-Rejtö (HUN) 2 wins	Helga Mees (GER) 2	Antonella Ragno (ITA) 2
1968	Elena Novikova (URS) 4 wins	Pilar Roldan (MEX) 3	Ildikó Ujlaki-Rejtö (HUN) 3
1972	Antonella Ragno-Lonzi (ITA) 4 wins	Ildikó Bóbis (HUN) 3	Galina Gorokhova (URS) 3
1976	Ildikó Schwarczenberger (HUN) 4 wins	Maria C. Collino (ITA) 4	Elene Novikova-Belova (URS) 3
1980	Pascale Trinquet (FRA) 4 wins	Magda Maros (HUN) 3	Barbara Wysoczanska (POL) 3

FOIL (TEAM)

	GOLD	SILVER	BRONZE
1896–1956	Event not held		
1960	U.S.S.R. Valentina Rastvorova Tatyana Petrenko Valentina Prudskova Lyudmila Shishova Galina Gorokhova Alexandra Zabelina	HUNGARY Katalin Juhász-Nagy Lidia Dömölky Ildikó Ujlaki-Rejtö Magda Kovács-Nyári Tiborné Székély	ITALY Irene Camber Velleda Cesari Antonella Ragno Bruna Colombetti Claudia Pasini
1964	HUNGARY Ilkidó Ujlaki-Rejtö Katalin Juhász-Nagy Lidia Dömölky-Sakovics Judit Medelényi-Agoston Paula Földessy-Marosi	U.S.S.R. Galina Gorokhova Valentina Prudskova Tatyana Samusenko Lyudmila Shishova Valentina Rastvorova	GERMANY Heidi Schmid Helga Mees Rosemarie Scherberger Gudrun Theuerkauff
1968	U.S.S.R. Alexandra Zabelina Tatyana Samusenko Elena Novikova Galina Gorokhova Svetlana Chirkova	HUNGARY Lidia Dömölky-Sakovics Ildikó Bóbis Ildikó Ujlaki-Rejtö Mária Gulácsy Paula Földessy-Marosi	RUMANIA Clara Stahl-Iencic Ileana Drimba Maria Vicol Olga Szabo Ana Ene-Dersidan
1972	U.S.S.R. Elena Novikova-Belova Alexandra Zabelina Galina Gorokhova Tatyana Samusenko Svetlana Chirkova	HUNGARY Ildikó Sagine-Retjo Ildikó Schwarczenberger Maria Szolnoki Ildikó Bóbis Ildikó Matuscakene-Ronay	RUMANIA Olga Szabo Ileana Gyulai Ana Pascu Ecaterina Stahl

GOLD	SILVER	BRONZE
1976 **U.S.S.R.**	**FRANCE**	**HUNGARY**
Elena Novikova-Belova	Brigitte Latrille	Ildikó Schwarczenberger
Olga Kniazeva	Brigitte Dumont	Edit Kovacs
Valentina Sidorova	Christi Muzio	Magda Maros
Nailia Guilazova	Veronique Trinquet	Ildikó Sagi-Retjö
1980 **FRANCE**	**U.S.S.R.**	**HUNGARY**
Brigitte Gaudin	Valentina Sidorova	Ildikó Schwarczenberger
Pascale Trinquet	Vailia Gilyasova	Magda Maros
Isabelle Boeri-Begard	Yelena Belova	Gertrud Stefanek
Veronique Brouquier	Irina Ushakova	Zsuzsa Szocz

Viktor Chukarin (URS), shown here on the pommelled horse, won a total of 7 gold medals in the gymnastics competitions of 1952 and 1956.

8. Gymnastics (Men)

In gymnastics there are eight events for men which are interlinked. First is the Team Competition which comprises one compulsory and one optional exercise for each of the six events: Floor Exercises, Side Horse, Rings, Horse Vault, Parallel Bars and Horizontal Bars. Each team competitor gets marks out of 10 for both his compulsory and optional exercise for each of the six events. The team of six with the greatest *total* of marks wins the gold medal.

Next, the best 36 competitors from the Team Competition qualify for the Individual All-Round Competition. They each complete a further optional exercise for each of the six events and gain new marks (out of 10) per event. These are then added to the *average* (not total) of their previous total marks in the compulsory and optional sections brought forward from the Team Competition previously decided.

Finally, the six best on each apparatus in the Team Competition qualify for the individual Final on that apparatus. This is decided by adding a new mark (out of 10) for a further optional exercise on that apparatus to the *average* (not total) of their previous marks in the compulsory and optional performances on that apparatus within the Team Competition previously decided.

In 1948 points for an event were marked out of 20 instead of 10 as in other recent years; otherwise scores since 1936 are of same comparative value.

TEAM COMPETITION

There was no team event in 1896 and 1900. From 1904 to 1932 this event often differed substantially from the current event as to program content, number of competitors and scoring values.

GOLD	SILVER	BRONZE
1936 **GERMANY** 657.430 pts.	**SWITZERLAND** 654.802	**FINLAND** 638.468
Franz Beckert	Walter Bach	Martti Uosikinen
Konrad Frey	Albert Bachmann	Heikki Savolainen
Alfred Schwarzmann	Eugen Mack	Mauri Noroma-Nyberg
Willi Stadel	Georges Miez	Aleksanteri Saarvala
Walter Steffens	Michael Reusch	Esa Seeste
Matthias Volz	Edi Seinemann	Veikkö Pakarinen
1948 **FINLAND** 1,358.3 pts.	**SWITZERLAND** 1,356.7	**HUNGARY** 1,330.35
A. Veikkö Huhtanen	Walter Lehmann	Lajos Tóth
Paavo Aaltonen	Josef Stalder	Lajos Sántha
Heikki Savolainen	Christian Kipfer	László Baranyai
Olavi Rove	Emil Studer	Ferenc Pataki
Einari Teräsvirta	Robert Lucy	János Mogyorósi-Klencs
Kalevi Laitinen	Michael Reusch	Ferenc Várköi
1952[1] **U.S.S.R.** 574.4 pts.	**SWITZERLAND** 567.5	**FINLAND** 564.2
Viktor Chukarin	Josef Stalder	Onni Lappalainen
Grant Shaginyan	Hans Eugster	Berndt Lindfors
Valentin Muratov	Jean Tschabold	Paavo Aaltonen
Yevgeniy Korolkov	Jack Günthard	Kaino Lempinen
Vladimir Belyakov	Melchior Thalmann	Heikki Savolainen
Yosif Berdiyev	Ernst Gebendinger	Kalevi Laitinen
Mikhail Perelman	Hans Schwarzentruber	Kalevi Viskari
Dimitriy Leonkin	Ernst Fivian	Olavi Rove
1956 **U.S.S.R.** 568.25 pts.	**JAPAN** 566.40	**FINLAND** 555.95
Viktor Chukarin	Takashi Ono	Raimo Heinonen
Valentin Muratov	Masao Takemoto	Onni Lappalainen
Boris Shakhlin	Akira Kono	Olavi Leimuvirta
Albert Azaryan	Nobuyuki Aihara	Berndt Lindfors
Yuriy Titov	Shinsaku Tsukawaki	Martti Mansikka
Pavel Stolbov	Masami Kubota	Kelevi Suoniemi
1960 **JAPAN** 575.20 pts.	**U.S.S.R.** 572.70	**ITALY** 559.05
Takashi Ono	Boris Shakhlin	Franco Menichelli
Shuji Tsurumi	Yuriy Titov	Giovanni Carminucci
Yukio Endo	Albert Azaryan	Gianfranco Marzolla
Masao Takemoto	Vladimir Portnoi	Angelo Vicardi
Nobuyuki Aihara	Valeriy Kerdemilidi	Orlando Polmonari
Takashi Mitsukuri	Nikolaya Miligulo	Pasquale Carminucci
1964 **JAPAN** 577.95 pts.	**U.S.S.R.** 575.45	**GERMANY** 565.10
Yukio Endo	Yury Tsapenko	Siegfried Fülle
Shuji Tsurumi	Boris Shakhlin	Klaus Köste
Haruhiro Yamashita	Victor Leontyev	Erwin Koppe
Takashi Mitsukuri	Victor Lisitsky	Peter Weber
Takuji Hayata	Sergey Diomidov	Philipp Fürst
Takashi Ono	Yuriy Titov	Günter Lyhs
1968 **JAPAN** 575.90 pts.	**U.S.S.R.** 571.10	**E. GERMANY** 557.15
Sawao Kato	Mikhail Voronin	Matthias Brehme
Akinori Nakayama	Sergey Diomidov	Klaus Köste
Eizo Kenmotsu	Vladimir Klimenko	Siegfried Fülle
Takeshi Kato	Valeryi Karassev	Peter Weber
Yukio Endo	Victor Lisitsky	Gerhard Dietrich
Mitsuo Tsukahara	Valeryi Iljinykh	Günter Beier

---

[1]In 1952 eight competitors counted instead of 6 as in other years.

GOLD	SILVER	BRONZE
1972 **JAPAN** 571.25 pts.	U.S.S.R. 564.05	**E. GERMANY** 559.70
Sawao Kato	Nikolai Andrianov	Klaus Köste
Eizo Kenmotsu	Mikhail Voronin	Matthias Brehme
Shigeru Kasamatsu	Viktor Klimenko	Wolfgang Thune
Akinori Nakayama	Edvard Mikhaelian	Wolfgang Klotz
Mitsuo Tsukahara	Aleksandre Maleev	Reinhard Rychly
Teriuihi Okamura	Vladimir Schukin	Jürgen Paeke
1976 **JAPAN** 576.85 pts.	U.S.S.R. 576.45	**E. GERMANY** 564.65
Hisato Igarashi	Vladimir Tikhonov	Bernd Jager
Shun Fujimoto	Gennadi Kryssin	Wolfgang Klotz
Sawao Kato	Alexandr Ditiatin	Rainer Hanschke
Hiroshi Kajiyama	Vladimir Marchenko	Michail Nikolay
Eizo Kenmotsu	Vladimir Markelov	Lutz Mack
Mitsuo Tsukahara	Nikolai Andrianov	Roland Bruckner
1980 **U.S.S.R.** 589.60 pts.	**EAST GERMANY** 581.15	**HUNGARY** 575.00
Nikolai Andrianov	Roland Bruckner	Ferenc Donath
Alexandr Ditiatin	Michael Nikolay	Zoltan Magyar
Eduard Asaryan	Lutz Hoffmann	Peter Kovacs
Alexandr Tkachyov	Ralf-Peter Hemmann	Gyorgy Guczoghy
Bogdan Makuts	Andreas Bronst	Istvan Vamos
Vladimir Markelov	Lutz Mack	Zoltan Kelemen

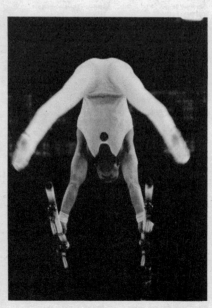

Soviet gymnast Alexandr Ditiatin won a medal in each of the eight gymnastics categories in 1980, setting an all-Olympic record for the most medals won at one Games.

COMBINED EXERCISES (INDIVIDUAL)

This event was not held in 1896. From 1900 to 1932 this event often differed substantially from the current event as to program content and scoring values.

	GOLD	SILVER	BRONZE
1936	Alfred Schwarzmann (GER) 113.100	Eugen Mack (SUI) 112.334	Konrad Frey (GER) 111.532
1948	A. Veikkö Huhtanen (FIN) 229.7	Walter Lehmann (SUI) 229.0	Paavo Aaltonen (FIN) 228.8
1952	Viktor Chukarin (URS) 115.70	Grant Shaginyan (URS) 114.95	Josef Stalder (SUI) 114.75
1956	Viktor Chukarin (URS) 114.25	Takashi Ono (JPN) 114.20	Yuriy Titov (URS) 113.80
1960	Boris Shakhlin (URS) 115.95	Takashi Ono (JPN) 115.90	Yuriy Titov (URS) 115.60
1964	Yukio Endo (JPN) 115.95	Shuji Tsurumi (JPN) 115.40 Boris Shakhlin (URS) 115.40 Victor Lisitsky (URS) 115.40	
1968	Sawao Kato (JPN) 115.90	Mikhail Voronin (URS) 115.85	Akinori Nakayama (JPN) 115.65
1972	Sawao Kato (JPN) 114.650	Eizo Kenmotsu (JPN) 114.575	Akinori Nakayama (JPN) 114.325
1976	Nikolai Andrianov (URS) 116.650	Sawao Kato (JPN) 115.650	Mitsuo Tsukahara (JPN) 115.575
1980	Alexandr Ditiatin (URS) 118.650	Nikolai Andrianov (URS) 118.225	Stoyan Deltchev (BUL) 118.000

FLOOR COMPETITION

1896–1928	Event not held		
1932	István Pelle (HUN) 9.60	Georges Miez (SUI) 9.47	Mario Lertora (ITA) 9.23
1936	Georges Miez (SUI) 18.666	Josef Walter (SUI) 18.5	Konrad Frey (GER) 18.466 Eugen Mack (SUI) 18.466
1948	Ferenc Pataki (HUN) 38.7	János Mogyorósi-Klencs (HUN) 38.4	Zdenek Ružička (TCH) 38.1
1952	William Thoresson (SWE) 19.25	Tadao Uesako (JPN) 19.15 Jerzy Jokiel (POL) 19.15	—
1956	Valentin Muratov (URS) 19.20	Nobuyuki Aihara (JPN) 19.10 William Thoresson (SWE) 19.10 Viktor Chukarin (URS) 19.10	—
1960	Nobuyuki Aihara (JPN) 19.450	Yuriy Titov (URS) 19.325	Franco Menichelli (ITA) 19.275
1964	Franco Menichelli (ITA) 19.45	Victor Lisitsky (URS) 19.35 Yukio Endo (JPN) 19.35	—
1968	Sawao Kato (JPN) 19.475	Akinori Nakayama (JPN) 19.400	Takeshi Kato (JPN) 19.275
1972	Nikolai Andrianov (URS) 19.175	Akinori Nakayama (JPN) 19.125	Shigeru Kasamatsu (JPN) 19.025
1976	Nikolai Andrianov (URS) 19.450	Vladimir Marchenko (URS) 19.425	Peter Kormann (USA) 19.300
1980	Roland Bruckner (GDR) 19.750	Nikolai Andrianov (URS) 19.725	Alexandr Ditiatin (URS) 19.700

RIGHT: Nikolai Andrianov
(URS) has won more
Olympic medals than any
other male competitor,
earning 15 in three Games
from 1972 through 1980.

LEFT: Boris Shakhlin (URS)
dominated the 1960
gymnastics competition
with his 1 bronze,
2 silver, and 4 gold
medals.

SIDE HORSE

	GOLD	SILVER	BRONZE
1896	Jules A. Zutter (SUI) d.n.a.	Hermann Weingärtner (GER)	
1900	Event not held		
1904	Anton Heida (USA) 42 pts	George Eyser (USA) 33	William A. Merz (USA)29
1906–1920	Event not held		
1924	Josef Wilhelm (SUI) 21.23	Jean Gutweniger (SUI) 21.13	Antoine Rebetez (SUI) 20.73
1928	Hermann Hänggi (SUI) 19.75	Georges Miez (SUI) 19.25	Heikki Savolainen (FIN) 18.83

	GOLD	SILVER	BRONZE
1932	István Pelle (HUN) 19.07	Omero Bonoli (ITA) 18.87	Frank Haubold (USA) 18.57
1936	Konrad Frey (GER) 19.333	Eugen Mack (SUI) 19.167	Albert Bachmann (SUI) 19.067
1948	Paavo Aaltonen (FIN) 38.7 A. Veikkö Huhtanen (FIN) 38.7 Heikki Savolainen (FIN) 38.7	Luigi Zanetti (ITA) 38.3	Guido Figone (ITA) 38.2
1952	Viktor Chukarin (URS) 19.50	Yevgeniy Korolkov (URS) 19.40 Grant Shaginyan (URS) 19.40	—
1956	Boris Shakhlin (URS) 19.25	Takashi Ono (JPN) 19.20	Viktor Chukarin (URS) 19.10
1960	Eugen Ekman (FIN) 19.375 Boris Shakhlin (URS) 19.375		Shuji Tsurumi (JPN) 19.150
1964	Miroslav Cerar (YUG) 19.525	Shuji Tsurumi (JPN) 19.325	Yury Tsapenko (URS) 19.200
1968	Miroslav Cerar (YUG) 19.325	Olli E. Laiho (FIN) 19.225	Mikhail Voronin (URS) 19.200
1972	Viktor Klimenko (URS) 19.125	Sawao Kato (JPN) 19.000	Eizo Kenmotsu (JPN) 18.950
1976	Zoltan Magyar (HUN) 19.700	Eizo Kenmotsu (JPN) 19.575	Nikolai Andrianov (URS) 19.525
1980	Zoltan Magyar (HUN) 19.925	Alexandr Ditiatin (URS) 19.800	Michael Nikolay (GDR) 19.775

RINGS

	GOLD	SILVER	BRONZE
1896	Ioannis Mitropoulos (GRE) d.n.a.	Hermann Weingärtner (GER)	Petros Persakis (GRE)
1900	Event not held		
1904	Herman Glass (USA) 45	William A. Merz (USA) 35	Emil Voight (USA) 32
1906–1920	Event not held		
1924	Franco Martino (ITA) 21.553	Robert Pražák (TCH) 21.483	Ladislav Vácha (TCH) 21.430
1928	Leon Škutelj (YUG) 19.25	Ladislav Vácha (TCH) 19.17	Emanuel Löffler (TCH) 18.83
1932	George Gulack (USA) 18.97	William Denton (USA) 18.60	Giovanni Lattuada (ITA) 18.50
1936	Alois Hudec (TCH) 19.433	Leon Škutelj (YUG) 18.867	Matthias Volz (GER) 18.667
1948	Karl Frei (SUI) 39.60	Michael Reusch (SUI) 39.10	Zdenek Ružička (TCH) 38.50
1952	Grant Shaginyan (URS) 19.75	Viktor Chukarin (URS) 19.55	Hans Eugster (SUI) 19.40 Dimitriy Leonkin (URS) 19.40
1956	Albert Azaryan (URS) 19.35	Valentin Muratov (URS) 19.15	Masao Takemoto (JPN) 19.10 Masami Kubota (JPN) 19.10
1960	Albert Azaryan (URS) 19.725	Boris Shakhlin (URS) 19.500	Velik Kapsazov (BUL) 19.425 Takashi Ono (JPN) 19.425
1964	Takuji Hayata (JPN) 19.475	Franco Menichelli (ITA) 19.425	Boris Shakhlin (URS) 19.400

ABOVE: Olympic champion of the rings in both 1956 and 1960 was Albert Azaryan of Russia.

RIGHT: Akinori Nakayama (JPN) repeated his 1968 triumph on the rings in 1972 at Munich.

	GOLD	SILVER	BRONZE
1968	Akinori Nakayama (JPN) 19.450	Mikhail Voronin (URS) 19.325	Sawao Kato (JPN) 19.225
1972	Akinori Nakayama (JPN) 19.350	Mikhail Voronin (URS) 19.275	Mitsuo Tsukahara (JPN) 19.225
1976	Nikolai Andrianov (URS) 19.650	Aleksandr Ditiatin (URS) 19.550	Danut Grecu (ROM) 19.500
1980	Alexandr Ditiatin (URS) 19.875	Alexandr Tkachyov (URS) 19.725	Jiri Tabak (TCH) 19.600

HORSE VAULT

	GOLD	SILVER	BRONZE
1896	Karl Schumann (GER) d.n.a.	Jules A. Zutter (SUI)	—
1900	Event not held		
1904	Anton Heida (USA) 36 George Eyser (USA) 36	—	William A. Merz (USA) 31
1906–1920	Event not held		
1924	Frank Kriz (USA) 9.98	Jan Koutny (TCH) 9.97	Bohumil Mořkovsky (TCH) 9.93
1928	Eugen Mack (SUI) 9.58	Emanuel Löffler (TCH) 9.50	Stane Derganc (YUG) 9.46
1932	Savino Guglielmetti (ITA) 18.03	Alfred Jochim (GER) 17.77	Edward Carmichael (USA) 17.53
1936	Alfred Schwarzmann (GER) 19.200	Eugen Mack (SUI) 18.967	Matthias Volz (GER) 18.467
1948	Paavo Aaltonen (FIN) 39.10	Olavi Rove (FIN) 39.00	János Mogyorósi-Klencs (HUN) 38.50 Ferenc Pataki (HUN) 38.50 Leos Sotornik (TCH) 38.50
1952	Viktor Chukarin (URS) 19.20	Masao Takemoto (JPN) 19.15	Tadao Uesako (JPN) 19.10 Takashi Ono (JPN) 19.10
1956	Helmuth Bantz (GER) 18.85 Valentin Muratov (URS) 18.85	—	Yuriy Titov (URS) 18.75
1960	Takashi Ono (JPN) 19.350 Boris Shakhlin (URS) 19.350	—	Vladimir Portnoi (URS) 19.225
1964	Haruhiro Yamashita (JPN) 19.600	Victor Lisitsky (URS) 19.325	Hannu Rantakari (FIN) 19.300
1968	Mikhail Voronin (URS) 19.000	Yukio Endo (JPN) 18.950	Sergey Diomidov (URS) 18.925
1972	Klaus Köste (GDR) 18.850	Viktor Klimenko (URS) 18.825	Nikolai Andrianov (URS) 18.800
1976	Nikolai Andrianov (URS) 19.450	Mitsuo Tsukahara (JPN) 19.375	Hiroshi Kajiyama (JPN) 19.275
1980	Nikolai Andrianov (URS) 19.825	Alexandr Ditiatin (URS) 19.800	Roland Bruckner (GDR) 19.775

PARALLEL BARS

	GOLD	SILVER	BRONZE
1896	Alfred Flatow (GER) d.n.a.	Jules A. Zutter (SUI)	Hermann Weingärtner (GER)
1900	Event not held		
1904	George Eyser (USA) 44	Anton Heida (USA) 43	John Duha (USA) 40
1906–1920	Event not held		
1924	August Güttinger (SUI) 21.63	Robert Pražák (TCH) 21.61	Giorgio Zampori (ITA) 21.45
1928	Ladislav Vácha (TCH) 18.83	Josip Primožič (YUG) 18.50	Hermann Hänggi (SUI) 18.08
1932	Romeo Neri (ITA) 18.97	István Pelle (HUN) 18.60	Heikki Savolainen (FIN) 18.27
1936	Konrad Frey (GER) 19.067	Michael Reusch (SUI) 19.034	Alfred Schwarzmann (GER) 18.967
1948	Michael Reusch (SUI) 39.5	Veikkö Huhtanen (FIN) 39.3	Christian Kipfer (SUI) 39.1 Josef Stalder (SUI) 39.1
1952	Hans Eugster (SUI) 19.65	Viktor Chukarin (URS) 19.60	Josef Stalder (SUI) 19.50
1956	Viktor Chukarin (URS) 19.20	Masami Kubota (JPN) 19.15	Takashi Ono (JPN) 19.10 Masao Takemoto (JPN) 19.10
1960	Boris Shakhlin (URS) 19.400	Giovanni Carminucci (ITA) 19.375	Takashi Ono (JPN) 19.350
1964	Yukio Endo (JPN) 19.675	Shuji Tsurumi (JPN) 19.450	Franco Menichelli (ITA) 19.350
1968	Akinori Nakayama (JPN) 19.475	Mikhail Voronin (URS) 19.425	Vladimir Klimenko (URS) 19.225
1972	Sawao Kato (JPN) 19.475	Shigeru Kasamatsu (JPN) 19.375	Eizo Kenmotsu (JPN) 19.250
1976	Sawao Kato (JPN) 19.675	Nikolai Andrianov (URS) 19.500	Mitsuo Tsukahara (JPN) 19.475
1980	Alexandr Tkachyov (URS) 19.775	Alexandr Ditiatin (URS) 19.750	Roland Bruckner (GDR) 19.650

HORIZONTAL BAR

1896	Hermann Weingärtner (GER) d.n.a.	Alfred Flatow (GER)	
1900	Event not held		
1904	Anton Heida (USA) 40 Edward Hennig (USA) 40	—	George Eyser (USA) 39
1906–1920	Event not held		
1924	Leon Štukelj (YUG) 19.730	Jean Gutweniger (SUI) 19.236	André Higelin (FRA) 19.163
1928	Georges Miez (SUI) 19.17	Romeo Neri (ITA) 19.00	Eugen Mack (SUI) 18.92
1932	Dallas Bixler (USA) 18.33	Heikki Savolainen (FIN) 18.07	Einari Teräsvirta (FIN) 18.07[1]
1936	Aleksanteri Saarvala (FIN) 19.367	Konrad Frey (GER) 19.267	Alfred Schwarzmann (GER) 19.233
1948	Josef Stalder (SUI) 39.7	Walter Lehmann (SUI) 39.4	Veikkö Huhtanen (FIN) 39.2
1952	Jack Günthard (SUI) 19.55	Josef Stalder (SUI) 19.50 Alfred Schwarzmann (GER) 19.50	—

---

[1]Teräsvirta conceded second place to Savolainen.

Mitsuo Tsukahara (JPN), gold medallist on the horizontal bar in 1972 and 1976, is seen here in the floor exercise competition, part of his bronze medal performance in the Individual Combined Exercises event in 1976.

	GOLD	SILVER	BRONZE
1956	Takashi Ono (JPN) 19.60	Yuriy Titov (URS) 19.40	Masao Takemoto (JPN) 19.30
1960	Takashi Ono (JPN) 19.60	Masao Takemoto (JPN) 19.525	Boris Shakhlin (URS) 19.475
1964	Boris Shakhlin (URS) 19.625	Yuriy Titov (URS) 19.55	Miroslav Cerar (YUG) 19.50
1968	Mikhail Voronin (URS) 19.550 Akinori Nakayama (JPN) 19.550	—	Eizo Kenmotsu (JPN) 19.375
1972	Mitsuo Tsukahara (JPN) 19.725	Sawao Kato (JPN) 19.525	Shigeru Kasamatsu (JPN) 19.450
1976	Mitsuo Tsukahara (JPN) 19.675	Eizo Kenmotsu (JPN) 19.500	Eberhard Gienger (GER) 19.475
1980	Stoyan Deltchev (BUL) 19.825	Alexandr Ditiatin (URS) 19.750	Nikolai Andrianov (URS) 19.675

Gymnastics (Women)

In women's gymnastics there are six events which are interlinked. First is the Team Competition which comprises one compulsory and one optional exercise for each of the four events: Horse Vault, Uneven Bars, Balance Beam and Floor Exercises. Each team competitor gets marks out of 10 for both her compulsory and optional exercise for each of the four events. The team of six with the greatest *total* of marks wins the gold medal.

Next the best 36 competitors from the Team Competition qualify for the Individual All-Round Competition. They each complete a further optional exercise for each of the four events and gain new marks (out of 10) per event. These are then added to the *average* (not total) of their previous total marks in the compulsory and optional sections brought forward from the Team Competition previously decided.

Finally, the six best on each apparatus in the Team Competition qualify for the individual Final on that apparatus. This is decided by adding a new mark (out of 10) for a further optional exercise on that apparatus and the *average* (not total) of their previous marks in the compulsory and optional performances on that apparatus within the Team Competition previously decided.

COMBINED EXERCISES (TEAM)

There was no team event from 1896 to 1924 nor in 1932. A team event was introduced in 1928 and was also held in 1936 to 1956 but the fundamental conditions make the results not comparable with the current event and conditions which started in 1960.

	GOLD	SILVER	BRONZE
1960	U.S.S.R. 382.320	CZECHOSLOVAKIA 373.323	RUMANIA 372.053
	Larissa Latynina	Vera Čáslavská	Sonia Iovan
	Sofia Muratova	Eva Bosáková	Elena Leustean
	Polina Astakhova	Ludmila Švedová	Antanasia Ionescu
	Margarita Nikolayeva	Adolfina Tkačiková	Uta Poreceanu
	Lydia Ivanova	Mathydla Matoušková-Šinová	Emilia Lita
	Tamara Lyukhina	Hana Ružičková	Elena Niculescu
1964	U.S.S.R. 380.890	CZECHOSLOVAKIA 379.989	JAPAN 377.889
	Larissa Latynina	Vera Čáslavská	Keiko Ikeda-Tanaka
	Elena Volchetskaya	Hana Ružičková	Toshiko Aihara-Shirasu
	Polina Astakhova	Jaroslava Sedlačková	
	Tamara Lyukhina	Adolfina Tkačiková	Kiyoko Ono
	Tamara Manina	Mária Krajčirová	Taniko Nakamura
	Ludmila Gromova	Jana Posnerová	Hiroko Tsuji
			Ginko Chiba-Abukawa
1968	U.S.S.R. 382.85	CZECHOSLOVAKIA 382.20	E. GERMANY 379.10
	Zinaida Voronina	Vera Čáslavská	Erika Zuchold
	Natalya Kuchinskaya	Bohumila Rimnácova	Karin Janz
	Larissa Petrik	Miroslava Skleničková	Maritta Bauerschmidt
	Olga Karasseva	Maria Krajčirová	Ute Starke
	Lyudmila Tourischeva	Hana Lišková	Marianne Noack
	Ljubov Burda	Jana Kubičková	Magdalena Schmidt
1972	U.S.S.R. 380.50	E. GERMANY 376.55	HUNGARY 368.25
	Lyudmila Tourischeva	Karin Janz	Ilona Bekesi
	Olga Korbut	Erika Zuchold	Monika Csaszar
	Tamara Lazakovitch	Angelika Hellmann	Krisztina Medveczky
	Ljubov Burda	Irene Abel	Aniko Kery
	Elvira Saadi	Christine Schmitt	Marta Kelemen
	Antonina Koshel	Richarda Schmeisser	Zsuzsa Nagy
1976	U.S.S.R. 390.35	RUMANIA 387.15	E. GERMANY 385.10
	Svetlana Grozdova	Gabriela Trusca	Angelika Hellmann
	Elvira Saadi	Georgeta Gabor	Marion Kische
	Maria Filatova	Anca Grigoras	Kerstin Gerschau
	Olga Corbut	Mariana Constantin	Gitta Escher
	Lyudmila Tourischeva	Teodora Ungureanu	Steffi Kraker
	Nelli Kim	Nadia Comaneci	Carola Dombeck
1980	U.S.S.R. 394.90	RUMANIA 393.50	EAST GERMANY 392.55
	Natalya Shaposhnikova	Emilia Eberle	Maxi Gnauck
	Yelena Davydova	Nadia Comaneci	Katharina Rensch
	Nelli Kim	Rodica Dunka	Steffi Kraker
	Maria Filatova	Melita Ruhn	Birgit Suss
	Stella Zacharova	Cristina Grigoras	Silvia Hindorff
	Yelena Naimushina	Dumitrita Turner	Karola Sube

COMBINED EXERCISES (INDIVIDUAL)

1896–1948	Event not held		
1952	Maria Gorokhovskaya (URS) 76.78	Nina Bocharova (URS) 75.94	Margit Korondi (HUN) 75.82
1956	Larissa Latynina (URS) 74.933	Agnes Keleti (HUN) 74.633	Sofia Muratova (URS) 74.466

At the 1976 Games in Montreal, 14-year-old Nadia Comaneci of Rumania became the first gymnast to be awarded a perfect score in Olympic competition.

	GOLD	SILVER	BRONZE
1960	Larissa Latynina (URS) 77.031	Sofia Muratova (URS) 76.696	Polina Astakhova (URS) 76.164
1964	Vera Časlavská (TCH) 77.564	Larissa Latynina (URS) 76.998	Polina Astakhova (URS) 76.965
1968	Vera Čáslavská (TCH) 77.025	Zinaida Voronina (URS) 76.85	Natalya Kuchinskaya (URS) 76.75
1972	Lyudmila Tourischeva (URS) 77.025	Karin Janz (GDR) 76.875	Tamara Lazakovitch (URS) 76.850
1976	Nadia Comaneci (ROM) 79.275	Nelli Kim (URS) 78.675	Lyudmila Tourischeva (URS) 78.625
1980	Yelena Davydova (URS) 79.150	Maxi Gnauck (GDR) 79.075 Nadia Comaneci (ROM) 79.075	—

HORSE VAULT

	GOLD	SILVER	BRONZE
1896–1948	Event not held		
1952	Yekaterina Kalinchuk (URS) 19.20	Maria Gorokhovskaya (URS) 19.19	Galina Minaitscheva (URS) 19.16
1956	Larissa Latynina (URS) 18.833	Tamara Manina (URS) 18.800	Ann-Sofi Colling (SWE) 18.733 Olga Tass (HUN) 18.733
1960	Margarita Nikolayeva (URS) 19.316	Sofia Muratova (URS) 19.049	Larissa Latynina (URS) 19.016
1964	Vera Čáslavská (TCH) 19.483	Larissa Latynina (URS) 19.283 Birgit Radochla (GER) 19.283	—
1968	Vera Čáslavská (TCH) 19.775	Erika Zuchold (GDR) 19.625	Zinaida Voronina (URS) 19.500

RIGHT: The Soviet gymnast Larissa Semyonovna Latynina has won more medals than any other Olympic competitor— 9 gold, 5 silver, and 4 bronze. She now coaches the U.S.S.R. team.

BELOW: Lyudmila Tourischeva (URS), winner of 4 gold medals in 3 Games, married Soviet track and field gold medallist Valery Borzov after the 1976 Olympics.

	GOLD	SILVER	BRONZE
1972	Karin Janz (GDR) 19.525	Erika Zuchold (GDR) 19.275	Lyudmila Tourischeva (URS) 19.250
1976	Nelli Kim (URS) 19.800	Lyudmila Tourischeva (URS) 19.650 Carola Dombeck (GDR) 19.650	—
1980	Natalia Shaposhnikova (URS) 19.725	Steffi Kraker (GDR) 19.675	Melita Ruhn (ROM) 19.650

ASYMMETRICAL BARS

1896–1948	Event not held		
1952	Margit Korondi (HUN) 19.40	Maria Gorokhovskaya (URS) 19.26	Agnes Keleti (HUN) 19.16
1956	Agnes Keleti (HUN) 18.966	Larissa Latynina (URS) 18.833	Sofia Muratova (URS) 18.800
1960	Polina Astakhova (URS) 19.616	Larissa Latynina (URS) 19.416	Tamara Lyukhina (URS) 19.399
1964	Polina Astakhova (URS) 19.332	Katalin Makray (HUN) 19.216	Larissa Latynina (URS) 19.199
1968	Vera Cáslavská (TCH) 19.650	Karin Janz (GDR) 19.500	Zinaida Voronina (URS) 19.425
1972	Karin Janz (GDR) 19.675	Olga Korbut (URS) 19.450 Erika Zuchold (GDR) 19.450	—
1976	Nadia Comaneci (ROM) 20.000	Teodora Ungureanu (ROM) 19.800	Marta Egervari (HUN) 19.775
1980	Maxi Gnauck (GDR) 19.875	Emilia Eberle (ROM) 19.850	Steffi Kraker (GDR) 19.775 Melita Ruhn (ROM) 19.775 Maria Filatova (URS) 19.775

BALANCE BEAM

1896–1948	Event not held		
1952	Nina Bocharova (URS) 19.22	Maria Gorokhovskaya (URS) 19.13	Margit Korondi (HUN) 19.02
1956	Agnes Keleti (HUN) 18.80	Eva Bosáková (TCH) 18.63 Tamara Manina (URS) 18.63	—
1960	Eva Bosáková (TCH) 19.283	Larissa Latynina (URS) 19.233	Sofia Muratova (URS) 19.232
1964	Vera Cáslavská (TCH) 19.449	Tamara Manina (URS) 19.399	Larissa Latynina (URS) 19.382
1968	Natalya Kuchinskaya (URS) 19.650	Vera Cáslavská (TCH) 19.575	Larissa Petrik (URS) 19.250
1972	Olga Korbut (URS) 19.575	Tamara Lazakovitch (URS) 19.375	Karin Janz (GDR) 18.975
1976	Nadia Comaneci (ROM) 19.950	Olga Korbut (URS) 19.725	Teodora Ungureanu (ROM) 19.700
1980	Nadia Comaneci (ROM) 19.800	Yelena Davydova (URS) 19.750	Natalia Shaposhnikova (URS) 19.725

FLOOR EXERCISES

	GOLD	SILVER	BRONZE
1896–1948	Event not held		
1952	Ágnes Keleti (HUN) 19.36	Maria Gorokhovskaya (URS) 19.20	Margit Korondi (HUN) 19.00
1956	Larissa Latynina (URS) 18.733 Ágnes Keleti (HUN) 18.733	—	Elena Leustean (ROM) 18.70
1960	Larissa Latynina (URS) 19.583	Polina Astakhova (URS) 19.532	Tamara Lyukhina (URS) 19.449
1964	Larissa Latynina (URS) 19.599	Polina Astakhova (URS) 19.500	Anikó Jánosi (HUN) 19.300
1968	Larissa Petrik (URS) 19.675 Vera Cáslavská (TCH) 19.675	—	Natalya Kuchinskaya (URS) 19.650
1972	Olga Korbut (URS) 19.575	Lyudmila Tourischeva (URS) 19.550	Tamara Lazakovitch (URS) 19.450
1976	Nelli Kim (URS) 19.850	Lyudmila Tourischeva (URS) 19.825	Nadia Comaneci (ROM) 19.750
1980	Nelli Kim (URS) 19.875 Nadia Comaneci (ROM) 19.875	—	Natalia Shaposhnikova (URS) 19.825 Maxi Gnauck (GDR) 19.825

Floor exercise medalists (left to right) Lyudmila Tourischeva (URS), Nelli Kim (URS), and Nadia Comaneci (ROM) receive their awards in 1976. Among them they hold a total of 14 gold, 8 silver, and 2 bronze medals.

9. Handball, Men (Indoor)

It should be noted that in 1936 there was a Field Handball (i.e. outdoor) competition.
The medals went to Germany (gold), Austria (silver) and Switzerland (bronze).

	GOLD	SILVER	BRONZE
1972	**YUGOSLAVIA** Zoran Zivkovic Abaz Arslanagic Miroslav Pribanic Petar Fajfric Milorad Karalic Djoko Lavrnic Slobodan Miskovic Hrvoje Horvat Branislav Pokrajac Zdravko Miljak Milan Lazarevic Nebojsa Popovic	**CZECHOSLOVAKIA** František Krabik Peter Pospisil Ivan Satrapa Vladimir Jary Jiri Kavan Andrej Lukosik Vladimir Haber Jindrich Krepinal Ladislav Benes Vincent Lavko Jaroslav Konecny Pavel Mikes	**RUMANIA** Cornel Penu Alexandru Dinca Gavril Kicsid Ghita Licu Cristian Gatu Roland Gunnesch Radu Voina Simion Schobel Gheorghe Gruia Werner Stockl Dan Marin Adrian Cosma
1976	**U.S.S.R.** Mikhail Istchenko Anatoli Fedjukin Vladimir Maximov Sergei Kushnirjuk Vladimir Kravsov Yuri Klimov Aleksandr Anpilogov Evgeniy Tchernyshov Valeriy Gassiy Anatoli Tomin Yuri Kidjayev Aleksandr Rezanov	**RUMANIA** Cornel Penu Gavril Kicsid Cristian Gatu Ghita Licu Radu Voina Roland Gunnesch Stefan Birtalan Adrian Cosma Constantin Tudosie Nicolae Munteanu Werner Stockl Mircea Grabovschi	**POLAND** Andrzej Szymczak Piotr Ciesla Zdzislaw Antczak Zygfryd Kuchta Jerzy Klempel Janusz Brzozowski Ryszard Przybysz Jerzy Melcer Andrzej Sokolowski Jan Gmyrek Henryk Rozmiarek Alfred Kaluzinski
1980	**EAST GERMANY** Siegfried Voigt Gunter Dreibrodt Peter Rost Klaus Gruner Hans-Georg Beyer Dietmar Schmidt Hartmut Kruger Lothar Doering Ernst Gerlach Frank Wahl Ingolf Wiegert Wieland Schmidt Rainer Hoft Georg Jaunich	**U.S.S.R.** Mikhail Istchenko Viktor Machorin Sergei Kushnirjuk Aleksandr Karshakevich Vladimir Belov Anatoli Fedjukin Aleksandr Anpilogov Yevgeniy Cheryshov Aleksey Zhuk Nikolai Tomin Yuri Kidjayev Valdemar Novitsky Vladimir Kravsov Vladimir Repiyev	**RUMANIA** Nicolae Munteanu Marian Dumitru Iosif Boros Maricel Voinea Vasile Stinga Radu Voina Cornel Durau Stefan Birtalan Alexandru Folker Neculai Vasilca Adrian Cosma Claudiu Eugen Ionescu Cezar Draganita Lucian Vasilache

Handball, Women (Indoor)

GOLD	SILVER	BRONZE
1896–1972 Event not held		

1976 U.S.S.R.
GOLD	SILVER	BRONZE
Natalia Sherstjuk	**EAST GERMANY** Hannelore Zober	**HUNGARY** Agota Bujdoso
Rafiga Shabanova	Gabriele Badorek	Marta Megyeri
Lubov Berezhnaya	Evelyn Matz	Borbala Toth-Harsanyi
Zinaida Turchina	Roswitha Krause	Katalin Laki
Tatyana Makarets	Christina Rost	Amalia Sterbinszky
Maria Litoshenko	Petra Uhlig	Marianna Nagy
Ludmila Bobrus	Christina Voss	Klaru Csik
Tatyana Glustchenko	Liane Michaelis	Rozalia Lelkes
Ludmila Shubina	Silvia Siebert	Maria Vadasz
Galina Zakharova	Marion Tietz	Erzsebet Nemeth
Aldona Chesaitite	Kristina Richter	Eva Angyal
Nina Lobova	Eva Paskuy	Maria Berzsenyi
Ludmila Pantchuk	Waltraud Kretzschmar	Ilona Nagy
Larisa Karlova	Hannelore Burosch	Zsuzsa Kezi

1980 U.S.S.R.
GOLD	SILVER	BRONZE
Natalia Timoshkina	**YUGOSLAVIA** Ana Titlic	**EAST GERMANY** Hannelore Zober
Larisa Karlova	Slavica Jeremic	Katrin Kruger
Irina Palchikova	Zorica Vojinovic	Evelyn Matz
Tatiana Kochergina	Radmila Drljaca	Roswitha Krause
Ludmila Poradnik	Katica Iles	Christina Rost
Larisa Savkina	Mirjana Ognjenovic	Petra Uhlig
Aldona Nenenene	Svetlana Anastasovski	Claudia Wunderlich
Yulia Safina	Svetlana Kitic	Savine Rother
Olga Zubareva	Mirjana Djurica	Kornelia Kunisch
Valentina Lutaeva	Biserka Visnjic	Marion Tietz
Lubov Odinokova	Jasna Merdan	Kristina Richter
Sigita Strechen	Vesna Radovic	Waltraud Kretzschmar
Natalia Lukianenko	Vesna Milosevic	Birgit Heinicke
Zinaida Turchina	Rada Savic	Renate Rudolph

---

10. Hockey (Field)

GOLD	SILVER	BRONZE
1896–1906 Event not held		

1908 ENGLAND
GOLD	SILVER	BRONZE
H. I. Wood	**IRELAND** E. P. C. Holmes	**SCOTLAND & WALES** (tied for third place)
L. C. Baillon	Henry J. Brown	d.n.a.
Harold Scott-Freeman	Walter E. Peterson	
Alan H. Noble	Henry L. Murphy	
Edgar W. Page	Walter J. H. Campbell	
John Y. Robinson	William E. Graham	
Eric Green	Robert L. Kennedy	
Reginald G. Pridmore	Frank L. Robinson	
Stanley H. Shoveller	Eric P. Allman-Smith	
Gerald Logan	G. S. Gregg	
Percy M. Rees	C. F. Power	
	W. G. McCormick	

1912 Event not held

GOLD	SILVER	BRONZE

1920 ENGLAND
Harry E. Haslam
John H. Bennett
Charles S. Atkin
Harold D. R. Cooke
Eric B. Crockford
Cyril T. A. Wilkinson
William F. Smith
George F. McGrath
John McBryan
Stanley H. Shoveller
Rex W. Crummack
Arthur F. Leighton
Colin H. Campbell
Charles Marcon
Harold K. Cassels

DENMARK
Andreas Rasmussen
Hans-Christian Herlak
Frans Faber
Erik Husted
Henning Holst
Hans-Jörgen Hansen
Hans-Adolf Bjerrum
Thorvald Eigenbrod
Sven Blach
Steen Due
Ejvind Blach

BELGIUM
Charles Delelienne
Maurice van den
       Bemden
Raoul Daufresne de la
       Chevalerie
René Strauwen
Fernand de Montigny
Adolphe Goemaere
Pierre Chibert
André Becquet
Raymond Keppens
Pierre Valcke
Jean van Nerom
Robert Gevers
Louis Diercxens

1924 Event not held

1928 INDIA
Richard J. Allen
Michael E. Rocque
Leslie C. Hammond
Rex A. Norris
Broome E. Pinniger
Sayed M. Yusuf
E. John Goodsir-Cullen
Maurice A. Gateley
George E. Marthins
Dhyan Chand
Frederick S. Seaman
Khair Singh
Jaipal Singh
Shaukat Ali
Feroze Khan

NETHERLANDS
Adriaan J. L. Katte
Albert W. Tresling
Reindert B. J. de Waal
Johannes W. Brand
Emile P. J. Duson
Jan G. Ankerman
Hendrik P. Visser t'Hooft
Robert van der Veen
Paulus van de Rovaert
Gerrit J. A. Jannink
August J. Kop

GERMANY
George Brunner
Werner Proft
Heinz Wöltje
Werner Freyberg
Theo Haag
Erich Zander
Friedrich Horn
Herbert Müller
Bruno Boche
Herbert Hobein
Herbert Kemmer
Erwin Franzkowiak
Hans Haussmann
Karl Heinz Immer
Aribert Heymann
Kurt Haverbeck
Rolf Wollner
Gerd Strantzen
Heinz Förstendorf

Grahannandan Singh (left) scores one of India's four winning goals in the 1948 finals.

	GOLD	SILVER	BRONZE
1932	**INDIA**	**JAPAN**	**UNITED STATES**
	Sayed Mohammed Jaffar	Junzo Inohara	David McMullin
		Toshio Usami	William Boddington
	Roop Singh	Kenichi Konishi	James Gentle
	Dhyan Chand	Hiroshi Nagata	Charles Shaeffer
	Gurmit Singh	Haruhiko Kon	Lawrence Knapp
	Richard J. Carr	Eiichi Nakamura	Horace Disston
	Lal Shah Bokhari	Yoshio Sakai	Samuel Ewing
	Broome E. Pinniger	Katsumi Shibata	Henry Greer
	M. A. K. Minhas	Sadayoshi Kobayashi	Leonard O'Brien
	Leslie C. Hammond	Akio Sohda	Frederick Wolters
	Carlyle C. Tapsell	Shumkichi Hamada	Harold Brewster
	Arthur C. Hind		Amos Deacon
	Richard Allen		
	Masud Minhas		
1936	**INDIA**	**GERMANY**	**NETHERLANDS**
	Richard J. Allen	Karl Dröse	Jan de Looper
	Carlyle C. Tapsell	Erich Zander	Reindert B. J. de Waal
	Mohammed Hussain	Herbert Kemmer	Max Westerkamp
	Baboo N. Nimal	Heinz Schmalix	Hendrik C. de Looper
	E. John Goodsir-Cullen	Erwin Keller	Rudolf J. van der Haar
	Joseph Galibardy	Alfred Gerdes	Anton R. van Lierop
	Shabban Shahab ud Din	Fritz Messner	Pieter A. Gunning
	Dara ali Iqtidar Shah	Hans Scherbart	Henri C. W. Schnitger
	Dhyan Chand	Kurt Weiss	Ernst W. van den Berg
	Roop Singh	Werner Hamel	Agathon de Roos
	Sayed Mohammed Jaffar	Harald Huffmann	René Sparenberg
		Werner Kubitzki	Carl E. Heybroek
	Ahmed Sher Khan	Tito Warnholtz	
	Garewal Gurcharan Singh	Detlef Okrent	
		Hermann Auf der Heide	
	Ahsan Mohomed Khan	Heinrich Peter	
	Lionel C. Emmett	Carl Menke	
	Mirza Nasir ud Din Masood	Heinz Raack	
		Paul Mehlitz	
	Cyril J. Michie	Ludwig Beisiegel	
	Fernandes Paul Peter	Karl Ruck	
	Joseph Phillip	Erich Cuntz	
1948	**INDIA**	**GREAT BRITAIN**	**NETHERLANDS**
	Leo H. K. Pinto	David L. S. Brodie	Antonius M. Richter
	Trilochan Singh	George B. Sime	Henri J. J. Derckx
	Randhir Singh Gentle	William L. C. Lindsay	Johan F. Drijver
	Keshav C. Datt	Michael M. Walford	Jenne Langhout
	Amir C. Kumar	Frank O. Reynolds	Hermanus P. Loggere
	Maxie Vaz	F. Robin Lindsay	Edvard H. Tiel
	Kishan Lal	John M. Peak	Willem van Heel
	Kunwa Digvijai Singh	W. Neil White	Andries C. Boerstra
	Grahanandan Singh	Robert E. Adlard	Pieter M. J. Bromberg
	Patrick A. Jansen	Norman F. Borrett	Jan H. Kruize
	Lawrie Fernandes	William S. Griffiths	Rius T. Esser
	Ranganadhan Francis	Ronald Davies	Henricus N. Bouwman
	Akhtar Hussain	G. Hudson	
	Leslie W. Claudius	R. T. Lake	
	Jaswant S. Rajput	Peter Whitbread	
	Reginald Rodrigues		
	Latifur Rehman		
	Balbir Singh		
	Walter J. L. D'Souza		
	Gerry R. Glacken		

	GOLD	SILVER	BRONZE
1952	**INDIA**	**NETHERLANDS**	**GREAT BRITAIN**
	Ranganadhan Francis	Laurens S. Mulder	Graham B. Dadds
	Dharam Singh	Henri J. J. Derckx	Roger K. Midgley
	Randhir S. Gentle	Johan F. Drijver	Denys J. Carnill
	Leslie W. Claudius	Julius T. Ancion	John A. Cockett
	Keshav C. Datt	Hermanus P. Loggere	Dennis M. R. Eagan
	Govind Perumal	Edvard H. Tiel	Anthony J. B.Robinson
	Raghbir Lal	Willem van Heel	Anthony S. Nunn
	Kunwar D. Singh	Rius T. Esser	Robin A. Fletcher
	Balbir Singh	Jan H. Kruize	Richard O. A. Norris
	Udham Singh	Andries C. Boerstra	John V. Conroy
	Muniswamy Rajagopal	Leonard H. Wery	John P. Taylor
	Meldric St. C. Daluz		Derek M. Day
	Grahanandan Singh		S. T. Theobald
	Chinadorai Deshmutu		
1956	**INDIA**	**PAKISTAN**	**GERMANY**
	Shankar Laxman	Zakir Hussain	Alfred Lücker
	Bakshish Singh	Ghulam Rasul	Helmut Nonn
	Randhir S. Gentle	Anwar Ahmad Khan	Günther Ullerich
	Leslie W. Claudius	Hussain Mussarat	Günther Brennecke
	Amir Kumar	Noor Alam	Werner Delmes
	Govind Perumal	Abdul Hamid	Eberhard Ferstl
	Charles Stephen	Habibur Rehman	Hugo Dollheiser
	Gurdev Singh	Mutih Ullah	Heinz Radzikowski
	Balbir Singh	Hussain Akhtar	Wolfgang Nonn
	Udham Singh	Nasir Ahmad	Hugo Budinger
	Raghbir S. Bhola	Manzur H. Atif	Werner Rozenbaum
	Ranganadhan Francis	Habib Alikiddi	
	Balkishan Singh	Munir Ahmad Dar	
	Amit Singh Bakshi	Latifur Rehman	
	Kaushi Haripal		
	Hardyal Singh		
	Raghbir Lal		
1960	**PAKISTAN**	**INDIA**	**SPAIN**
	Abdul Rashid	Shankar Laxman	Carlos Del Coso Iglesias
	Bashir Ahmad	Prithipal Singh	José Colomer Rivas
	Manzur H. Atif	Jamanlal Sharma	Rafael Egusquiza
	Ghulam Rasul	Leslie W. Claudius	Basterva
	Anwar Ahmad Khan	Joseph Antic	Juan Angel Calzado
	Ali Habib Kidi	Mohinder Lal	de Castro
	Noor Alam	Joginder Singh	José Antonio Dinares
	Abdul Hamid	John V. Peter	Massaqué
	Abdul Waheed	Jaswant Singh	Edouardo Dualde
	Nasir Ahmad	Udham Singh	Santos de Lamadrid
	Mutih Ullah	Raghbir S. Bhola	Joachim Dualde
	Khurshid Aslam	Charanjit Singh	Santos de Lamadrid
	Mushtaq Ahmad	Govind Savant	Pedro Amat Fontanais
	Munir Ahmad Dar		Francisco Caballer
			Soteras
			Ignacio Macaya
			Santos de Lamadrid
			Pedro Murúa
			Leguizamón
			Pedro Roig Junyent
			Luis Maria Usoz
			Quintana
			Narciso Ventalló
			Surralles

	GOLD	SILVER	BRONZE

1964

GOLD	SILVER	BRONZE
INDIA	**PAKISTAN**	**AUSTRALIA**
Shankar Laxman	Abdul Hamid	Paul Dearing
Prithipal Singh	Munir Ahmad Dar	Donald McWatters
Dhara M. Singh	Manzur H. Atif	Brian Glencross
Mohinder Lal	Saeed Anwar	John McBride
Charanjit Singh	Anwar Ahmad Khan	Julian Pearce
Gurbux Singh	Muhammad Rashid	Graham Wood
Joginder Singh	Khalid Mahmood Hussain	Robin Hodder
John V. Peter	Zaka-ud-Din	Raymond Evans
Harbinder Singh	Muhammad Afzal	Eric Pearce
Kashik Haripal	Manna	Patrick Nilan
Darshan Singh	Mohammad Asad Malik	Donald Smart
Jagjit Singh	Mutih Ullah	Antony Waters
Bandu Patil	Tariq Niazi	Mervyn Crossman
Udham Singh	Zafar Hayat	Desmond Piper
Ali Sayeed	Khizar Nawaz	
	Kurshid Aslam	

1968

GOLD	SILVER	BRONZE
PAKISTAN	**AUSTRALIA**	**INDIA**
Zakir Hussain	Paul Dearing	Rajendra A. Christy
Tanvir A. Dar	James Mason	Gurbux Singh
Tariq Aziz	Brian Glencross	Prithipal Singh
Saeed Anwar	Gordon Pearce	Balbir Singh II
Riaz Ahmed	Julian Pearce	Ajitpal Singh
Bulrez Akhtar	Robert Haigh	Krishna Murtay
Khalid Mahmood Hussain	Donald Martin	Perumal
	Eric Pearce	Balbir Singh III
Mohammad Ashfaq	Raymond Evans	Balbir Singh I
Abdul Rashid	Frederick Quinn	Harbinder Singh
Mohammad Asad Malik	Ronald Riley	Inamur Rehman
Jahangir Ahmad Butt	Patrick Nilan	Inder Singh
Riaz Ud Din	Donald Smart	Munir Sait
Tariq Niazi	Desmond Piper	Harmik Singh
		John V. Peter
		Tarsem Singh

1972

GOLD	SILVER	BRONZE
WEST GERMANY	**PAKISTAN**	**INDIA**
Peter Kraus	Saleem Sherwan	Cornelius Charles
Michael Peter	Akhtarul Islam	Mukhbain Singh
Dieter Freise	Munawaruz Zaman	Michael Kindo
Michael Krause	Saeed Anwar	Krishna Murtay
Eduard Thelen	Riaz Ahmed	Perumal
Horst Droese	Fazalur Rehman	Ajitpal Singh
Carsten Keller	Islahud Din	Harmik Singh
Ulrich Klaes	Mudasser Asqhar	Ganesh
Wolfgang Baumgart	Abdul Rashid	Mollerapoovayya
Uli Vos	Mohammad Asad Malik	Harbinder Singh
Peter Trump	Muhammad Shahnaz	Govin
		Billimogaputtaswamy
		Kumar Ashok
		Harcharn Singh

GOLD	SILVER	BRONZE
1976 NEW ZEALAND	**AUSTRALIA**	**PAKISTAN**
Paul Ackerley	Robert Haigh	Saleem Sherwan
Jeff Archibald	Richard Charlesworth	Manzoor Hassan
Thur Borren	David Bell	Munawar Zaman Khan
Alan Chesney	Gregory Browning	Saleem Nazim
John Christensen	Ian Cooke	Akhtar Rasool
Greg Dayman	Barry Dancer	Iftikhar Syed
Tony Ineson	Douglas Golder	Islah Islahuddin
Alan McIntyre	Wayne Hammond	Manzoor Hussain
Barry Maister	James Irvine	Abdul Rashid
Selwyn Maister	Malcolm Poole	Shanaz Sheikh
Trevor Manning	Robert Proctor	Samiulah Khan
Arthur Parkin	Graham Reid	Qamar Zia
Mohan Patel	Ronald Riley	Arshad Mahmood
Ramesh Patel	Trevor Smith	Arshad Ali Chaudry
	Terry Walsh	Mudassar Asghar
		Haneef Khan
1980 INDIA	**SPAIN**	**U.S.S.R.**
Schofield Allan	Jose Garcia	Vladimir Pleshakov
Chettri Bir Bhadur	Juan Amat	Vyacheslav Lampeyev
Dung Dung Sylvanus	Santiago Malgosa	Leonid Pavlovsky
Rajinder Singh	Rafael Garralda	Sos Airapetyan
Deavinder Singh	Francisco Fabregas	Farit Zigangirov
Gurmail Singh	Juan Luis Coghen	Valeriy Belyakov
Ravinder Pal Singh	Ricardo Cabot	Sergey Klevtsov
Baskaran Vasudevan	Jaime Arbos	Oleg Zagorodny
Somaya Maneypanda	Carlos Roca	Aleksandr Gusev
Maharaj Krishon Kaushik	Miguel Chaves	Sergey Pleshakov
Charanjit Kumar	Juan Arbos	Mikhail Nichepurenko
Mervyn Fernandis	Javier Cabot	Aleksandr Sytchev
Amarjit Rana Singh	Juan Pellon	Aleksandr Myasnikov
Shahid Mohamed	Miguel De Paz	Minnuela Azizov
Zafar Iqbal	Paulino Monsalve	Viktor Deputatov
Surinder Singh	Jaime Zumalacarregui	Aleksandr Goncharov

Hockey (Field) Women

1896–1976 Event not held

GOLD	SILVER	BRONZE
1980 ZIMBABWE	**CZECHOSLOVAKIA**	**U.S.S.R.**
Sarah English	Berta Hruba	Nelli Gorbatkova
Anne Mary Grant	Jirina Kadlecova	Valentina Zazdravnykh
Brenda Joan Phillips	Jirina Cermakova	Nadyezda Ovechkina
Patricia Jean McKillop	Marta Urbanova	Natella Krasnikova
Sonia Robertson	Kveta Petrickova	Natalya Bykova
Patricia Joan Davies	Marie Sykorova	Lidiya Glubokova
Maureen Jean George	Ida Hubackova	Galina Vyuzhanina
Linda Margaret Watson	Milada Blazkova	Natalya Bozunova
Susan Huggett	Jana Lahodova	Lyailya Akhmerova
Gillian Margaret Cowley	Alena Kyselicova	Nadyezda Filipova
Elizabeth Murial Chase	Jirina Hajkova	Tatyana Yembakhtova
Sandra Chick	Viera Podhanyiova	Tatyana Shviganova
Helen Volk	Jarmila Kralickova	Ludmila Frolova
Christine Prinsloo	Iveta Srankova	Galina Inzhuvatova
Arlene Nadine Boxhall	Lenka Vymazalova	Yelena Gureva
Anthea Doreen Stewart	Jirina Krizova	Alina Kham

The first Olympic field hockey competition for women was held at the 1980 Games. Here, a match between India and the eventual bronze medallists, the Soviet Union.

11. Judo

Sport introduced in 1964.

OPEN CATEGORY, NO WEIGHT LIMIT

	GOLD	SILVER	BRONZE
1964	Antonius Geesink (HOL)	Akio Kaminaga (JPN)	Theodore Boronovskis (AUS) Klaus Glahn (GER)
1968	Event not held		
1972	Wilhelm Ruska (HOL)	Vitali Kusnezov (URS)	Jean-Claude Brondani (FRA) Angelo Parisi (GBR)
1976	Haruki Uemura (JPN)	Keith Remfry (GBR)	Shota Chochoshvili (URS) Jeaki Cho (KOR)
1980	Dietmar Lorenz (GDR)	Angelo Parisi (FRA)	Arthur Mapp (GBR) Andras Ozsvar (HUN)

New weight categories were introduced in 1980

OVER 95 kg (209¼ lb)

	GOLD	SILVER	BRONZE
1980	Angelo Parisi (FRA)	Dimitar Zaprianov (BUL)	Vladimir Kocman (TCH) Radomir Kovacevic (YUG)

UP TO 95 kg (209¼ lb)

1980	Robert Van De Walle (BEL)	Tengiz Khubuluri (URS)	Dietmar Lorenz (GDR) Henk Numan (HOL)

UP TO 86 kg (189½ lb)

1980	Juerg Roethlisberger (SUI)	Issac Azcuy (CUB)	Alexandr Iatskevich (URS) Detlef Ultsch (GDR)

UP TO 78 kg (171¾ lb)

1980	Shota Khabareli (URS)	Juan Ferrer (CUB)	Bernard Tchoullouyan (FRA) Harald Heinke (GDR)

UP TO 71kg (156½ lb)

1980	Ezio Gamba (ITA)	Neil Adams (GBR)	Karl-Heinz Lehmann (GDR) Ravdan Davaadalai (MGL)

UP TO 65 kg (143¼ lb)

1980	Nikolay Solodukhin (URS)	Tsendying Damdin (MGL)	Ilian Nedkov (BUL) Janusz Pawlowski (POL)

UP TO 60 kg (132¼ lb)

1980	Thierry Rey (FRA)	Jose Rodriguez (CUB)	Aramby Emizh (URS) Tibor Kinces (HUN)

Wilhelm Ruska of the Netherlands exults at the moment of victory over Vitali Kusnezov in the 1972 open weight judo final.

PREVIOUS WINNERS

OVER 93 kg (205 lb)

	GOLD	SILVER	BRONZE
1964	Isao Inokuma (JPN)	A. H. Douglas Rogers (CAN)	Parnaoz Chikviladze (URS) Anzor Kiknadze (URS)
1968	Event not held		
1972	Wilhelm Ruska (HOL)	Klaus Glahn (GER)	Givi Onashvili (URS) Motoki Nishimura (JPN)
1976	Sergei Novikov (URS)	Gunther Neureuther (GER)	Sumio Endo (JPN) Allen Coage (USA)

80 to 93 kg (176¼ to 205 lb)

	GOLD	SILVER	BRONZE
1964–1968	Event not held		
1972	Shota Chochoshvili (URS)	David C. Starbrook (GBR)	Chiaki Ishii (BRA) Paul Barth (GER)
1976	Kazuhiro Ninomiya (JPN)	Ramaz Harshiladze (URS)	David C. Starbrook (GBR) Juerg Roethlisberger (SUI)

Shinobu Sekine of Japan (left) defeated Brian Jacks of Great Britain (right) in this semi-final match and went on to win the gold medal in the middleweight category in 1972.

70 to 80 kg (154¼ to 176¼ lb)

	GOLD	SILVER	BRONZE
1964	Isao Okano (JPN)	Wolfgang Hofmann (GER)	James Bregman (USA) Eui Tae Kim (KOR)
1968	Event not held		
1972	Shinobu Sekine (JPN)	Seung-Lip Oh (KOR)	Brian Jacks (GBR) Jean-Paul Coche (FRA)
1976	Isamu Sonoda (JPN)	Valeriy Dvoinikov (URS)	Slavko Obadov (YUG) Youngchul Park (KOR)

63 to 70 kg (138¾ to 154¼ lb)

	GOLD	SILVER	BRONZE
1964–1968	Event not held		
1972	Toyokazu Nomura (JPN)	Anton Zajkowski (POL)	Dietmar Hoetger (GDR) Anatoli Novikov (URS)
1976	Vladimir Nevzorov (URS)	Koji Kuramoto (JPN)	Patrick Vial (FRA) Marian Talaj (POL)

Up to 63 kg (138¾ lb)

	GOLD	SILVER	BRONZE
1964	Takehide Nakatani (JPN)	Eric Haenni (SUI)	Oleg Stepanov (URS) Aron Bogulubov (URS)
1968	Event not held		
1972	Takao Kawaguchi (JPN)	—[1]	Yong Ik Kim (PRK) Jean-Jacques Mounier (FRA)
1976	Hector Rodriguez (CUD)	Eunkyung Chang (KOR)	Felice Mariani (ITA) Jozsef Tuncsik (HUN)

----

[1]Bakhaavaa Buidaa (MGL) disqualified after positive drug test.

---

12. Modern Pentathlon

The five events [currently in the order Riding (800 m course), Fencing (epée), Shooting (pistol 25 m), Swimming (300 m free-style), and Cross-country running (4,000 m)] have remained constant although there have inevitably been changes of rules, time allowed and order over the years.

Competitors were placed by lowest number of placing points (e.g. 1 for 1st in an event and 10 for a 10th place in another) until an international graduated points scoring table was introduced in 1956.

1896–1908	Event not held		
1912	Gustaf Lilliehöök (SWE) 27	Gösta Åsbrink (SWE) 28	Georg de Laval (SWE) 30
1920	Gustaf Dryssen (SWE) 18	Erik de Laval (SWE) 23	Gösta Rüno (SWE) 27
1924	Bo Lindman (SWE) 18	Gustaf Dryssen (SWE) 39.5	Bertil Uggla (SWE) 45
1928	Sven Thofelt (SWE) 47	Bo Lindman (SWE) 50	Helmuth Kahl (GER) 52
1932	Johan Gabriel Oxenstierna (SWE) 32	Bo Lindman (SWE) 35.5	Richard Mayo (USA) 38.5
1936	Gotthard Handrick (GER) 31.5	Charles Leonard (USA) 39.5	Silvano Abba (ITA) 45.5
1948	William Grut (SWE) 16	George Moore (USA) 47	Gösta Gärdin (SWE) 49
1952	Lars Hall (SWE) 32	Gábor Benedek (HUN) 39	István Szondi (HUN) 41
Teams—HUNGARY 166	Gábor Benedek István Szondi Aladár Kovácsi	SWEDEN 182 Lars Hall Torsten Lindqvist Cläes Egnell	FINLAND 213 Olavi Mannonen Lauri Vikko Olavi Rokka
1956	Lars Hall (SWE) 4,843	Olavi Mannonen (FIN) 4,774.5	Väinö Korhonen (FIN) 4,750
Teams—U.S.S.R. 13,690.5	Igor Novikov Aleksandr Tarassov Ivan Deryugin	UNITED STATES 13,482 George H. Lambert William Andre Jack T. Daniels	FINLAND 13,185.5 Olavi Mannonen Väinö Korhonen Berndt Katter

Andras Balczo (HUN) was the most successful of all modern pentathletes with 3 gold and 2 silver medals.

GOLD	SILVER	BRONZE
1960 Ferenc Németh (HUN) 5,024	Imre Nagy (HUN) 4,988	Robert L. Beck (USA) 4,981
Teams—HUNGARY 14,863	U.S.S.R. 14,309	UNITED STATES 14,192
Ferenc Németh	Igor Novikov	Robert L. Beck
Imre Nagy	Nikolai Tatarinov	George H. Lambert
András Balczó	Hanno Selg	Jack T. Daniels
1964 Ferenc Török (HUN) 5,116	Igor Novikov (URS) 5,067	Albert Mokeyev (URS) 5,039
Teams—U.S.S.R. 14,961	UNITED STATES 14,189	HUNGARY 14,173
Igor Novikov	James Moore	Ferenc Török
Albert Mokeyev	David Kirkwood	Imre Nagy
Victor Mineyev	Paul Pesthy	Otto Török
1968 Björn Ferm (SWE) 4,964	András Balczó (HUN) 4,953	Pavel Lednev (URS) 4,795
Teams—HUNGARY 14,325	U.S.S.R. 14,248	FRANCE 13,289
András Balczó	Boris Onischenko	Raoul Gueguen
István Móna	Pavel Lednev	Lucien Guiguet
Ferenc Török	Stasis Shaparnis	Jean-Pierre Giudicelli
1972 András Balczó (HUN) 5,412	Boris Onischenko (URS) 5,335	Pavel Lednev (URS) 5,328
Teams—U.S.S.R. 15,968	HUNGARY 15,348	FINLAND 14,812
Boris Onischenko	András Balczó	Risto Hurme
Pavel Lednev	Zsigmond Villanyi	Veikko Salminen
Vladimir Shmelev	Pal Bako	Martti Ketelae
1976 Janusz Pyciak-Peciak (POL) 5,520	Pavel Lednev (URS) 5,485	Jan Bartu (TCH) 5,466
Teams—GREAT BRITAIN 15,559	CZECHOSLOVAKIA 15,451	HUNGARY 15,395
Adrian Parker	Jan Bartu	Tamas Kancsal
Robert Nightingale	Bohumil Starnovsky	Tibor Maracsko
Jeremy Fox	Jiri Adam	Szvetiszlav Sasics
1980 Anatoly Starostin (URS) 5,568	Tamas Szmobathelyi (HUN) 5,502	Pavel Lednev (URS) 5,382
Teams—U.S.S.R. 16,126	HUNGARY 15,912	SWEDEN 15,845
Anatoliy Starostin	Tamas Szombathelyi	Svante Rasmuson
Pavel Lednev	Tibor Maracsko	Lennart Pettersson
Yevgeniy Lipeyev	Laszlo Horvath	George Horvath

13. Rowing (Men)

The standard Olympic course is now 1 mile 427 yards *2 000 m* in length.

In 1904, however, the course was 2 miles *3 218,7 m;* in 1908 1½ miles *2 414 m;* and in 1948 1 mile 350 yards *1 929 m.*

Times: The water conditions can vary sufficiently from one Games to another, even over a course of the same length, so as to make comparison between Games of little value.

There can thus be no Olympic *records* as such, but as a matter of interest the following are the *fastest times* achieved in any Olympic regatta over 2,000 meters:

Single Sculls	6:52.46	S. Drea (IRL)	1976
Double Sculls	6:12.48	Norway	1976
Quadruple Sculls	5:47.83	U.S.S.R.	1976
Coxless Pairs	6:33.02	East Germany	1976
Coxed Pairs	7:01.10	Bulgaria	1976
Coxless Fours	5:53.65	East Germany	1976
Coxed Fours	6:09.28	U.S.S.R.	1976
Eights	5:32.17	East Germany	1976

The times given of the Bronze medal winners in 1928 are those achieved in a losing semi-final or race between beaten semi-finalists.

SINGLE SCULLS

	GOLD	SILVER	BRONZE
1896	Event not held		
1900	Henri Barrelet (FRA) 7:35.6	André Gaudin (FRA) 7:41.6	St. George Ashe (GBR) 8:15.6
1904	Frank Greer (USA) 10:08.5	James Juvenal (USA) 2 lengths	Constance Titus (USA) 1 length
1906	Gaston Delaplane (FRA) 5:53.4	Joseph Larran (FRA) 6:07.2	
1908	Harry Blackstaffe (GBR) 9:26.0	Alexander McCulloch (GBR) 1 length	Bernhard von Gaza (GER) d.n.a. Károly Levitzky (HUN) d.n.a.
1912	William D. Kinnear (GBR) 7:47.6	Polydore Veirman (BÉL) 1 length	Everard B. Butler (CAN) d.n.a. Mikhail Kusik (URS) d.n.a.

One of only five oarsmen to take three gold medals, Jack Beresford of Great Britain won rowing events in 1924, 1932, and 1936.

	GOLD	SILVER	BRONZE
1920	John Kelly (USA) 7:35.0	Jack Beresford (GBR) 7:36.0	Clarence Hadfield d'Arcy (NZL) 7:48.0
1924	Jack Beresford (GBR) 7:49.2	William E. Garrett-Gilmore (USA) 7:54.0	Josef Schneider (SUI) 8:01.1
1928	Henry Pearce (AUS) 7:11.10	Kenneth Myers (USA) 7:20.8	T. David Collet (GBR) 7:19.8
1932	Henry Pearce (AUS) 7:44.4	William Miller (USA) 7:45.2	Guillermo Douglas (URU) 8:13.6
1936	Gustav Schäfer (GER) 8:21.5	Josef Hasenöhrl (AUT) 8:25.8	Daniel Barrow (USA) 8:28.0
1948	Mervyn Wood (AUS) 7:24.4	Eduardo Risso (URU) 7:38.2	Romolo Catasta (ITA) 7:51.4
1952	Yuri Tyukalov (URS) 8:12.8	Mervyn Wood (AUS) 8:14.5	Teodor Kocerka (POL) 8:19.4
1956	Vyacheslav Ivanov (URS) 8:02.5	Stuart Mackenzie (AUS) 8:07.7	John B. Kelly (USA) 8:11.8
1960	Vyacheslav Ivanov (URS) 7:13.96	Achim Hill (GER) 7:20.21	Teodor Kocerka (POL) 7:21.26
1964	Vyacheslav Ivanov (URS) 8:22.51	Achim Hill (GER) 8:26.34	Gottfried Kottmann (SUI) 8:29.68
1968	Henri Jan Wienese (HOL) 7:47.80	Jochen Meissner (GER) 7:52.00	Alberto Demiddi (ARG) 7:57.19
1972	Yuri Malishev (URS) 7:10.12	Alberto Demiddi (ARG) 7:11.53	Wolfgang Gueldenpfennig (GDR) 7:14.45
1976	Pertti Karppinen (FIN) 7:29.03	Peter Kolbe (GER) 7:31.67	Joachim Dreifke (GDR) 7:38.03
1980	Pertti Karppinen (FIN) 7:09.61	Vasily Yakusha (URS) 7:11.66	Peter Kersten (GDR) 7:14.88

Vyacheslav Ivanov (URS), the only man ever to win three Olympic single sculls titles, celebrates his 1960 victory on Lake Albano, Italy.

DOUBLE SCULLS

<table>
<thead>
<tr><th>GOLD</th><th>SILVER</th><th>BRONZE</th></tr>
</thead>
<tbody>
<tr><td colspan="3">1896–1900 Event not held</td></tr>
<tr><td>1904 UNITED STATES
10:03.2</td><td>UNITED STATES
d.n.a.</td><td>UNITED STATES
d.n.a.</td></tr>
<tr><td>John Mulcahy
William Varley</td><td>John Hoben
James McLoughlin</td><td>John Wells
Joseph Ravanack</td></tr>
<tr><td colspan="3">1906–1912 Event not held</td></tr>
<tr><td>1920 UNITED STATES
7:09.0</td><td>ITALY 7:19.0</td><td>FRANCE 7:21.0</td></tr>
<tr><td>John Kelly
Paul Costello</td><td>Erminio Dones
Pietro Annoni</td><td>Alfred Plé
Gaston Giran</td></tr>
<tr><td>1924 UNITED STATES
7:45.0</td><td>FRANCE 7:54.8</td><td>SWITZERLAND d.n.a.</td></tr>
<tr><td>John Kelly
Paul Costello</td><td>Jean-Pierre Stock
Marc Detton</td><td>Rudolf Bosshard
Heini Thoma</td></tr>
<tr><td>1928 UNITED STATES
6:41.4</td><td>CANADA 6:51.0</td><td>AUSTRIA 6:48.8</td></tr>
<tr><td>Charles J. McIlvaine
Paul Costello</td><td>Jack Guest
Joseph Wright</td><td>Viktor Flessl
Leo Losert</td></tr>
<tr><td>1932 UNITED STATES
7:17.4</td><td>GERMANY 7:22.8</td><td>CANADA 7:27.6</td></tr>
<tr><td>William E.
Garrett-Gilmore
Kenneth Myers</td><td>Gerhard Boetzelen
Herbert Buhtz</td><td>Nöel de Mille
Charles Pratt</td></tr>
<tr><td>1936 GREAT BRITAIN
7:20.8</td><td>GERMANY 7:26.2</td><td>POLAND 7:36.2</td></tr>
<tr><td>Leslie F. Southwood
Jack Beresford</td><td>Joachim Pirsch
Willy Kaidel</td><td>Jerzy Ustupski
Roger Verey</td></tr>
<tr><td>1948 GREAT BRITAIN
6:51.3</td><td>DENMARK 6:55.3</td><td>URUGUAY 7:12.4</td></tr>
<tr><td>B. Herbert T. Bushnell
Richard D. Burnell</td><td>Aage E. Larsen
Ebbe Parsner</td><td>Juan Rodriguez
William Jones</td></tr>
<tr><td>1952 ARGENTINA 7:32.2</td><td>U.S.S.R. 7:38.3</td><td>URUGUAY 7:43.7</td></tr>
<tr><td>Tranquilo Capozzo
Eduardo Guerrero</td><td>Georgiy Zhilin
Igor Emchuk</td><td>Miguel Seijas
Juan Rodriguez</td></tr>
<tr><td>1956 U.S.S.R. 7:24.0</td><td>UNITED STATES
7:32.3</td><td>AUSTRALIA 7:37.4</td></tr>
<tr><td>Aleksandr Berkutov
Yuri Tyukalov</td><td>Bernard Costello
James Gardiner</td><td>Murray Riley
Mervyn Wood</td></tr>
<tr><td>1960 CZECHOSLOVAKIA
6:47.50</td><td>U.S.S.R. 6:50.49</td><td>SWITZERLAND
6:50.59</td></tr>
<tr><td>Václav Kozák
Pavel Schmidt</td><td>Aleksandr Berkutov
Yuri Tyukalov</td><td>Ernst Huerlimann
Rolf Larcher</td></tr>
<tr><td>1964 U.S.S.R. 7:10.66</td><td>UNITED STATES
7:13.16</td><td>CZECHOSLOVAKIA
7:14.23</td></tr>
<tr><td>Oleg Tyurin
Boris Dubrovsky</td><td>Seymour Cromwell
James Storm</td><td>Vladimir Andrs
Pavel Hofman</td></tr>
<tr><td>1968 U.S.S.R. 6:51.82</td><td>NETHERLANDS
6:52.80</td><td>UNITED STATES
6:54.21</td></tr>
<tr><td>Anatoly Sass
Aleksandr Timoshinin</td><td>Henricus A. Droog
Leendert F. van Dis</td><td>John Nunn
William Maher</td></tr>
<tr><td>1972 U.S.S.R. 7:01.77</td><td>NORWAY 7:02.58</td><td>EAST GERMANY
7:05.55</td></tr>
<tr><td>Aleksandr Timoshinin
Gennadi Korshikov</td><td>Frank Hansen
Svein Thogersen</td><td>Joachim Boehmer
Hans-Ulrich Schmied</td></tr>
<tr><td>1976 NORWAY 7:13.20</td><td>GREAT BRITAIN
7:15.26</td><td>EAST GERMANY
7:17.45</td></tr>
<tr><td>Frank Hansen
Alf Hansen</td><td>Chris Baillieu
Michael Hart</td><td>Hans-Ulrich Schmied
Jurgen Bertow</td></tr>
<tr><td>1980 EAST GERMANY
6:24.33</td><td>YUGOSLAVIA 6:26.34</td><td>CZECHOSLOVAKIA
6:29.07</td></tr>
<tr><td>Joachim Dreifke
Klaus Kroppelien</td><td>Zoran Pancic
Milorad Stanulov</td><td>Zdenek Pecka
Vaclav Vochoska</td></tr>
</tbody>
</table>

COXLESS QUADRUPLE SCULLS

GOLD	SILVER	BRONZE
1896–1972 Event not held		
1976 **EAST GERMANY** 6:18.65	U.S.S.R. 6:19.89	CZECHOSLOVAKIA 6:21.77
Wolfgang Guldenpfennig Rudiger Reiche Karl-Heinz Bussert Michael Wolfgramm	Yevgeni Duleyev Yuri Yakimov Aivar Lazdenieks Vitautas Butkus	Jaroslav Helebrand Vaclav Vochoska Zdenek Pecka Vladek Lacina
1980 **EAST GERMANY** 5:49.81	U.S.S.R. 5:51.47	BULGARIA 5:52.38
Frank Dundr Karsten Bunk Uwe Heppner Martin Winter	Yuriy Shapochka Yevgeniy Barbakov Valeriy Kleshnev Nikolai Dovgan	Mintscho Nikolov Lubomir Petrov Ivo Russev Bogdan Dobrev

COXLESS PAIRS

GOLD	SILVER	BRONZE
1896–1906 Event not held		
1908 **GREAT BRITAIN** 9:41.0	GREAT BRITAIN 2½ lengths	——
(Leander I) J. R. K. Fenning Gordon L. Thomson	(Leander II) George E. Fairbairn Philip E. Verdon	
1912–1920 Event not held		
1924 **NETHERLANDS** 8:19.4	FRANCE 8:21.6	——
Wilhelm H. Rösingh Antonie C. Beijnen	Maurice Bouton George Piot	
1928 **GERMANY** 7:06.4	GREAT BRITAIN 7:08.8	UNITED STATES 7:20.4
Bruno Müller Kurt Moeschter	R. Archibald Nisbet Terence O'Brien	John Schmitt Paul McDowell
1932 **GREAT BRITAIN** 8:00.0	NEW ZEALAND 8:02.4	POLAND 8:08.2
H. R. Arthur Edwards Lewis Clive	Frederick Thompson Cyril Stiles	Janusz Mikolajczyk Henryk Budzynski
1936 **GERMANY** 8:16.1	DENMARK 8:19.2	ARGENTINA 8:23.0
Hugo Strauss Willi Eichhorn	Harry J. Larsen Richard Olsen	Julio Curatella Horacio Podestá
1948 **GREAT BRITAIN** 7:21.1	SWITZERLAND 7:23.9	ITALY 7:31.5
John H. T. Wilson William G. R. M. Laurie	Josef Kalt Hans Kalt	Bruno Boni Felice Fanetti
1952 **UNITED STATES** 8:20.7	BELGIUM 8:23.5	SWITZERLAND 8:32.7
Charles Logg Thomas Price	Michel Knuysen Robert Baetens	Kurt Schmid Hans Kalt
1956 **UNITED STATES** 7:55.4	U.S.S.R. 8:03.9	AUSTRIA 8:11.8
James Fifer Duvall Hecht	Igor Buldakov Viktor Ivanov	Josef Kloimstein Alfred Sageder
1960 **U.S.S.R.** 7:02.01	AUSTRIA 7:03.69	FINLAND 7:03.80
Valentin Boreyko Olyeg Golovanov	Josef Kloimstein Alfred Sageder	Veli Lehtelä Toimi Pitkänen
1964 **CANADA** 7:32.94	NETHERLANDS 7:33.40	GERMANY 7:38.63
George Hungerford Roger C. Jackson	Steven Blaisse Ernst W. Veenemans	Michael Schwan Wolfgang Hottenrott
1968 **EAST GERMANY** 7:26.56	UNITED STATES 7:26.71	DENMARK 7:31.84
Jörg Lucke Hans-Jürgen Bothe	Lawrence Hough Philip Johnson	Peter F. Christiansen Ib Ivan Larsen

	GOLD	SILVER	BRONZE
1972	**EAST GERMANY** 6:53.16	**SWITZERLAND** 6:57.06	**NETHERLANDS** 6:58.70
	Siegfried Brietzke	Heinrich Fischer	Roelof Luyernburg
	Wolfgang Mager	Alfred Bachmann	Rund Stokvis
1976	**EAST GERMANY** 7:23.31	**UNITED STATES** 7:26.73	**GERMANY** 7:30.03
	Jorg Landvoigt	Calvin Coffey	Peter Vanroye
	Bernd Landvoigt	Michael Staines	Thomas Strauss
1980	**EAST GERMANY** 6:48.01	**U.S.S.R.** 6:50.50	**GREAT BRITAIN** 6:51.47
	Jorg Landvoigt	Yuriy Pimenov	Charles Wiggin
	Bernd Landvoigt	Nikolai Pimenov	Malcolm Carmichael

COXED PAIRS

	GOLD	SILVER	BRONZE
1896	Event not held		
1900	**NETHERLANDS** 7:34.2	**FRANCE I** 7:34.4	**FRANCE II** 7:57.2
	(Minerva, Amsterdam)	(Soc. Nautique de la Marne)	(Rowing Club Castillonais)
1904–1912	Event not held		
1920	**ITALY** 7:56.0	**FRANCE** 7:57.0	**SWITZERLAND** d.n.a.
	Ercole Olgeni	Gabriel Poix	Edouard Candeveau
	Giovanni Scatturin	Maurice Bouton	Alfred Felber
	Guido de Filip (cox)	Ernest Barberolle (cox)	Paul Piaget (cox)
1924	**SWITZERLAND** 8:39.0	**ITALY** 8:39.1	**UNITED STATES** d.n.a.
	Edouard Candeveau	Ercole Olgeni	Leon Butler
	Alfred Felber	Giovanni Scatturin	Harold Wilson
	Emil Lachapelle (cox)	Gino Sopracordevole (cox)	Edward Jennings (cox)
1928	**SWITZERLAND** 7:42.6	**FRANCE** 7:48.4	**BELGIUM** 7:59.4
	Hans Schöchlin	Armand Marcelle	Léon Flament
	Karl Schöchlin	Edouard Marcelle	François de Coninck
	Hans Bourquin (cox)	Henri Préaux (cox)	Georges Anthony (cox)
1932	**UNITED STATES** 8:25.8	**POLAND** 8:31.2	**FRANCE** 8:41.2
	Charles Kieffer	Janusz Slazak	André Giriat
	Joseph Schauers	Jerzy Braun	Anselme Brusa
	Edward Jennings (cox)	Jerzy Skolimowski (cox)	Pierre Brunet (cox)
1936	**GERMANY** 8:36.9	**ITALY** 8:49.7	**FRANCE** 8:54.0
	Herbert Adamski	Guido Santin	Georges Tapie
	Gerhard Gustmann	Almiro Bergamo	Marceau Fourcade
	Dieter Arend (cox)	Luciano Negrini (cox)	Nöel Vandernotte (cox)
1948	**DENMARK** 8:00.5	**ITALY** 8:12.2	**HUNGARY** 8:25.2
	Tage Henriksen	Aldo Tarlao	Béla Zsitnik
	Finn Pedersen	Giovanni Steffe	Antal Szendey
	Carl Ebbe Andersen (cox)	Alberto Radi (cox)	Róbert Zimonyi (cox)
1952	**FRANCE** 8:28.6	**GERMANY** 8:32.1	**DENMARK** 8:34.9
	Raymond Salles	Heinz Manchen	Svend Petersen
	Gaston Mercier	Helmut Heinhold	Paul Svendsen
	Bernard Malivoire (cox)	Helmut Noll (cox)	Jörgen Frandsen (cox)
1956	**UNITED STATES** 8:26.1	**GERMANY** 8:29.2	**U.S.S.R.** 8:31.0
	Arthur Ayrault	Karl-Heinrich von Groddeck	Igor Yemtschuk
	F. Conn Findlay	Horst Arndt	Georgiy Zhilin
	Kurt Seiffert (cox)	Rainer Borkowsky (cox)	Vladimir Petrov (cox)
1960	**GERMANY** 7:29.14	**U.S.S.R.** 7:30.17	**UNITED STATES** 7:34.58
	Bernhard Knubel	Antanas Bogdanavichus	F. Conn Findlay
	Heinz Renneberg	Zigmas Yukna	Richard Draeger
	Klaus Zerta (cox)	Igor Rudakov (cox)	H. Kent Mitchell (cox)

GOLD	SILVER	BRONZE
1964 **UNITED STATES** 8:21.23	**FRANCE** 8:23.15	**NETHERLANDS** 8:23.42
Edward Ferry	Georges Morel	Jan J. Bos
F. Conn Findlay	Jacques Morel	Herman J. Rouwé
H. Kent Mitchell (cox)	Jean-Claude Darouy (cox)	Frederik Hartsuiker (cox)
1968 **ITALY** 8:04.81	**NETHERLANDS** 8:06.80	**DENMARK** 8:08.07
Primo Baran	Herman J. Suselbeek	Jörn Krab
Renzo Sambo	Hadriaan van Nes	Harry Jörgensen
Bruno Cipolla (cox)	Roderick Rijnders (cox)	Preben Krab (cox)
1972 **EAST GERMANY** 7:17.25	**CZECHOSLOVAKIA** 7:19.57	**RUMANIA** 7:21.36
Wolfgang Gunkel	Oldrich Svojanovsky	Stefan Tudor
Joerg Lucke	Pavel Svojanovsky	Petre Ceapura
Klaus-Dieter Neubert (cox)	Vladimir Petricek (cox)	Ladislau Lowrenschi (cox)
1976 **EAST GERMANY** 7:58.99	**U.S.S.R.** 8:01.82	**CZECHOSLOVAKIA** 8:03.28
Harald Jahrling	Dmitri Bekhterev	Oldrich Svojanovsky
Friedrich Ulrich	Yuri Shurkalov	Pavel Svojanovsky
George Spohr (cox)	Yuri Lorentson (cox)	Ludvik Vebr (cox)
1980 **EAST GERMANY** 7:02.54	**U.S.S.R.** 7:03.35	**YUGOSLAVIA** 7:04.92
Harald Jahrling	Viktor Prevertsev	Dusko Mrduljas
Friedrich-Wilhelm Ulrich	Gennadiy Kryuchkin	Zlatko Celent
Georg Spohr (cox)	Aleksandr Lukyanov (cox)	Josip Reic (cox)

COXLESS FOURS

1896–1900 Event not held		
1904 **UNITED STATES** 9:53.8	**UNITED STATES** d.n.a.	——
(Century B.C., St. Louis)	(Mound City R.C., St. Louis)	
Arthur M. Stockhoff	Frederick Suerig	
August C. Erker	Martin Fromanack	
George Dietz	Charles Aman	
Albert Nasse	Michael Begley	
1906 Event not held		
1908 **GREAT BRITAIN** 8:34.0	**GREAT BRITAIN** 1½ lengths	
(Magdalen B.C., Oxford)	(Leander)	
C. Robert Cudmore	Philip R. Filleul	
James A. Gillan	Harold R. Barker	
Duncan McKinnon	J. R. K. Fenning	
John R. Somers-Smith	Gordon L. Thomson	
1912–1920 Event not held		
1924 **GREAT BRITAIN** 7:08.6	**CANADA** 7:18.0	**SWITZERLAND** d.n.a.
Charles R. M. Eley	Archibald C. Black	Emile Albrecht
James A. McNabb	Colin H. B. Finlayson	Alfred Probst
Robert E. Morrison	George F. McKay	Eugen Sigg
T. Robert B. Sanders	William Wood	Hans Walter
1928 **GREAT BRITAIN** 6:36.0	**UNITED STATES** 6:37.0	**ITALY** 6:31.6
Edward V. Bevan	Charles Karle	Cesare Rossi
Richard Beesly	William Miller	Pietro Freschi
Michael H. Warriner	George Heales	Umberto Bonadè
John G. H. Lander	Ernest Bayer	Paolo Gennari
1932 **GREAT BRITAIN** 6:58.2	**GERMANY** 7:03.0	**ITALY** 7:04.0
Rowland D. George	Hans Maier	Antonio Provenzani
Jack Beresford	Walter Flinsch	Giliante d'Este
Hugh R. A. Edwards	Ernst Gaber	Francesco Cossu
John C. Badcock	Karl Aletter	Antonio Ghiardello

East Germany, the eventual gold medalist, leads Great Britian in a preliminary heat of coxless fours at the 1972 Games in Munich.

	GOLD	SILVER	BRONZE
1936	GERMANY 7:01.8	GREAT BRITAIN 7:06.5	SWITZERLAND 7:10.6
	Wilhelm Menne	Thomas Bristow	Karl Schmid
	Martin Karl	Alan Barrett	Alex Homberger
	Anton Rom	Peter Jackson	Hans Homberger
	Rudolf Eckstein	John D. Sturrock	Hermann Betschart
1948	ITALY 6:39.0	DENMARK 6:43.5	UNITED STATES 6:47.7
	Franco Faggi	Ib Storm Larsen	Robert Perew
	Giovanni Invernizzi	Helge Schroeder	Gregory Gates
	Elio Morille	A. Bonde Hansen	Stuart Griffing
	Giuseppe Moioli	Helge Halkjaer	F. John Kingsbury
1952	YUGOSLAVIA 7:16.0	FRANCE 7:18.9	FINLAND 7:23.3
	Duje Bonačič	Pierre Blondiaux	Veikko Lommi
	Vleimir Valenta	Jacques Guissart	Kauko Wahlsten
	Mate Trojanovič	Marc Bouissou	Oiva Lommi
	Peter Šegvič	Roger Gautier	Lauri Nevalainen
1956	CANADA 7:08.8	UNITED STATES 7:18.4	FRANCE 7:20.9
	Archibald McKinnon	John Welchli	Guy Guillabert
	Lorne Loomer	John McKinlay	Gaston Mercier
	I. Walter d'Hondt	Arthur McKinlay	Yves Delacour
	Donald Arnold	James McIntosh	René Guissart
1960	UNITES STATES 6:26.26	ITALY 6:28.78	U.S.S.R. 6:29.62
	Arthur Ayrault	Tullio Baraglia	Igor Akhremchik
	Theodore Nash	Renato Bosatta	Yuriy Batschurov
	John Sayre	Giancarlo Crosta	Valentin Morkovkin
	Richard Wailes	Giuseppe Galante	Anatoliy Tarabrin
1964	DENMARK 6:59.30	GREAT GRITAIN 7:00.47	UNITED STATES 7:01.37
	John Orsted Hansen	John M. Russell	Geoffrey Picard
	Björn Haslöv	Hugh A. Wardell-Yerburgh	Richard Lyon
	Erik Petersen	William Barry	Theodore Mittet
	Kurt Helmudt	John James	Theodore Nash
1968	EAST GERMANY 6:39.18	HUNGARY 6:41.64	ITALY 6:44.01
	Frank Forberger	Zoltán Melis	Renato Bosatta
	Dieter Grahn	György Sarlós	Tullio Baraglia
	Frank Rühle	József Csermely	Pier Angelo Conti Manzini
	Dieter Schubert	Antal Melis	Abramo Albini

GOLD	SILVER	BRONZE
1972 **EAST GERMANY** 6:24.27	**NEW ZEALAND** 6:25.64	**WEST GERMANY** 6:28.41
Frank Forberger	Dick Tonks	Joachim Ehrig
Frank Rühle	Dudley Storey	Peter Funnekoetter
Dieter Grahn	Ross Collinge	Franz Weld
Dieter Schubert	Noel Mills	Wolfgang Plottke
1976 **EAST GERMANY** 6:37.42	**NORWAY** 6:41.22	**U.S.S.R.** 6:42.52
Siegfried Brietzke	Ole Nafstad	Raul Arnemann
Andreas Decker	Arne Bergodd	Nikolai Kuznetsov
Stefan Semmler	Finn Tveter	Valeri Dolinin
Wolfgang Mager	Rolf Andreassen	Anushavan Gasan-Dzhalalov
1980 **EAST GERMANY** 6:08.17	**U.S.S.R.** 6:11.81	**GREAT BRITAIN** 6:16.58
Jurgen Thiele	Aleksey Kamkin	John Beattie
Andreas Decker	Valeri Dolinin	Ian McNuff
Stefan Semmler	Aleksandr Kulagin	David Townsend
Siegfried Brietzke	Vitaliy Yeliseyev	Martin Cross

COXED FOURS

GOLD	SILVER	BRONZE
1896 Event not held		
1900 **GERMANY** 5:59.0 (Germania, Hamburg)	**NETHERLANDS** 6:33.0 (Minerva, Amsterdam)	**GERMANY** 6:35.0 (Ruderverein, Ludwigshafen)
Oskar Gossler		
Katzenstein		
Tietgens		
G. Gossler		
G. Gossler (cox)		
1904 Event not held		
1906 **ITALY** 8:13.0 (Bucintoro)	**FRANCE** d.n.a. (Soc. Nautique de la Basse Siene)	**FRANCE** d.n.a. (Soc. Nautique de Bayonne)
Enrico Bruna	Gaston Delaplane	Adolphe Bernard
Emilio Fontanella	Charles Delaporte	Joseph Halcet
Riccardo Jandinoni	León Deliguières	Jean-Baptiste Laporte
Giorgio Cesana	Paul Echard	Jean-Baptiste Mathieu
Giuseppe Poli (cox)	Marcel Frébourg (cox)	Pierre Sourbé (cox)
1908 Event not held		
1912 **GERMANY** 6:59.4 (Ludwigshafener R.C.)	**GREAT BRITAIN** 2 lengths (Thames R.C.)	**NORWAY** d.n.a. (Christiania R.C.)
Albert Arnheiter	Julius Beresford	Henry Larsen
Otto Fickeisen	Charles Rought	Matias Torstensen
Rudolf Fickeisen	Bruce Logan	Theodor Klem
Herman Wilker	Charles G. Vernon	Haakon Tonsager
Otto Maier (cox)	Geoffrey Carr (cox)	Ejnar Tonsager (cox)
		DENMARK (Polyteknic R.C.)
		Erik Bisgaard
		Rasmus P. Frandsen
		Magnus Simonsen
		Poul Thymann
		Eigil Clemmensen (cox)
1920 **SWITZERLAND** 6:54.0	**UNITED STATES** 6:58.0	**NORWAY** 7:02.0
Hans Walter	Kenneth Myers	Henry Larsen
Max Rudolf	Carl O. Klose	Per Gulbrandsen
Willy Brüderlin	Franz Federschmidt	Theodor Klem
Paul Rudolf	Erich Federschmidt	Birger Var
Paul Staub (cox)	Sherman Clark (cox)	Thoralf Hagen (cox)

GOLD	SILVER	BRONZE

1924 **SWITZERLAND** 7:18.4 — **FRANCE** 7:21.6 — **UNITED STATES** 1 length

Hans Walter	Louis Gressier	Robert Gerhardt
Alfred Probst	Georges Lecointe	Sidney Jelinek
Emile Albrecht	Raymond Thalleux	Edward Mitchell
Eugen Sigg	Eugène Constant	Henry Welsford
Walter Loosli (cox)	Marcel Lepan (cox)	John Kennedy (cox)

1928 **ITALY** 6:47.8 — **SWITZERLAND** 7:03.4 — **POLAND** 7:12.8

Valerio Perentin	Ernst Haas	František Bronikowski
Giliante d'Este	Joseph Meyer	Edmund Jankowski
Nicolo Vittori	Otto Bucher	Leszek Birkholz
Giovanni Delise	Karl Schwegler	Bernard Ormanowski
Renato Petronio (cox)	Fritz Boesch (cox)	Bronislaw Drewek (cox)

1932 **GERMANY** 7:19.0 — **ITALY** 7:19.2 — **POLAND** 7:26.8

Joachim Spemberg	Bruno Parovel	Edward Kobylinski
Walter Meyer	Riccardo Divora	Stanislaw Urban
Horst Hoeck	Giovanni Plazzer	Janusz Ślazak
Hans Eller	Bruno Vattovaz	Jerzy Braun
Karlheinz Neumann (cox)	Giovanni Scherl (cox)	Jerzy Skolimowski (cox)

1936 **GERMAY** 7:16.2 — **SWITZERLAND** 7:24.3 — **FRANCE** 7:33.3

Paul Söllner	Karl Schmid	Fernand Vandernotte
Ernst Gaber	Hans Homberger	Marcel Vandernotte
Walter Volle	Alex Homberger	Marcel Cosmat
Hans Maier	Hermann Betschart	Marcel Chauvigné
Fritz Bauer (cox)	Rolf Spring (cox)	Noel Vandernotte (cox)

1948 **UNITED STATES** 6:50.3 — **SWITZERLAND** 6:53.3 — **DENMARK** 6:58.6

Gordon Giovanelli	Pierre Stebler	Harry M. Knudsen
Robert W. Eill	Erich Schriever	Henry C. Larsen
Robert Martin	Emile Knecht	Börge R. Nielsen
Warren Westlund	Rudolf Reichling	Erik C. Larsen
Allen Morgan (cox)	André Moccand (cox)	Jörgen Ib Olsen (cox)

1952 **CZECHOSLOVAKIA** 7:33.4 — **SWITZERLAND** 7:36.5 — **UNITED STATES** 7:37.0

Karel Mejta	Enrico Bianchi	Carl Lovested
Jiři Havlis	Karl Weidmann	Alvin Ulbrickson
Jan Jindra	Heinrich Scheller	Richard Wahlström
Stanislav Lusk	Emile Ess	Matthew Leanderson
Miroslav Koranda (cox)	Walter Leiser (cox)	Albert Rossi (cox)

1956 **ITALY** 7:19.4 — **SWEDEN** 7:22.4 — **FINLAND** 7:30.9

Alberto Winkler	Olof Larsson	Kauko Hänninen
Romano Sgheiz	Gösta Eriksson	Reino Poutanen
Angelo Vanzin	Ivar Aronsson	Veli Lehtelä
Franco Trincavelli	Sven E. Gunnarsson	Toimi Pitkänen
Ivo Stefanoni (cox)	Bertil Göransson (cox)	Matti Niemi (cox)

1960 **GERMANY** 6:39.12 — **FRANCE** 6:41.62 — **ITALY** 6:43.72

Gerd Cintl	Robert Dumantois	Fulvio Balatti
Horst Effertz	Claude Martin	Romano Sgheiz
Jürgen Litz	Jacques Morel	Franco Trincavelli
Klaus Riekemann	Guy Nosbaum	Giovanni Zucchi
Michael Obst (cox)	Jean Klein (cox)	Ivo Stefanoni (cox)

1964 **GERMANY** 7:00.44 — **ITALY** 7:02.84 — **NETHERLANDS** 7:06.46

Peter Neusel	Renato Bosatta	Alex Mullink
Bernhard Britting	Emilio Trivini	Jan van de Graaf
Joachim Werner	Giuseppe Galante	Frederick R. van de Graaf
Egbert Hirschfelder	Franco de Pedrina	Robert van de Graaf
Jürgen Oelke (cox)	Giovanni Spinola (cox)	Marius Klumperbeek (cox)

1968 **N. ZEALAND** 6:45.62 — **E. GERMANY** 6:48.20 — **SWITZERLAND** 6:49.04

Richard J. Joyce	Peter Kremtz	Denis Oswald
Dudley L. Storey	Roland Göhler	Hugo Waser
Warren J. Cole	Klaus Jacob	Jakob Grob
Ross H. Collinge	Manfred Gelpke	Peter Bolliger
Simon C. Dickie (cox)	Dieter Semetzky (cox)	Gottlieb Fröhlich (cox)

GOLD	SILVER	BRONZE
1972 W. GERMANY 6:31.85	E. GERMANY 6:33.30	CZECHOSLOVAKIA 6:35.64
Peter Berger	Dietrich Zander	Otakar Marecek
Hans-Johann Faerber	Reinhard Gust	Karel Neffe
Gerhard Auer	Eckhard Martens	Vladimir Janos
Alois Bierl	Rolf Jobst	František Provaznik
Uwe Benter (cox)	Klaus-Dieter Ludwig (cox)	Vladimir Petricek (cox)
1976 U.S.S.R. 6:40.22	E. GERMANY 6:42.70	W. GERMANY 6:46.96
Vladimir Eshinov	Andreas Schulz	Johann Faerber
Nikolai Ivanov	Rudiger Kunze	Ralph Kubail
Mikhail Kuznetsov	Walter Diessner	Siegfried Frickle
Alexandr Klepikov	Ullrich Diessner	Peter Niehusen
Alexandr Lukianov (cox)	Johannes Thomas (cox)	Hartmut Wenzel (cox)
1980 EAST GERMANY 6:14.51	U.S.S.R. 6:19.05	POLAND 6:22.52
Dieter Wendisch	Artur Garonskis	Grzegorz Stellak
Ullrich Diessner	Dimant Krisianis	Adam Tomasiak
Walter Diessner	Dzintars Krisianis	Grzegorz Nowak
Gottfried Dohn	George Tikmers	Ryszard Stadniuk
Andreas Gregor (cox)	Juris Berzynsh (cox)	Ryszard Kubiak (cox)

The United States wins by a nose over Italy, Canada, and Great Britain in the final eights race at Los Angeles in 1932.

EIGHTS

1896 Event not held

1900 **UNITED STATES**
6:09.8
(Vesper B.C.,
Philadelphia)
Roscoe Lockwood
Edward Marsh
Edward Hedley
William Carr
John E. Geiger
James Juvenal
Harry Debaecke
John N. Exley
Louis G. Abell

BELGIUM 6:13.8
(Royal Club Nautique
de Ghent)
Marcel van
Crombrugghe
Maurice Hemelsoet
Oscar de Cock
Maurice Verdonck
Prospère Bruggeman
Oscar de Somville
Frank Odberg
Jules de Bisschop
Alfred Vanlandeghem

NETHERLANDS
6:23.0
(Minerva, Amsterdam)
Walker M. Timmerman
Thijssen
Ruurd G. Leegstra
Johannes W. van Djik
Henricus Tromp
Hendrick K. Offerhaus
Roelof Klein
François A. Brandt
Walter Middelberg
Hermanus G.
Brockmann

1904 **UNITED STATES**
7:50.0
(Vesper B.C.,
Philadelphia)
Fred Cresser
M. D. Gleason
Frank Schell
J. S. Flanigan
C. E. Armstrong
H. H. Lott
J. F. Dempsey
John N. Exley
Louis G. Abell

CANADA d.n.a.
(Argonaut, R.C.
Toronto)
Joseph Wright
Donald Mackenzie
William Wadsworth
Geroge Strange
Phil Boyd
C. R. 'Pat' Reiffensteim
W. Rice
R. Bailey
Thomas Loudon

———

1906 Even not held

1908 **GREAT BRITAIN I**
7:52.0
(Leander Club)
Albert C. Gladstone
Frederick S. Kelly
Banner C. Johnstone
Guy Nickalls
Charles D. Burnell
Ronald H. Sanderson
Raymond B.
Etherington-Smith
Henry C. Bucknall
Gilchrist S. Maclagen
(cox)

BELGIUM 2 lenghts
(Royal C.N. Gand)

Oscar Taelman
Marcel Morimont
Rémy Orban
Georges Mijs
François Vergucht
Polydore Veirman
Oscar de Somville
Rodolphe Poma
Alfred Vanlandeghem
(cox)

GREAT BRITAIN II
(Cambridge University
B.C.)
Frederick Jerwood
Eric W. Powell
Guy A. Carver
Edward G. Williams
Henry M. Goldsmith
Harold E. Kitching
John S. Burn
Douglas C. R. Stuart
Richard F. Boyle (cox)
CANADA
(Argonaut R. C.
Toronto)
Irvine R. Robertson
George F. Wright
Julius A. Thomson
Walter A. Lewis
Gordon B. Balfour
Becher R. Gale
Charles Riddy
Geoffrey Taylor
Douglas E. Kertland (cox)

1912 **GREAT BRITAIN I**
6:15.0
(Leander Club)
Sidney E. Swann
Leslie G. Wormald
Ewart D. Horsfall
James A. Gillan
Arthur S. Garton
Alister G. Kirby
Philip Fleming
Edgar R. Burgess
Henry B. Wells (cox)

GREAT BRITAIN II
1 length
(New College, Oxford)
Sir William Parker
William Fison
Thomas Gillespie
Beaufort Burdekin
Frederick Pitman
Arthur Wiggins
Charles Littlejohn
Robert Bourne
John Walker (cox)

GERMANY d.n.a.
(Berliner R.V. 1876)

Otto Leibing
Max Broeske
Max Vetter
Wilhelm Bartholomae
Fritz Bartholomae
Werner Dehn
Rudolf Reichelt
Hans Mathiae
Kurt Runge (cox)

GOLD	SILVER	BRONZE

1920 UNITED STATES (Navy) 6:02.6
Virgil Jacomini
Edwin Graves
Willian Jordan
Edward Moore
Allen Sanborn
Donald Johnston
Vincent Gallagher
Clyde King
Sherman Clark (cox)

GREAT BRITAIN (Leander Club) 6:05.0
Rev. Sidney Swann
Ralph Shove
Sebastian Earl
John Campbell
Walter James
Richard Lucas
Guy O. Nickalls
Ewart Horsfall
Robin Johnston (cox)

NORWAY 6:36.0
Theodor Nag
Conrad Olsen
Adolf Nilsen
Haakon Ellingsen
Thore Michelsen
Arne Mortensen
Karl Nag
Tollef Tollefsen
Thoralf Hagen (cox)

1924 UNITED STATES (Yale B.C.) 6:33.4
Leonard G. Carpentier
Howard T. Kingsbury
Alfred M. Wilson
J. David Lindley
John L. Miller
James S. Rockefeller
Frederick Sheffield
Benjamin M. Spock
Laurence R. Stoddard (cox)

CANADA 6:49.0 (Toronto B.C.)
Arthur Bell
Robert Hunter
William Langford
Harold Little
John Smith
Warren Snyder
Norman Taylor
William Wallace
Ivor Campbell (cox)

ITALY d.n.a. (Zara R.C.)
Antonio Cattalinich
Francesco Cattalinich
Simeone Cattalinich
Guiseppe Crivelli
Latino Galasso
Pietro Ivanov
Bruno Sorich
Carlo Toniatti
Vittorio Gliubich (cox)

1928 UNITED STATES (Univ. of Calif.) 6:03.2
Marvin Stalder
John Brinck
Francis Frederick
Walter Thompson
William Dally
James Workman
Hubert Caldwell
Peter Donlon
Donald Blessing (cox)

GREAT BRITAIN (Thames R.C.) 6:05.6
Harold West
Jack Beresford
Gordon Killick
Harold Lane
Donald Gollan
John Badcock
Guy O. Nickalls
James Hamilton
Arthur Sulley (cox)

CANADA 6:03.8
Frederick Hedges
Frank Fiddes
John Hand
Herbert Richardson
Jack Murdock
Athol Meech
Edgar Norris
William Ross
Jack Donelly (cox)

1932 UNITED STATES (Univ. of Calif.) 6:37.6
Winslow Hall
Harold Tower
Charles Chandler
Burton Jastram
David Dunlap
Duncan Gregg
James Blair
Edwin Salisbury
Norris Graham (cox)

ITALY 6:37.8
Renato Barbieri
Enrico Garzelli
Guglielmo del Bimbo
Roberto Vestrini
Dino Barsotti
Renato Bracci
Mario Balleri
Vittorio Cioni
Cesare Milani (cox)

CANADA 6:40.4
Albert Taylor
Donald Boal
William Thoburn
Cedric Liddell
Harry Fry
Stanley Stanyar
Joseph Harris
Earl Eastwood
George MacDonald (cox)

1936 UNITED STATES 6:25.4 (Univ. Washington)
Donald Hume
Joseph Rantz
George Hunt
James McMillin
John White
Gordon Adam
Charles Day
Herbert Morris
Robert Moch (cox)

ITALY 6:26.0
Guglielmo del Bimbo
Dino Barsotti
Oreste Grossi
Enzo Bartolini
Mario Checcacci
Dante Secchi
Ottorino Quaglierini
Enrico Garzelli
Cesare Milani (cox)

GERMANY 6:26.4
Herbert Schmidt
Hans-Joachim Hannemann
Werner Loeckle
Gerd Völs
Hein Kaufmann
Hans Kuschke
Helmut Radach
Alfred Rieck
Wilhelm Mahlow (cox)

GOLD	SILVER	BRONZE
1948 **UNITED STATES** (Univ. of Calif.) 5:56.7	**GREAT BRITAIN** 6:06.9	**NORWAY** 6:10.3
John Stack	Andrew Mellows	Carl H. Monssen
Justus Smith	David Meyrick	Thor Pedersen
David Brown	C. Brian Lloyd	Leif Naess
Lloyd Butler	Paul Massey	Harald Kråkenes
George Ahlgren	E. A. Paul Bircher	Halfdan Gran-Olsen
James Hardy	Guy Richardson	Hans E. Hansen
David Turner	Maurice Lapage	Torstein Kråkenes
Ian Turner	Christopher Barton	Kristoffer Lepsöe
Ralph Purchase (cox)	Jack Dearlove(cox)	Sigurd Monssen (cox)
1952 **UNITED STATES** (Navy) 6:25.9	**U.S.S.R.** 6:31.2	**AUSTRALIA** 6:33.1
Frank Shakespeare	Yevgeniy Brago	Robert Tinning
William Fields	Vladimir Rodimushkin	Ernest Chapman
James Dunbar	Aleksey Komarov	Nimrod Greenwood
Richard Murphy	Igor Borisov	Mervyn Finlay
Robert Detweiler	Slava Amiragov	Edward Pain
Henry Proctor	Leonid Gissen	Philip Cayzer
Wayne Frye	Yevgeniy Samsonov	Thomas Chessel
Edward Stevens	Vladimir Krukov	David Anderson
Charles Manring (cox)	Igor Polyakov (cox)	Geoffrey Williamson (cox)
1956 **UNITED STATES** (Yale Univ.) 6:35.2	**CANADA** 6:37.1	**AUSTRALIA** 6:39.2
Thomas Charlton	Philip Kueber	Michael Aikman
David Wight	Richard McClure	David Boykett
John Cooke	Robert Wilson	Angus Benfield
Donald Beer	David Helliwell	James Howden
Caldwell Esselstyn	Donald Pretty	Garth Manton
Charles Grimes	William McKerlich	Walter Howell
Richard Wailes	Douglas McDonald	Adrian Monger
Robert Morey	Lawrence West	Bryan Doyle
William Becklean (cox)	Carlton Ogawa (cox)	Harold Hewitt (cox)
1960 **GERMANY** 5:57.18	**CANADA** 6:01.52	**CZECHOSLOVAKIA** 6:04.84
Klaus Bittner	Donald Arnold	Josef Ventus
Karl-Heinz Hopp	I. Walter d'Hondt	Bohumil Janoušek
Hans Lenk	Nelson Kuhn	Jan Jindra
Manfred Rulffs	John Lecky	Jiri Lundák
Frank Schepke	Lorne Loomer	Stanislav Lusk
Kraft Schepke	Archibald McKinnon	Václav Pavkovič
Walter Schröeder	William McKerlich	Ludek Pojezny
Karl-Heinz von Groddeck	Glen Mervyn	Jan Švéda
Willi Padge (cox)	Sohen Biln (cox)	Miroslav Koniček (cox)
1964 **UNITED STATES** 6:18.23	**GERMANY** 6:23.29	**CZECHOSLOVAKIA** 6:25.11
Joseph Amlong	Klaus Aeffke	Petr Čermák
Thomas Amlong	Klaus Bittner	Jiri Lundák
Harold Budd	Karl-Heinz von Groddeck	Jan Mrvik
Emory Clark	Hans-Jürgen Wallbrecht	Julnis Toček
Stanley Cwiklinski	Klaus Behrens	Josef Ventus
Hugh Foley	Jürgen Schroeder	Ludek Pojezny
William Knecht	Jürgen Plagemann	Bohumil Janoušek
William Stowe	Horst Meyer	Richard Novy
Robert Zimonyi (cox)	Thomas Ahrens (cox)	Miroslav Koniček (cox)

	GOLD	SILVER	BRONZE
1968	**W. GERMANY** 6:07.00	**AUSTRALIA** 6:07.98	**U.S.S.R.** 6:09,11
	Horst Meyer	Alfred Duval	Zigmas Yukna
	Dirk Schreyer	Michael Morgan	Antanas Bagdonavichus
	Ruediger Henning	Joseph Fazio	Vladimir Sterlik
	Lutz Ulbricht	Peter Dickson	Yozanas Yagelavichus
	Wolfgang Hottenrott	David Douglas	Alexander Matryshkin
	Egbert Hirschfelder	John Ranch	Vitautas Briedis
	Joerg Siebert	Gary Pearce	Valentin Kravtschuk
	Nico Ott	Robert Shirlaw	Victor Suslin
	Gunther Thiersch (cox)	Alan Grover (cox)	Yury Lorentsson (cox)
1972	**NEW ZEALAND** 6:08.94	**UNITED STATES** 6:11.61	**EAST GERMANY** 6:11.67
	Tony Hurt	Lawrence Terry	Hans-Joachim Borzym
	Wybo Veldman	Fritz Hobbs	Joerg Landvoigt
	Dick Joyce	Peter Raymond	Harold Dincke
	John Hunter	Timothy Mickelson	Manfred Schneider
	Lindsay Wilson	Eugene Clapp	Hartmut Schreiber
	Arhol Earl	William Hobbs	Manfred Schmorde
	Trevor Coker	Cleve Livingstone	Bernd Landvoigt
	Gary Robertson	Michael Livingstone	Heinrich Mederow
	Simon C. Dickie (cox)	Paul Hoffman (cox)	Dietmar Schwartz (cox)
1976	**EAST GERMANY** 5:58.29	**GREAT BRITAIN** 6:00.82	**NEW ZEALAND** 6:03.51
	Bernd Baumgart	Richard Lester	Ivan Sutherland
	Gottfried Döhn	John Yallop	Trevor Coker
	Werner Klatt	Timothy Crooks	Peter Dignan
	Hans-Joachim Lück	Hugh Matheson	Lindsay Wilson
	Dieter Wendisch	David Maxwell	Athol Earl
	Roland Kostulski	James Clark	Dave Rodger
	Ulrich Karnatz	Fred Smallbone	Alex McLean
	Karl-Heinz Prudohl	Leonard Robertson	Tony Hurt
	Karl-Heinz Danielowski (cox)	Patrick Sweeney (cox)	Simon Dickie (cox)
1980	**EAST GERMANY** 5:49.05	**GREAT BRITAIN** 5:51.92	**U.S.S.R.** 5:52.66
	Bernd Krauss	Duncan McDougall	Viktor Kokoshkin
	Hans-Peter Koppe	Allan Whitwell	Andrej Tishchenko
	Ulrich Kons	Henry Clay	Aleksandr Tkachenko
	Jorg Friedrich	Chris Mahoney	Ionas Pintskus
	Jens Doberschutz	Andrew Justice	Ionas Normantas
	Ulrich Karnatz	John Pritchard	Andrej Lugin
	Uwe Duhring	Malcolm McGowan	Aleksandr Manzevich
	Bernd Hoing	Richard Stanhope	Igor Maistrenko
	Klaus-Dieter Ludwig (cox)	Colin Moynihan (cox)	Grigori Dmitrenko (cox)

Rowing (Women)

Women's rowing was introduced in 1976 over a course of 1,000 meters.

SINGLE SCULLS

1976	Christine Scheiblich (GDR) 4:05.56	Joan Lind (USA) 4:06.21	Elena Antonova (URS) 4:10.24
1980	Sanda Toma (ROM) 3:40.69	Antonina Makhina (URS) 3:41.65	Martina Schroter (GDR) 3:43.54

DOUBLE SCULLS

GOLD	SILVER	BRONZE
1976 **BULGARIA** 3:44.36	**EAST GERMANY** 3:47.86	**U.S.S.R.** 3:49.93
Svetla Otzetova	Sabine Jahn	Leonora Kaminskaite
Zdravka Yordanova	Petra Boesler	Genovate Ramoshkene
1980 **U.S.S.R.** 3:16.27	**EAST GERMANY** 3:17.63	**RUMANIA** 3:18.91
Elena Khloptseva	Cornelia Linse	Olga Homeghi
Larisa Popova	Heidi Westphal	Valeria Rosca-Racila

COXLESS PAIRS

GOLD	SILVER	BRONZE
1976 **BULGARIA** 4:01.22	**EAST GERMANY** 4:01.64	**WEST GERMANY** 4:02.35
Siika Kelbetcheva	Angelika Noack	Edith Eckbauer
Stoyanka Grouitcheva	Sabine Dahne	Thea Einoeder
1980 **EAST GERMANY** 3:30.49	**POLAND** 3:30.95	**BULGARIA** 3:32.39
Ute Steindorf	Malgorzata Dluzewska	Siika Barboulova
Cornelia Klier	Czeslawa Koscianska	Stoyanka Kubatova

COXED QUADRUPLE SCULLS

GOLD	SILVER	BRONZE
1976 **EAST GERMANY** 3:29.99	**U.S.S.R.** 3:32.49	**RUMANIA** 3:32.76
Anke Borchmann	Anna Kondrachina	Ioana Tudoran
Jutta Lau	Mira Bryunina	Maria Micsa
Viola Poley	Larisa Alexandrova	Felicia Afrasiloaia
Roswitha Zobelt	Galina Ermolaeva	Elisabeta Lazar
Liane Weigelt (cox)	Nadyezda Chernysheva (cox)	Elena Giurca (cox)
1980 **EAST GERMANY** 3:15.32	**U.S.S.R** 3:15.73	**BULGARIA** 3:16.10
Sybille Reinhardt	Antonina Pustovit	Mariana Serbezova
Jutta Ploch	Yelena Matyevskaya	Rumeliana Boneva
Jutta Lau	Olga Vasilchenko	Dolores Nakova
Roswitha Zobelt	Nadyezda Lubimova	Ani Bakova
Liane Buhr (cox)	Nina Cheremisina (cox)	Anka Georgieva (cox)

COXED FOURS

GOLD	SILVER	BRONZE
1976 **EAST GERMANY** 3:45.08	**BULGARIA** 3:48.24	**U.S.S.R.** 3:49.38
Karin Metze	Ginka Gurova	Nadyezda Sevostyanova
Bianka Schwede	Liliana Vasseva	Ludmila Krokhina
Gabriele Lohs	Reni Yordanova	Galina Mishenina
Andrea Kurth	Mariika Modeva	Anna Pasokha
Sabine Hess (cox)	Kapka Gueorguieva (cox)	Lidia Krylova (cox)
1980 **EAST GERMANY** 3:19.27	**BULGARIA** 3:20.75	**U.S.S.R.** 3:20.92
Ramona Kapheim	Ginka Gurova	Mariya Fadeyeva
Silvia Frohlich	Mariika Modeva	Galina Sovetnikova
Angelika Noack	Rita Todorova	Marina Studneva
Romy Saalfeld	Iskra Velinova	Svetlana Semyonova
Kristen Wenzel (cox)	Nadelda Filipova (cox)	Nina Cheremisina (cox)

EIGHTS

	GOLD	SILVER	BRONZE
1976	**EAST GERMANY** 3:33.32	U.S.S.R. 3:36.17	UNITED STATES 3:38.68
	Viola Goretzki	Lubov Tatalayeva	Jacqueline Zoch
	Christiane Knetsch	Nadyezda Roshchina	Anita DeFrantz
	Ilona Richter	Klavdiya Kozenkova	Carie Graves
	Brigitte Ahrenholz	Elena Zubko	Marion Greig
	Monika Kallies	Olga Kolkova	Anne Warner
	Henrietta Ebert	Nelli Tarakanova	Peggy Ann McCarthy
	Helma Lehmann	Nadyezda Rozgon	Carol Brown
	Irina Muller	Olga Guzenko	Gail Ricketson
	Marina Wilke (cox)	Olga Pugovskaya (cox)	Lynn Silliman (cox)
1980	**EAST GERMANY** 3:03.32	U.S.S.R. 3:04.39	RUMANIA 3:05.63
	Martina Boesler	Olga Pivovarova	Angelica Aposteanu
	Kersten Neisser	Nina Umanets	Marlena Zagoni
	Christiane Kopke	Nadyezda Prischepa	Rodica Frintu
	Birgit Schutz	Valentina Zhulina	Florica Bucur
	Gabriele Kuhn	Tatyana Stetzenko	Rodica Puscatu
	Ilona Richter	Yelena Tereshina	Ana Iliuta
	Marita Sandig	Nina Preobrazhenskaya	Maria Constantinescu
	Karin Metze	Maria Pazyun	Elena Bondar
	Marina Wilke (cox)	Nina Frolova (cox)	Elena Dobritoiu (cox)

14. Shooting

FREE PISTOL (50 meters)

1896	Summer Paine (USA) 442	Viggo Jensen (DEN) 285	Holger Nielsen (DEN) d.n.a.
1900	Karl Röderer (SUI) 503	Achille Paroche (FRA) 466	Konrad Stäheli (SUI) 453
1904	Event not held		
1906	Georgios Orphanidis (GRE) 221	Jean Fouconnier (FRA) 219	Aristides Rangavis (GRE) 218
1908	Event not held		
1912	Alfred Lane (USA) 499	Peter J. Dolfen (USA) 474	Charles E. Stewart (GBR) 470
1920	Karl T. Frederick (USA) 496	Afranio da Costa (BRA) 489	Alfred P. Lane (USA) 481
1924–1932	Event not held		
1936	Torsten Ullmann (SWE) 559	Erich Krempel (GER) 544	Charles des Jammonières
1948	Edwin Vazquez Cam (PER) 545	Rudolf Schnyder (SUI) 539	Torsten Ullmann (SWE) 539
1952	Huelet Benner (USA) 553	Angel Léon de Gozalo (ESP) 550	Ambrus Balogh (HUN) 549
1956	Pentti Linnosvuo (FIN) 556	Makhmud Oumarov (URS) 556	Offutt Pinion (USA) 551
1960	Aleksey Gushchin (URS) 560	Makhmud Oumarov (URS) 552	Yoshihisa Yoshikawa (JPN) 552
1964	Väinö Markkanen (FIN) 560	Franklin Green (USA) 557	Yoshihisa Yoshikawa (JPN) 554
1968	Grigory Kossykh (URS) 562	Heinz Mertel (GER) 562	Harald Vollmar (GDR) 560

GOLD	SILVER	BRONZE
1972 Ragnar Skanakar (SWE) 567*	Dan Iuga (ROM) 562	Rudolf Dollinger (AUT) 560
1976 Uwe Potteck (GDR) 573*	Harald Vollmar (GDR) 567	Rudolf Dollinger (AUT) 562
1980 Aleksandr Melentev (URS) 581*	Harald Vollmar (GDR) 568	Lubtcho Diakov (BUL) 565

LEFT: Ragnar Skanakar (SWE) won the 1972 free pistol gold medal with an Olympic record score of 567 out of a possible 600.

BELOW: Willy Rogeberg of Norway won the prone small-bore rifle competition in 1936.

SMALL-BORE RIFLE—PRONE POSITION

	GOLD	SILVER	BRONZE
1896–1920	Event not held		
1924	Pierre Coquelin de Lisle (FRA) 398	Marcus W. Dinwiddie (USA) 396	Josias Hartmann (SUI) 394
1928	Event not held		
1932	Bertil Rönnmark (SWE) 294	Gustavo Huet (MEX) 294	Zoltán Hradetsky-Soós (HUN) 293
1936	Willy Rögeberg (NOR) 300	Ralph Berzsenyi (HUN) 296	Wladyslaw Karás (POL) 296
1948	Arthur Cook (USA) 599	Walter Tomsen (USA) 599	Jonas Jonsson (SWE) 597
1952	Iosif Sarbu (ROM) 400	Boris Andreyev (URS) 400	Arthur Jackson (USA) 399
1956	Gerald Rouellette (CAN) 600[1]	Vasiliy Borissov (URS) 599	Gilmour S. Boa (CAN) 598
1960	Peter Kohnke (GER) 590	James Hill (USA) 589	Enrico Forcella Pelliccione (VEN) 587
1964	László Hammerl (HUN) 597	Lones Wigger (USA) 597	Tommy Pool (USA) 596
1968	Jan Kurka (TCH) 598	László Hammerl (HUN) 598	Ian Ballinger (NZL) 597
1972	Ho Jun Li (PRK) 599*	Victor Auer (USA) 598	Nicolae Rotaru (ROM) 598
1976	Karlheinz Smieszek (GER) 599*	Ulrich Lind (GER) 597	Gennadi Lushchikov (URS) 595
1980	Karoly Varga (HUN) 599*	Hellfried Heilfort (GDR) 599*	Petar Zaprianov (BUL) 598

[1] Range found to be slightly short—record not allowed.

Lones Wigger (USA) receiving the silver medal for small-bore rifle shooting from the prone position at Tokyo in 1964. He earned a gold medal for small-bore rifle shooting in the three-position event at the same Games.

SMALL-BORE RIFLE—THREE POSITIONS
(prone, kneeling, standing)

GOLD	SILVER	BRONZE
1896–1948 Event not held		
1952 Erling Kongshaug (NOR) 1,164	Vilho Ylönen (FIN) 1,164	Boris Andreyev (URS) 1,163
1956 Anatoliy Bogdanov (URS) 1,172	Otakar Hořinek (TCH) 1,172	Nils J. Sundberg (SWE) 1,167
1960 Viktor Shamburkin (URS) 1,149	Marat Niyasov (URS) 1,145	Klaus Zähringer (GER) 1,139
1964 Lones Wigger (USA) 1,164	Velitchko Khristov (BUL) 1,152	László Hammerl (HUN) 1,151
1968 Bernd Klingner (GER) 1,157	John Writer (USA) 1,156	Vitaly Parkhimovich (URS) 1,154
1972 John Writer (USA) 1,166*	Lanny Bassham (USA) 1,157	Werner Lippoldt (GDR) 1,153
1976 Lanny Bassham (USA), 1,162	Margaret Murdock (USA) 1,162	Werner Seibold (GER) 1,160
1980 Viktor Vlasov (URS) 1,173*	Bernd Hartstein (GDR) 1,166	Sven Johansson (SWE) 1,165

RAPID-FIRE PISTOL

1896 Jean Phrangoudis (GRE) 344	Georgios Orphanidis (GRE) 249	Holger Nielsen (DEN) d.n.a.
1900 Maurice Larony (FRA) 58	Léon Moreaux (FRA) 57	Eugène Balne (FRA) 57
1904 Event not held		
1906 Maurice Lecoq (FRA) 250	Léon Moreaux (FRA) 249	Aristides Rangavis (GRE) 245
1908 Paul van Asbroeck (BEL) 490	Réginald Storms (BEL) 487	James E. Gorman (USA) 485
1912 Alfred Lane (USA) 287	Paul Palén (SWE) 286	Johan H. von Holst (SWE) 283
1920 Guilherne Paraense (BRA) 274	Raymond C. Bracken (USA) 272	Fritz Zulauf (SUI) 269
1924 H. M. Bailey (USA) 18	Vilhelm Carlberg (SWE) 18	Lennart Hannelius (FIN) 18
1928 Event hot held		
1932 Renzo Morigi (ITA) 36	Heinz Hax (GER) 36	Domenico Matteucci (ITA) 36
1936 Cornelius van Oyen (GER) 36	Heinz Hax (GER) 35	Torsten Ullmann (SWE) 34
1948 Károly Takács (HUN) 580	Carlos E. Diaz Sáenz Valiente (ARG) 571	Sven Lundqvist (SWE) 569
1952 Károly Takács (HUN) 579	Szilárd Kun (HUN) 578	Gheorghe Lichiardopol (ROM) 578
1956 Stefan Petrescu (ROM) 587	Evgeniy Shcherkasov (URS) 585	Gheorghe Lichiardopol (ROM) 581
1960 William McMillan (USA) 587	Pentti Linnosvuo (FIN) 587	Aleksandr Zabelin (URS) 587
1964 Pentti Linnosvuo (FIN) 592	Ion Tripsa (ROM) 591	Lubomi T. Nacovsky (TCH) 590
1968 Jozef Zapedzki (POL) 593	Marcel Rosca (ROM) 591	Renart Suleimanov (URS) 591
1972 Josef Zapedzki (POL) 595*	Ladislav Faita (TCH) 594	Victor Torshin (URS) 593
1976 Norbert Klaar (GDR) 597*	Jurgen Wiefel (GDR) 596	Roberto Ferraris (ITA) 595
1980 Corneliu Ion (ROM) 596	Jurgen Wiefel (GDR) 596	Gerhard Petritsch (AUT) 596

OLYMPIC TRAP SHOOTING

	GOLD	SILVER	BRONZE
1896	Event not held		
1900	Roger de Barbarin (FRA) 17	René Guyot (FRA) 17	Justinien de Clary (FRA) 17
1904	Event not held		
1906	Two events were held under different conditions.		
1908	Walter H. Ewing (CAN) 72	George Beattie (CAN) 60	Alexander Maunder (GBR) 57 Anastassios Metaxas (GRE) 57
1912	James Graham (USA) 96	Alfred Goeldel (GER) 94	Harry Blau (URS) 91
1920	Mark Arie (USA) 95	Frank Troeh (USA) 93	Frank Wright (USA) 87
1924	Gyula Halasy (HUN) 98	Konrad Huber (FIN) 98	Frank Hughes (USA) 97
1928–1948	Event not held		
1952	George P. Généreux (CAN) 192	Knut Holmqvist (SWE) 191	Hans Liljedahl (SWE) 190
1956	Galliano Rossini (ITA) 195	Adam Smelczynski (POL) 190	Alessandro Ciceri (ITA) 188
1960	Ion Dumitrescu (ROM) 192	Galliano Rossini (ITA) 191	Sergey Kalinin (URS) 190
1964	Ennio Mattarelli (ITA) 198	Pavel Senichev (URS) 194	William Morris (USA) 194
1968	J. Robert Braithwaite (GBR) 198	Thomas Garrigus (USA) 196	Kurt Czekalla (GDR) 196
1972	Angelo Scalzone (ITA) 199	Michel Carrega (FRA) 198	Silvano Basagni (ITA) 195
1976	Donald Haldeman (USA) 190	Armando Silva Marques (POR) 189	Ubaldesc Baldi (ITA) 189
1980	Luciano Giovannetti (ITA) 198	Rustan Yambulatov (URS) 196	Jorg Damme (GDR) 196

SKEET SHOOTING

1896–1964	Event not held		
1968	Evgeny Petrov (URS) 198*	Romano Garagnani (ITA) 198*	Konrad Wirnhier (GER) 198*
1972	Konrad Wirnhier (GER) 195	Evgeny Petrov (URS) 195	Michael Buchheim (GDR) 195
1976	Josef Panacek (TCH) 198	Eric Swinkels (HOL) 198	Wieslaw Gawlikowski (POL) 196
1980	Hans Kjeld Rasmussen (DEN) 196	Lars-Goran Carlsson (SWE) 196	Roberto Castrillo (CUB) 196

RUNNING GAME TARGET

1896	Event not held		
1900	Louis Debray (FRA) 20	P. Nivet (FRA) 20	de Lambert (FRA) 19
1904–1968	Event not held		
1972	Lakov Zhelezniak (URS) 569*	Hanspeter Bellingrodt (COL) 565	John Kynoch (GBR) 562
1976	Alexander Gazov (URS) 579*	Alexander Kedyarov (URS) 576	Jerzy Greszkiewicz (POL) 571
1980	Igor Sokolov (URS) 589*	Thomas Pfeffer (GDR) 589*	Alexandr Gazov (URS) 587

15. Soccer

There was no Soccer event in 1896. In the 1900, 1904 and 1906 Games most of the medal winning teams were merely clubs rather than strictly international teams.

	GOLD	SILVER	BRONZE
1896	Event not held		

	GOLD	SILVER	BRONZE
1908	**GREAT BRITAIN**	**DENMARK**	**NETHERLANDS**
	Harold P. Bailey	Ludwig Drescher	Reinier B. Beeuwkes
	Walter S. Corbett	Charles Buchwald	Karel Heijting
	Herbert Smith	Harald Hansen	Lou Otten
	Kenneth R. G. Hunt	Harald Bohr	Johan W. E. Sol
	Frederick W. Chapman	Christian Middelboe	Johannes M. de Korver
	Robert M. Hawkes	Nils Middelboe	Emil G. Mundt
	Arthur Berry	Oscar Nielsen-Nörland	Jan H. Welcker
	Vivian J. Woodward	August Lindgreen	Edu Snethlage
	Harold S. Stapley	Sophus Nielsen	Gerard S. Reeman
	Claude H. Parnell	Vilhelm Wolffhagen	Jan Thomée
	Harold P. Hardman	Björn Rasmussen	Georges F. de
		Marius Andersen	Bruyn Kops
		Johannes Gandil	Johan A. F. Kok

	GOLD	SILVER	BRONZE
1912	**GREAT BRITAIN**	**DENMARK**	**NETHERLANDS**
	Ronald G. Brebner	Sophus Hansen	Marius J. Göbel
	Thomas C. Burn	Nils Middelboe	David Wijnfeldt
	Arthur E. Knight	Harald Hansen	Piet Bouman
	Douglas McWhirter	Charles Buchwald	Gerardus Fortgens
	Horace C. Littlewort	Emil Jörgensen	Constant W. Feith
	James Dines	Paul Berth	Nicolaas de Wolff
	Arthur Berry	Oscar Nielsen-Nörland	Dick N. Lotsy
	Vivian J. Woodward	Axel Thufason	Johannes W. Boutmy
	Harold A. Walden	Anton Olsen	Jan G. van Bredakolff
	Gordon R. Hoare	Sophus Nielsen	Huug F. de Groot
	Ivan G. A. Sharpe	Vilhelm Wolffhagen	Caesar H. ten Cate
	Edward Hanney	Askel M. Petersen	Jan van der Sluis
	Harold Stamper	Hjalmar Christoffersen	Jan Vos
	E. Gordon D. Wright	Poul Nielsen	Nico J. Bouvy
		Ivar L. Seidelin-Neilsen	Johannes M. de Korver

	GOLD	SILVER	BRONZE
1916	Event not held		

	GOLD	SILVER	BRONZE
1920	**BELGIUM**	**SPAIN**	**NETHERLANDS**
	Jan de Bie	Ricardo Zamora	Robert McNeill
	Armand Swartenbroeks	Pedro Vallana	Henri L. B. Denis
	Oscar Verbeek	Mariano Arrate	Leonard F. G. Bosschart
	Joseph Musch	Juan Artola	Frederick C. Kuipers
	Emile Hanse	Agustin Sancho	Hermanus H. Steeman
	André Fierens	Ramón Eguiazábal	Johannes D. de Natris
	Louis van Hege	Francisco	Jacob E. Bulder
	Robert Coppée	Pagazaurtundúa	Bernardus Groosjohan
	Mathieu Bragard	Felix Sesúmaga	Jan L. van Dort
	Henri Larnoe	Patricio Arbolaza	Oscar E. van Rappard
	Désiré Bastin	Rafael Moreno	Herman C. G. van
	Fernand Nisot	Domingo Acedo	Heijden
	Georges Hebden	José Samitier	Bernard W. J. Verweij
	Félix Balyu	José M. Belausteguigoitia	Evert J. Bulder
		Louis Otero	Adrianus G. Bieshaar
		Joaquin Vázquez	
		Ramón Moncho Gil	
		Sabino Bilbao	
		Silverio Izaguirre	

This British soccer team took home the gold medal in 1912 with a final victory of 18 to 1 over Denmark.

The Italian goalkeeper protects his team's 2-to-1 edge from Austrian attack in the 1936 soccer final.

GOLD	SILVER	BRONZE
1924 URUGUAY	**SWITZERLAND**	**SWEDEN**
Andrés Mazali	Hans Pulver	Sigfrid Lindberg
José Nasazzi	Adolphe Reymond	Axel Alfredsson
Pedro Arispe	Rudolf Ramseyer	Fritjof Hillén
José L. Andrade	August Oberhauser	Sven Friberg
José Vidal	Paul Schmiedlin	Gustaf Carlson
Alfredo Ghierra	Aron Pollitz	Harry Sundberg
Santos Urdinarán	Karl Ehrenbolger	Charles Brommesson
Hector Scarone	Robert Pache	Sven Rydell
Pedro Petrone	Walter Dietrich	Per Kaufeldt
Pedro Céa	Max Abbeglen	Albin Dahl
Alfredo Romano	Paul Fässler	Rudolf Kock
Umberto Tomasina	Paul Sturzenegger	Gunnar Holmberg
Juan Naya	Edmond Kramer	Evert Lundqvist
Alfredo Zibechi	Félix Bédouret	Tore Keller
Antonio Urdinarán	Adolphe Mengotti	Thorsten Svensson
		Konrad Hirsch
		Sven Linqvist
		Sten Mellgren
1928 URUGUAY	**ARGENTINA**	**ITALY**
Andrés Mazali	Angel Bossio	Giampiero Combi
José Nasazzi	Fernando Paternoster	Delfo Bellini
Pedro Arispe	Ludovico Bidoglio	Umberto Caligaris
José L. Andrade	Juan Evaristo	Alfredo Pitto
Lorenzo Fernández	Luis F. Monto	Fulvio Bernardini
Alvaro Gestido	Segundo Medici	Pietro Genovesi
Santos Urdináran	Raimundo Orsi	Adolfo Baloncieri
Hector Castro	Enrique Gainzarain	Elvio Banchero
Pedro Petrone	Manuel Ferreira	Angelo Schiavio
Pedro Céa	Domingo Tarasconi	Mario Magnozzi
Hector Scarone	Adolfo Carricaberri	Virgilio F. Levratto
Antonio Campolo	Feliciano A. Perducca	Giovanni Deprà
Juan Arremón	Saúl Calandra	Antonio Janni
René Borjas	Roberto Cherro	Silvio Pietroboni
Juan Piriz	Rodolfo Orlandini	Enrico Rivolta
Adhemar Canavesi	Octavio Diaz	Virginio Rosetta
Roberto Figueroa		Gino Rossetti
1932 Event not held		
1936 ITALY	**AUSTRIA**	**NORWAY**
Bruno Venturini	Eduard Kainberger	Henry Johansen
Alfredo Foni	Ernst Künz	Nils Ériksen
Pietro Rava	Martin Kargl	Öivind Holmsen
Giuseppe Baldo	Anton Krenn	Frithjof Ulleberg
Achille Piccini	Karl Wahlmüller	Jörgen Juve
Ugo Locatelli	Max Hofmeister	Rolf Holmberg
Annibale Frossi	Walter Werginz	Magdalon Monsen
Libero Marchini	Adolf Laudon	Reidar Kvammen
Sergio Bertoni	Klement Steinmetz	Alf Martinsen
Carlo Biagi	Karl Kainberger	Odd Frantzen
Francesco Gabriotti	Franz Fuchsberger	Arne Brustad
Luigi Scarabello	Josef Kitzmüller	Frederik Horn
Giulio Cappelli	Franz Mandl	Sverre Hansen
Alfonso Negro		Magnar Isaksen

GOLD	SILVER	BRONZE
1948 **SWEDEN**	**YUGOSLAVIA**	**DENMARK**
Torsten Lindberg	Ljubomir Lovrič	Ejgil Nielsen
Knut Nordahl	Miroslav Brozovič	Viggo Jensen
Erik Nilsson	Branislav Stankovič	Knud B. Overgaard
Birger Rosengren	Zlatko Cajkoviski	Axel Pilmark
Bertil Nordahl	Miodrag Jovanovič	Dion Örnvold
Sune Andersson	Aleksandar Atanakovič	Ivan Jensen
Kjell Rosén	Zvonko Cimermančič	Johannes Plöger
Gunnar Grén	Rajko Mitič	Knud Lundberg
Gunnar Nordahl	Stejpan Bobek	Carl A. Praest
Henry Carlsson	Željko Čajkovski	John Hansen
Nils Liedholm	Bernard Vukas	Jörgen Sörensen
Börje Leander	Franjo Soštarič	Holger Seebach
	Prvoslav Mihajlovič	Karl Aage Hansen
	Franjo Völfl	
	Kosta Tomasevič	

This hard-fought match resulted in a bronze medal for Denmark (dark shirts) in the 1948 Games.

GOLD	SILVER	BRONZE
1952 **HUNGARY**	**YUGOSLAVIA**	**SWEDEN**
Gyula Grosics	Vladimir Beara	Karl Svensson
Jenö Buzánszky	Branko Stankovič	Lennart Samuelsson
Gyula Lóránt	Tomislav Crnkovič	Erik Nilsson
Mihály Lantos	Zlatko Cajkovski	Olle Åhlund
József Bozsik	Ivan Horvat	Bengt Gustavsson
Nándor Hidegkuti	Vujadin Boškov	Gösta Lindh
Sándor Kocsis	Tihomir Ognjanov	Sylve Bengtsson
Péter Palotás	Rajko Mitič	Gösta Löfgren
Ferenc Puskás	Bernard Vukas	Ingvar Rydell
Zoltán Csibor	Stjepan Bobek	Yngve Brodd
József Zakariás	Branko Zebec	Gösta Sandberg
Jenö Dalnoki		Holger Hansson
Imre Kovács		
László Budai		
Lajos Csordás		

Italy vs. U.S. in the 1952 soccer competition in Helsinki.

GOLD	SILVER	BRONZE
1956 U.S.S.R.	**YUGOSLAVIA**	**BULGARIA**
Lev Yashin	Petar Radenkovič	Georgi Naydenov
Boris Kuznyetsov	Mladen Koščak	Kiril Rakarov
Mikhail Ogognikov	Nikola Radovič	Yosif Yosifor
Aleksey Paramanov	Ivan Santek	Stefan Stefanov
Anatoliy Bashashkin	Ljubiša Spajič	Manol Manolov
Igor Netto	Dobrošlav Krstič	Nikola Kovatchev
Boris Tatushin	Dragoslav Sekularac	Gavril Stojanov
Anatoliy Issayev	Zlatko Papec	Miltcho Goranov
Edouard Streltsov	Sava Antič	Panayot Panayotov
Sergey Salnikov	Todor Vaselinovič	Ivan Kolev
Anatoliy Ilin	Muhamed Mujič	Kroum Yanev
Anatoliy Maslenkin	Blagoje Vidinič	Todor Diyev
Nikita Simonian	Ibrahim Biogradlič	Dimiter Milanov
Nikolay Tyshenko	Luka Liposinovič	Georgy Dimitrov
Vladimir Ryjkin		
Iosif Betsa		
Valentin Ivanov		
Boris Rasinsky		
1960 YUGOSLAVIA	**DENMARK**	**HUNGARY**
Blagoje Vidinič	Poul Andersen	Gábor Török
Vladimir Djurkovic	Poul Jensen	Zoltán Dudás
Fahrudin Jusufi	Bent Hansen	Jenö Dalnoki
Ante Zanetic	Hans C. Nielsen	Ernö Sölymösi
Novak Roganovič	Flemming Nielsen	Pál Várhidi
Želijko Perušič	Poul Pedersen	Ferenc Kovács
Andreja Ankovič	Tommy Troelsen	Imre Sátori
Zelijko Matuš	Harald Nielsen	János Göröcs
Milan Galič	Henning Enoksen	Flórián Albert
Tomislav Knez	Jörn Sörensen	Pál Orosz
Borivoje Kostič	Henry Fröm	János Dunai
Velimir Sombolac	John Danielsen	Dezsö Novák
Alexsandar Kozlina		Oszkár Vilezsál
Dušan Maravič		Gyula Rákosi
Silvester Takač		Lajos Faragó
Milutin Soskič		László Pál
		Tibor Pál

	GOLD	SILVER	BRONZE
1964	**HUNGARY**	**CZECHOSLOVAKIA**	**GERMANY**
	Antal Szentmihàlyi	František Schmucker	Hans J. Heinsch
	Dezsö Novák	Anton Urban	Peter Rock
	Kálmán Ihász	Karel Z. Pičman	Manfred Geisler
	Árpád Orban	Josef Vojta	Herbert Pankau
	Ferenc Nógrádi	Vladimir Weiss	Manfred Walter
	János Farkas	Jan Geleta	Gerhard Koerner
	Tibor Csernai	Jan Bramovsky	Hermann Stoeker
	Ferenc Bene	Ivan Mráz	Otto Fraessdorf
	Imre Komora	Karel Lichtnégl	Henning Frenzel
	Gustáv Szepesi	Vojtech Masny	Jürgen Noeldner
	Sándor Katona	František Valóšek	Eberhard Vogel
	József Gelei	Anton Svajlen	Horst Weigang
	Károly Palotai	Karel Knesl	Klaus Urbanczyk
	Zoltán Varga	Stefan Matlák	Klaus-Dieter Seehaus
		Karel Nepomucky	Werner Unger
		Ludevit Cvet	Dieter Engelhardt
		František Knebort	Wolfgang Bartels
			Bernd Bauchspiess
			Klaus Lisiewicz
1968	**HUNGARY**	**BULGARIA**	**JAPAN**
	Károly Fatér	Stoyan Yordanov	Kenzo Yokayama
	Dezsö Novák	Atanas Gerov	Hirosci Katayama
	Lajos Dunai	Gueorgui Christakiev	Yoshitada Yamaguchi
	Miklós Pancsics	Milko Gaidarski	Mitsuo Kamata
	Iván Menczel	Kiril Ivkov	Takaji Mori
	Lajos Szücs	Ivailo Georgiev	Aritatsu Ogi
	László Fazekas	Tzvetan Dimitrov	Teruki Miyamoto
	Antal Dunai	Evgueni Yantchovski	Masashi Watanabe
	László Nagy	Petar Jekov	Kunishige Kamamoto
	Ernö Noskó	Atanas Christov	Ikuo Matsumoto
	István Juhász	Asparukh Donev	Ryuichi Sugiyama
	Lajos Kocsis	Georgi Vassilev	Masakatsu Miyamoto
	László Keglovich	Kiril Christov	Shigeo Yaegashi
	István Sárközi	Mikhail Giionin	Yasuyuki Kuwahara
	István Basti	Yantcho Dimitrov	
		Georgi Ivanov	
		Ivan Zafirov	
		Todor Nikolov	
1972	**POLAND**	**HUNGARY**	**EAST GERMANY**[1]
	Hubert Kostka	Istvan Geczi	Jürgen Croy
	Zbigniew Gut	Peter Vepi	Manfred Zapf
	Jerzy Gorgon	Miklós Pancsics	Konrad Weise
	Zygmunt Anczok	Peter Juhasz	Bernd Bransch
	Leslaw Cmikiewicz	Lajos Szucs	Jürgen Pommerenke
	Jerzy Kraska	Mihaly Kozma	Jürgen Sparwasser
	Kazimierz Deyna	Antal Dunai	Hans-Jürgen Kreische
	Zygfryd Szoltysik	Lajos Ku	Achim Streich
	Wlodzimierz Lubanski	Bela Varadi	Wolfgang Seguin
	Robert Gadocha	Ede Dunai	Peter Ducke
	Ryszard Szymczak	Laszlo Balint	Frank Ganzera
	Antoni Szymanowski	Lajos Kocsis	Lothar Kurbjuweit
	Marian Ostafinski	Kalman Toth	Eberhard Vogel
	Kazimierz Kmiecik	Jozsef Kovacs	Ralf Schulenberg
	Zygmunt Maszczyk	Laszlo Branikovics	Reinhard Häfner
	Joachim Marx	Csaba Vidacs	Harald Irmscher
	Grzegorz Lato	Adam Rothermel	Siegmar Wätzlich

DELIVERS PATIENT ACCEPTABILITY

95% of patients preferred Slow-K[1,2]

Slow-K overwhelmingly preferred to liquid KCl or a potassium gluconate elixir on the basis of palatability and convenience.

Over 90% of patients reported no nausea with Slow-K[3]

Incidence of nausea among patients taking KCl		
	Slow-K patients (n = 103)	Liquid KCl- preparation patients (n = 100)
Never	95	59
Occasionally	7	36
Almost Always	1	5
Note: Three patients taking liquid KCl did not report.		

Patients tolerated Slow-K better

In an open-label, crossover study versus liquid KCl: "Gastrointestinal tolerability was superior with the tablet, particularly with respect to the relative incidence of nausea, abdominal pain or cramps, diarrhea, and heartburn...."[1]

Slow-K®
potassium chloride
slow-release tablets 8 mEq (600 mg)

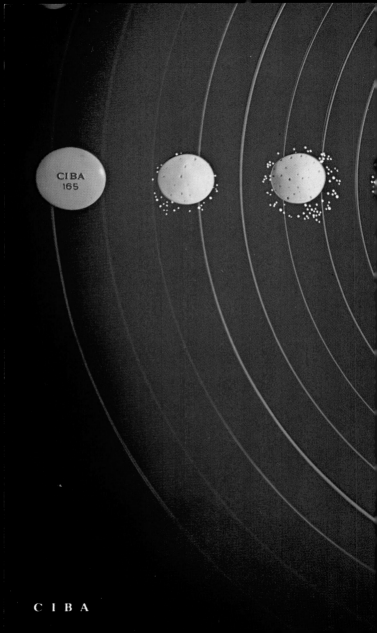

CIBA

IT DELIVERS...

—the potassium your patient needs:
slowly, gradually, dependably* dispersed
through the GI tract, minimizing high local concentrations

—the right salt
which provides potassium and the essential chloride ion

—the right taste
unlike liquids, there is no taste or aftertaste

—the right price
still under 30¢ a day for the average patient†

Slow-K® 50 million new and refill U.S. prescriptions since 1975
potassium chloride
slow-release tablets 8 mEq (600 mg)

*Capsule or tablet slow-release potassium chloride prepara-
tions should be reserved for patients who cannot tolerate,
refuse to take or have compliance problems with liquid or
effervescent potassium preparations, because of reports of
intestinal and gastric ulceration and bleeding with slow-
release KCl preparations.

†The second quarter 1983 National Prescription Audit reported the average daily cost of Slow-K therapy to the patient is $.27.

Before prescribing, please consult Prescribing Information on last pages
of this book.

K DELIVERY YOU CAN DEPEND ON

Protective coating
Slow-K is not enteric coated, but sugar coated. The sugar coating dissolves upon digestion, revealing the wax-matrix core.

Wax-matrix core
600 mg (8 mEq) of KCl crystals are evenly dispersed in an inert, insoluble wax matrix.

Gradual release
Upon passing through the GI tract, the wax matrix comes in contact with intestinal fluids, which slowly dissolve the KCl crystals.

Slow-release system minimizes high local KCl concentrations
The Slow-K system is designed to prevent sudden release of KCl, thus minimizing high potassium concentrations, which could irritate the GI mucosa.

Slow-K®
potassium chloride slow-release tablets
8 mEq (600 mg)

Before prescribing, please consult Prescribing Information on last pages of this book.

CIBA

GAMES OF THE XXIIIrd OLYMPIAD
LOS ANGELES 1984 JULY 28-AUGUST 12

*Data shown for all Olympic events is complete and accurate as of the time of printing.
It may change in the future.* **Bold type** *indicates a final or the final stages of an event.*

Date	Event	Time

Archery, El Dorado Park, Long Beach

August 8 Wednesday	70m women, 90m men 60m women, 70m men	10:00 a.m.-12:45 p.m. 2:30 p.m.-5:00 p.m.
August 9 Thursday	50m women, 50m men 30m women, 30m men	10:00 a.m.-1:00 p.m. 2:30 p.m.-5:15 p.m.
August 10 Friday	70m women, 90m men 60m women, 70m men	10:00 a.m.-12:45 p.m. 2:30 p.m.-5:00 p.m.
August 11 Saturday	50m women, 50m men 30m women, 30m men	10:00 a.m.-1:00 p.m. 2:30 p.m.-5:15 p.m.

Baseball, Dodger Stadium

July 31 Tuesday	2 games—preliminaries	4:00 p.m.-11:00 p.m.
August 1 Wednesday	2 games—preliminaries	4:00 p.m.-11:00 p.m.
August 2 Thursday	2 games—preliminaries	4:00 p.m.-11:00 p.m.
August 3 Friday	2 games—preliminaries	1:00 p.m.-8:00 p.m.
August 4 Saturday	2 games—preliminaries	10:00 a.m.-5:00 p.m.
August 5 Sunday	2 games—preliminaries	1:00 p.m.-8:00 p.m.
August 6 Monday	2 games—semifinals	1:00 p.m.-8:00 p.m.
August 7 Tuesday	**2 games—finals**	**4:00 p.m.-11:00 p.m.**

Basketball, The Forum, Inglewood

July 29 Sunday	2 games—preliminaries, men	9:00 a.m.-12:30 p.m.
	2 games—preliminaries, men	2:30 p.m.-6:00 p.m.
	2 games—preliminaries, men	8:00 p.m.-11:30 p.m.
July 30 Monday	1 game—round robin, women 1 game—preliminary, men	9:00 a.m.-12:30 p.m.
	1 game—round robin, women 1 game—preliminary, men	2:30 p.m.-6:00 p.m.
	1 game—round robin, women 1 game—preliminary, men	8:00 p.m.-11:30 p.m.
July 31 Tuesday	1 game—round robin, women 1 game—preliminary, men	9:00 a.m.-12:30 p.m.
	1 game—round robin, women 1 game—preliminary, men	2:30 p.m.-6:00 p.m.
	1 game—round robin, women 1 game—preliminary, men	8:00 p.m.-11:30 p.m.
August 1 Wednesday	2 games—preliminaries, men	9:00 a.m.-12:30 p.m.
	2 games—preliminaries, men	2:30 p.m.-6:00 p.m.
	2 games—preliminaries, men	8:00 p.m.-11:30 p.m.

August 2 Thursday	1 game—round robin, women 1 game—preliminary, men	9:00 a.m.-12:30 p.m.
	1 game—round robin, women 1 game—preliminary, men	2:30 p.m.-6:00 p.m.
	1 game—round robin, women 1 game—preliminary, men	8:00 p.m.-11:30 p.m.
August 3 Friday	1 game—round robin, women 1 game—preliminary, men	9:00 a.m.-12:30 p.m.
	1 game—round robin, women 1 game—preliminary, men	2:30 p.m.-6:00 p.m.
	1 game—round robin, women 1 game—preliminary, men	8:00 p.m.-11:30 p.m.
August 4 Saturday	2 games—preliminaries, men	9:00 a.m.-12:30 p.m.
	2 games—preliminaries, men	2:30 p.m.-6:00 p.m.
	2 games—preliminaries, men	8:00 p.m.-11:30 p.m.
August 5 Sunday	2 games—round robin, women 1 game—semifinal, men consolation	9:00 a.m.-12:30 p.m. 2:30 p.m.-4:15 p.m.
	1 game—round robin, women 1 game—semifinal, men consolation	6:30 p.m.-10:00 p.m.
August 6 Monday	2 games—quarterfinals, men 2 games—quarterfinals, men	10:00 a.m.-1:30 p.m. 5:00 p.m.-8:30 p.m.
August 7 Tuesday	**2 games—finals (1-4 places), women**	**5:00 p.m.-8:30 p.m.**
August 8 Wednesday	2 games—semifinals, men 2 games—semifinals, men	10:00 a.m.-1:30 p.m. 5:00 p.m.-8:30 p.m.
August 9 Thursday	**2 games—finals (9-12 places), men** **1 game—final (3-4 places), men**	**10:00 a.m.-1:30 p.m.** **7:00 p.m.-8:45 p.m.**
August 10 Friday	**2 games—finals (5-8 places), men** **1 game—final (1-2 places), men**	**10:00 a.m.-1:30 p.m.** **7:00 p.m.-8:45 p.m.**

Boxing, Los Angeles Sports Arena

July 29 Sunday	Preliminary bouts Preliminary bouts	11:00 a.m.-2:00 p.m. 6:00 p.m.-9:30 p.m.
July 30 Monday	Preliminary bouts Preliminary bouts	11:00 a.m.-2:00 p.m. 6:00 p.m.-9:30 p.m.
July 31 Tuesday	Preliminary bouts Preliminary bouts	11:00 a.m.-2:00 p.m. 6:00 p.m.-9:30 p.m.
August 1 Wednesday	Preliminary bouts Preliminary bouts	11:00 a.m.-2:00 p.m. 6:00 p.m.-9:30 p.m.
August 2 Thursday	Preliminary bouts Preliminary bouts	11:00 a.m.-2:00 p.m. 6:00 p.m.-9:30 p.m.
August 3 Friday	Preliminary bouts Preliminary bouts	11:00 a.m.-2:00 p.m. 6:00 p.m.-9:30 p.m.
August 4 Saturday	Preliminary bouts Preliminary bouts	11:00 a.m.-2:00 p.m. 6:00 p.m.-9:30 p.m.
August 5 Sunday	Preliminary bouts Preliminary bouts	11:00 a.m.-2:00 p.m. 6:00 p.m.-9:30 p.m.
August 6 Monday	Preliminary bouts Preliminary bouts	11:00 a.m.-2:00 p.m. 6:00 p.m.-9:30 p.m.
August 7 Tuesday	Quarterfinal bouts Quarterfinal bouts	11:00 a.m.-2:00 p.m. 6:00 p.m.-9:00 p.m.
August 8 Wednesday	Quarterfinal bouts Quarterfinal bouts	11:00 a.m.-2:00 p.m. 6:00 p.m.-9:00 p.m.

| August 9
Thursday | Semifinal bouts
Semifinal bouts | 11:00 a.m.-2:00 p.m.
6:00 p.m.-9:00 p.m. |
| August 11
Saturday | Final bouts
Final bouts | 11:00 a.m.-2:00 p.m.
6:00 p.m.-9:00 p.m. |

Canoeing, Lake Casitas, Ventura County

August 6 Monday	500m heats, men & women 500m repechage, men & women	7:30 a.m.-10:45 a.m. 4:30 p.m.-6:45 p.m.
August 7 Tuesday	1,000m heats, men 500m heats, women	7:30 a.m.-10:45 a.m.
	1,000m repechage, men 500m repechage, women	4:30 p.m.-6:45 p.m.
August 8 Wednesday	500m semifinals, men & women	7:30 a.m.-10:30 a.m.
August 9 Thursday	1,000m semifinals, men 500m semifinals, women	7:30 a.m.-10:30 a.m.
August 10 Friday	**500m finals, men & women**	**8:00 a.m.-10:30 a.m.**
August 11 Saturday	1,000m finals, men	8:00 a.m.-10:30 a.m.

Cycling, California State University, Dominguez Hills 7-Eleven Velodrome

July 29 Sunday	190 km individual road race, men 70 km individual road race, women (Held in Mission Viejo, Orange County)	9:00 a.m.-2:00 p.m. 3:00 p.m.-5:30 p.m.
July 30 Monday	**Individual pursuit—qualification 1 km time trial—final**	**10:00 a.m.-1:00 p.m.**
July 31 Tuesday	Individual pursuit—quarterfinals Spring repechage Points race—qualification	10:00 a.m.-3:00 p.m.
August 1 Wednesday	**Individual pursuit—semifinals & finals** Sprint—quarterfinals **Points race—qualification**	**10:00 a.m.-3:00 p.m.**
August 2 Thursday	Spring—semifinals Team pursuit—qualification & quarterfinals	10:00 a.m.-3:00 p.m.
August 3 Friday	Sprint—finals Team pursuit—semifinals & finals Points race—final	10:00 a.m.-3:00 p.m.
August 5 Sunday	100 km road race team time trial (Held on Artesia Freeway, Route 91)	8:00 a.m.-1:00 p.m.

Diving, University of Southern California McDonald's Swim Stadium

August 5 Sunday	Springboard preliminaries, women Springboard preliminaries, women	10:00 a.m.-12:30 p.m. 3:00 p.m.-5:30 p.m.
August 6 Monday	Springboard finals, women	4:30 p.m.-6:00 p.m.
August 7 Tuesday	Springboard preliminaries, men Springboard preliminaries, men	10:00 a.m.-1:00 p.m. 4:00 p.m.-6:30 p.m.
August 8 Wednesday	Springboard finals, men	4:30 p.m.-6:30 p.m.
August 9 Thursday	Platform preliminaries, women Platform preliminaries, women	10:00 a.m.-12:00 noon 4:30 p.m.-6:30 p.m.
August 10 Friday	Platform finals, women	4:30 p.m.-6:30 p.m.
August 11 Saturday	Platform preliminaries, men Platform preliminaries, men	10:00 a.m.-12:00 noon 3:00 p.m.-5:00 p.m.
August 12 Sunday	Platform finals, men	11:00 a.m.-1:00 p.m.

Equestrian Events, Santa Anita Park, Arcadia

July 29 Sunday	Three-day event—dressage test	8:00 a.m.-6:00 p.m.
July 30 Monday	Three-day event—dressage test	8:00 a.m.-6:00 p.m.
August 1 Wednesday	Three-day event—endurance test (Held at Fairbanks Country Club— San Diego)	10:00 a.m.-6:00 p.m.
August 3 Friday	Three-day event—jumping test	11:30 a.m.-2:30 p.m.
Three-Day Event Pass	All three-day event tests	—
August 4 Saturday	Jumping training competition	2:00 p.m.-6:00 p.m.
August 7 Tuesday	Team jumping competition	10:00 a.m.-2:00 p.m.
August 8 Wednesday	Team dressage competition	2:00 p.m.-6:00 p.m.
August 9 Thursday	Team dressage competition	2:00 p.m.-6:00 p.m.
August 10 Friday	Individual dressage competition	2:00 p.m.-5:00 p.m.
August 12 Sunday	Individual jumping competition	7:00 a.m.-2:00 p.m.

Fencing, Long Beach Convention Center

August 1 Wednesday	Foil—individual preliminaries, men	9:00 a.m.-6:00 p.m.
August 2 Thursday	Foil—individual preliminaries, men & women	9:00 a.m.-5:00 p.m.
	Foil—individual finals, men	8:00 p.m.-11:00 p.m.
August 3 Friday	Foil—individual preliminaries, women Sabre—individual preliminaries, men	9:00 a.m.-5:00 p.m.
	Foil—individual finals, women	8:00 p.m.-11:00 p.m.
August 4 Saturday	Foil—team preliminaries, men Sabre—individual preliminaries, men	9:00 a.m.-5:00 p.m.
	Sabre—individual finals, men	8:00 p.m.-11:00 p.m.
August 5 Sunday	Foil—team preliminaries, men & women Foil—team finals, men	9:00 a.m.-6:00 p.m. 8:00 p.m.-11:00 p.m.
August 7 Tuesday	Foil—team preliminaries, women Epee—individual preliminaries, men	9:00 a.m.-6:00 p.m.
	Foil—team finals, women	8:00 p.m.-11:00 p.m.
August 8 Wednesday	Sabre—team preliminaries, men Epee—individual preliminaries, men	9:00 a.m.-5:00 p.m.
	Epee—individual finals, men	8:00 p.m.-11:00 p.m.
August 9 Thursday	Sabre—team preliminaries, men Sabre—team finals, men	12:00 noon-6:00 p.m. 8:00 p.m.-11:00 p.m.
August 10 Friday	Epee—team preliminaries, men	10:00 a.m.-4:00 p.m.
August 11 Saturday	Epee—team preliminaries, men Epee—team finals, men	10:00 a.m.-6:00 p.m. 8:00 p.m.-11:00 p.m.

Gymnastics, University of California, Los Angeles

July 29 Sunday	Compulsory exercises, men	9:30 a.m.-11:30 a.m.
	Compulsory exercises, men	2:00 p.m.-4:00 p.m.
	Compulsory exercises, men	6:30 p.m.-8:30 p.m.
July 30 Monday	Compulsory exercises, women	10:00 a.m.-12:45 p.m.
	Compulsory exercises, women	5:30 p.m.-8:15 p.m.

July 31 Tuesday	Optional exercises, men	9:30 a.m.-11:30 a.m.
	Optional exercises, men	2:00 p.m.-4:00 p.m.
	Optional exercises—team finals, men	6:30 p.m.-8:30 p.m.
August 1 Wednesday	Optional exercises, women	10:00 a.m.-12:45 p.m.
	Optional exercises—team finals, women	5:30 p.m.-8:15 p.m.
August 2 Thursday	All-around finals, men	5:30 p.m.-8:30 p.m.
August 3 Friday	**All-around finals, women**	**5:30 p.m.-8:00 p.m.**
August 4 Saturday	**Apparatus finals, men**	**5:30 p.m.-8:30 p.m.**
August 5 Sunday	**Apparatus finals, women**	**5:30 p.m.-7:30 p.m.**
August 9 Thursday	Rhythmic preliminaries, women	6:30 p.m.-10:30 p.m.
August 10 Friday	Rhythmic preliminaries, women	6:30 p.m.-10:30 p.m.
August 11 Saturday	**Rhythmic finals, women**	**8:00 p.m.-10:30 p.m.**

Handball (Team), California State University, Fullerton

July 31 Tuesday	3 games—preliminaries, men	11:00 a.m.-3:30 p.m.
	3 games—preliminaries, men	6:30 p.m.-11:00 p.m.
August 1 Wednesday	3 games—round robin, women	6:30 p.m.-11:00 p.m.
August 2 Thursday	3 games—preliminaries, men	11:00 a.m.-3:30 p.m.
	3 games—preliminaries, men	6:30 p.m.-11:00 p.m.
August 3 Friday	3 games—round robin, women	6:30 pm.-11:00 p.m.
August 4 Saturday	3 games—preliminaries, men	11:00 a.m.-3:30 p.m.
	3 games—preliminaries, men	6:30 p.m.-11:00 p.m.
August 5 Sunday	3 games—round robin, women	6:30 p.m.-11:00 p.m.
August 6 Monday	3 games—preliminaries, men	11:00 a.m.-3:30 p.m.
	3 games—preliminaries, men	6:30 p.m.-11:00 p.m.
August 7 Tuesday	3 games—round robin, women	6:30 p.m.-11:00 p.m.
August 8 Wednesday	3 games—preliminaries, men	11:00 a.m.-3:30 p.m.
	3 games—preliminaries, men	6:30 p.m.-11:00 p.m.
August 9 Thursday	3 games—round robin, women	6:30 p.m.-11:00 p.m.
August 10 Friday	**2 games—finals (9-12 places), men**	**11:00 a.m.-2:00 p.m.**
	2 games—finals (5-8 places), men	**6:30 p.m.-9:30 p.m.**
	The Forum, Inglewood	
August 11 Saturday	**2 games—finals (1-4 places), men**	**2:00 p.m.-5:00 p.m.**

Hockey (Field), East Los Angeles College, Monterey Park

| July 29
Sunday | 3 games—preliminaries, men | 1:45 p.m.-6:45 p.m. |
| July 30
Monday | 3 games—preliminaries, men | 1:45 p.m.-6:45 p.m. |

July 31 Tuesday	2 games—preliminaries, men 1 game—round robin, women 1 game—preliminary, men	8:30 a.m.-11:45 a.m. 2:30 p.m.-5:45 p.m.
August 1 Wednesday	1 game—preliminary, men 1 game—round robin, women	8:00 a.m.-11:15 a.m.
	2 games—preliminaries, men 1 game—round robin, women	1:45 p.m.-6:45 p.m.
August 2 Thursday	2 games—preliminaries, men 1 game—round robin, women 1 game—preliminary, men	8:30 a.m.-11:45 a.m. 2:30 p.m.-5:45 p.m.
August 3 Friday	1 game—round robin, women 1 game—preliminary, men	8:00 a.m.-11:15 a.m.
	2 games—preliminaries, men 1 game—round robin, women	1:45 p.m.-6:45 p.m.
August 4 Saturday	2 games—preliminaries, men 1 game—preliminary, men 1 game—round robin, women	8:30 a.m.-11:45 a.m. 2:30 p.m.-5:45 p.m.
August 5 Sunday	1 game—preliminary, men 1 game—round robin, women	8:00 a.m.-11:15 a.m.
	2 games—preliminaries, men 1 game—round robin, women	1:45 p.m.-6:45 p.m.
August 6 Monday	2 games—preliminaries, men 1 game—preliminary, men 1 game—round robin, women	8:30 a.m.-11:45 a.m. 2:30 p.m.-5:45 p.m.
August 7 Tuesday	1 game—preliminary, men 1 game—round robin, women	8:00 a.m.-11:15 a.m.
	1 game—round robin, women 2 games—preliminaries, men	1:45 p.m.-6:45 p.m.
August 8 Wednesday	2 games—semifinals, men	7:00 p.m.-10:30 p.m.
August 9 Thursday	2 games—semifinals, men 1 game—round robin, women 2 games—semifinals, men	8:00 a.m.-11:15 a.m. 1:15 p.m.-6:15 p.m.
August 10 **Friday**	1 game—final (11-12 places), men 1 game—round robin, women	8:00 a.m.-11:15 a.m.
	2 games—finals (7-10 places), men 1 game—round robin, women	1:15 p.m.-6:15 p.m.
August 11 Saturday	3 games—finals (1-6 places), men	9:15 a.m.-2:45 p.m.

Judo, California State University, Los Angeles

August 4 Saturday	Extra lightweight	4:00 p.m.-8:00 p.m.
August 5 Sunday	Half lightweight	4:00 p.m.-8:00 p.m.
August 6 Monday	Lightweight	4:00 p.m.-8:00 p.m.
August 7 Tuesday	Half middleweight	4:00 p.m.-8:00 p.m.
August 8 Wednesday	Middleweight	4:00 p.m.-8:00 p.m.
August 9 Thursday	Half heavyweight	4:00 p.m.-8:00 p.m.
August 10 Friday	Heavyweight	4:00 p.m.-8:00 p.m.
August 11 Saturday	Open category	4:00 p.m.-8:00 p.m.

Modern Pentathlon, Coto de Caza, Orange County

July 29 Sunday	Riding Riding	9:00 a.m.-11:00 a.m. 4:00 p.m.-6:00 p.m.
July 30 Monday	Fencing	8:00 a.m.-8:30 p.m.
July 31 Tuesday	Swimming	2:00 p.m.-4:00 p.m.
August 1 Wednesday	Shooting Running	9:00 a.m.-12:00 noon 5:00 p.m.-6:00 p.m.

Rowing, Lake Casitas, Ventura County

July 30 Monday	Elimination heats, women	7:30 a.m.-10:00 a.m.
July 31 Tuesday	Elimination heats, men	7:30 a.m.-10:30 a.m.
August 1 Wednesday	Repechage, men & women	7:30 a.m.-10:30 a.m.
August 2 Thursday	Semifinals, men & women	7:30 a.m.-10:30 a.m.
August 3 Friday	**Finals (7-12 places), men & women**	**8:00 a.m.-10:30 a.m.**
August 4 Saturday	**Finals (1-6 places), women**	**8:00 a.m.-10:00 a.m.**
August 5 Sunday	**Finals (1-6 places), men**	**8:00 a.m.-10:30 a.m.**

Shooting, Prado Recreational Area, San Bernardino County

July 29 Sunday	Free pistol Sport pistol Clay target-trap	9:00 a.m.-4:00 p.m.
July 30 Monday	Small-bore rifle English match Clay target-trap Running game target	9:00 a.m.-4:00 p.m.
July 31 Tuesday	Clay target-trap Running game target Air rifle	9:00 a.m.-4:00 p.m.
August 1 Wednesday	Small-bore rifle 3 positions Rapid-fire pistol	9:00 a.m.-4:00 p.m.
August 2 Thursday	Small-bore rifle 3 positions Rapid-fire pistol Clay target-skeet	9:00 a.m.-4:00 p.m.
August 3 Friday	Air rifle Clay target-skeet	9:00 a.m.-4:00 p.m.
August 4 Saturday	Clay target-skeet	9:00 a.m.-3:00 p.m.

Soccer (Football), Rose Bowl Pasadena, California

July 29 Sunday	Preliminary match	7:00 p.m.-9:00 p.m.
July 30 Monday	Preliminary match	7:00 p.m.-9:00 p.m.
July 31 Tuesday	Preliminary match	7:00 p.m.-9:00 p.m.
August 1 Wednesday	Preliminary match	7:00 p.m.-9:00 p.m.
August 2 Thursday	Preliminary match	7:00 p.m.-9:00 p.m.
August 3 Friday	Preliminary match	7:00 p.m.-9:00 p.m.

August 5 Sunday	Quarterfinal match	7:00 p.m.-9:00 p.m.
August 6 Monday	Quarterfinal match	7:00 p.m.-9:00 p.m.
August 8 Wednesday	Semifinal match	6:00 p.m.-8:00 p.m.
August 10 **Friday**	**Final match (3-4 places)**	**7:00 p.m.-9:00 p.m.**
August 11 **Saturday**	**Final match (1-2 places)**	**7:00 p.m.-9:00 p.m.**

Soccer (Football), Harvard University
Cambridge, Massachusetts

July 29 Sunday	Opening ceremonies and preliminary match	7:00 p.m.-9:00 p.m.
July 30 Monday	Preliminary match	7:00 p.m.-9:00 p.m.
July 31 Tuesday	Preliminary match	7:00 p.m.-9:00 p.m.
August 1 Wednesday	Preliminary match	7:00 p.m.-9:00 p.m.
August 2 Thursday	Preliminary match	7:00 p.m.-9:00 p.m.
August 3 Friday	Preliminary match	7:00 p.m.-9:00 p.m.

Soccer (Football), U.S. Naval Academy
Annapolis, Maryland

July 29 Sunday	Opening ceremonies and preliminary match	7:00 p.m.-9:00 p.m.
July 30 Monday	Preliminary match	7:00 p.m.-9:00 p.m.
July 31 Tuesday	Preliminary match	7:00 p.m.-9:00 p.m.
August 1 Wednesday	Preliminary match	7:00 p.m.-9:00 p.m.
August 2 Thursday	Preliminary match	7:00 p.m.-9:00 p.m.
August 3 Friday	Preliminary match	7:00 p.m.-9:00 p.m.

Soccer (Football), Stanford University
Palo Alto, California

July 29 Sunday	Opening ceremonies and preliminary match	7:00 p.m.-9:00 p.m.
July 30 Monday	Preliminary match	7:00 p.m.-9:00 p.m.
July 31 Tuesday	Preliminary match	7:00 p.m.-9:00 p.m.
August 1 Wednesday	Preliminary match	7:00 p.m.-9:00 p.m.
August 2 Thursday	Preliminary match	7:00 p.m.-9:00 p.m.
August 3 Friday	Preliminary match	7:00 p.m.-9:00 p.m.
August 5 Sunday	Quarterfinal match	3:00 p.m.-5:00 p.m.
August 6 Monday	Quarterfinal match	5:00 p.m.-7:00 p.m.
August 8 Wednesday	Semifinal match	8:30 p.m.-10:30 p.m.

Swimming, University of Southern California, McDonald's Swim Stadium

July 29 Sunday	Heats—100m freestyle, women Heats—100m breaststroke, men Heats—400m I. medley, women Heats—200m freestyle, men	8:30 a.m.-11:30 a.m.
	Finals—100m freestyle, women **Finals—100m breaststroke, men** **Finals—400m I. medley, women** **Finals—200m freestyle, men**	4:15 p.m.-6:00 p.m.
July 30 Monday	Heats—100m butterfly, men Heats—200m freestyle, women Heats—400m I. medley, men Heats—200m breaststroke, women Heats—4×200m freestyle relay, men	8:30 a.m.-11:30 a.m.
July 30 Monday	**Finals—100m butterfly, men** **Finals—200m freestyle, women** **Finals—400m I. medley, men** **Finals—200m breaststroke, women** **Finals—4×200m freestyle relay, men**	4:15 p.m.-6:00 p.m.
July 31 Tuesday	Heats—400m freestyle, women Heats—100m freestyle, men Heats—100m backstroke, women Heats—200m backstroke, men Heats—4×100m freestyle relay, women	8:30 a.m.-11:30 a.m.
	Finals—400m freestyle, women **Finals—100m freestyle, men** **Finals—100m backstroke, women** **Finals—200m backstroke, men** **Finals—4×100m freestyle relay, women**	4:15 p.m.-6:00 p.m.
August 2 Thursday	Heats—400m freestyle, men Heats—100m butterfly, women Heats—200m breaststroke, men Heats—100m breaststroke, women Heats—4×100m freestyle relay, men Heats—800m freestyle, women	8:30 a.m.-11:30 a.m.
	Finals—400m freestyle, men **Finals—100m butterfly, women** **Finals—200m breaststroke, men** **Finals—100m breaststroke, women** **Finals—4×100m freestyle relay, men**	4:15 p.m.-6:00 p.m.
August 3 Friday	Heats—200m I. medley, women Heats—200m butterfly, men Heats—100m backstroke, men Heats—4×100m medley relay, women Heats—1500m freestyle, men	8:30 a.m.-11:30 a.m.
	Finals—200m I. medley, women **Finals—200m butterfly, men** **Finals—800m freestyle, women** **Finals—100m backstroke, men** **Finals—4×100m medley relay, women**	5:00 p.m.-7:00 p.m.
August 4 Saturday	Heats—200m I. medley, men Heats—200m butterfly, women Heats—200m backstroke, women Heats—4×100m medley relay, men	8:30 a.m.-11:30 a.m.
	Finals—200m I. medley, men **Finals—200m butterfly, women** **Finals—1500m freestyle, men** **Finals—200m backstroke, women** **Finals—4×100m medley relay, men**	5:00 p.m.-7:00 p.m.

Synchronized Swimming, University of Southern California, McDonald's Swim Stadium

August 6 Monday	Duet routines preliminary	10:00 a.m.-2:00 p.m.

| August 9 Thursday | Duet routines final | 1:30 p.m.-2:30 p.m. |

Tennis, University of California, Los Angeles

August 6 Monday	16 matches—grounds pass —center court —center court	9:00 a.m.-5:30 p.m.
August 7 Tuesday	16 matches—grounds pass —center court —center court	9:00 a.m.-5:30 p.m.
August 8 Wednesday	16 matches—grounds pass —center court —center court	9:00 a.m.-5:30 p.m.
August 9 Thursday	8 matches, quarterfinals— —grounds pass —center court —center court	9:00 a.m.-5:30 p.m.
August 10 Friday	4 matches, semifinals— —center court —center court	9:00 a.m.-5:30 p.m.
August 11 Saturday	matches, finals— —center court —center court	10:00 a.m.-2:00 p.m.

Track and Field (Athletics), Los Angeles Memorial Coliseum

| August 3 Friday | Heptathlon 100m hurdles, high jump **9:30 a.m.-1:00 p.m.**
Triple jump qualifying, 400m hurdles 1st round, men, 400m 1st round, women, Shot put qualifying, women, 100m 1st & 2nd rounds, men

800m 1st round, women **4:00 p.m.-8:15 p.m.**
Heptathlon shot put, 200m, 800m 1st round, men, **20km walk final (start & finish), Shot put final, women,** 10,000m 1st round |
| August 4 Saturday | Heptathlon long jump **9:30 a.m.-1:00 p.m.**
400m 1st round, men, 400m 2nd round, women, Javelin throw qualifying, men, 100m 1st round, women

100m 2nd round, women **4:00 p.m. - 8:15 p.m.**
Heptathlon javelin throw, 800m (final event), 100m semifinal, men, 800m semifinal, women, 800m 2nd round, men, **Triple jump final,** 400m hurdles semifinal, men, **100m final, men** |
| August 5 Sunday | **Marathon, women (finish)** **8:00 a.m.-12:30 p.m.**
Javelin throw qualifying, women, 400m hurdles 1st round, women, 110m hurdles 1st round, men, Hammer throw qualifying

100m semifinal & final, women **4:00 p.m.-7:30 p.m.**
Long jump qualifying, men, 110m hurdles 2nd round, 400m 2nd round, men, 400m semifinal, women, **Javelin throw final, men,** 800m semifinal, men, **400m hurdles final, men** |
| August 6 Monday | Pole vault qualifying **9:30 a.m.-12:30 p.m.**
200m 1st & 2nd rounds, men, 3000m 1st round,

110m hurdles semifinal & final **4:00 p.m.-8:15 p.m.**
Hammer throw final, 400m hurdles semifinal, women, 400m semifinal, men, **400m final, women, 800m final, women, Long jump final, men, 800m final, men, Javelin throw final, women,** 3,000m steeplechase 1st round, **10,000m final** |
| August 8 Wednesday | Decathlon 100m, long jump, shot put **9:30 a.m.-1:00 p.m.**
Discus throw qualifying, men, 200m 1st & 2nd rounds, women, 1,500m 1st round, women,

200m semifinal & final, men **4:00 p.m.-8:30 p.m.**
Decathlon high jump, 400m, **Pole vault final, 400m hurdles final, women, 400m final, men,** 5,000m 1st round, Long jump qualifying, women, 3,000m semifinal, 3,000m steeplechase semifinal |
| August 9 Thursday | Decathlon, discus throw, 110m hurdles, **9:30 a.m.-5:00 p.m.**
pole vault, 100m hurdles 1st round, High jump qualifying, women, **200m semifinal & final, women, Decathlon javelin throw, 1,500m (final event),** 1,500m 1st round, men, 1,500m semifinal, women, **Long jump final, women,** 5,000m semifinal |

August 10 Friday	High jump qualifying, men	9:30 a.m.-12:30 p.m.
	4×400m relay 1st round, women, 4×400m relay 1st round, men, Discus throw qualifying, men, 4×100m relay 1st round, women, 4×100m relay 1st round, men,	
	High jump final, women	4:00 p.m.-7:45 p.m.
	100m hurdles semifinal, 4×400m relay semifinal, men, 4×400m relay semifinal, women, **Discus throw final, men**, 1,500m semifinal, men, 100m hurdles final, 3,000m final, 3,000m steeplechase final	
August 11 Saturday	50km walk final (start & finish)	8:00 a.m.-12:30 p.m.
	Shot put qualifying, men, 4×100m relay semifinal, women, 4×100m relay semifinal, men,	
	Discus throw final, women	4:00 p.m.-8:00 p.m.
	4×100m relay final, women, High jump final, men, 4×100m relay final, men, 4×400m relay final, women, 4×400m relay final, men, Shot put final, men, 1,500m final, women, 1,500m final, men, 5,000m final	
August 12 Sunday	Marathon, men (finish)	

Volleyball, Long Beach Sports Arena

July 29 Sunday	2 matches—preliminaries, men	10:00 a.m.-2:00 p.m.
	2 matches—preliminaries, men	6:30 p.m.-10:30 p.m.
July 30 Monday	2 matches—preliminaries, women	10:00 a.m.-2:00 p.m.
	2 matches—preliminaries, women	6:30 p.m.-10:30 p.m.
July 31 Tuesday	2 matches—preliminaries, men	10:00 a.m.-2:00 p.m.
	2 matches—preliminaries, men	6:30 p.m.-10:30 p.m.
August 1 Wednesday	2 matches—preliminaries, women	10:00 a.m.-2:00 p.m.
	2 matches—preliminaries, women	6:30 p.m.-10:30 p.m.
August 2 Thursday	2 matches—preliminaries, men	10:00 a.m.-2:00 p.m.
	2 matches—preliminaries, men	6:30 p.m.-10:30 p.m.
August 3 Friday	2 matches—preliminaries, women	10:00 a.m.-2:00 p.m.
	2 matches—preliminaries, women	6:30 p.m.-10:30 p.m.
August 4 Saturday	2 matches—preliminaries, men	10:00 a.m.-2:00 p.m.
	2 matches—preliminaries, men	6:30 p.m.-10:30 p.m.
August 5 Sunday	2 matches—semifinals (5-8 places), women	10:00 a.m.-2:00 p.m.
	2 matches—semifinals (1-4 places), women	6:30 p.m.-10:30 p.m.
August 6 Monday	2 matches—preliminaries, men	10:00 a.m.-2:00 p.m.
	2 matches—preliminaries, men	6:30 p.m.-10:30 p.m.
August 7 Tuesday	**2 matches—finals (5-8 places), women**	10:00 a.m.-2:00 p.m.
	1 match—final (3-4 places), women	4:00 p.m.-6:00 p.m.
	1 match—final (1-2 places), women	8:30 p.m.-10:30 p.m.
August 8 Wednesday	2 matches—semifinals, men	9:00 a.m.-3:00 p.m.
	1 match—final (9-10 places), men	
	2 matches—semifinals, men	6:30 p.m.-10:30 p.m.
August 10 Friday	**2 matches—finals (5-8 places), men**	6:30 p.m.-10:30 p.m.
August 11 Saturday	**1 match—final (3-4 places), men**	12:00 noon-2:00 p.m.
	1 match—final (1-2 places), men	6:30 p.m.-8:30 p.m.

Water Polo, Pepperdine University, Malibu

August 1 Wednesday	2 games—preliminaries	8:30 a.m.-11:00 a.m.
	2 games—preliminaries	1:30 p.m.-4:00 p.m.
	2 games—preliminaries	7:30 p.m.-10:00 p.m.
August 2 Thursday	2 games—preliminaries	8:30 a.m.-11:00 a.m.
	2 games—preliminaries	1:30 p.m.-4:00 p.m.
	2 games—preliminaries	7:30 p.m.-10:00 p.m.

August 3 Friday	2 games—preliminaries	8:30 a.m.-11:00 a.m.
	2 games—preliminaries	1:30 p.m.-4:00 p.m.
	2 games—preliminaries	7:30 p.m.-10:00 p.m.
August 6 Monday	2 games—preliminaries	8:30 a.m.-11:00 a.m.
	2 games—preliminaries	1:30 p.m.-4:00 p.m.
	2 games—preliminaries	7:30 p.m.-10:00 p.m.
August 7 Tuesday	2 games—preliminaries	8:30 a.m.-11:00 a.m.
	2 games—preliminaries	1:30 p.m.-4:00 p.m.
	2 games—preliminaries	7:30 p.m.-10:00 p.m.
August 9 Thursday	2 games—final round	8:30 a.m.-11:00 a.m.
	2 games—final round	1:30 p.m.-4:00 p.m.
	2 games—final round	7:30 p.m.-10:00 p.m.
August 10 Friday	2 games—final round	8:30 a.m.-11:00 a.m.
	2 games—final round	1:30 p.m.-4:00 p.m.
	2 games—final round	7:30 p.m.-10:00 p.m.

Weightlifting, Loyola Marymount University, Westchester

July 29 Sunday	Flyweight (up to 52 kg), group B	2:00 p.m.-4:00 p.m.
	Flyweight, group A	6:00 p.m.-9:00 p.m.
July 30 Monday	Bantamweight (up to 56 kg), group B	2:00 p.m.-4:00 p.m.
	Bantamweight, group A	6:00 p.m.-9:00 p.m.
July 31 Tuesday	Featherweight (up to 60 kg), group B	2:00 p.m.-4:00 p.m.
	Featherweight, group A	6:00 p.m.-9:00 p.m.
August 1 Wednesday	Lightweight (up to 67.5 kg), group C	11:00 a.m.-1:00 p.m.
	Lightweight, group B	2:00 p.m.-4:00 p.m.
	Lightweight, group A	6:00 p.m.-8:00 p.m.
August 2 Thursday	Middleweight (up to 75 kg), group C	11:00 a.m.-1:00 p.m.
	Middleweight, group B	2:00 p.m.-4:00 p.m.
	Middleweight, group A	6:00 p.m.-8:00 p.m.
August 4 Saturday	Light heavyweight (up to 82.5 kg), group C	11:00 a.m.-1:00 p.m.
	Light heavyweight, group B	2:00 p.m.-4:00 p.m.
	Light heavyweight, group A	6:00 p.m.-8:00 p.m.
August 5 Sunday	Middle heavyweight (up to 90 kg), group C	11:00 a.m.-1:00 p.m.
	Middle heavyweight, group B	2:00 p.m.-4:00 p.m.
	Middle heavyweight, group A	6:00 p.m.-8:00 p.m.
August 6 Monday	First heavyweight (up to 100 kg), group B	2:00 p.m.-4:00 p.m.
	First heavyweight, group A	6:00 p.m.-9:00 p.m.
August 7 Tuesday	Second heavyweight (up to 110 kg), group B	2:00 p.m.-4:00 p.m.
	Second heavyweight, group A	6:00 p.m.-9:00 p.m.
August 8 Wednesday	Super heavyweight (over 110 kg), group B	2:00 p.m.-4:00 p.m.
	Super heavyweight, group A	6:00 p.m.-9:00 p.m.

Wrestling, Anaheim Convention Center

Greco-Roman Style

July 30 Monday	Preliminaries—48, 62, 90 kg	12:00 noon-3:00 p.m.
	Preliminaries—48, 62, 90 kg	6:00 p.m.-8:30 p.m.
July 31 Tuesday	Preliminaries—48, 52, 62, 74, 90, over 100 kg	12:00 noon-3:00 p.m.
	Preliminaries—48, 52, 62, 74, 90 over 100 kg	6:00 p.m.-8:30 p.m.

August 1 Wednesday	Preliminaries—52, 57, 68, 74, 82, 100, over 100 kg Semifinals—48, 62, 90 kg	12:00 noon-3:00 p.m.
	Preliminaries—52, 57, 68, 74, 82, 100, over 100 kg **Finals—48, 62, 90 kg**	**6:00 p.m.-8:30 p.m.**
August 2 Thursday	Preliminaries—57, 68, 82, 100 kg Semifinals—52, 74, over 100 kg	12:00 noon-3:00 p.m.
	Preliminaries—57, 68, 82, 100 kg **Finals—52, 74, over 100 kg**	**6:00 p.m.-8:30 p.m.**
August 3 Friday	Preliminaries—57, 68, 82, 100 kg **Semifinals/finals—57, 68, 82, 100 kg** **Freestyle**	12:00 noon-3:00 p.m. **6:00 p.m.-8:30 p.m.**
August 7 Tuesday	Preliminaries—48, 62, 90 kg Preliminaries—48, 62, 90 kg	12:00 noon-3:00 p.m. 6:00 p.m.-8:30 p.m.
August 8 Wednesday	Preliminaries—48, 52, 62, 74, 90, over 100 kg	12:00 noon-3:00 p.m.
	Preliminaries—48, 52, 62, 74, 90, over 100 kg	6:00 p.m.-8:30 p.m.
August 9 Thursday	Preliminaries—52, 57, 68, 74, 82, 100, over 100 kg Semifinals—48, 62, 90 kg	12:00 noon-3:00 p.m.
	Preliminaries— 52, 57, 68, 74, 82, 100, over 100 kg **Finals—48, 62, 90 kg**	**6:00 p.m.-8:30 p.m.**
August 10 Friday	Preliminaries—57, 68, 82, 100 kg Semifinals—52, 74, over 100 kg	12:00 noon-3:00 p.m.
	Preliminaries—57, 68, 82, 100 kg **Finals—52, 74, over 100 kg**	**6:00 p.m.-8:30 p.m.**
August 11 Saturday	Preliminaries—57, 68, 82, 100 kg **Semifinals/finals—57, 68, 82, 100 kg**	12:00 noon-3:00 p.m. 6:00 p.m.-8:30 p.m.

Yachting, Olympic Yachting Center, Long Beach
All Races Held at Sea

July 31 Tuesday	First race	1:30 p.m.-6:30 p.m.
August 1 Wednesday	Second race	1:30 p.m.-6:30 p.m.
August 2 Thursday	Third race	1:30 p.m.-6:30 p.m.
August 3 Friday	Fourth race	1:30 p.m.-6:30 p.m.
August 6 Monday	Fifth race	1:30 p.m.-6:30 p.m.
August 7 Tuesday	Sixth race	1:30 p.m.-6:30 p.m.
August 8 Wednesday	Seventh race	1:30 p.m.-6:30 p.m.

Opening and Closing Ceremonies,
Los Angeles Memorial Coliseum

| July 28
Saturday | Opening ceremony | 4:00 p.m. |
| August 12
Sunday | Closing ceremony
(Men's marathon finish included) | 6:30 p.m. |

GAMES OF THE XXIIIrd OLYMPIAD
YUGOSLAVIA 1984 FEBRUARY 8-FEBRUARY 19

Date	Event	Time
Ski Jumps, Malo Polje Igman		
February 12 Sunday	70m	1:00 p.m.-3:00 p.m.
February 18 Saturday	90m	12:30 p.m.-3:00 p.m.
Nordic Combined, Malo & Veliko Polje Igman		
February 11 Saturday	70m	12:30 p.m.-2:30 p.m.
February 12 Sunday	15km	12:00 noon-2:00 p.m.
Cross-Country, Veliko Polje Igman		
February 9 Thursday	10km women	9:00 a.m.-10:00 a.m.
February 10 Friday	30km men	9:00 a.m.-11:30 a.m.
February 12 Sunday	5km women	9:00 a.m.-9:40 a.m.
February 13 Monday	15km men	9:00 a.m.-10:40 a.m.
February 15 Wednesday	Relay 4×5 women	9:00 a.m.-10:30 a.m.
February 16 Thursday	Relay 4×10 men	9:00 a.m.-11:20 a.m.
February 18 Saturday	20km women	9:00 a.m.-12:00 p.m.
February 19 Sunday	50km men	8:00 a.m.-11:30 a.m.
Biathlon, Voliko Polje Igman		
February 11 Saturday	20 km	9:00 a.m.-12:00 p.m.
February 14 Tuesday	10 km	9:00 a.m.-12:00 p.m.
February 17 Friday	Relay 4×7.5	9:00 a.m.-12:00 p.m.
Downhill, Bjelašnica		
February 9 Thursday	men	12:00 p.m.-2:00 p.m.
Giant Slalom, Bjelašnica		
February 15 Wednesday	men	12:00 p.m.-1:30 p.m.
February 16 Thursday	men	12:00 p.m.-1:30 p.m.

Slalom, Bjelašnica

| February 19
Sunday | men | 10:30 a.m.-12:30 p.m. |

Downhill, Jahorina

| February 11
Saturday | women | 10:30 a.m.-12:30 p.m. |

Giant Slalom, Jahorina

| February 13
Monday | women | 12:00 p.m.-1:30 p.m. |
| February 14
Tuesday | women | 12:00 p.m.-1:30 p.m. |

Slalom, Jahorina

| February 17
Friday | women | 11:30 a.m.-1:30 p.m. |

Luge, Trebević

February 9 Thursday	1 run men & women	2:00 p.m.-4:00 p.m.
February 10 Friday	2 run men & women	9:00 a.m.-11:00 a.m.
February 11 Saturday	3 run men & women	9:00 a.m.-11:00 a.m.
February 12 Sunday	4 run men & women	2:00 p.m.-4:00 p.m.
February 15 Wednesday	Double	10:00 a.m.-12:00 p.m.

Bobsleigh, Trebević

February 10 Friday	1-2 run	1:30 p.m.-4:00 p.m.
February 11 Saturday	3-4 run	1:30 p.m.-4:00 p.m.
February 17 Friday	1-2 run	1:30 p.m.-4:00 p.m.
February 18 Saturday	3-4 run	1:30 p.m.-4:00 p.m.

Speed Skating, Zetra

February 9 Thursday	1500m women	9:30 a.m.-11:30 a.m.
February 10 Friday	500m men & women	9:30 a.m.-10:30 a.m.(w) 11:00 a.m.-12:00 p.m. (m)
February 12 Sunday	5000m men	9:30 a.m.-12:30 p.m.
February 13 Monday	1000m women	9:30 a.m.-11:00 a.m.
February 14 Tuesday	1000m men	9:30 a.m.-11:30 a.m.
February 15 Wednesday	3000m women	9:30 a.m.-11:30 a.m.
February 16 Thursday	1500m men	9:30 a.m.-12:00 p.m.
February 18 Saturday	10,000m men	9:00 a.m.-1:00 p.m.

Figure Skating, Skenderija 2

| February 13
Monday | Compulsory Figures men | 7:00 a.m.-3:00 p.m. |
| February 15
Wednesday | Compulsory Figures women | 7:00 a.m.-4:00 p.m. |

Figure Skating, Zetra

February 10 Friday	Compulsory Dances (Ice Dancing)	1:00 p.m.-6:00 p.m.
February 12 Sunday	Original Set Pattern (Ice Dancing)	3:00 p.m.-6:00 p.m.
February 14 Tuesday	Short Program men	3:30 p.m.-6:30 p.m.
February 16 Thursday	Short Program women	2:00 p.m.-6:30 p.m.
February 19 Sunday	Exhibition	6:00 p.m.-8:00 p.m.

Figure Skating, Zetra

February 10 Friday	Short Program (pairs)	8:00 p.m.-11:00 p.m.
February 12 Sunday	Free Skating (pairs)	7:30 p.m.-11:00 p.m.
February 14 Tuesday	Free Dance (Ice Dancing)	7:30 p.m.-11:00 p.m.
February 16 Thursday	Free Skating men	7:30 p.m.-11:00 p.m.
February 18 Saturday	Free Skating women	7:00 p.m.-11:00 p.m.

Ice Hockey, Zetra

February 7 Tuesday	1:30 p.m./5:00 p.m./8:30 p.m.
February 9 Thursday	1:30 p.m./5:00 p.m./8:30 p.m.
February 11 Saturday	1:30 p.m./5:00 p.m./8:30 p.m.
February 13 Monday	1:30 p.m./5:00 p.m./8:30 p.m.
February 15 Wednesday	1:30 p.m./5:00 p.m./8:30 p.m.
February 17 Friday	1:30 p.m./5:00 p.m./8:30 p.m.
February 19 Sunday	10:00 a.m./1:30 p.m.

Ice Hockey, Skenderija 1

February 7 Tuesday	1:00 p.m./4:30 p.m./8:00 p.m.
February 9 Thursday	1:00 p.m./4:30 p.m./8:00 p.m.
February 11 Saturday	1:00 p.m./4:30 p.m./8:00 p.m.
February 13 Monday	1:00 p.m./4:30 p.m./8:00 p.m.
February 15 Wednesday	1:00 p.m./4:30 p.m./8:00 p.m.

Opening and Closing Ceremonies
Opening Ceremony, Stadion Koševo

| February 8
Wednesday | Opening Ceremony | 2:30 p.m.-4:00 p.m. |

Closing Ceremony, Zetra

| February 19
Sunday | Closing Ceremony | 8:00 p.m.-9:00 p.m. |

P　■　Schedule

	GOLD	SILVER	BRONZE
			U.S.S.R.[1]
			Oleg Blohin
			Murtaz Hurcilava
			Yuri Istomin
			Vladimir Kaplichnyi
			Viktor Kolotov
			Evgeniy Lovchev
			Sergei Olshanskiy
			Evgeniy Rudakov
			Viacheslav Semenov
			Gennadi Yevrushikhin
			Oganes Zanazanian
			Andrei Yakubik
			Arkadiy Andriasian
			Revaz Dsodzuashvili
			Iojef Sabo
			Vladimir Onischenko
			Anatoliy Kuksov
			Yuri Eliseev
			Vladimir Pilguy
1976	EAST GERMANY	POLAND	U.S.S.R.
	Jurgen Croy	Jan Tomaszewski	Vladimir Astapovski
	Hans Jurgen Dorner	Piotr Mowlik	Viktor Matvienko
	Konrad Weise	Antoni Szymanowski	Mikhail Fomenko
	Lothar Kurbjuweit	Wladyslaw Zmuda	Stefan Reshko
	Reinhard Lauck	Zygmunt Maszczyk	Vladimir Troshkin
	Reinhard Häfner	Grzegorz Lato	Vladimir Onischenko
	Hans Jurgen Riediger	Henryk Kasperczak	Leonid Nazarenko
	Bernd Bransch	Kazimierz Deyna	Viktor Kolotov
	Martin Hoffmann	Andrzej Szarmach	Oleg Blokhin
	Gerd Kische	Kazimierz Kmiecik	Leonid Buriak
	Wolfram Lowe	Henryk Wawrowski	Aleksandr Minayev
	Wilfried Grobner	Henryk Wieczorek	Viktor Zviagintsev
	Hartmut Schade		
1980	CZECHOSLOVAKIA	EAST GERMANY	U.S.S.R.
	Stanislav Seman	Bodo Rudwaleit	Rinat Dasayev
	Ludek Macela	Artur Ullrich	Tengiz Sulakvelidze
	Josef Mazura	Lothar Hause	Aleksandr Chivadze
	Libor Radimec	Frank Baum	Vagiz Khidiyatullin
	Zdenek Rygel	Rudiger Schnuphase	Oleg Romantsev
	Petr Nemec	Frank Terletzki	Sergey Shavlo
	Ladislav Vizek	Wolfgang Steinbach	Sergey Andreyev
	Jan Berger	Werner Peter	Vladimir Bessonov
	Jindrich Svoboda	Dieter Kuhn	Yuriy Gavrilov
	Lubos Pokluda	Norbert Trieloff	Feodor Chernenkov
	Werner Licka	Matthias Muller	Valeriy Gazzayev
	Rostislav Vaclavicek	Matthias Liebers	Sergey Baltacha
	Jaroslav Netolicka	Wolf-Rudiger Netz	Khoren Oganesyan
	Oldrich Rott	Frank Uhlig	Vladimir Pilgu
	Frantisek Stambacher	Jurgen Bahringer	Sergey Nikulin
	Frantisek Kunzo	Bernd Jakubowski	Aleksandr Prokopenko

---

[1]Third place declared a tie after extra time played.

16. Swimming and Diving (Men)

100 METERS FREE-STYLE (109 yd. 1 ft.)

GOLD	SILVER	BRONZE
1896 Alfréd Hajós (HUN) 1:22.2*	Efstathios Choraphas (GRE) 1:23.0	Otto Herschmann (AUT) d.n.a.
1900–1904 Event not held		
1906 Charles M. Daniels (USA) 1:13.4*	Zoltán von Halmay (HUN) 1:14.2	Cecil Healy (AUS) d.n.a.
1908 Charles M. Daniels (USA) 1:05.6*	Zoltán von Halmay (HUN) 1:06.2	Harald Julin (SWE) 1:08.0
1912 Duke P. Kahanamoku (USA) 1:03.4	Cecil Healy (AUS/NZL) 1:04.6	Kenneth Huszagh (USA) 1:05.6
1920 Duke P. Kahanamoku (USA) 1:01.4	Pua K. Kealoha (USA) 1:02.2	William W. Harris (USA) 1:03.0
1924 Johnny Weissmuller (USA) 59.0*	Duke P. Kahanamoku (USA) 1:01.4	Samuel Kahanamoku (USA) 1:01.8
1928 Johnny Weissmuller (USA) 58.6*	István Bárány (HUN) 59.8	Katsuo Takaishi (JPN) 1:00.0
1932 Yasuji Miyazaki (JPN) 58.2	Tatsugo Kawaishi (JPN) 58.6	Albert Schwartz (USA) 58.8
1936 Ferenc Csik (HUN) 57.6	Masanori Yusa (JPN) 57.9	Shigeo Arai (JPN) 58.0
1948 Walter Ris (USA) 57.3*	Alan Ford (USA) 57.8	Géza Kádas (HUN) 58.1
1952 C. Clarke Scholes (USA) 57.4	Hiroshi Suzuki (JPN) 57.4	Göran Larsson (SWE) 58.2
1956 Jon Henricks (AUS) 55.4*	John Devitt (AUS) 55.8	Gary Chapman (AUS) 56.7
1960 John Devitt (AUS) 55.2*	Lance M. Larson (USA) 55.2*	Manuel dos Santos (BRA) 55.4
1964 Donald Schollander (USA) 53.4*	Robert McGregor (GBR) 53.5	Hans-Joachim Klein (GER) 54.0
1968 Michael V. Wenden (AUS) 52.2*	Kenneth Walsh (USA) 52.8	Mark A. Spitz (USA) 53.0
1972 Mark A. Spitz (USA) 51.22*	Jerry Heidenreich (USA) 51.65	Vladimir Bure (URS) 51.77
1976 Jim Montgomery (USA) 49.99*	Jack Babashoff (USA) 50.81	Peter Nocke (GER) 51.31
1980 Jorg Woithe (GDR) 50.40	Per Holmertz (SWE) 50.91	Per Johansson (SWE) 51.29

The following Olympic records were set in addition to those medal-winning performances marked with an asterisk*.

1:08.2	von Halmay 1908	1:00.4	Kahanamoku 1920 (in a final prior to a re-swim)	57.5	Ris 1948
1:05.8	Daniels 1908			57.1	Scholes 1952
1:04.8	Perry McGillivray (USA) 1912	58.6	Weissmuller 1928	56.8	L. Reid Patterson (USA) 1956
		58.0	Miyazaki 1932		
		57.7	Peter Fick (USA) 1936	55.7	Henricks 1956
1:02.6	Kahanamoku 1912			54.0	Gary Ilman (USA) 1964
1:02.4	Kahanamoku 1912	57.7	Arai 1936	53.9	Ilman 1964
		57.5	Masaharu Taguchi (JPN) 1936	53.4	Zachary Zorn (USA) 1968
1:01.8	Kahanamoku 1920				
		57.5	Yusa 1936	52.9	Wenden 1968
1:01.4	Kahanamoku 1920			50.39	Montgomery 1976

American Brian Goodell won gold medals in the 400 meters and 1,500 meters freestyle swimming events in 1976, setting Olympic and world records in both.

LEFT: Mark Spitz (USA) won 7 gold medals at the Munich Games in 1972, an Olympic record for a single year in any sport.

ABOVE: The dominant free-style swimmers at 400 meters and 1,500 meters in 1956 and 1960 were (left to right) George Breen (USA), I. Murray Rose (AUS) and Tsuyoshi Yamanaka (JPN).

200 METERS FREE-STYLE (218 yd. 2 ft.)

	GOLD	SILVER	BRONZE
1896	Event not held		
1900	Frederick C. V. Lane (AUS) 2:25.2	Zóltán von Halmay (HUN) 2:31.4	Karl Ruberl (AUT) 2:32.0
1904–1964	Event not held		
1968[1]	Michael V. Wenden (AUS) 1:55.2*	Donald A. Schollander (USA) 1:55.8	John M. Nelson (USA) 1:58.1
1972	Mark A. Spitz (USA) 1:52.78*	Steven Genter (USA) 1:53.73	Werner Lampe (GER) 1:53.99
1976	Bruce Furniss (USA) 1:50.29*	John Naber (USA) 1:50.50	Jim Montgomery (USA) 1:50.58
1980	Sergei Kopliakov (URS) 1:49.81*	Andrei Krylov (URS) 1:50.76	Graeme Brewer (AUS) 1:51.60

The following Olympic records were set in addition to those medal-winning performances already marked with an asterisk*.

1:59.5	Nelson	1968	1:52.71	Andrei Bogdanov (URS) 1976	1:51.41	Klaus Steinbach (GER) 1976
1:59.3	Wenden	1968			1:50.93	Furniss 1976

400 METERS FREE-STYLE (437 yd. 1 ft.)

	GOLD	SILVER	BRONZE
1896–1904	Event not held		
1906	Otto Scheff (AUT) 6:23.8*	Henry Taylor (GBR) 6:24.4	John A. Jarvis (GBR) 6:27.2
1908	Henry Taylor (GBR) 5:36.8*	Frank E. Beaurepaire (AUS/NZL) 5:44.2	Otto Scheff (AUT) 5:46.0
1912	George R. Hodgson (CAN) 5:24.4*	John G. Hatfield (GBR) 5:25.8	Harold H. Hardwick (AUS/NZL) 5:31.2
1920	Norman Ross (USA) 5:26.8	Ludy Langer (USA) 5:29.2	George Vernot (CAN) 5:29.8
1924	Johnny Weissmuller (USA) 5:04.2*	Arne Borg (SWE) 5:05.6	Andrew M. Charlton (AUS) 5:06.6
1928	V. Alberto Zorilla (ARG) 5:01.6*	Andrew M. Charlton (AUS) 5:03.6	Arne Borg (SWE) 5:04.6
1932	Clarence L. Crabbe (USA) 4:48.4*	Jean Taris (FRA) 4:48.5	Tautomu Oyokota (JPN) 4:52.3
1936	Jack Medica (USA) 4:44.5*	Shumpei Uto (JPN) 4:45.6	Shozo Makino (JPN) 4:48.1
1948	William Smith (USA) 4:41.0*	James McLane (USA) 4:34.4	John B. Marshall (AUS) 4:47.7
1952	Jean Boiteaux (FRA) 4:30.7*	Ford Konno (USA) 4:31.3	Per-Olof Ostrand (SWE) 4:35.2
1956	I. Murray Rose (AUS) 4:27.3*	Tsuyoshi Yamanaka (JPN) 4:30.4	George T. Breen (USA) 4:32.5
1960	I. Murray Rose (AUS) 4:18.3*	Tsuyoshi Yamanaka (JPN) 4:21.4	John Konrads (AUS) 4:21.8
1964	Donald A. Schollander (USA) 4:12.2*	Frank Wiegand (GER) 4:14.9	Allan Wood (AUS) 4:15.1
1968	Michael J. Burton (USA) 4:09.0*	Ralph W. Hutton (CAN) 4:11.7	Alain Mosconi (FRA) 4:13.3
1972[1]	Bradford P. Cooper (AUS) 4:00.27*	Steven Genter (USA) 4:01.94	Tom McBreen (USA) 4:02.64
1976	Brian Goodell (USA) 3:51.93*	Tim Shaw (USA) 3:52.54	Vladimir Raskatov (URS) 3:55.76
1980	Vladimir Salnikov (URS) 3:51.31*	Andrei Krylov (URS) 3:53.24	Ivar Stukolkin (URS) 3:53.95

[1]Rick DeMont (USA) finished first but was subsequently disqualified.

The following Olympic records were set in addition to those medal-winning performances already marked with an asterisk *.

5:48.8 T. Sydney Battersby (GBR) 1908	5:13.6 Weissmuller 1924	4:17.2 Wiegand 1964
5:42.2 Taylor 1908	4:53.2 Takashi Yokoyama (JPN) 1932	4:15.8 Schollander 1964
5:40.6 Scheff 1908	4:51.4 Yokoyama 1932	4:06.59 Bengt Gingsjoe (SWE) 1972
5:36.0 Hardwick 1912	4:45.5 Uto 1936	4:05.89 Genter 1972
5:34.0 Cecil Healy (AUS/NZL) 1912	4:42.2 McLane 1948	4:04.59 Cooper 1972
5:25.4 Hodgson 1912	4:38.6 Ostrand 1952	3:59.62 Djan Madruga (BRA) 1976
5:22.4 Breyer (USA) 1924	5:33.1 Boiteaux 1952	3:57.56 Raskatov 1976
5:22.2 Weissmuller 1924	4:21.0 Yamanaka 1960	3:56.40 Shaw 1976
	4:19.2 Alan Somers (USA) 1960	3:55.24 Goodell 1976

1,500 METERS FREE-STYLE (1,640 yd. 1 ft.)

	GOLD	SILVER	BRONZE
1896–1906	Event not held		
1908	Henry Taylor (GBR) 22:48.4*	T. Sydney Battersby (GBR) 22:51.2	Frank E. Beaurepaire (AUS/NZL) 22:56.2
1912	George R. Hodgson (CAN) 22:00.0*	John G. Hatfield (GBR) 22:39.0	Harold Hardwick (AUS/NZL) 23:15.4
1920	Norman Ross (USA) 22:23.2	George Vernot (CAN) 22:36.4	Frank E. Beaurepaire (AUS) 23:04.0
1924	Andrew M. Charlton (AUS) 20:06.6*	Arne Borg (SWE) 20:41.4	Frank E. Beaurepaire (AUS) 21:48.4
1928	Arne Borg (SWE) 19:51.8*	Andrew M. Charlton (AUS) 20:02.6	Clarence L. Crabbe (USA) 20:28.8
1932	Kusuo Kitamura (JPN) 19:12.4*	Shozo Makino (JPN) 19:14.1	James C. Christy (USA) 19:39.5

Vladimir Salnikov (URS) earned one of his three 1980 gold medals by becoming the first swimmer ever to complete the 1,500 meter free-style in less than 15 minutes.

	GOLD	SILVER	BRONZE
1936	Noboru Terada (JPN) 19:13.7	Jack Medica (USA) 19:34.0	Shumpei Uto (JPN) 19:34.5
1948	James McLane (USA) 19:18.5	John B. Marshall (AUS) 19:31.3	György Mitró (HUN) 19:43.2
1952	Ford Konno (USA) 18:30.0*	Shiro Hashizume (JPN) 18:41.4	Tetsuo Okamoto (BRA) 18:51.3
1956	I. Murray Rose (AUS) 17:58.9	Tsuyoshi Yamanaka (JPN) 18:00.3	George T. Breen (USA) 18:08.2
1960	John Konrads (AUS) 17:19.6*	I. Murray Rose (AUS) 17:21.7	George T. Breen (USA) 17:30.6
1964	Robert Windle (AUS) 17:01.7*	John Nelson (USA) 17:03.0	Allan Wood (AUS) 17:07.7
1968	Michael J. Burton (USA) 16:38.9*	John Kinsella (USA) 16:57.3	Gregory Brough (AUS) 17:04.7
1972	Michael J. Burton (USA) 15:52.58*	Graham Windeatt (AUS) 15:58.48	Douglas Northway (USA) 16:09.25
1976	Brian Goodell (USA) 15:02.40*	Bobby Hackett (USA) 15:03.91	Stephen Holland (AUS) 15:04.66
1980	Vladimir Salnikov (URS) 14:58.27*	Alexandr Chaev (URS) 15:14.30	Max Metzker (AUS) 15:14.49

The following Olympic records were set in addition to those medal-winning performances already marked with an asterisk *.

25:02.6	Paul Radmilovic (GBR) 1908	21:11.4	Borg 1924	17:15.9	Windle 1964
		19:51.6	Kitamura 1932	16:34.63	Hans-Joachim Fassnacht (GER) 1972
		19:38.7	Makino 1932		
23:45.8	Beaurepaire 1908	18:34.0	Hashizume 1952	15:59.63	Windeatt 1972
23:42.8	Battersby 1908	18:04.1	Rose 1956	15:37.61	Zoltan Wladar (HUN) 1976
23:24.4	Taylor 1908	17:52.9	Breen 1956		
22:54.0	Taylor 1908	17:46.5	Yamanaka 1960		
22:23.0	Hodgson 1912			15:20.74	Paul Hartloff (USA) 1976
21:20.4	Charlton 1924	17:32.8	Rose 1960		

Michael Burton of the United States doubled in 1968 in the 400 meters and 1,500 meters free-style, and won a third gold medal in 1972, again in the 1,500 meters free-style.

100 METERS BACK STROKE (109 yd. 1 ft.)

	GOLD	SILVER	BRONZE
1896–1906	Event not held		
1908	Arno Bieberstein (GER) 1:24.6*	Ludvig Dam (DEN) 1:26.6	Herbert Haresnape (GBR) 1:27.0
1912	Harry J. Hebner (USA) 1:21.2	Otto Fahr (GER) 1:22.4	Paul Kellner (GER) 1:24.0
1920	Warren P. Kealoha (USA) 1:15.2	Ray Kegeris (USA) 1:16.2	Gérard Blitz (BEL) 1:19.0
1924	Warren P. Kealoha (USA) 1:13.2*	Paul Wyatt (USA) 1:15.4	Károly Bartha (HUN) 1:17.8
1928	George H. Kojac (USA) 1:08.2*	Walter Laufer (USA) 1:10.0	Paul Wyatt (USA) 1:12.0
1932	Masaji Kiyokawa (JPN) 1:08.6	Toshio Irie (JPN) 1:09.8	Kentaro Kawatsu (JPN) 1:10.0
1936	Adolf Kiefer (USA) 1:05.9*	Albert Van de Weghe (USA) 1:07.7	Masaji Kiyokawa (JPN) 1:08.4
1948	Allen Stack (USA) 1:06.4	Robert Cowell (USA) 1:06.5	Georges Vallerey (FRA) 1:07.8
1952	Yoshinobu Oyakawa (USA) 1:05.4*	Gilbert Bozon (FRA) 1:06.2	Jack Taylor (USA) 1:06.4
1956	David Thiele (AUS) 1:02.2*	John Monckton (AUS) 1:03.2	Frank E. McKinney (USA) 1:04.5
1960	David Thiele (AUS) 1:01.9*	Frank E. McKinney (USA) 1:02.1	Robert E. Bennett (USA) 1:02.3
1964	Event not held		
1968	Roland Matthes (GDR) 58.7*	Charles Hickcox (USA) 1:00.2	Ronnie P. Mills (USA) 1:00.5
1972	Roland Matthes (GDR) 56.58*	Mike Stamm (USA) 57.70	John Murphy (USA) 58.35
1976	John Naber (USA) 55.49*	Peter Rocca (USA) 56.34	Roland Matthes (GDR) 57.22
1980	Bengt Baron (SWE) 56.53	Viktor Kuznetsov (URS) 56.99	Vladimir Dolgov (URS) 57.63

The following Olympic records were set in addition to those medal-winning performances already marked with an asterisk *

1:25.6 (twice)	Bieberstein	1908	1:06.9	Kiefer	1936	1:01.9	Larry Barbiere (USA)	1968
1:21.1	Hebner	1912	1:06.8	Kiefer	1936	1:01.0	Matthes	1968
1:20.8	Hebner	1912	1:05.7	Oyakawa	1952	58.63	Stamm	1972
1:17.8	Ray Kegeris (USA)	1920	1:04.2	Robert Christophe (FRA)	1956	58.15	Mitchell Ivey (USA)	1972
1:14.8	Kealoha	1920	1:03.4	Monckton	1956	57.99	Ivey	1972
1:13.4	Kealoha	1924	1:02.0	Bennett	1960	56.30†	Matthes	1972
1:09.2	Kojac	1928				56.19	Naber	1976

†In medley relay.

200 METERS BACK STROKE (218 yd. 2 ft.)

	GOLD	SILVER	BRONZE
1896	Event not held		
1900	Ernst Hoppenberg (GER) 2:47.0*	Karl Ruberl (AUT) 2:56.0	Johannes Drost (HOL) 3:01.0
1904–1960	Event not held		
1964	Jed Graef (USA) 2:10.3*	Gary Dilley (USA) 2:10.5	Robert E. Bennett (USA) 2:13.1
1968	Roland Matthes (GDR) 2:09.6*	Mitchell Ivey (USA) 2:10.6	Jack Horsley (USA) 2:10.9
1972	Roland Matthes (GDR) 2:02.82*	Mike Stamm (USA) 2:04.09	Mitchell Ivey (USA) 2:04.33

Two of the greatest back stroke experts ever seen in Olympic competition are Roland Matthes (GDR) at left and John Naber (USA) at right. Matthes won the gold medal at 100 meters and 200 meters in both 1968 and 1972. Naber set Olympic and world records at both distances at the 1976 Games.

In the 100 meters breast stroke event in 1976, John Hencken (USA) in lane 3 beat David Wilkie (GBR) in lane 5 by just over half a second. At 200 meters Wilkie beat the defending champion Hencken.

GOLD	SILVER	BRONZE
1976 John Naber (USA) 1:59.19*	Peter Rocca (USA) 2:00.55	Don Harrigan (USA) 2:01.35
1980 Sandor Wladar (HUN) 2:01.93	Zoltan Verraszto (HUN) 2:02.40	Mark Kerry (AUS) 2:03.14

The following Olympic records were set in addition to those medal-winning perform-ances already marked with an asterisk *.

2:16.1	Bennett	1964	2:14.5	Graef	1964	2:07.51	Stamm	1972
2:14.7	Shigeo		2:14.2	Dilley	1964	2:06.62	Matthes	1972
	Fukushima		2:13.8	Dilley	1964	2:02.25	Harrigan	1976
	(JPN)	1964	2:13.7	Graef	1964	2:02.01	Naber	1976

100 METERS BREAST STROKE (109 yd. 1 ft.)

1896–1964 Event not held

GOLD	SILVER	BRONZE
1968 Donald McKenzie (USA) 1:07.7*	Vladimir Kossinsky (URS) 1:08.0	Nickolay Pankin (URS) 1:08.0
1972 Nobutaka Taguchi (JPN) 1:04.94*	Tom Bruce (USA) 1:05.43	John Hencken (USA) 1:05.61
1976 John Hencken (USA) 1:03.11*	David Wilkie (GBR) 1:03.43	Arvidas Iuozaytis (URS) 1:04.23
1980 Duncan Goodhew (GBR) 1:03.34	Arsen Miskarov (URS) 1:03.82	Peter Evans (AUS) 1:03.96

The following Olympic records were set in addition to those medal-winning perform-ances already marked with an asterisk *.

1:08.9	Pankin	1968	1:05.89	Mark		1:04.92	Duncan	
1:08.1	McKenzie	1968		Chatfield			Goodhew	
1:08.1	Pankin	1968		(USA)	1972		(GBR)	1976
1:07.9	Kossinsky	1968	1:05.68	Hencken	1972	1:04.78	Iuozaytis	1976
			1:05.13	Taguchi	1972	1:03.88	Hencken	1976
						1:03.62	Hencken	1976

200 METERS BREAST STROKE (218 yd. 2 ft.)

1896–1906 Event not held

GOLD	SILVER	BRONZE
1908 Frederick Holman (GBR) 3:09.2*	William W. Robinson (GBR) 3:12.8	Pontus Hansson (SWE) 3:14.6
1912 Walter Bathe (GER) 3:01.8*	Wilhelm Lützow (GER) 3:05.0	Kurt Malisch (GER) 3:08.0
1920 Häken Malmroth (SWE) 3:04.4	Thor Henning (SWE) 3:09.2	Arvo Aaltonen (FIN) 3:12.2
1924 Robert D. Skelton (USA) 2:56.5	Joseph de Combe (BEL) 2:59.2	William Kirschbaum (USA) 3:01.0
1928 Yoshiyuki Tsuruta (JPN) 2:48.8*	Erich Rademacher (GER) 2:50.6	Teofilo Yldefonzo (PHI) 2:56.4
1932 Yoshiyuki Tsuruta (JPN) 2:45.4	Reizo Koike (JPN) 2:46.4	Teofilo Yldefonzo (PHI) 2:47.1
1936 Tetsuo Hamuro (JPN) 2:42.5*	Erwin Sietas (GER) 2:42.9	Reizo Koike (JPN) 2:44.2
1948 Joseph Verdeur (USA) 2:39.3*	Keith Carter (USA) 2:40.2	Robert Sohl (USA) 2:43.9
1952 John Davies (AUS) 2:34.4*	Bowen Stassforth (USA) 2:34.7	Herbert Klein (GER) 2:35.9
1956 Masura Furukawa (JPN) 2:34.7*	Masahiro Yoshimura (JPN) 2:36.7	Charis Yunitschev (URS) 2:36.8

	GOLD	SILVER	BRONZE
1960	William D. Mulliken (USA) 2:37.4	Yoshihiko Osaki (JPN) 2:38.0	Wieger E. Mensonides (HOL) 2:39.7
1964	Ian O'Brien (AUS) 2:27.8*	Georgy Prokopenko (URS) 2:28.2	Chester Jastremski (USA) 2:29.6
1968	Felipe Muñoz (MEX) 2:28.7	Vladimir Kossinsky (URS) 2:29.2	Brian Job (USA) 2:29.9
1972	John Hencken (USA) 2:21.55*	David A. Wilkie (GBR) 2:23.67	Nobutaka Taguchi (JPN) 2:23.88
1976	David Wilkie (GBR) 2:15.11*	John Hencken (USA) 2:17.26	Rick Colella (USA) 2:19.20
1980	Robertas Zulpa (URS) 2:15.85	Alban Vermes (HUN) 2:16.93	Arsen Miskarov (URS) 2:17.28

The following Olympic records were set in addition to those medal-winning performances already marked with an asterisk *.

3:10.0	Holman	1908	2:46.2	Koike	1932	2:38.0	Mulliken	1960
3:10.6	Holman	1908	2:44.9	Koike	1932	2:37.2	Mulliken	1960
3:07.4	Lützow	1912	2:42.5	Hamuro	1936	2:31.4	O'Brien	1964
3:03.4	Bathe	1912	2:40.0†	Verdeur	1948	2:30.1	Egon	
3:02.2	Bathe	1912	2:38.9†	L. Komadel			Henninger	
2:56.0	Skelton	1924		(TCH)	1952		(GER)	1964
2:52.0	Rademacher		2:36.8†	G. Holan		2:28.7	O'Brien	1964
		1928		(USA)	1952	2:26.32	Klaus Katzur	
2:50.0	Tsuruta	1928	2:36.8†	Davies	1952		(GDR)	1972
2:49.2	Tsuruta	1928	2:36.1†	Furukawa		2:23.45	Taguchi	1972
2:46.2	Tsuruta	1932			1956	2:21.08	Colella	1976
						2:18.29	Wilkie	1976

† In the 1948 and 1952 Games the records for this event were achieved by the then permissible butterfly stroke. Furukawa's 1956 record was achieved by the now also disallowed underwater technique.

100 METERS BUTTERFLY (109 yd. 1 ft.)

1896–1964	Event not held		
1968	Douglas A. Russell (USA) 55.9*[1]	Mark A. Spitz (USA) 56.4	Ross Wales (USA) 57.2
1972	Mark A. Spitz (USA) 54.27*	Bruce Robertson (CAN) 55.56	Jerry Heidenreich (USA) 55.74
1976	Matt Vogel (USA) 54.35	Joseph Bottom (USA) 54.50	Gary Hall (USA) 54.65
1980	Par Arvidsson (SWE) 54.92	Roger Pyttel (GDR) 54.94	David Lopez (ESP) 55.13

[1] In 1968 Russell set an inaugural record of 57.3 which he improved to 55.9 in the semi-finals.

200 METERS BUTTERFLY (218 yd. 2 ft.)

1896–1952	Event not held		
1956	William Yorzyk (USA) 2:19.3	Takashi Ishimoto (JPN) 2:23.8	György Tumpek (HUN) 2:23.9
1960	Michael F. Troy (USA) 2:12.8*	Neville Hayes (AUS) 2:14.6	J. David Gillanders (USA) 2:15.3
1964	Kevin J. Berry (AUS) 2:06.6*	Carl Robie (USA) 2:07.5	Fred Schmidt (USA) 2:09.3
1968	Carl Robie (USA) 2:08.7	Martyn Woodroffe (GBR) 2:09.0	John Ferris (USA) 2:09.3
1972	Mark A. Spitz (USA) 2:00.70*	Gary Hall (USA) 2:02.86	Robin Backhaus (USA) 2:03.23

At the 1976 Games, Rod Strachan (USA) won the gold medal in the 400 meters individual medley in Olympic record time.

Charles Hickcox (USA) (right) beat his compatriot Gary Hall to win the 400 meters individual medley at Mexico City in 1968.

GOLD	SILVER	BRONZE
1976 Michael Bruner (USA) 1:59.23*	Steven Gregg (USA) 1:59.54	William Forrester (USA) 1:59.96
1980 Sergei Fesenko (URS) 1:59.76	Philip Hubble (GBR) 2:01.20	Roger Pyttel (GDR) 2:01.39

There were six record butterfly performances (then permissible) in the 1948 and 1952 breast stroke events culminating in John Davies' (AUS) 2:34.4 in 1952. Thereafter the non-medal-winning records were:

2:18.6	Yorzyk	1956	2:09.3	Robie	1964	2:03.11	Backhaus	1972
2:15.5	Troy	1960	2:03.70	Hall	1972	2:02.11	Spitz	1972
2:10.0	Robie	1964				2:00.24	Gregg	1976

400 METERS INDIVIDUAL MEDLEY (437 yd. 1 ft.)

1896–1960 Event not held

1964 Richard Roth (USA) 4:45.4*	Roy Saari (USA) 4:47.1	Gerhard Hetz (GER) 4:51.0
1968 Charles Hickcox (USA) 4:48.4	Gary Hall (USA) 4:48.7	Michael Holthaus (GER) 4:51.4
1972 Gunnar Larsson (SWE) 4:31.98*	Tim McKee (USA) 4:31.98*	Andras Hargitay (HUN) 4:32.70
1976 Rod Strachan (USA) 4:23.68*	Tim McKee (USA) 4:24.62	Andrei Smirnov (URS) 4:26.90
1980 Aleksandr Sidorenko (URS) 4:22.89*	Sergei Fesenko (URS) 4:23.43	Zoltan Verraszto (HUN) 4:24.24

The following non-medal-winning performances were also Olympic Records:

4:52.0	Robie	1964	4:34.99	Larsson	1972	4:27.15	Strachan	1976
4:37.51	Hargitay	1972	4:27.76	Steve Furniss (USA)	1976			

4 × 100 METERS MEDLEY RELAY (4 × 109 yd. 1 ft.)
(Order of strokes: back stroke, breast stroke, butterfly, free-style.)

1896–1956 Event not held

1960 UNITED STATES 4:05.4*	AUSTRALIA 4:12.0	JAPAN 4:12.2
Frank E. McKinney	David Theile	Kazuo Tomita
Paul W. Hait	Terry Gathercole	Koichi Hirakida
Lance M. Larson	Neville Hayes	Yoshihiko Osaki
F. Jeffrey Farrell	Gary Shipton	Keigo Shimizu
1964 UNITED STATES 3:58.4*	GERMANY 4:01.6	AUSTRALIA 4:02.3
Harold T. Mann	Ernst-Joachim Küppers	Peter Reynolds
William Craig	Egon Henninger	Ian O'Brien
Fred Schmidt	Horst-Günther Gregor	Kevin J. Berry
Stephen Clark	Hans-Joachim Klein	David Dickson
1968 UNITED STATES 3:54.9*	EAST GERMANY 3:57.5	U.S.S.R. 4:00.7
Charles Hickcox	Roland Matthes	Yuri Gromak
Donald McKenzie	Egon Henninger	Vladimir Kossinsky
Douglas A. Russell	Horst-Günther Gregor	Vladimir Nemshilov
Kenneth Walsh	Frank Wiegand	Leonid Ilyichev
1972 UNITED STATES 3:48.16*	EAST GERMANY 3:52.12	CANADA 3:52.26
Mike Stamm	Roland Matthes	Eric Fish
Tom Bruce	Klaus Katzur	William Mahony
Mark A. Spitz	Hartmut Floekner	Bruce Robertson
Jerry Heidenerich	Lutz Unger	Robert A. Kasting

GOLD	SILVER	BRONZE
1976 **UNITED STATES** 3:42.22*	**CANADA** 3:45.94	**WEST GERMANY** 3:47.29
John Naber	Stephen Pickell	Klaus Steinbach
John Hencken	Graham Smith	Walter Kusch
Matt Vogel	Clay Evans	Michael Kraus
Jim Montgomery	Gary MacDonald	Peter Nocke
1980 **AUSTRALIA** 3:45.70	**U.S.S.R.** 3:45.92	**GREAT BRITAIN** 3:47.71
Mark Kerry	Viktor Kuznetsov	Gary Abraham
Peter Evans	Arsen Miskarov	Duncan Goodhew
Mark Tonelli	Yevgeniy Seredin	David Lowe
Neil Brooks	Sergei Kopliakov	Martin Smith

The following Olympic records were set in addition to those medal-winning performances already marked with an asterisk*.

4:14.8	Australia	1960	4:05.1	United States 1964		3:51.98	United States 1972
4:08.2	United States	1960				3:47.28	United States 1976

4 × 200 METERS FREE-STYLE RELAY (4 × 218 yd. 2 ft.)

1896–1906 Event not held

1908 **GREAT BRITAIN** 10:45.6	**HUNGARY** 10:59.0	**UNITED STATES** 11:02.8
John H. Derbyshire	József Munk	Harry Hebner
Paul Radmilovic	Imre Zachár	Leo Goodwin
William Foster	Béla von Las Torres	Charles M. Daniels
Henry Taylor	Zóltán von Halmay	Leslie G. Rich
1912 **AUSTRALASIA** 10:11.6*	**UNITED STATES** 10:20.2	**GREAT BRITAIN** 10:28.2
Cecil Healy	Kenneth Huszagh	William Foster
Malcolm Champion[1]	Harry J. Hebner	T. Sydney Battersby
Leslie Boardman	Perry McGillivray	John Hatfield
Harold Hardwick	Duke P. Kahanamoku	Henry Taylor
1920 **UNITED STATES** 10:04.4*	**AUSTRALIA** 10:25.4	**GREAT BRITAIN** 10:37.2
Perry McGillivray	Henry Hay	Leslie Savage
Pua K. Kealoha	William Herald	E. Percy Peter
Norman Ross	Ivan Stedman	Henry Taylor
Duke P. Kahanamoku	Frank E. Beaurepaire	Harold E. Annison
1924 **UNITED STATES** 9:53.4*	**AUSTRALIA** 10:02.2	**SWEDEN** 10:06.8
Wallace O'Connor	Maurice Christie	George Werner
Harry Glancy	Ernest Henry	Orvar Trolle
Ralph Breyer	Frank E. Beaurepaire	Åke Borg
Johnny Weissmuller	Andrew M. Charlton	Arne Borg
1928 **UNITED STATES** 9:36.2*	**JAPAN** 9:41.4	**CANADA** 9:47.8
Austin Clapp	Hiroshi Yoneyama	F. Munro Bourne
Walter Laufer	Nobuo Arai	James Thompson
George Kojac	Tokuhei Sada	Garnet Ault
Johnny Weissmuller	Katsuo Takaishi	Walter Spence
1932 **JAPAN** 8:58.4*	**UNITED STATES** 9:10.5	**HUNGARY** 9:31.4
Yasuji Miyazaki	Frank Booth	András Wannié
Masanori Yusa	George Fissier	László Szabados
Takashi Yokoyama	Marola Kalili	András Székely
Hisakichi Toyoda	Manuella Kalili	István Bárány

---

[1] A New Zealander; the other three members of the team were Australians. The two countries entered a composite team in the Olympic Games until 1920.

GOLD	SILVER	BRONZE
1936 **JAPAN** 8:51.5*	**UNITED STATES** 9:03.0	**HUNGARY** 9:12.3
Masanori Yusa	Ralph Flanagan	Arpád Lengyel
Shigeo Sugiura	John Macionis	Oszkár Abay-Nemes
Masaharu Taguchi	Paul Wolf	Ödön Gróf
Shigeo Arai	Jack Medica	Ferenc Csík
1948 **UNITED STATES** 8:46.0*	**HUNGARY** 8:48.4	**FRANCE** 9:08.0
Walter Ris	Elemér Szathmári	Joseph Bernardo
James McLane	György Mitró	Henri Padou
Wallace Wolf	Imre Nyéki	René Cornu
William Smith	Géza Kádas	Alexandre Jany
1952 **UNITED STATES** 8:31.1*	**JAPAN** 8:33.5	**FRANCE** 8:45.9
Wayne Moore	Hiroshi Suzuki	Joseph Bernardo
William Woolsey	Yoshihiro Hamaguchi	Aldo Eminente
Ford Konno	Toru Goto	Alexandre Jany
James McLane	Teijiro Tanikawa	Jean Boiteaux
1956 **AUSTRALIA** 8:23.6*	**UNITED STATES** 8:31.5	**U.S.S.R.** 8:34.7
Kevin O'Halloran	Richard Hanley	Vitaliy Sorokin
John Devitt	George T. Breen	Vladimir Struschanov
I. Murray Rose	William Woolsey	Gennadiy Nikolayev
Jon Henricks	Ford Konno	Boris Nikitin
1960 **UNITED STATES** 8:10.2*	**JAPAN** 8:13.2	**AUSTRALIA** 8:13.8
George P. Harrison	Makoto Fukui	David G. Dickson
Richard A. Blick	Hiroshi Ishii	John Devitt
Michael F. Troy	Tsuyoshi Yamanaka	I. Murray Rose
F. Jeffrey Farrell	Tatsuo Fujimoto	John Konrads
1964 **UNITED STATES** 7:52.1*	**GERMANY** 7:59.3	**JAPAN** 8:03.8
Stephen Clark	Horst-Günther Gregor	Makoto Fukui
Roy Saari	Gerhard Hetz	Kunihiro Iwasaki
Gary Ilman	Frank Wiegand	Toshio Shoji
Donald A. Schollander	Hans-Joachim Klein	Yukiaki Okabe

The Japanese retained their 4 × 200 meters free-style relay title in world record time at Berlin in 1936. Masanori Yusa (second from right) was on both champion teams.

GOLD	SILVER	BRONZE
1968 **UNITED STATES** 7:52.3	**AUSTRALIA** 7:53.7	**U.S.S.R.** 8:01.6
John M. Nelson	Gregory Rogers	Vladimir Bure
Stephen Rerych	Graham White	Semyon Belitz-Geiman
Mark A. Spitz	Robert Windle	Georgy Kulikov
Donald A. Schollander	Michael V. Wenden	Leonid Ilyichev
1972 **UNITED STATES** 7:35.78*	**WEST GERMANY** 7:41.69	**U.S.S.R.** 7:45.76
John Kinsella	Klaus Steinbach	Igor Grivennilkov
Frederick Tyler	Werner Lampe	Viktor Mazanov
Steven Genter	Hans-Günter Vosseler	Georgy Kulikov
Mark Spitz	Hans-Joachim Fassnacht	Vladimir Bure
1976 **UNITED STATES** 7:23.22*	**U.S.S.R.** 7:27.97	**GREAT BRITAIN** 7:32.11
Michael Bruner	Vladimir Raskatov	Alan McClatchey
Bruce Furniss	Andrei Bogdanov	David Dunne
John Naber	Sergei Kopliakov	Gordon Downie
Jim Montgomery	Andrei Krylov	Brian Brinkley
1980 **U.S.S.R.** 7:23.50	**EAST GERMANY** 7:28.60	**BRAZIL** 7:29.30
Sergei Kopliakov	Frank Pfutze	Jorge Fernades
Vladimir Salnikov	Jorg Woithe	Marcus Mattioli Laborne
Ivar Stukolkin	Detlef Grabs	Cyro Delgado Marques
Andrei Krylov	Rainer Strohbach	Djan Madruga Garrido

The following Olympic records were set in addition to those medal-winning performances already marked with an asterisk*.

11:35.0	Australasia 1908	9:59.4	United States 1924	8:09.0	United States 1964
10.53.4	Great Britain 1908	9:38.8	United States 1928	7:49.03	Australia 1972
10:26.4	United States 1912	8:56.1	Japan 1936	7:46.42	United States 1972
		8:42.1	Japan 1952	7:33.21	U.S.S.R. 1976
10:14.0	Australasia 1912	8:17.1	Japan 1960	7:30.33	United States 1976
		8:09.7	Germany 1964		

SPRINGBOARD DIVING

1896–1906	Event not held		
1908	Albert Zurner (GER) 85.5	Kurt Behrens (GER) 85.3	George Gaidzik (USA) 80.8 Gottlob Walz (GER) 80.8
1912	Paul Günther (GER) 79.23	Hans Luber (GER) 76.78	Kurt Behrens (GER) 73.73
1920	Louis E. Kuehn (USA) 675.4	Clarence Pinkston (USA) 655.3	Louis J. Balbach (USA) 649.5
1924	Albert C. White (USA) 696.4	Peter Desjardins (USA) 693.2	Clarence Pinkston (USA) 653
1928	Peter Desjardins (USA) 185.04	Michael Galitzen (USA) 174.06	Farid Simaika (EGY) 172.46
1932	Michael Galitzen (USA) 161.38	Harold Smith (USA) 158.54	Richard Degener (USA) 151.82
1936	Richard Degener (USA) 163.57	Marshall Wayne (USA) 159.56	Al Greene (USA) 146.29
1948	Bruce Harlan (USA) 163.64	Miller Anderson (USA) 157.29	Samuel Lee (USA) 145.52
1952	David Browning (USA) 205.29	Miller Anderson (USA) 199.84	Robert Clotworthy (USA) 184.92
1956	Robert Clotworthy (USA) 159.56	Donald Harper (USA) 156.23	Joaquín Capilla Pérez (MEX) 150.69
1960	Gary M. Tobian (USA) 170.00	Samuel N. Hall (USA) 167.08	Juan Botella (MEX) 162.30

	GOLD	SILVER	BRONZE
1964	Kenneth Sitzberger (USA) 159.90	Francis Gorman (USA) 157.63	Larry Andreasen (USA) 143.77
1968	Bernard Wrightson (USA) 170.15	Klaus Dibiasi (ITA) 159.74	James Henry (USA) 158.09
1972	Vladimir Vasin (URS) 594.09	Franco Cagnotto (ITA) 591.63	Craig Lincoln (USA) 577.29
1976	Philip Boggs (USA) 619.05	Franco Cagnotto (ITA) 570.48	Aleksandr Kosenkov (URS) 567.24
1980	Aleksandr Portnov (URS) 905.025	Carlos Giron (MEX) 892.140	Franco Cagnotto (ITA) 871.500

PLATFORM DIVING

1896–1904 Event not held

	GOLD	SILVER	BRONZE
1906	Gottlob Walz (GER) 156.00	Georg Hoffman (GER) 150.20	Otto Satzinger (AUT) 147.40
1908	Hjalmar Johansson (SWE) 83.75	Karl Malström (SWE) 78.73	Arvid Spångberg (SWE) 74.00
1912	Erik Adlerz (SWE) 73.94	Albert Zürner (GER) 72.60	Gustaf Blomgren (SWE) 69.56
1920	Clarence Pinkston (USA) 100.67	Erik Adlerz (SWE) 99.08	Haig Prieste (USA) 93.73
1924	Albert C. White (USA) 97.46	David Fall (USA) 97.30	Clarence Pinkston (USA) 94.60
1928	Peter Desjardins (USA) 98.74	Farid Simaika (EGY) 99.58	Michael Galitzen (USA) 92.34
1932	Harold Smith (USA) 124.80	Michael Galitzen (USA) 124.28	Frank Kurtz (USA) 121.98
1936	Marshall Wayne (USA) 113.58	Elbert Root (USA) 110.60	Hermann Stork (GER) 110.31
1948	Samuel Lee (USA) 130.05	Bruce Harlan (USA) 122.30	Joaquin Capilla Pérez (MEX) 113.52
1952	Samuel Lee (USA) 156.28	Joaquin Capilla Pérez (MEX) 145.21	Günther Haase (GER) 141.31
1956	Joaquin Capilla Pérez (MEX) 152.44	Gary M. Tobian (USA) 152.41	Richard Connor (USA) 149.79
1960	Robert D. Webster (USA) 165.56	Gary M. Tobian (USA) 165.25	Brian E. Phelps (GBR) 157.13
1964	Robert D. Webster (USA) 148.58	Klaus Dibiasi (ITA) 147.54	Thomas Gompf (USA) 146.57
1968	Klaus Dibiasi (ITA) 164.18	Alvaro Gaxiola (MEX) 154.49	Edwin Young (USA) 153.93
1972	Klaus Dibiasi (ITA) 504.12	Richard Rydze (USA) 480.75	Franco Cagnotto (ITA) 475.83
1976	Klaus Dibiasi (ITA) 600.51	Gregory Louganis (USA) 576.99	Vladimir Aleynik (URS) 548.61
1980	Falk Hoffmann (GDR) 835.65	Vladimir Aleinik (URS) 819.705	David Ambartsumyan (URS) 817.44

Swimming and Diving (Women)

100 METERS FREE-STYLE (109 yd. 1 ft.)

1896–1908 Event not held

	GOLD	SILVER	BRONZE
1912	Fanny Durack (AUSTRALASIA) 1:22.2	Wilhelmina Wylie (AUSTRALASIA) 1:25.4	Jennie Fletcher (GBR) 1:27.0
1920	Ethelda M. Bleibtrey (USA) 1:13.6*	Irene M. Guest (USA) 1:17.0	Frances C. Schroth (USA) 1:17.2
1924	Ethel Lackie (USA) 1:12.4	Mariechen Wehselau (USA) 1:12.8	Gertrude C. Ederle (USA) 1:14.2

GOLD	SILVER	BRONZE
1928 Albina Osipowich (USA) 1:11.0*	Eleanor A. Gerratti (USA) 1:11.4	M. Joyce Cooper (GBR) 1:13.6
1932 Helene Madison (USA) 1:06.8*	Willemijntje den Ouden (HOL) 1:07.8	Eleanor A. Saville (USA) 1:08.2
1936 Hendrika W. Mastenbroek (HOL) 1:05.9*	Jeanette Campbell (ARG) 1:06.4	Gisela Arendt (GER) 1:06.6
1948 Greta M. Andersen (DEN) 1:06.3	Ann E. Curtis (USA) 1:06.5	Marie-Louise J. Vaessen (HOL) 1:07.6
1952 Katalin Szöke (HUN) 1:06.8	Johanna Termeulen (HOL) 1:07.0	Judit Temes (HUN) 1:07.1
1956 Dawn Fraser (AUS) 1:02.0*	Lorraine J. Crapp (AUS) 1:02.3	Faith Leech (AUS) 1:05.1
1960 Dawn Fraser (AUS) 1:01.2*	S. Christine von Saltza (USA) 1:02.8	Natalie Steward (GBR) 1:03.1
1964 Dawn Fraser (AUS) 59.5*	Sharon Stouder (USA) 59.9	Kathleen Ellis (USA) 1:00.8
1968 Jan M. Henne (USA) 1:00.0	Susan Pedersen (USA) 1:00.3	Linda Gustavson (USA) 1:00.3
1972 Sandra Neilson (USA) 58.59*	Shirley Babashoff (USA) 59.02	Shane E. Gould (AUS) 59.06
1976 Kornelia Ender (GDR) 55.65*	Petra Priemer (GDR) 56.49	Enith Brigitha (HOL) 56.65
1980 Barbara Krause (GDR) 54.78*	Caren Metschuck (GDR) 55.16	Ines Diers (GDR) 55.65

The following Olympic records were set in addition to those medal-winning performances already marked with an asterisk*.

1:29.8	Bella Moore (GBR)	1912	1:08.5	Saville	1932	59.9	Fraser	1964
1:23.6	Daisy Curwen (GBR)	1912	1:07.6	den Ouden	1932	59.5 (.47)	Magdolna Patoh (HUN)	1972
1:19.8	Durack	1912	1:06.4	(twice) Mastenbroek	1936	59.5 (.51)	Neilson	1972
1:18.0	Schroth	1920	1:05.9	Andersen	1948	59.5 (.51)	Babashoff	1972
1:14.4	Bleibtrey	1920	1:05.5	Temes	1952			
1:12.2	Wehselau	1924	1:03.4	Crapp	1956	59.44	Gould	1972
1:12.2	Osipowich	1928	1:02.4	Fraser	1956	59.05	Babashoff	1972
1:11.4	Gerratti	1928	1:01.9	von Saltza	1960	56.95	Priemer	1976
1:09.0	Cooper	1932	1:01.4	Fraser	1960	56.61	Brigitha	1976
1:08.9	Madison	1932	1:00.6	Fraser	1964	55.81	Ender	1976
						54.98	Krause	1980

200 METERS FREE-STYLE (218 yd. 2 ft.)

1896–1964 Event not held

1968 Debbie Meyer (USA) 2:10.5*	Jan M. Henne (USA) 2:11.0	Jane Barkman (USA) 2:11.2
1972 Shane E. Gould (AUS) 2:03.56*	Shirley Babashoff (USA) 2:04.33	Keena Rothhammer (USA) 2:04.92
1976 Kornelia Ender (GDR) 1:59.26*	Shirley Babashoff (USA) 2:01.22	Enith Brigitha (HOL) 2:01.40
1980 Barbara Krause (GDR) 1:58.33*	Ines Diers (GDR) 1:59.64	Carmela Schmidt (GDR) 2:01.44

The following Olympic records were set in addition to those medal-winning performances already marked with an asterisk*.

2:13.1	Meyer	1968	2:07.48	Rothhammer	1972	2:07.05	Andrea Eife (GDR)	1972
2:08.12	Ann Marshall (USA)	1972				2:01.54	Brigitha	1976

The first time women's swimming made the Olympic schedule was in 1912 at Stockholm. This is the final of the 100 meters free-style event.

400 METERS FREE-STYLE (437 yd. 1 ft.)

GOLD	SILVER	BRONZE
1896–1920 Event not held		
1924 Martha Norelius (USA) 6:02.2*	Helen Wainwright (USA) 6:03.8	Gertrude C. Ederle (USA) 6:04.8
1928 Martha Norelius (USA) 5:42.8*	Marie J. Braun (HOL) 5:57.8	Josephine McKim (USA) 6:00.2
1932 Helene Madison (USA) 5:28.5*	Lenore Kight (USA) 5:28.6	Jennie Maakal (SAF) 5:47.3
1936 Hendrika W. Maestenbrock (HOL) 5:26.4*	Ragnhild Hveger (DEN) 5:27.5	Lenore Wingard (USA) 5:29.0
1948 Ann E. Curtis (USA) 5:17.8*	Karen-Margrete Harup (DEN) 5:21.2	Catherine Gibson (GBR) 5:22.5
1952 Valéria Gyenge (HUN) 5:12.1*	Eva Novák (HUN) 5:13.7	Evelyn T. Kawamoto (USA) 5:14.6

At the 1976 Montreal Games, Kornelia Ender (GDR) became one of only 3 women to win 4 Olympic gold medals in swimming.

	GOLD	SILVER	BRONZE
1956	Lorraine J. Crapp (AUS) 4:54.6*	Dawn Fraser (AUS) 5:02.5	Sylvia Ruuska (USA) 5:07.1
1960	S. Christine von Saltza (USA) 4:50.6*	Jane Cederqvist (SWE) 4:53.9	Catharina Lagerberg (HOL) 4:56.9
1964	Virginia Duenkel (USA) 4:43.3*	Marilyn Ramenofsky (USA) 4:44.6	Terri L. Stickles (USA) 4:47.2
1968	Debbie Meyer (USA) 4:31.8*	Linda Gustavson (USA) 4:35.5	Karen L. Moras (AUS) 4:37.0
1972	Shane E. Gould (AUS) 4:19.04*	Novella Calligaris (ITA) 4:22.44	Gudrun Wegner (GDR) 4:23.11
1976	Petra Thuemer (GDR) 4:09.89*	Shirley Babashoff (USA) 4:10.46	Shannon Smith (CAN) 4:14.60
1980	Ines Diers (GDR) 4:08.76*	Petra Schneider (GDR) 4:09.16	Carmela Schmidt (GDR) 4:10.86

The following Olympic records were set in addition to those medal-winning performances already marked with an asterisk*.

6:12.2	Ederle	1924	5:02.5	Fraser	1956	4:27.53	Jenny Wylie	
5:45.4	Norelius	1928	5:00.2	Crapp	1956		(USA)	1972
5:40.9	Kight	1932	4:53.6	von Saltza	1960	4:24.14	Calligaris	1972
5:28.0	Hveger	1936	4:48.6	Duenkel	1964	4:15.71	Rebecca	
5:25.7	Harup	1948	4:47.7	Ramenofsky	1964		Perrott	
5:16.6	Kawamoto	1952	4:35.0	Meyer	1968		(NZL)	1976
5:07.6	Marley L. Shriver (USA)	1956						

800 METERS FREE-STYLE (874 yd. 2 ft.)

1896–1964	Event not held		
1968	Debbie Meyer (USA) 9:24.0*	Pamela Kruse (USA) 9:35.7	Maria T. Ramirez (MEX) 9:38.5
1972	Keena Rothhammer (USA) 8:53.68*	Shane E. Gould (AUS) 8:56.39	Novella Calligaris (ITA) 8:57.46
1976	Petra Thuemer (GDR) 8:37.14*	Shirley Babashoff (USA) 8:37.59	Wendy Weinberg (USA) 8:42.60
1980	Michelle Ford (AUS) 8:28.90*	Ines Diers (GDR) 8:32.55	Heike Dahne (GDR) 8:33.48

The following Olympic records were set in addition to those medal-winning performances already marked with an asterisk*.

9:42.8	Meyer	1968	9:02.96	Calligaris 1972		8:46.81	Nicole Kramer	
9:38.3	Karen L. Moras (AUS)	1968	8:59.69	Rothhammer	1972	8:46.58	(USA) Thuemer	1976 1976

100 METERS BACK STROKE (109 yd. 1 ft.)

1896–1920	Event not held		
1924	Sybil Bauer (USA) 1:23.2*	Phyllis Harding (GBR) 1:27.4	Aileen Riggin (USA) 1:28.2
1928	Marie J. Braun (HOL) 1:22.0	Ellen King (GBR) 1:22.2	M. Joyce Cooper (GBR) 1:22.8
1932	Eleanor Holm (USA) 1:19.4	Philomena Mealing (AUS) 1:21.3	Elizabeth V. Davies (GBR) 1:22.5
1936	Dina W. J. Senff (HOL) 1:18.9	Hendrika W. Maestenbroek (HOL) 1:19.2	Alice Bridges (USA) 1:19.4

Free-styler Ines Diers (GDR) won 2 gold medals, 2 silvers and a bronze in Moscow as the East German women swept 12 of the 15 swimming gold medals and 29 of the 45 total swimming medals available.

Shane Gould (AUS) dominated women's swimming in 1972 with a bronze, a silver and 3 gold medals in the six events she entered.

GOLD	SILVER	BRONZE
1948 Karen M. Harup (DEN) 1:14.4*	Suzanne W. Zimmermann (USA) 1:16.0	Judy-Joy Davies (AUS) 1:16.7
1952 Joan C. Harrison (SAF) 1:14.3	Geertje Wielema (HOL) 1:14.5	Jean Stewart (NZL) 1:15.8
1956 Judith B. Grinham (GBR) 1:12.9*	Carin Cone (USA) 1:12.9*	Margaret Edwards (GBR) 1:13.1
1960 Lynn E. Burke (USA) 1:09.3	Natalie Steward (GBR) 1:10.8	Satoko Tanaka (JPN) 1:11.4
1964 Cathy Ferguson (USA) 1:07.7*	Christine Caron (FRA) 1:07.9	Virginia Duenkel (USA) 1:08.0
1968 Kaye Hall (USA) 1:06.2*	Elaine B. Tanner (CAN) 1:06.7	Jane Swaggerty (USA) 1:08.1
1972 Melissa Belote (USA) 1:05.78*	Andrea Gyarmati (HUN) 1:06.26	Susie Atwood (USA) 1:06.34
1976 Ulrike Richter (GDR) 1:01.83*	Birgit Treiber (GDR) 1:03.41	Nancy Garapick (CAN) 1:03.71
1980 Rica Reinisch (GDR) 1:00.86*	Ina Kleber (GDR) 1:02.07	Petra Reidel (GDR) 1:02.64

The following Olympic records were set in addition to those medal-winning performances already marked with an asterisk*.

1:24.0	Bauer	1924	1:13.0	Edwards	1956	1:07.6	Tanner	1968
1:22.0	King	1928	1:12.0	Laura Ranwell		1:07.4	Tanner	1968
1:21.6	Braun	1928		(SAF)	1960	1:06.08	Belote	1972
1:18.3	Holm	1932	1:09.4	Burke	1960	1:05.00	Tauna	
1:16.6	Senff	1936	1:09.0	Burke			Vandeweghe	
1:15.6	Harup	1948		(relay leg)	1960		(USA)	1976
1:15.5	Harup	1948	1:08.9	Duenkel	1964	1:03.28	Garapick	1976
1:13.8	Wielema	1952	1:08.8	Ferguson	1964	1:02.39	Richter	1976
1:13.1	Grinham	1956	1:08.5	Caron	1964	1:01.50	Reinisch	1980

200 METERS BACK STROKE (218 yd. 2 ft.)

1896–1964 Event not held

1968 Lillian D. Watson (USA) 2:24.8*	Elaine B. Tanner (CAN) 2:27.4	Kaye Hall (USA) 2:28.9
1972 Melissa Belote (USA) 2:19.19*	Susie Atwood (USA) 2:20.38	Donna Marie Gurr (CAN) 2:23.22
1976 Ulrike Richter (GDR) 2:13.43*	Birgit Treiber (GDR) 2:14.97	Nancy Garapick (CAN) 2:15.60
1980 Rica Reinisch (GDR) 2:11.77*	Cornelia Polit (GDR) 2:13.75	Birgit Treiber (GDR) 2:14.14

The following Olympic records were set in addition to those medal-winning performances already marked with an asterisk*.

2:31.1	Hall	1968	2:29.2	Watson	1968	2:20.58	Belote	1972
2:30.9	Tanner	1968	2:22.13	Atwood	1972	2:16.49	Garapick	1976

100 METERS BREAST STROKE (109 yd. 1 ft.)

1896–1964 Event not held

1968 Djurdjica Bjedov (YUG) 1:15.8*	Galina Prozumenshchikova (URS) 1:15.9	Sharon Wichman (USA) 1:16.1
1972 Catherine Carr (USA) 1:13.58*	Galina Stepanova (URS) 1:14.99	Beverley J. Whitfield (AUS) 1:15.73

GOLD	SILVER	BRONZE
1976 Hannelore Anke (GDR) 1:11.16	Lyubov Rusanova (URS) 1:13.04	Marina Koshevaia (URS) 1:13.30
1980 Ute Geweniger (GDR) 1:10.22	Elvira Vasilkova (URS) 1:10.41	Susanne Nielsson (DEN) 1:11.16

The following Olympic records were set in addition to those medal-winning performances already marked with an asterisk*.

1:18.8 Catie Ball (USA) 1968	1:17.4 Ana Maria Norbis (URU) 1968	1:16.7 Norbis 1968
1:17.7 Bjedov 1968	1:16.8 Wichman 1968	1:15.00 Carr 1972
		1:11.11 Anke 1976
		1:10.86 Anke 1976
		1:10.11 Geweniger 1980

200 METERS BREAST STROKE (218 yd. 2 ft.)

1896–1920 Event not held		
1924 Lucy Morton (GBR) 3:33.2	Agnes Geraghty (USA) 3:34.0	Gladys H. Carson (GBR) 3:35.4
1928 Hilde Schrader (GER) 3:12.6	Mietje Baron (HOL) 3:15.2	Lotte Mühe (GER) 3:17.6
1932 Claire Dennis (AUS) 3:06.3*	Hideko Maehata (JPN) 3:06.4	Else Jacobson (DEN) 3:07.1
1936 Hideko Maehata (JPN) 3:03.6	Martha Genenger (GER) 3:04.2	Inge Sörensen (DEN) 3:07.8

LEFT: Ulrike Richter (GDR) won both gold medals in the back stroke at the 1976 Games.

RIGHT: Beverley Whitfield of Australia won the 200 meters breast stroke in record time in 1972.

GOLD	SILVER	BRONZE
1948 Petronella van Vliet (HOL) 2:57.2	Beatrice Lyons (AUS) 2:57.7	Éva Novák (HUN) 2:00.2
1952 Éva Székely (HUN) 2:51.7*†	Éva Novák (HUN) 2:54.4	Helen O. Gordon (GBR) 2:57.6
1956 Ursula Happe (GER) 2:53.1*‡	Éva Székely (HUN) 2:54.8	Éva-Maria ten Elsen (GER) 2:55.1
1960 Anita Lonsbrough (GBR) 2:49.5*	Wiltrud Urselmann (GER) 2:50.0	Barbara Göbel (GER) 2:53.6
1964 Galina Prozumenshchikova (URS) 2:46.4*	Claudia A. Kolb (USA) 2:47.6	Svetlana Babanina (URS) 2:48.6
1968 Sharon Wichman (USA) 2:44.4*	Djurdjica Bjedov (YUG) 2:46.4	Galina Prozumenshchikova (URS) 2:47.0
1972 Beverley J. Whitfield (AUS) 2:41.71*	Dana Schoenfield (USA) 2:42.05	Galina Stepanova (URS) 2:42.36
1976 Marina Koshevaia (URS) 2:33.35*	Marina Iurchenia (URS) 2:36.08	Lyubov Rusanova (URS) 2:36.22
1980 Lina Kachushite (URS) 2:29.54*	Svetlana Varganova (URS) 2:29.61	Yulia Bogdanova (URS) 2:32.39

The following Olympic records were set in addition to those medal-winning performances already marked with an asterisk*.

3:27.6	Geraghty	1924	2:57.4	van Vliet	1948	2:48.3	Babanina	1964
3:11.6	Schrader	1928	2:57.0	van Vliet	1948	2:43.13	Agnes Kissne-	
3:11.2	Schrader	1928	2:54.0	Novák	1952		Kaczander	
3:08.2	Dennis	1932	2:54.0†	Székely	1952		(HUN)	1972
3:03.0	Genenger	1936	2:52.0	Urselmann	1960	2:35.14	Koshevaia	1976
3:01.9	Machata	1936	2:48.6	Bärbel Grimmer		2:29.77	Varganova	1980
3:01.2†	Székely	1948		(GER)	1964			

†Butterfly stroke (then permitted) used.
‡Underwater technique (then permitted) used.

100 METERS BUTTERFLY (109 yd. 1 ft.)

1896–1952 Event not held		
1956 Shelley Mann (USA) 1:11.0	Nancy J. Ramey (USA) 1:11.9	Mary J. Sears (USA) 1:14.4
1960 Carolyn J. Schuler (USA) 1:09.5*	Marianne Heemskerk (HOL) 1:10.4	Janice Andrew (AUS) 1:12.2
1964 Sharon Stouder (USA) 1:04.7*	Aagje Kok (HOL) 1:05.6	Kathleen Ellis (USA) 1:06.0
1968 Lynette McClements (AUS) 1:05.5	Ellie Daniel (USA) 1:05.8	Susan Shields (USA) 1:06.2
1972 Mayumi Aoki (JPN) 1:03.34*	Roswitha Beier (GDR) 1:03.61	Andrea Gyarmati (HUN) 1:03.73
1976 Kornelia Ender (GDR) 1:00.13*	Andrea Pollack (GDR) 1:00.98	Wendy Boglioli (USA) 1:01.17
1980 Caren Metschuk (GDR) 1:00.42	Andrea Pollack (GDR) 1:00.90	Christiane Knacke (GDR) 1:01.44

The following Olympic records were set in addition to those medal-winning performances already marked with an asterisk*.

1:11.2	Mann	1956	1:07.0	Stouder	1964	1:01.84	Boglioli	1976
1:09.8	Schuler	1960	1:05.6	Stouder	1964	1:01.43	Pollack	1976
1:07.8	Ellis	1964	1:04.00	Aoki	1972	1:01.03	Ender	1976
1:07.5	Donna De Varona (USA)	1964	1:03.80	Gyarmati	1972			

Aagje Kok (HOL) won the 200 meters butterfly when it was introduced in the Olympic program in 1968.

200 METERS BUTTERFLY (218 yd. 2 ft.)

	GOLD	SILVER	BRONZE
1896–1964	Event not held		
1968	Aagje Kok (HOL) 2:24.7*	Helga Lindner (GDR) 2:24.8	Ellie Daniel (USA) 2:25.9
1972	Karen Moe (USA) 2:15.57*	Lynn Colella (USA) 2:16.34	Ellie Daniel (USA) 2:16.74
1976	Andrea Pollack (GDR) 2:11.41*	Ulrike Tauber (GDR) 2:12.50	Rosemarie Gabriel (GDR) 2:12.86
1980	Ines Geissler (GDR) 2:10.44*	Sybille Schonrock (GDR) 2:10.45	Michelle Ford (AUS) 2:11.66

The following Olympic records were set in addition to those medal-winning performances already marked with an asterisk *. The butterfly stroke was permissible in the 1948 and 1952 breast stroke competition. The fastest time then recorded was 2:54.0 by Éva Székely in 1952.

2:33.0	Diane Giebel (USA)	1968	2:26.3	Kok	1968	2:14.53	Karen Thornton (USA) 1976
2:29.4	Daniel	1968.	2:18.32	Rosemarie Kother		2:14.39	Tamara Shelofastova
2:29.1	Toni Hewitt (USA)	1968		(GDR)	1972		(URS) 1976
			2:17.18	Daniel	1972	2:11.56	Pollack 1976

400 METERS INDIVIDUAL MEDLEY

	GOLD	SILVER	BRONZE
1896–1960	Event not held		
1964	Donna De Varona (USA) 5:18.7*	Sharon Finneran (USA) 5:24.1	Martha Randall (USA) 5:24.2
1968	Claudia A. Kolb (USA) 5:08.5*	Lynn Vidali (USA) 5:22.2	Sabine Steinbach (GDR) 5:25.3
1972	Gail Neall (AUS) 5:02.97*	Leslie Cliff (CAN) 5:03.57	Novella Calligaris (ITA) 5:03.99
1976	Ulrike Tauber (GDR) 4:42.77*	Cheryl Gibson (CAN) 4:48.10	Becky Smith (CAN) 4:50.48
1980	Petra Schneider (GDR) 4:36.29*	Sharron Davies (GBR) 4:46.83	Agnieszka Czopek (POL) 4:48.17

The following Olympic records were set in addition to those medal-winning performances already marked with an asterisk *.

5:30.6	Anita Lonsbrough (GBR)	1964	5:26.8	Veronika Holletz (GDR)	1964
5:27.8	Randall	1964	5:24.2	De Varona	1964

5:17.2	Kolb	1968
5:06.96	Evelin Stolze (GDR)	1972
4:52.90	Smith	1976
4:51.24	Tauber	1976

4 × 100 METERS FREE-STYLE RELAY

GOLD	SILVER	BRONZE
1896–1908 Event not held		
1912 GREAT BRITAIN 5:52.8*	GERMANY 6:04.6	AUSTRIA 6:17.0
Bella Moore	Wally Dressel	Margarete Adler
Jennie Fletcher	Louise Otto	Klara Milch
Annie Spiers	Hermine Stindt	Josephine Sticker
Irene Steer	Grete Rosenberg	Berta Zahourek
1920 UNITED STATES 5:11.6*	GREAT BRITAIN 5:40.8	SWEDEN 5:43.6
Margaret D. Woodbridge	Hilda James	Aina Berg
Frances C. Schroth	Constance M. Jeans	Emy Machnow
Irene M. Guest	Charlotte Radcliffe	Karin Nilsson
Ethelda M. Bleibtrey	Grace McKenzie	Jane Gylling
1924 UNITED STATES 4:58.8*	GREAT BRITAIN 5:17.0	SWEDEN 5:35.6
Gertrude C. Ederle	Florence Barker	Aina Berg
Euphrasia Donnelly	Grace McKenzie	Vivan Petersson
Ethel Lackie	Iris V. Tanner	Gulli Everlund
Mariechen Wehselau	Constance M. Jeans	Hjördis Töppel
1928 UNITED STATES 4:47.6*	GREAT BRITAIN 5:02.8	SOUTH AFRICA 5:13.4
Adelaide Lambert	M. Joyce Cooper	Katharine Russell
Eleonora Gerratti	Sarah Stewart	Rhoda Rennie
Albina Osipowich	Iris V. Tanner	Marie Bedford
Martha Norelius	Ellen E. King	Frederica J. van der Goes
1932 UNITED STATES 4:38.0*	NETHERLANDS 4:47.5	GREAT BRITAIN 4:52.4
Josephine McKim	Maria Vierdag	Elizabeth V. Davies
Helen Johns	Maria Oversloot	Helen Varcoe
Eleonora Saville	Cornelia Ladde	M. Joyce Cooper
Helene Madison	Willemijntje den Ouden	Edna Hughes
1936 NETHERLANDS 4:36.0*	GERMANY 4:36.8	UNITED STATES 4:40.2
Johanna K. Selbach	Ruth Halbsguth	Katherine L. Rawls
Catherina W. Wagner	Leni M. Lohmar	Bernice R. Lapp
Willemijntje den Ouden	Ingeborg Schmitz	Mavis Freeman
Hendrika W. Mastenbroek	Gisela Arendt	Olive M. McKean
1948 UNITED STATES 4:29.2*	DENMARK 4:29.6	NETHERLANDS 4:31.6
Marie L. Corridon	Eva J. Riise	Irma Schuhmacher
Thelma M. Kalama	Karen M. Harup	Margot Marsman
Brenda M. Helser	Greta M. Andersen	Marie-Louise J. Vaessen
Ann E. Curtis	Fritze W. Carstensen	Johanna M. Termeulen
1952 HUNGARY 4:24.4*	NETHERLANDS 4:29.0	UNITED STATES 4:30.1
Ilona Novák	Marie-Louise Linssen	Jacqueline La Vine
Judit Temes	Koosje van Voorn	Marilee Stepan
Éva Novák	Johanna M. Termeulen	Joan Alderson
Katalin Szöke	Irma Heijting	Evelyn Kawamoto

The United States' swimmer is first in the water as the team sets a world-record pace in picking up the gold medal for the women's 4 × 100 meters relay in 1932.

Shirley Babashoff (USA) holds a total of 8 Olympic medals, including 2 golds in the 4 × 100 meters free-style relay events in 1972 and 1976 and 6 silvers in team and individual competition.

GOLD	SILVER	BRONZE
1956 **AUSTRALIA** 4:17.1*	**UNITED STATES** 4:19.2	**SOUTH AFRICA** 4:25.7
Dawn Fraser	Sylvia Ruuska	Jeanette Myburgh
Faith Leech	Shelley Mann	Susan Roberts
Sandra Morgan	Nancy Simons	Natalie Myburgh
Lorraine J. Crapp	Joan Rosazza	Moira Abernethy
1960 **UNITED STATES** 4:08.9*	**AUSTRALIA** 4:11.3	**GERMANY** 4:19.7
Joan A. Spillane	Dawn Fraser	Christel Steffin
Shirley A. Stobs	Ilsa Konrads	Heidi Pechstein
Carolyn V. Wood	Lorraine J. Crapp	Gisela Weiss
S. Christine von Saltza	Alva Colquhoun	Ursula Brunner
1964 **UNITED STATES** 4:03.8*	**AUSTRALIA** 4:06.9	**NETHERLANDS** 4:12.0
Sharon Stouder	Robyn Thorn	Paulina van der Wildt
Donna De Varona	Janice Murphy	Catharina Beumer
Lillian Watson	Lynette Bell	Winnie Van Weerdenburg
Kathleen Ellis	Dawn Fraser	Erica Terpstra
1968 **UNITED STATES** 4:02.5*	**EAST GERMANY** 4:05.7	**CANADA** 4:07.2
Jane Barkman	Gabriele Wetzko	Angela Coughlan
Linda Gustavson	Roswitha Krause	Marilyn Corson
Susan Pedersen	Uta Schmuck	Elaine B. Tanner
Jan M. Henne	Martina Grunert	Marion Lay
1972 **UNITED STATES** 3:55.19*	**EAST GERMANY** 3:55.55	**WEST GERMANY** 3:57.93
Sandra Neilson	Gabriele Wetzko	Jutta Weber
Jennifer Kemp	Andrea Eife	Heidemarie Reineck
Jane Barkman	Elke Sehmisch	Gudrun Beckmann
Shirley Babashoff	Kornelia Ender	Angela Steinbach
1976 **UNITED STATES** 3:44.82*	**EAST GERMANY** 3:45.50	**CANADA** 3:48.81
Kim Peyton	Kornelia Ender	Gail Amundrud
Wendy Boglioli	Petra Priemer	Barbara Clark
Jill Sterkel	Andrea Pollack	Becky Smith
Shirley Babashoff	Claudia Hempel	Anne Jardin
1980 **EAST GERMANY** 3:42.71*	**SWEDEN** 3:48.93	**NETHERLANDS** 3:49.51
Barbara Krause	Carina Ljungdahl	Conny van Bentum
Caren Metschuck	Tina Gustafsson	Wilma van Velsen
Ines Diers	Agneta Martensson	Reggie de Jong
Sarina Hulsenbeck	Agneta Eriksson	Annelies Maas

The following Olympic records were set in addition to those medal-winning performances already marked with an asterisk *.

4:55.6	United States 1928	4:28.1	United States 1952	3:50.27	United States 1976
4:33.5	Denmark 1948	3:58.11	East Germany 1972	3:48.95	East Germany 1976
4:31.3	Netherlands 1948				

4 × 100 METERS MEDLEY RELAY

(Order of strokes: back stroke, breast stroke, butterfly, free-style.)

	GOLD	SILVER	BRONZE

1896–1956 Event not held

1960 UNITED STATES 4:41.1*   **AUSTRALIA** 4:45.9   **GERMANY** 4:47.6

Lynn E. Burke	Marilyn Wilson	Ingrid Schmidt
Patty Kempner	Rosemarie Lassig	Ursula Küper
Carolyn J. Schuler	Janice Andrew	Bärbel Fuhrmann
S. Christine von Saltza	Dawn Fraser	Ursula Brunner

1964 UNITED STATES 4:33.9*   **NETHERLANDS** 4:37.0   U.S.S.R. 4:39.2

Cathy Ferguson	Kornelia Winkel	Tatyana Savelieva
Cynthia Goyette	Klena Bimolt	Svetlana Babanina
Sharon Stouder	Aagje Kok	Tatyana Deviatova
Kathleen Ellis	Erica Terpstra	Natalya Ustinova

1968 UNITED STATES 4:28.3*   **AUSTRALIA** 4:30.0   **WEST GERMANY** 4:36.4

Kaye Hall	Lynette P. Watson	Angelika Kraus
Catie Ball	Lynette McClements	Uta Frommater
Ellie Daniel	Judy Playfair	Heike Hustede
Susan Pedersen	Janet Steinbeck	Heidi Reineck

1972 UNITED STATES 4:20.75*   **EAST GERMANY** 4:24.91   **WEST GERMANY** 4:26.46

Melissa Belote	Christine Herbst	Silke Pielen
Catherine Carr	Renate Vogel	Verena Eberle
Deena Deardurff	Roswitta Beier	Gudrun Beckmann
Sandra Neilsen	Kornelia Ender	Heidi Reineck

1976 EAST GERMANY 4:07.95*   **UNITED STATES** 4:14.55   **CANADA** 4:15.22

Ulrike Richter	Linda Jeszek	Wendy Hogg
Hannelore Anke	Lauri Siering	Robin Corsiglia
Andrea Pollack	Camille Wright	Susan Sloan
Kornelia Ender	Shirley Babashoff	Anne Jardin

1980 EAST GERMANY 4:06.67*   **GREAT BRITAIN** 4:12.24   U.S.S.R. 4:13.61

Rica Reinisch	Helen Jameson	Yelena Kruglova
Ute Geweniger	Margaret Kelly	Elvira Vasilkova
Andrea Pollack	Ann Osgerby	Alla Grishchenkova
Caren Metschuck	June Croft	Natalya Strunnikova

The following Olympic records were set in addition to those medal-winning performances already marked with an asterisk *.

4:49.0	Gt. Britain 1960	4:27.58	East Germany 1972	4:20.10	Canada 1976
4:47.7	Holland 1960			4:13.98	East Germany 1976
4:39.1	U.S.S.R. 1964	4:27.57	United States 1972		

SPRINGBOARD DIVING

1896–1912 Event not held

	GOLD	SILVER	BRONZE
1920	Aileen M. Riggin (USA) 539.9	Helen E. Wainwright (USA) 534.8	Thelma R. Payne (USA) 534.1
1924	Elizabeth Becker (USA) 474.5	Aileen M. Riggin (USA) 460.4	Caroline Fletcher (USA) 434.4
1928	Helen Meany (USA) 78.62	Dorothy Poynton (USA) 75.62	Georgia Coleman (USA) 73.38
1932	Georgia Coleman (USA) 87.52	Katherine Rawls (USA) 82.56	Jane Fauntz (USA) 82.12
1936	Marjorie Gestring (USA) 89.27	Katherine Rawls (USA) 88.35	Dorothy Hill (USA) 82.36
1948	Victoria Draves (USA) 108.74	Zoe Ann Olsen (USA) 108.23	Patricia Elsener (USA) 101.30

Milena Duchkova, the little Czech highboard diver, won her gold medal in 1968 with remarkable ease and with the full sympathy of the crowd in view of the then recent invasion of her country by the U.S.S.R.

Jennifer Chandler's gold medal in the 1976 springboard diving event gave the title to the U.S.A. for the eleventh time.

	GOLD	SILVER	BRONZE
1952	Patricia McCormick (USA) 147.30	Madeleine Moreau (FRA) 139.34	Zoe Ann Jensen (USA) 127.57
1956	Patricia McCormick (USA) 142.36	Jeanne Stunyo (USA) 125.89	Irene Macdonald (CAN) 121.40
1960	Ingrid Krämer (GER) 155.81	Paula J. Pope (USA) 141.24	Elizabeth Ferris (GBR) 139.09
1964	Ingrid Engel (GER) 145.00	Jeanne Collier (USA) 138.36	Mary Willard (USA) 138.18
1968	Sue Gossick (USA) 150.77	Tamara Pogozheva (URS) 145.30	Keala O'Sullivan (USA) 145.23
1972	Micki J. King (USA) 450.03	Ulrika Knape (SWE) 434.19	Marina Janicke (GDR) 430.92
1976	Jennifer Chandler (USA) 506.19	Christa Kohler (GDR) 469.41	Cynthia McIngvale (USA) 466.83
1980	Irina Kalinina (URS) 725.910	Martina Proeber (GDR) 698.895	Karin Guthke (GDR) 685.245

PLATFORM DIVING

	GOLD	SILVER	BRONZE
1896–1908	Event not held		
1912	Greta Johansson (SWE) 39.9	Lisa Regnell (SWE) 36.0	Isabelle White (GBR) 34.0
1920	Stefani Fryland-Clausen (DEN) 34.6	Eileen Armstrong (GBR) 33.3	Eva Ollivier (SWE) 33.3
1924	Caroline Smith (USA) 10.5	Elizabeth Becker (USA) 11.0	Hjördis Töpel (SWE) 15.5
1928	Elizabeth Pinkston (USA) 31.6	Georgia Coleman (USA) 30.6	Lala Sjöqvist (SWE) 29.2
1932	Dorothy Poynton (USA) 40.26	Georgia Coleman (USA) 35.56	Marion Roper (USA) 35.22
1936	Dorothy Hill (USA) 33.93	Velma Dunn (USA) 33.63	Käthe Köhler (GER) 33.43
1948	Victoria Draves (USA) 68.87	Patricia Elsener (USA) 66.28	Birte Christoffersen (DEN) 66.04
1952	Patricia McCormick (USA) 79.37	Paula J. Myers (USA) 71.63	Juno Irwin (USA) 70.49
1956	Patricia McCormick (USA) 84.85	Juno Irwin (USA) 81.64	Paula J. Myers (USA) 81.58
1960	Ingrid Krämer (GER) 91.28	Paula J. Pope (USA) 88.94	Ninel Krutova (URS) 86.99
1964	Lesley Bush (USA) 99.80	Ingrid Engel (GER) 98.45	Galina Alekseyeva (URS) 97.60
1968	Milena Duchková (TCH) 109.59	Natalia Lobanova (URS) 105.14	Ann Peterson (USA) 101.11
1972	Ulrika Knape (SWE) 390.00	Milena Duchková (TCH) 370.92	Marina Janicke (GDR) 360.54
1976	Elena Vaytsekhovskaya (URS) 406.59	Ulrika Knape (SWE) 402.60	Deborah Wilson (USA) 401.07
1980	Martina Jaschke (GDR) 596.250	Servard Emirzyan (URS) 576.465	Liana Tsotadze (URS) 575.925

The following married medalists also won medals under their maiden names:

Eleanor Saville, formerly Gerratti

Lenore Wingard, formerly Kight

Marie-Louise Linssen, formerly Vaessen

Irma Heijting, formerly Schuhmacher

Paula Pope, formerly Myers

Dorothy Hill, formerly Poynton

Elizabeth Pinkston, formerly Becker

Zoe Ann Jensen, formerly Olsen

Ingrid Engel, formerly Krämer

Water Polo

Water Polo tournaments were held in 1900 and 1904 but entries were Clubs rather than International teams.

	GOLD	SILVER	BRONZE
1908	**GREAT BRITAIN** Charles S. Smith George Nevinson George Cornet Thomas Thould George Wilkinson Paul Radmilovic Charles G. E. Forsyth	**BELGIUM** Albert Michant Herman Meyboom Victor Boin Joseph Pletincx Fernand Feyaerts Oscar Grégoire Herman Donners	**SWEDEN** Thorsten Kumfeldt Axel Runström Harald Julin Pontus Hansson Gunnar Wennerström Robert Andersson Erik Bergvall
1912	**GREAT BRITAIN** Charles S. Smith George Cornet Charles Bugbee Arthur Hill George Wilkinson Paul Radmilovic Isaac Bentham	**SWEDEN** Thorsten Kumfeldt Harald Julin Max Gumpel Pontus Andersson Wilhelm Andersson Robert Andersson Eric Bergqvist	**BELGIUM** Albert Durant Herman Donners Victor Boin Joseph Pletincx Oscar Grégoire Herman Meyboom Félicien Courbet Jean Hoffman Pierre Nijs
1920	**GREAT BRITAIN** Charles S. Smith Paul Radmilovic Charles Bugbee Noel M. Purcell Christopher Jones William Peacock William H. Dean	**BELGIUM** Gérard Blitz Maurice Blitz Albert Durant Joseph Pletincx Paul Gailly Pierre Nijs René Bauwens Pierre Dewin	**SWEDEN** Harald Julin Robert Andersson Wilhelm Andersson Eric Bergqvist Max Gumpel Pontus Hansson Erik Andersson Nils Backlund Theodor Nauman
1924	**FRANCE** Paul Dujardin Henri Padou Georges Rigal Albert Deborgies Nöel Delberghe Robert Desmettre Albert Mayraud	**BELGIUM** Gérard Blitz Maurice Blitz Albert Durant Joseph Pletincx Joseph Cludts Joseph de Combe Pierre Dewin Georges Fleurix Paul Gailly Jules Thiry Pierre Vermetten	**UNITED STATES** Arthur Austin Oliver Horn Frederick Lauer Clarence Mitchell John Norton Wallace O'Connor George Schroth Herbert Vollmer Johnny Weissmuller
1928	**GERMANY** Erich Rademacher Fritz Gunst Otto Cordes Emil Benecke Joachim Rademacher Karl Bähre Max Amann Johann Blank	**HUNGARY** István Barta Sándor Ivády Márton Hommonay Alajos Keserü Olivér Halasy József Vértesy Ferenc Keserü	**FRANCE** Paul Dujardin Henri Padou Jules Keignaert Emile Bulteel Achille Tribouillet Henri Cuvelier Ernest Rogez Albert van de Plancke Albert Thévenon

GOLD	SILVER	BRONZE
1932 HUNGARY György Bródy Sándor Ivády Márton Hommonay Olivér Halasy József Vértesy János Németh Ferenc Keserü Alajos Keserü István Barta Miklós Sárkány	**GERMANY** Erich Rademacher Fritz Gunst Otto Cordes Emil Benecke Joachim Rademacher Heiko Schwartz Hans Schulze Hans Eckstein	**UNITED STATES** Herbert Wildman Wallace O'Connor Calvert Strong Philip Daubenspeck Harold McCallister Charles Finn Austin Clapp
1936 HUNGARY György Bródy Kálmán Hazai Márton Hommonay Olivér Halasy Jenö Brandi János Németh György Kutasi Mihály Bozsi István Molnár Sándor Tarics Miklós Sárkány	**GERMANY** Paul Klingenburg Bernhard Baier Gustav Schürger Fritz Gunst Josef Hauser Hans Schneider Hans Schulze Alfred Kienzle Heinrich Krug Helmuth Schwenn Fritz Stolze	**BELGIUM** Albert Castelens Gérard Blitz Pierre Coppieters Fernand Isselé Joseph de Combe Henry Stoelen Henry Disy Henri de Pauw Edmond Michiels
1948 ITALY Pasquale Buonocore Emilio Bulgarelli Cesare Rubini Geminio Ognio Ermenegildo Arena Aldo Ghira Tulio Pandolfini Mario Majoni Gianfranco Pandolfini	**HUNGARY** László Jenei Miklós Holop Dezsö Gyarmati Károly Szittya Oszkár Csuvik István Szivós Dezsö Lemhényi Jenö Brandi Dezsö Fábián Endre Györfi	**NETHERLANDS** Johannes J. Rohner Cornelius Korevaar Cor Braasem Hans Stam Alfred F. Ruimschotel Rudolph van Feggelen Frits Smol Hendrikus Z. Keetelaar Pieter J. Salomons
1952 HUNGARY László Jenei György Vizvári Dezsö Gyarmati Kálmán Markovits Antal Bolvári István Szivós György Kárpáti Róbert Antal Dezsö Fábián Károly Szittya Dezsö Lemhényi Miklós Martin István Hosznos	**YUGOSLAVIA** Zdravko Kovačić Veljiko Bakašun Ivo Stakula Ivo Kurtini Boško Vuksanović Zdravko Ježić Lovro Radonić Vlado Ivković Marko Brainović	**ITALY** Raffaello Gambino Cesare Rubini Maurizio Mannelli Geminio Ognio Ermenegildo Arena Renato de Sanzuane Carlo Peretti Renato Traiola Vincenzo Polito Salvatore Gionta
1956 HUNGARY Ottó Boros Dezsö Gyarmati Kálmán Markovits István Hevesi György Kárpáti Mihály Mayer Antal Bolvári László Jenei Tivadar Kanisza István Szivós Ervin Zádor	**YUGOSLAVIA** Zdravko Kovačić Hrvoje Kačić Marijan Žužej Ivo Cipci Tomislav Franjković Lovro Radonić Zdravko Ježić Vlado Ivković	**U.S.S.R.** Boris Goikhman Vyacheslav Kurrenoy Yuriy Schlyapin Valentin Prokopov Boris Markarov Petr Mchvenieradze Petr Breus Mikkhail Ryzhak Viktor Ageyev Nodar Gvakharia

This was one of the eight goals scored in a 1932 match between Germany and the U.S.A., the eventual silver and bronze medalists. The game ended in a tie.

1960	ITALY	U.S.S.R.	HUNGARY
	Danio Bardi	Vladimir Semyenov	Ottó Boros
	Giuseppe d'Altrui	Anatoliy Kartashyov	István Hevesi
	Franco Lavoratori	Vladimir Novikov	Mihály Mayer
	Gianni Lonzi	Petr Mchvenieradze	Kálmán Markovits
	Rosario Parmegiani	Yuriy Grigorovskiy	Tivadar Kanizsa
	Eraldo Pizzo	Viktor Ageyev	Zoltán Dömötör
	Dante Rossi	Givi Chikvanaya	György Kárpáti
	Amadeo Ambron	Leri Gogoladze	László Jenei
	Salvatore Gionta	Vyacheslav Kurrenoy	Péter Rusorán II
	Luigi Mannelli	Boris Goikhman	András Katona
	Brunello Spinelli	Evgeniy Saltsyn	Dezsö Gyarmati
	Giancario Guerrini		László Felkai
			János Konrád
			András Bodnár

Györgi Kárpáti (right) and Dezsö Gyarmati (left) played together on Hungary's Olympic gold medal teams in 1952, 1956 and 1964. They also won the bronze medal in 1960.

	GOLD	SILVER	BRONZE
1964	**HUNGARY**	**YUGOSLAVIA**	**U.S.S.R.**
	Miklós Ambrus	Milan Muškatirović	Igor Grabovsky
	László Felkai	Ivo Trumbić	Vladimir Kuznetsov
	János Konrád	Vinco Rosić	Boris Grishin
	Zoltán Dömötör	Slatco Šimenć	Boris Popov
	Tivadar Kanizsa	Božidor Stanišić	Nikolay Kalashnikov
	Péter Rusorán II	Ante Nardeli	Zenon Bortevich
	György Kárpáti	Zoran Janković	Nicolay Kuznetsov
	Dezső Gyarmati	Frane Nonković	Vladimir Semyenov
	Dénes Pócsik	Karlo Stipanić	Viktor Ageyev
	Mihály Mayer	Mirko Sandič	Leonid Ossipov
	András Bodnár	Ozren Bonačic	Eduard Yegorov
	Ottó Boros		
1968	**YUGOSLAVIA**	**U.S.S.R.**	**HUNGARY**
	Karlo Stipanić	Vadim Gulyaev	Endre Molnár
	Ivo Trumbić	Givi Chikvanaya	Mihály Mayer
	Ozren Bonačić	Boris Grishin	István Szivós
	Uroš Marović	Alexandr Dolgushin	János Konrád II
	Ronald Lopatny	Alexei Barkalov	László Sárosi
	Zoran Janković	Yuriy Grigorovskiy	László Felkai
	Miroslav Poljak	Vladimir Semyenov	Ferenc Konrád III
	Dejan Dabović	Alexandr Shidlovski	Dénes Pócsik
	Djordje Perišić	Vjacheslav Skok	András Bodnár
	Mirko Sandič	Leonid Ossipov	Zoltán Dömötör
	Zdravko Hebel	Oleg Bovin	János Steinmetz
1972	**U.S.S.R.**	**HUNGARY**	**UNITED STATES**
	Vadim Gulyaev	Endre Molnár	James Slatton
	Anatoli Akimov	András Bodnár	Stanley Cole
	Alexandr Dreval	István Goergenyi	Russell Webb
	Alexandr Dolgushin	Zoltàn Kasas	Barry Weitzenberger
	Vladimir Shmudski	Tamás Fárágo	Gary Sheerer
	Alexandr Kabanov	László Sárosi	Bruce Bradley
	Alexei Barkalov	István Szivós	Peter Asch
	Alexandr Shidlovski	István Magas	James Ferguson
	Nikolai Melnikov	Dénes Pócsik	Steven Barnett
	Leonid Ossipov	Ferenc Konrád	John Parker
	Vyacheslav Sobchenko	Tibor Czervenyak	Eric Lindroth
1976	**HUNGARY**	**ITALY**	**HOLLAND**
	Endre Molnár	Alberto Alberani	Evert Kroon
	István Szivós	Roldano Simeoni	Nico Landeweerd
	Tamás Fárágo	Silvio Baracchini	Jan Evert Veer
	Laszló Sárosi	Sante Marsili	Hans van Zeeland
	Gyorgy Horkai	Marcello del Duca	Ton Buunk
	Gábor Csapó	Gianni de Magistris	Piet de Zwarte
	Attila Sudár	Alessandro Ghibellini	Hans Smit
	Gyorgy Kenéz	Luigi Castagnola	Rik Toonen
	Gyorgy Gerendás	Riccardo de Magistris	Gyze Stroboer
	Ferenc Konrád	Vincenzo d'Angelo	Andy Hoepelman
	Tibor Czervenyák	Umberto Panerai	Alex Boegschoten
1980	**U.S.S.R.**	**YUGOSLAVIA**	**HUNGARY**
	Yevgeniy Sharanov	Luka Vezilic	Endre Molnár
	Sergey Kotenko	Zoran Gopcevic	István Szivós Jr
	Vladimir Akimov	Damir Polić	Attila Sudár
	Yevgeniy Grischin	Ratko Rudić	Gyorgy Gerendás
	Mait Riisman	Zoran Mustur	Gyorgy Horkai
	Aleksandr Kabanov	Zoran Roje	Gábor Csapó
	Aleksey Barkalov	Milivoj Bebic	István Kiss
	Erkin Shagayev	Slobodan Trifunovic	István Udvardi
	Georgy Mshvenieradze	Bosko Lozica	László Kuncz
	Mikhail Ivanov	Predrag Manojlović	Tamás Fárágó
	Vyacheslav Sobchenko	Milorad Krivokapic	Károly Hauszler

17. Track and Field Athletics (Men)

100 METERS (109 yd. 1 ft.)

GOLD	SILVER	BRONZE
1896 Thomas E. Burke (USA) 12.0	Fritz Hofmann (GER) d.n.a.	Alajos Szokolyi (HUN) d.n.a.
1900 Francis W. Jarvis (USA) 11.0	J. Walter B. Tewksbury (USA) 1 ft.	Stanley Rowley (AUS/NZL) inches
1904 Archie Hahn (USA) 11.0	Nathaniel J. Cartmell (USA) d.n.a.	William Hogenson (USA) d.n.a.
1906 Archie Hahn (USA) 11.2	Fay R. Moulton (USA) 11.3	Nigel Barker (AUS) 11.3
1908 Reginald E. Walker (SAF) 10.8*	James A. Rector (USA) 2 ft.	Robert Kerr (CAN) inches
1912 Ralph C. Craig (USA) 10.8	Alvah Meyer (USA) 10.9	Donald F. Lippincott (USA) 10.9
1920 Charles W. Paddock (USA) 10.8	Morris M. Kirksey (USA) 1 ft.	Harry F. V. Edward (GBR) d.n.a.
1924 Harold M. Abrahams (GBR) 10.6*	Jackson V. Scholz (USA) 2 ft.	Arthur E. Porritt (NZL) d.n.a.
1928 Percy Williams (CAN) 10.8	Jack E. London (GBR) 2 ft.	Georg Lammers (GER) inches
1932 Eddie Tolan (USA) 10.3*	Ralph H. Metcalfe (USA) 10.3*	Arthur Jonath (GER) 10.4
1936 Jesse Owens (USA) 10.3	Ralph H. Metcalfe (USA) 10.4	Martinus B. Osendarp (HOL) 10.5
1948 W. Harrison Dillard (USA) 10.3	H. Norwood Ewell (USA) 10.4	Lloyd B. LaBeach (PAN) 10.4
1952 Lindy J. Remigino (USA) 10.4	Herbert H. McKenley (JAM) 10.4	Emmanuel McDonald Bailey (GBR) 10.4
1956 Bobby-Joe Morrow (USA) 10.5	W. Thane Baker (USA) 10.5	Hector D. Hogan (AUS) 10.6
1960 Armin Hary (GER) 10.2*	David W. Sime (USA) 10.2*	Peter F. Radford (GBR) 10.3
1964 Robert L. Hayes (USA) 10.0*	Enrique Figuerola (CUB) 10.2	Harry W. Jerome (CAN) 10.2
1968 James R. Hines (USA) 9.9*	Lennox Miller (JAM) 10.0	Charles E. Greene (USA) 10.0
1972 Valeriy Borzov (URS) 10.14	Robert Taylor (USA) 10.24	Lennox Miller (JAM) 10.33
1976 Hasely Crawford (TRI) 10.06	Donald Quarrie (JAM) 10.08	Valeriy Borzov (URS) 10.14
1980 Allan Wells (GBR) 10.25	Silvio Leonard (CUB) 10.25	Petar Petrov (BUL) 10.39

The performances listed below were Olympic Records set additionally in preliminaries.

11.8	Burke	1896	10.6	Williams	1928	10.3	Ira J. Murchison	
10.8	Jarvis	1900	10.6	Robert			(USA)	1956
10.8	Tewksbury	1900		MacAllister		10.3	Morrow	1956
10.8	Rector	1908		(USA)	1928	10.2	Hary	1960
10.8	Walker	1908	10.6	London	1928	10.0	Greene	1968
10.8	Rector	1908	10.4	Tolan	1932		Hermes Ramirez	
10.6	Lippincott	1912	10.3	Owens	1936		(CUB)	1968
10.6	(twice)		10.3	Morrow	1956	10.0	Greene	1968
	Abrahams	1924				10.0	Hines	1968

Performances of 10.2 and 10.3 (final) by Owens in 1936 and 9.9 by Hayes in 1964 were wind assisted.

Jim Hines (USA) won the 1968 Olympic 100 meters in the world record time of 9.9 seconds. High altitude helped sprinters because of reduced air resistance.

Jesse Owens (USA) captured public attention by winning 4 gold medals in the 1936 Games at Berlin. Owens was the top vote-getter in an election held to select 20 charter members of the U.S. Olympic Hall of Fame.

Donald Quarrie of Jamaica, the gold medal winner at 200 meters at the 1976 Games, is shown here easily winning a preliminary heat.

200 METERS (218 yd. 2 ft.)

	GOLD	SILVER	BRONZE
1896	Event not held		
1900	J. Walter B. Tewksbury (USA) 22.2*	Norman G. Pritchard (IND) 5 yd.	Stanley Rowley (AUS/NZL) 1 yd.
1904	Archie Hahn (USA) 21.6*[1]	Nathaniel J. Cartmell (USA) 2 yd.	William Hogenson (USA) d.n.a.
1906	Event not held		
1908	Robert Kerr (CAN) 22.6	Robert Cloughen (USA) 1 ft.	Nathaniel J. Cartmell (USA) 1 ft.
1912	Ralph C. Craig (USA) 21.7	Donald F. Lippincott (USA) 21.8	William R. Applegarth (GBR) 22.0
1920	Allen Woodring (USA) 22.0	Charles W. Paddock (USA) d.n.a.	Harry F. V. Edward (GBR) d.n.a.
1924	Jackson V. Scholz (USA) 21.6*	Charles W. Paddock (USA) ½ yd.	Eric H. Liddell (GBR) 1½ yd.
1928	Percy Williams (CAN) 21.8	Walter Rangeley (GBR) 2 ft.	Helmut Körnig[2] (GER) 1 ft.
1932	Eddie Tolan (USA) 21.2*	George Simpson (USA) 21.4	Ralph H. Metcalfe[3] (USA) 21.5
1936	Jesse Owens (USA) 20.7*	Mack M. Robinson (USA) 21.1	Martinus B. Osendarp (HOL) 21.3
1948	Melvin E. Patton (USA) 21.1	H. Norwood Ewell (USA) 21.1	Lloyd B. LaBeach (PAN) 21.2
1952	Andrew W. Stanfield (USA) 20.7*	W. Thane Baker (USA) 20.8	James Gathers (USA) 20.8
1956	Bobby-Joe Morrow (USA) 20.6*	Andrew W. Stanfield (USA) 20.7	W. Thane Baker (USA) 20.9
1960	Livio Berutti (ITA) 20.5*	Lester N. Carney (USA) 20.6	Abdoulaye Seye (FRA) 20.7

[1] Race run over straight course.
[2] Awarded bronze medal when Scholz refused to re-run after third place tie.
[3] Metcalfe's lane was later found to be 1½ meters too long.

	GOLD	SILVER	BRONZE
1964	Henry Carr (USA) 20.3*	O. Paul Drayton (USA) 20.5	Edwin Roberts (TRI) 20.6
1968	Tommie C. Smith (USA) 19.8*	Peter G. Norman (AUS) 20.0	John W. Carlos (USA) 20.0
1972	Valeriy Borzov (URS) 20.00	Larry J. Black (USA) 20.19	Pietro Mennea (ITA) 20.30
1976	Donald Quarrie (JAM) 20.23	Millard Hampton (USA) 20.29	Dwayne Evans (USA) 20.43
1980	Pietro Mennea (ITA) 20.19	Allan Wells (GBR) 20.21	Donald Quarrie (JAM) 20.29

The performances listed below were Olympic Records set additionally in preliminaries.

22.2	Hahn	1904	21.4	Arthur Jonath (GER)	1932	20.3	Smith	1968
21.6	Körnig	1928				20.2	Norman	1968
21.5	Metcalfe	1932	21.1	(twice) Owens	1936	20.2	Smith	1968
21.5	Tolan	1932	21.1	Robinson	1936	20.1	Carlos	1968
21.4	Carlos B. Luti (ARG)	1932	20.5	Berutti	1960	20.1	Smith	1968
			20.5	Drayton	1964			

400 METERS (437 yd. 1 ft.)

	GOLD	SILVER	BRONZE
1896	Thomas E. Burke (USA) 54.2*	Herbert Jamison (USA) 15 yd.	Fritz Hofmann (GER) d.n.a.
1900	Maxwell W. Long (USA) 49.4*	William J. Holland (USA) 1 yd.	Ernst Schultz (DEN) 15 yd.
1904	Harry L. Hillman (USA) 49.2*	Frank Waller (USA) 5 yd.	Herman C. Groman (USA) 1 yd.
1906	Paul H. Pilgrim (USA) 53.2	Wyndham Halswell (GBR) 53.8	Nigel Barker (AUS) 54.1
1908	Wyndham Halswell (GBR) 50.0	No other competitors[1]	
1912	Charles D. Reidpath (USA) 48.2*	Hanns Braun (GER) 48.3	Edward F. Lindberg (USA) 48.4
1920	Bevil G. d'U. Rudd (SAF) 49.6	Guy M. Butler (GBR) d.n.a.	Nils Engdahl (SWE) d.n.a.
1924	Eric H. Liddell (GBR) 47.6*	Horatio M. Fitch (USA) 48.4	Guy M. Butler (GBR) 48.6
1928	Raymond J. Barbuti (USA) 47.8	James Ball (CAN) 48.0	Joachim Büchner (GER) 48.2
1932	William A. Carr (USA) 46.2*	Benjamin B. Eastman (USA) 46.4	Alexander Wilson (CAN) 47.4
1936	Archie F. Williams (USA) 46.5	A. Godfrey K. Brown (GBR) 46.7	James E. LuValle (USA) 46.8
1948	Arthur S. Wint (JAM) 46.2*	Herbert H. McKenley (JAM) 46.4	Malvin G. Whitfield (USA) 46.6
1952	V. George Rhoden (JAM) 45.9*	Herbert H. McKenley (JAM) 45.9*	Ollie A. Matson (USA) 46.8
1956	Charles L. Jenkins (USA) 46.7	Karl-Friedrich Haas (GER) 46.8	Voitto V. Hellsten (FIN) 47.0 Ardalion V. Ignatyev (URS) 47.0
1960	Otis C. Davis (USA) 44.9*	Carl Kaufmann (GER) 44.9*	Malcolm C. Spence (SAF) 45.5
1964	Michael D. Larrabee (USA) 45.1	Wendell A. Mottley (TRI) 45.2	Andrzej Badenski (POL) 45.6
1968	Lee E. Evans (USA) 43.8*	G. Lawrence James (USA) 43.9	Ronald J. Freeman (USA) 44.4

---

[1] Re-run ordered after J. C. Carpenter (USA) disqualified in original final. Only Halswell showed up and "walked over" for the title.

	GOLD	SILVER	BRONZE
1972	Vincent E. Matthews (USA) 44.66	Wayne C. Collett (USA) 44.80	Julius Sang (KEN) 44.92
1976	Alberto Juantorena (CUB) 44.26	Fred Newhouse (USA) 44.40	Herman Frazier (USA) 44.95
1980	Viktor Markin (URS) 44.60	Richard Mitchell (AUS) 44.84	Frank Schaffer (GDR) 44.87

The performances listed below were Olympic Records set additionally in preliminaries.

50.4	Long	1900	47.8	Fitch	1924	45.5	Davis	1960
48.4	Halswell	1908	47.2	Carr	1932	44.8	Evans	1968
48.0	Josef Imbach (SUI)	1924						

800 METERS (874 yd. 2 ft.)

1896	Edwin H. Flack (AUS/NZL) 2:11.0	Nándor Dáni (HUN) 2:11.8	Demitrios Golemis (GRE) 100 yd.
1900	Alfred E. Tysoe (GBR) 2:01.2	John F. Cregan (USA) 1 yd.	David C. Hall (USA) d.n.a.
1904	James D. Lightbody (USA) 1:56.0*	Howard V. Valentine (USA) 2 yd.	Emil W. Breitkreutz (USA) d.n.a.
1906	Paul H. Pilgrim (USA) 2:01.5	James D. Lightbody (USA) 2:01.6	Wyndham Halswell (GBR) 2:03.0
1908	Melvin W. Sheppard (USA) 1:52.8*	Emilio Lunghi (ITA) 1:54.2	Hanns Braun (GER) 1:55.4
1912	James E. Meredith (USA) 1:51.9*	Melvin W. Sheppard (USA) 1:52.0	Ira N. Davenport (USA) 1:52.0
1920	Albert G. Hill (GBR) 1:53.4	Earl W. Eby (USA) 1 yd.	Bevil G. d'U. Rudd (SAF) d.n.a.

Alberto Juantorena (CUB), known as "The Horse," defeated 2 USA runners for the gold medal at 400 meters in 1976. He also won the gold at 800 meters.

	GOLD	SILVER	BRONZE
1924	Douglas G. A. Lowe (GBR) 1:52.4	Paul Martin (SUI) 1:52.6	Schuyler C. Enck (USA) 1:53.0
1928	Douglas G. A. Lowe (GBR) 1:51.8*	Erik Byléhn (SWE) 1:52.8	Hermann Engelhardt (GER) 1:53.2
1932	Thomas Hampson (GBR) 1:49.7*	Alexander Wilson (CAN) 1:49.9	Philip A. Edwards (CAN) 1:51.5
1936	John Y. Woodruff (USA) 1:52.9	Mario Lanzi (ITA) 1:53.3	Philip A. Edwards (CAN) 1:53.6
1948	Malvin G. Whitfield (USA) 1:49.2*	Arthur S. Wint (JAM) 1:49.5	Marcel Hansenne (FRA) 1:49.8
1952	Malvin G. Whitfield (USA) 1:49.2*	Arthur S. Wint (JAM) 1:49.4	Heinz Ulzheimer (GER) 1:49.7
1956	Thomas W. Courtney (USA) 1:47.7*	Derek J. N. Johnson (GBR) 1:47.8	Audun Boysen (NOR) 1:48.1
1960	Peter G. Snell (NZL) 1:46.3*	Roger Moens (BEL) 1:46.5	George E. Kerr (BWI) 1:47.1
1964	Peter G. Snell (NZL) 1:45.1*	William Cothers (CAN) 1:45.6	Wilson Kiprugut (KEN) 1:45.9
1968	Ralph D. Doubell (AUS) 1:44.3*	Wilson Kiprugut (KEN) 1:44.5	Thomas F. Farrell (USA) 1:45.4
1972	David J. Wottle (USA) 1:45.9	Evgeni Arzhanov (URS) 1:45.9	Michael Boit (KEN) 1:46.0
1976	Alberto Juantorena (CUB) 1:43.5*	Ivo Van Damme (BEL) 1:43.9	Richard Wohlhuter (USA) 1:44.1
1980	Steven Ovett (GBR) 1:45.4	Sebastian Coe (GBR) 1:45.9	Nikolai Kirov (URS) 1:46.0

The performances listed below were Olympic Records set additionally in the preliminaries.

2:10.0	Flack	1896	1:47.1	Kerr	1960	1:46.1 Kiprugut	1964
1:59.0	Hall	1900	1:46.1	Kerr	1964		

1,500 METERS (1,640 yd. 1 ft.)

	GOLD	SILVER	BRONZE
1896	Edwin H. Flack (AUS/NZL) 4:33.2*	Arthur Blake (USA) d.n.a.	Albin Lermusiaux (FRA) d.n.a.
1900	Charles Bennett (GBR) 4:06.2*	Henri Deloge (FRA) 2 yd.	John Bray (USA) d.n.a.
1904	James D. Lightbody (USA) 4:05.4*	W. Frank Verner (USA) d.n.a.	Lacey E. Hearn (USA) d.n.a.
1906	James D. Lightbody (USA) 4:12.0	John McGough (GBR/IRL) 4:12.6	Kristian Hellström (SWE) 4:13.4
1908	Melvin W. Sheppard (USA) 4:03.4*	Harold A. Wilson (GBR) 4:03.6	Norman F. Hallows[1] (GBR) 4:04.0
1912	Arnold N. S. Jackson[2] (GBR) 3:56.8*	Abel R. Kiviat (USA) 3:56.9	Norman S. Taber (USA) 3:56.9
1920	Albert G. Hill (GBR) 4:01.8	Philip J. Baker[2] (GBR) 4:02.4	M. Lawrence Shields (USA) d.n.a.
1924	Paavo J. Nurmi (FIN) 3:53.6*	Willy Schärer (SUI) 3:55.0	Henry B. Stallard (GBR) 3:55.6
1928	Harri E. Larva (FIN) 3:53.2*	Jules Ladoumègue (FRA) 3:53.8	Eino Purje (FIN) 3:56.4
1932	Luigi Beccali (ITA) 3:51.2*	John F. Cornes (GBR) 3:52.6	Philip A. Edwards (CAN) 3:52.8
1936	John E. Lovelock (NZL) 3:47.8*	Glenn Cunningham (USA) 3:48.4	Luigi Beccali (ITA) 3:49.2

[1] The Olympic record has only been set in those winning performances marked * with the exception of Hallows, who achieved 4:03.4 in the 1908 preliminaries.
[2] A. N. S. Jackson (1912) changed name to A. N. S. Strode-Jackson and P. J. Baker (1920) changed name to P. J. Noel-Baker.

LEFT: Lauri Lehtinen (FIN) (left) was rightly awarded the gold medal in 1932 for the 5,000 meters run, although both he and runner-up Ralph Hill were clocked at the same Olympic record time. RIGHT: Kip Keino (KEN) won the 1,500 meters by the remarkable margin of nearly 20 yards at Mexico City in 1968.

Lasse Viren of Finland (number 301) repeated his 1972 gold medal success at 5,000 meters in Montreal. Earlier that week he had won the gold medal at 10,000 meters for the second consecutive time.

GOLD	SILVER	BRONZE
1948 Henry Eriksson (SWE) 3:49.8	Lennart Strand (SWE) 3:50.4	Willem F. Slijkhuis (HOL) 3:50.4
1952 Josef Barthel (LUX) 3:45.1*	Robert E. McMillen (USA) 3:45.2	Werner Lueg (GER) 3:45.4
1956 Ron Delany (IRL) 3:41.2*	Klaus Richtzenhain (GER) 3:42.0	John M. Landy (AUS) 3:42.0
1960 Herbert J. Elliott (AUS) 3:35.6*	Michel Jazy (FRA) 3:38.4	István Rózsavölgyi (HUN) 3:39.2
1964 Peter G. Snell (NZL) 3:38.1	Josef Odložil (TCH) 3:39.6	John Davies (NZL) 3:39.6
1968 H. Kipchoge Keino (KEN) 3:34.9*	James R. Ryun (USA) 3:37.8	Bodo Tümmler (GER) 3:39.0
1972 Pekka Vasala (FIN) 3:36.3	H. Kipchoge Keino (KEN) 3:36.8	Rodney Dixon (NZL) 3:37.5
1976 John Walker (NZL) 3:39.2	Ivo Van Damme (BEL) 3:39.3	Paul Heinz Wellmann (GER) 3:39.3
1980 Sebastian Coe (GBR) 3:38.4	Jurgen Straub (GDR) 3:38.8	Steven Ovett (GBR) 3:39.0

5,000 METERS (3 miles 188 yd.)

1896–1908 Event not held		
1912 Hannes Kolehmainen (FIN) 14:36.6*	Jean Bouin (FRA) 14:36.7	George W. Hutson (GBR) 15:07.6
1920 Joseph Guillemot (FRA) 14:55.6	Paavo J. Nurmi (FIN) 15:00.0	Erik Backman (SWE) 15:13.0
1924 Paavo J. Nurmi (FIN) 14:31.2*	Ville Ritola (FIN) 14:31.4	Edvin Wide (SWE) 15:01.8
1928 Ville Ritola (FIN) 14:38.0	Paavo J. Nurmi (FIN) 14:40.0	Edvin Wide (SWE) 14:41.2
1932 Lauri A. Lehtinen (FIN) 14:30.0*	Ralph Hill (USA) 14:30.0*	Lauri J. Virtanen (FIN) 14:44.0
1936 Gunnar Höckert (FIN) 14:22.2*	Lauri A. Lehtinen (FIN) 14:25.8	Henry Jonsson (SWE) 14:29.0
1948 Gaston E. G. Reiff (BEL) 14:17.6*	Emil Zátopek (TCH) 14:17.8	Willem F. Slijkhuis (HOL) 14:26.8
1952 Emil Zátopek (TCH) 14:06.6*	Allain Mimoun-o-Kacha (FRA) 14:07.4	Herbert Schade (GER) 14:08.6
1956 Vladimir P. Kuts (URS) 13:39.6*	D. A. Gordon Pirie (GBR) 13:50.6	G. Derek Ibbotson (GBR) 13:54.4
1960 Murray G. Halberg (NZL) 13:43.4	Hans Grodotzki (GER) 13:44.6	Kazimierz Zimny (POL) 13:44.8
1964 Robert K. Schul (USA) 13:48.8	Harald Norpoth (GER) 13:49.6	William Dellinger (USA) 13:49.8
1968 Mohamed Gammoudi (TUN) 14:05.0	H. Kipchoge Keino (KEN) 14:05.2	Naftali Temu (KEN) 14:06.4
1972 Lasse Viren (FIN) 13:26.4*	Mohamed Gammoudi (TUN) 13:27.4	Ian Stewart (GBR) 13:27.6
1976 Lasse Viren (FIN) 13:24.8	Dick Quax (NZL) 13:25.2	Klaus-Peter Hildenbrand (GER) 13:25.4
1980 Miruts Yifter (ETH) 13:21.0	Suleiman Nyambui (TAN) 13:21.6	Kaarlo Maaninka (FIN) 13:22.0

The Olympic record has only been set in those medal-winning performances marked * with the exception of Emiel Puttemans (BEL), 13:31.8 in the 1972 preliminaries and Brendan Foster (GBR), 13:20.3 in the 1976 preliminaries.

10,000 METERS (6 miles 376 yd.)

GOLD	SILVER	BRONZE
1896–1908 Event not held		
1912 Hannes Kolehmainen (FIN) 31:20.8*	Lewis Tewanima (USA) 32:06.6	Albin O. Stenroos (FIN) 32:21.8
1920 Paavo J. Nurmi (FIN) 31:45.8	Joseph Guillemot (FRA) 31:47.2	James Wilson (GBR) 31:50.8
1924 Ville Ritola (FIN) 30:23.2*	Edvin Wide (SWE) 30:55.2	Eero E. Berg (FIN) 31:43.0
1928 Paavo J. Nurmi (FIN) 30:18.8*	Ville Ritola (FIN) 30:19.4	Edvin Wide (SWE) 31:00.8
1932 Janusz Kusocinski (POL) 30:11.4*	Volmari Iso-Hollo (FIN) 30:12.6	Lauri J. Virtanen (FIN) 30:35.0
1936 Ilmari Salminen (FIN) 30:15.4	Arvo Askola (FIN) 30:15.6	Volmari Iso-Hollo (FIN) 30:20.2
1948 Emil Zátopek (TCH) 29:59.6*	Alain Mimoun-o-Kacha (FRA) 30:47.4	Bertil Albertsson (SWE) 30:53.6
1952 Emil Zátopek (TCH) 29:17.0*	Alain Mimoun-o-Kacha (FRA) 29:32.8	Aleksandr A. Anufriyev (URS) 29:48.2
1956 Vladimir P. Kuts (URS) 28:45.6*	József Kovács (HUN) 28:52.4	Allan Lawrence (AUS) 28:53.6
1960 Pyotr G. Bolotnikov (URS) 28:32.2*	Hans Grodotzki (GER) 28:37.0	W. David Power (AUS) 28:38.2
1964 William M. Mills (USA) 28:24.4*	Mohamed Gammoudi (TUN) 28:24.8	Ronald W. Clarke (AUS) 28:25.8
1968 Naftali Temu (KEN) 29:27.4	Mamo Wolde (ETH) 29:28.0	Mohamed Gammoudi (TUN) 29:34.2
1972 Lasse Viren (FIN) 27:38.4*	Emiel Puttemans (BEL) 27:39.6	Meruts Yifter (ETH) 27:41.0
1976 Lasse Viren (FIN) 27:40.4	Carlos Lopes (POR) 27:45.2	Brendan Foster (GBR) 27:54.9
1980 Miruts Yifter (ETH) 27:42.7	Kaarlo Maaninka (FIN) 27:44.3	Mohammed Kedir (ETH) 27:44.7

The Olympic record has only been set in those medal-winning performances marked * with the exception of: 33:49.0 by Kolehmainen, and 32:30.8 by Len Richardson (SAF) both in 1912; and 27:53.4 by Puttemans in 1972.

MARATHON (42,195 meters—26 miles 385 yd.)

The length of a Marathon was standardized at the 1908 distance of 26 miles 385 yards (42 195 m) from 1924.

The distances run in other years were:

1896 & 1904	24 miles 1,503 yards 40 000 m		1912	24 miles 1,723 yards 40 200 m
1900	25 miles 28 yards 40 260 m		1920	26 miles 991 yards 42 750 m
1906	26 miles 18 yards 41 860 m			

GOLD	SILVER	BRONZE
1896 Spyridon Louis (GRE) 2h 58:50.0	Charilaos Vasilakos (GRE) 3h 06:03.0	Gyula Kellner (HUN) 3h 09:35.0
1900 Michel Theato (FRA) 2h 59:45.0	Emile Champion (FRA) 3h 04:17.0	Ernst Fast (SWE) 3h 37:14.0
1904 Thomas J. Hicks (USA) 3h 28:35.0	Albert J. Corey (USA) 3h 34:52.0	Arthur L. Newton (USA) 3h 47:33.0
1906 William H. Sherring (CAN) 2h 51:23.6	John Svanberg (SWE) 2h 58:20.8	William Frank (USA) 3h 00:46.8
1908 John J. Hayes[1] (USA) 2h 55:18.4*	Charles A. Hefferon (SAF) 2h 56:06.0	Joseph Foreshaw (USA) 2h 57:10.4
1912 Kenneth K. McArthur (SAF) 2h 36:54.8	Christian W. Gitsham (SAF) 2h 37:52.0	Gaston Strobino (USA) 2h 38:42.4

---

[1] Dorando Pietri (ITA) finished 1st but was disqualified for assistance by officials over the final few hundred yards.

GOLD	SILVER	BRONZE
1920	Hannes Kolehmainen (FIN) 2h 32:35.8*	Jüri Lossman (EST) 2h 32:48.6	Valerio Arri (ITA) 2h 36:32.8
1924	Albin O. Stenroos (FIN) 2h 41:22.6	Romeo Bertini (ITA) 2h 47:19.6	Clarence H. DeMar (USA) 2h 48:14.0
1928	Mohamed El Ouafi (FRA) 2h 32:57.0	Miguel Plaza (CHI) 2h 33:23.0	Martti Marttelin (FIN) 2h 35:02.0
1932	Juan Carlos Zabala (ARG) 2h 31:36.0*	Samuel Ferris (GBR) 2h 31:55.0	Armas A. Toivonen (FIN) 2h 32:12.0
1936	Kitei Son (JPN) 2h 29:19.2*	Ernest Harper (GBR) 2h 31:23.2	Shoryu Nan (JPN) 2h 31:42.0
1948	Delfo Cabrera (ARG) 2h 34:51.6	Thomas Richards (GBR) 2h 35:07.6	Etienne Gailly (BEL) 2h 35:33.6
1952	Emil Zátopek (TCH) 2h 23:03.2*	Reinaldo B. Gorno (ARG) 2h 25:35.0	Gustaf N. Jansson (SWE) 2h 26:07.0
1956	Alain Mimoun-o-Kacha (FRA) 2h 25:00.0	Franjo Mihalič (YUG) 2h 26:32.0	Veikko Karvonen (FIN) 2h 27:47.0
1960	Abebe Bikila (ETH) 2h 15:16.2*	Rhadi Ben Abdesselem (MAR) 2h 15:41.6	A. Barry Magee (NZL) 2h 17:18.2
1964	Abebe Bikila (ETH) 2h 12:11.2*	Basil B. Heatley (GBR) 2h 16:19.2	Kokichi Tsuburaya (JPN) 2h 16:22.8
1968	Mamo Wolde (ETH) 2h 20:26.4	Kenji Kimihara (JPN) 2h 23:31.0	Michael Ryun (NZL) 2h 23:45.0
1972	Frank Shorter (USA) 2h 12:19.8	Karel Lismont (BEL) 2h 14:31.8	Mamo Wolde (ETH) 2h 15:08.4
1976	Waldemar Cierpinski (GDR) 2h 09:55.0*	Frank Shorter (USA) 2h 10:45.8	Karel Lismont (BEL) 2h 11:12.6
1980	Waldemar Cierpinski (GDR) 2h 11:03	Gerard Nijboer (HOL) 2h 11:20	Setymkul Dzhumanazarov (URS) 2h 11:35

Abebe Bikila (ETH) became the first of only two runners to retain the Olympic marathon championship by winning the race in the 1960 and 1964 Games.

This English foursome was the first 4 × 100 meters relay race in 1912. Sweden was second. The other finalists were disqualified for illegal baton passes.

4 × 100 METERS (109 yd. 1 ft.) RELAY

GOLD	SILVER	BRONZE
1896–1908 Event not held		
1912 **GREAT BRITAIN** 42.4	SWEDEN 42.6	
David H. Jacobs	Ivan Möller	
Harold M. Macintosh	Charles Luther	
Victor H. A. D'Arcy	Ture Persson	
William R. Applegarth	Knut Lindberg	
1920 **UNITED STATES** 42.2*	FRANCE 42.6	SWEDEN d.n.a.
Charles W. Paddock	René Tirard	Agne Holmström
Jackson V. Scholz	René Lorain	William Pettersson
Loren C. Murchison	René Mourlon	Sven Malm
Morris M. Kirksey	Emile Ali Khan	Nils Sandström
1924 **UNITED STATES** 41.0*	GREAT BRITAIN 41.2	NETHERLANDS 41.8
Francis Hussey	Harold M. Abrahams	Jakob Boot
Louis A. Clarke	Walter Rangeley	Henricus Broos
Loren C. Murchison	Lancelot C. Royle	Jan de Vries
J. Alfred Le Coney	William P. Nichol	Marinus van den Berge
1928 **UNITED STATES** 41.0*	GERMANY 41.2	GREAT BRITAIN 41.8
Frank C. Wykoff	Georg Lammers	Cyril W. Gill
James F. Quinn	Richard Corts	Eric R. Smouha
Charles E. Borah	Hubert Houben	Walter Rangeley
Henry A. Russell	Helmut Körnig	Jack E. London
1932 **UNITED STATES** 40.0*	GERMANY 40.9	ITALY 41.2
Robert A. Kiesel	Helmut Körnig	Giuseppe Castelli
Emmett Toppino	Walter Hendrix	Ruggero Maregatti
Hector M. Dyer	Erich Borchmeyer	Gabriele Salviati
Frank C. Wykoff	Arthur Jonath	Edgardo Toetti

	GOLD	SILVER	BRONZE
1936	**UNITED STATES** 39.8*	**ITALY** 41.1	**GERMANY** 41.2
	Jesse Owens	Orazio Mariani	Wilhelm Leichum
	Ralph H. Metcalfe	Gianni Caldana	Erich Borchmeyer
	Foy Draper	Elio Ragni	Erwin Gillmeister
	Frank C. Wykoff	Tullio Gonnelli	Gerd Hornberger
1948	**UNITED STATES**[1] 40.6	**GREAT BRITAIN** 41.3	**ITALY** 41.5
	H. Norwood Ewell	John Archer	Carlo Monti
	Lorenzo C. Wright	John A. Gregory	Enrico Perucconi
	W. Harrison Dillard	Alistair McCorquodale	Antonio Siddi
	Melvin E. Patton	Kenneth J. Jones	Michele Tito
1952	**UNITED STATES** 40.1	**U.S.S.R.** 40.3	**HUNGARY** 40.5
	F. Dean Smith	Boris Tokaryev	László Zarándi
	W. Harrison Dillard	Levan Kalyayev	Géza Varasdi
	Lindy J. Remigino	Levan Sanadze	György Csányi
	Andrew W. Stanfield	Vladimir Sukharyev	Béla Goldoványi
1956	**UNITED STATES** 39.5	**U.S.S.R.** 39.8	**GERMANY** 40.3
	Ira J. Murchison	Boris Tokaryev	Lothar Knörzer
	Leamon King	Vladimir Sukharyev	Leonhard Pohl
	W. Thane Baker	Leonid Bartenyev	Heinz Fütterer
	Bobby-Joe Morrow	Yuriy Konovalov	Manfred Germar
1960	**GERMANY** 39.5*	**U.S.S.R.** 40.1	**GREAT BRITAIN** 40.2
	Bernd Cullmann	Gusman Kosanov	Peter F. Radford
	Armin Hary	Leonid Bartenyev	David N. Jones
	Walter Mahlendorf	Yuriy Konovalov	David H. Segal
	Martin Lauer	Edvin Ozolin	J. Neville Whitehead
1964	**UNITED STATES** 39.0*	**POLAND** 39.3	**FRANCE** 39.3
	O. Paul Drayton	Andrzej Zielinski	Paul Genevay
	Gerald A. Ashworth	Wieslaw Maniak	Bernard Laidebeur
	Richard V. Stebbins	Marian Foik	Claude Piquemal
	Robert L. Hayes	Marian Dudziak	Jocelyn Delecour
1968	**UNITED STATES** 38.2*	**CUBA** 38.3	**FRANCE** 38.4
	Charles E. Greene	Hermes Ramirez	Gérard Fenouil
	Melvin Pender	Juan Morales	Jocelyn Delecour
	Ronnie Ray Smith	Pablo Montes	Claude Piquemal
	James R. Hines	Enriques Figuerola	Roger Bambuck
1972	**UNITED STATES** 38.19*	**U.S.S.R.** 38.50	**WEST GERMANY** 38.79
	Larry J. Black	Alexandr Korneliuk	Jobst Hirscht
	Robert Taylor	Vladimir Lovetski	Karl-Heinz Klotz
	Gerald Tinker	Yuri Silov	Gerhard Wucherer
	Eddie J. Hart	Valeriy Borzov	Klaus Ehl
1976	**UNITED STATES** 38.33	**EAST GERMANY** 38.66	**U.S.S.R.** 38.78
	Harvey Glance	Manfred Kokot	Alexandr Aksinin
	John Jones	Jorg Pfeifer	Nikolai Kolesnikov
	Millard Hampton	Klaus-Dieter Kurrat	Yuri Silov
	Steven Riddick	Alexander Thieme	Valeriy Borzov
1980	**U.S.S.R.** 38.26	**POLAND** 38.33	**FRANCE** 38.53
	Vladimir Muravyov	Krzysztof Zwolinski	Antoine Richard
	Nikolai Sidorov	Zenon Licznerski	Pascal Barré
	Aleksandr Aksinin	Leszek Dunecki	Patrick Barré
	Andre Prokofiev	Marian Woronin	Hermann Panzo

---

[1] USA was disqualified but later reinstated.

The performances listed below were Olympic Records set additionally in preliminaries.

43.0	Great Britain 1912	42.0	Netherlands 1924	38.6	Jamaica	1968
42.5	Sweden 1912	41.2	United States 1924		(Errol Stewart,	
42.3	Germany 1912	41.0	United States 1924		Michael Fray,	
	(K. Halt,	40.6	United States 1932		Clifton Forbes,	
	M. Hermann,	40.0	United States 1936		Lennox Miller)	
	E. Kern,	39.5	Germany 1960	38.3	Jamaica	1968
	Richard Rau)	39.5	United States 1964			
42.0	Great Britain 1924	38.7	Cuba 1968			

4 × 400 METERS (437 yd. 1 ft.) RELAY

	GOLD	SILVER	BRONZE
1896–1908	Event not held		
1912	**UNITED STATES** 3:16.6*	FRANCE 3:20.7	**GREAT BRITAIN** 3.23.2
	Melvin W. Sheppard	Charles L. Lelong	George Nicol
	Edward F. Lindberg	Robert Schurrer	Ernest J. Henley
	James E. Meredith	Pierre Failliot	James T. Soutter
	Charles D. Reidpath	Charles A. C. Poulenard	Cyril N. Seedhouse
1920	**GREAT BRITAIN** 3:22.2	S. AFRICA d.n.a.	FRANCE d.n.a.
	Cecil R. Griffiths	Harry Davel	George André
	Robert A. Lindsay	Clarence W. Oldfield	Gaston Féry
	John C. Ainsworth-Davis	Jack K. Oosterlaak	Maurice Delvart
	Guy M. Butler	Bevil G. d'U. Rudd	Jean Devaux
1924	**UNITED STATES** 3:16.0*	SWEDEN 3:17.0	**GREAT BRITAIN** 3:17.4
	Con S. Cochrane	Artur Svensson	Edward J. Toms
	Alan B. Helffrich	Erik Byléhn	George R. Renwick
	James O. McDonald	Gustaf Wejnarth	Richard N. Ripley
	William E. Stevenson	Nils Engdahl	Guy M. Butler
1928	**UNITED STATES** 3:14.2*	GERMANY 3:14.8	CANADA 3:15.4
	George Baird	Otto Neumann	Alexander Wilson
	Emerson Spencer	Richard Krebs	Philip A. Edwards
	Frederick P. Alderman	Harry Storz	Stanley Glover
	Raymond J. Barbuti	Hermann Engelhard	James Ball
1932	**UNITED STATES** 3:08.2*	**GREAT BRITAIN** 3:11.2	CANADA 3:12.8
	Ivan Fuqua	Crew H. Stoneley	Raymond Lewis
	Edgar A. Ablowich	Thomas Hampson	James Ball
	Karl D. Warner	Lord Burghley	Philip A. Edwards
	William A. Carr	Godfrey L. Rampling	Alexander Wilson
1936	**GREAT BRITAIN** 3:09.0	UNITED STATES 3:11.0	GERMANY 3:11.8
	Frederick F. Wolff	Harold Cagle	Helmut Hamann
	Godfrey L. Rampling	Robert C. Young	Friedrich von Stülpnagel
	William Roberts	Edward T. O'Brien	Harry C. Voigt
	A. Godfrey K. Brown	Alfred L. Fitch	Rudolf Harbig
1948	**UNITED STATES** 3:10.4	FRANCE 3:14.8	SWEDEN 3:16.3
	Arthur H. Harnden	Jean Kerebel	Kurt Lundqvist
	Clifford F. Bourland	Francis Schewetta	Lars-Enk Wolfbrandt
	Roy B. Cochran	Robert C. Chef d'Hôtel	Folke Alnevik
	Malvin G. Whitfield	Jacques J. Lunis	Rune Larsson
1952	**JAMAICA** 3:03.9*	UNITED STATES 3:04.0	GERMANY 3:06.6
	Arthur S. Wint	Ollie A. Matson	Hans Geister
	Leslie A. Laing	G. Eugene Cole	Günther Steines
	Herbert H. McKenley	Charles H. Moore	Heinz Ulzheimer
	V. George Rhoden	Malvin G. Whitfield	Karl-Friedrich Haas

	GOLD	SILVER	BRONZE
1956	UNITED STATES 3:04.8	AUSTRALIA 3:06.2	GREAT BRITAIN 3:07.2
	Lou Jones	Leslie S. Gregory	John E. Salisbury
	Jesse W. Mashburn	David F. Lean	Michael K. V. Wheeler
	Charles L. Jenkins	Graham Gipson	F. Peter Higgins
	Thomas W. Courtney	Kevin V. Gosper	Derek J. N. Johnson
1960	UNITED STATES 3:02.2*	GERMANY 3:02.7	BRITISH W.I. 3:04.0
	Jack L. Yerman	Hans-Joachim Reske	Malcolm Spence
	Earl V. Young	Manfred Kinder	James Wedderburn
	Glenn A. Davis	Johannes Kaiser	Keith A. St. H. Gardner
	Otis C. Davis	Carl Kaufmann	George E. Kerr

This successful baton pass helped the United States team to win the gold medal in the 4 × 400 meters relay in world record time in 1912.

	GOLD	SILVER	BRONZE
1964	UNITED STATES 3:00.7*	GREAT BRITAIN 3:01.6	TRINIDAD 3:01.7
	Ollan C. Cassell	Timothy J. M. Graham	Edwin Skinner
	Michael D. Larrabee	Adrian P. Metcalfe	Kent Bernard
	Ulis C. Williams	John H. Cooper	Edwin Roberts
	Henry Carr	Robbie I. Brightwell	Wendell A. Mottley
1968	UNITED STATES 2:56.1*	KENYA 2:59.6	WEST GERMANY 3:00.5
	Vincent E. Matthews	Daniel Rudisha	Helmar Müller
	Ronald J. Freeman	Munyoro L. Nyamau	Manfred Kinder
	G. Lawrence James	Naftali Bon	Gerhard Hennige
	Lee E. Evans	Charles Asati	Martin Jellinghaus
1972	KENYA 2:59.8	GREAT BRITAIN 3:00.5	FRANCE 3:00.7
	Charles Asati	Martin E. Reynolds	Gilles Bertould
	Hezakiah Nyamau	Alan P. Pascoe	Daniel Velasques
	Robert Ouko	David P. Hemery	Francis Kerbiriou
	Julius Sang	David A. Jenkins	Jacques Carette

GOLD	SILVER	BRONZE
1976 **UNITED STATES** 2:58.7	**POLAND** 3:01.4	**WEST GERMANY** 3:02.0
Herman Frazier	Ryszard Podlas	Franz-Peter Hofmeiste
Benjamin Brown	Jan Werner	Lothar Krieg
Fred Newhouse	Zbigniew Jaremski	Harald Schmid
Maxie Parks	Jerzy Pietrzyk	Bernd Herrmann
1980 **U.S.S.R.** 3:01.1	**EAST GERMANY** 3:01.3	**ITALY** 3:04.3
Remigius Valyulis	Klaus Thiele	Stefano Malinverni
Michail Linge	Andreas Knebel	Mauro Zuliani
Nikolai Chernyetsky	Frank Schaffer	Roberto Tozzi
Viktor Markin	Volker Beck	Pietro Mennea

The Olympic record has only been set in those winning performances marked * with the exception of:

3:19.0	Great Britain	1912
3:11.8	United States	1932
3:00.7	United States	1968

110 METERS (120 yd. 1 ft.) HURDLES

	GOLD	SILVER	BRONZE
1896	Thomas P. Curtis (USA) 17.6	Grantley T. Goulding (GBR) 17.7	—[1]
1900	Alvin C. Kraenzlein (USA) 15.4*	John McLean (USA) 1½ ft.	Fred G. Moloney (USA) d.n.a.
1904	Frederick W. Schule (USA) 16.0	Thaddeus Shideler (USA) 2 yd.	L. Ashburner (USA) d.n.a.
1906	R. G. Leavitt (USA) 16.2	A. H. Healey (GBR) 16.2	Vincent deV. Duncker (SAF) 16.3
1908	Forrest C. Smithson (USA) 15.0*	John C. Garrels (USA) 5 yd.	Arthur B. Shaw (USA) d.n.a.
1912	Frederick W. Kelly (USA) 15.1	James I. Wendell (USA) 15.2	Martin W. Hawkins (USA) 15.3
1920	Earl J. Thomson (CAN) 14.8*	Harold E. Barron (USA) 2½ yd.	Frederick S. Murray (USA) d.n.a.
1924	Daniel C. Kinsey (USA) 15.0	Sydney J. M. Atkinson (SAF) inches	Sten Pettersson (SWE) d.n.a.
1928	Sydney J. M. Atkinson (AF) 14.8	Stephen E. Anderson (USA) 14.8	John S. Collier (USA) 15.0
1932	George J. Saling (USA) 14.6	Percy M. Beard (USA) 14.7	Donald O. Finlay (GBR) 14.8
1936	Forrest G. Towns (USA) 14.2	Donald O. Finlay (GBR) 14.4	Frederick D. Pollard (USA) 14.4
1948	William F. Porter (USA) 13.9*	Clyde L. Scott (USA) 14.1	Craig K. Dixon (USA) 14.1
1952	W. Harrison Dillard (USA) 13.7*	Jack W. Davis (USA) 13.7*	Arthur Barnard (USA) 14.1
1956	Lee Q. Calhoun (USA) 13.5*	Jack W. Davis (USA) 13.5*	Joel W. Chankle (USA) 14.1
1960	Lee Q. Calhoun (USA) 13.8	Willie L. May (USA) 13.8	Hayes W. Jones (USA) 14.0
1964	Hayes W. Jones (USA) 13.6	H. Blaine Lindgren (USA) 13.7	Anatoly Mikhailov (URS) 13.7
1968	Willie Davenport (USA) 13.3*	Ervin Hall (USA) 13.4	Eddy Ottoz (ITA) 13.4
1972	Rodney Milburn (USA) 13.24*	Guy Drut (FRA) 13.34	Thomas L. Hill (USA) 13.48
1976	Guy Drut (FRA) 13.30	Alejandro Casanas (CUB) 13.33	Willie Davenport (USA) 13.38
1980	Thomas Munkelt (GDR) 13.39	Alejandro Casanas (CUB) 13.40	Aleksandr Puchkov (URS) 13.44

[1] Only two finalists.

Willie Davenport, the 1968 hurdles champion, shows his strong form in Mexico City.

The 400 meter hurdles being won in 1968 in world record time (48.1 seconds) by David Hemery (GBR) by the exceptional margin of nearly a second from Gerhard Hennige (GER) and John Sherwood (GBR).

The performances listed below were Olympic records set additionally in preliminaries.

15.6	Kraenzlein	1900	14.8	Leighton Dye		14.1	Towns	1936
15.4	Smithson	1908		(USA)	1928	14.1	Porter	1948
15.0	Barron	1920	14.8	Anderson	1928	13.9	Dillard	1952
15.0	Thomson	1920	14.6	Weightman-Smith		13.5	Ottoz	1968
14.8	George C.				1928	13.3	Hall	1968
	Weightman-Smith		14.5	Jack Keller				
	(SAF)	1928		(USA)	1932			
			14.4	Saling	1932			

400 METERS (437 yd. 1 ft.) HURDLES

	GOLD	SILVER	BRONZE
1896	Event not held		
1900	J. Walter B. Tewksbury (USA) 57.6*	Henri Tauzin (FRA) d.n.a.	George W. Orton (CAN) d.n.a.
1904[1]	Harry L. Hillman (USA) 53.0	Frank Waller (USA) 2 yd.	George Poage (USA) d.n.a.
1906	Event not held		
1908	Charles J. Bacon (USA) 55.0*	Harry L. Hillmann (USA) 1½ yd.	Leonard F. Tremeer (GBR) d.n.a.
1912	Event not held		
1920	Frank F. Loomis (USA) 54.0*	John K. Norton (USA) d.n.a.	August G. Desch (USA) d.n.a.
1924	F. Morgan Taylor (USA) 52.6[2]	Erik Vilén (FIN) 53.8*	Ivan H. Riley (USA) 54.2
1928	Lord Burghley (GBR) 53.4*	Frank J. Cuhel (USA) 53.6	F. Morgan Taylor (USA) 53.6
1932	Robert M. N. Tisdall (IRL) 51.7[2]	Glenn F. Hardin (USA) 51.9*	F. Morgan Taylor (USA) 52.0
1936	Glenn F. Hardin (USA) 52.4	John W. Loaring (CAN) 52.7	Miguel S. White (PHI) 52.8
1948	Roy B. Cochran (USA) 51.1*	Duncan White (CEY) 51.8	Rune Larsson (SWE) 52.2
1952	Charles H. Moore (USA) 50.8*	Yuriy N. Lituyev (URS) 51.3	John McF. Holland (NZL) 52.2
1956	Glenn A. Davis (USA) 50.1*	S. Eddie Southern (USA) 50.8	Joshua Culbreath (USA) 51.6
1960	Glenn A. Davis (USA) 49.3*	Clifton E. Cushman (USA) 49.6	Richard W. Howard (USA) 49.7
1964	Warren Cawley (USA) 49.6	John H. Cooper (GBR) 50.1	Salvadore Morale (ITA) 50.1
1968	David P. Hemery (GBR) 48.1*	Gerhard Hennige (GER) 49.0	John Sherwood (GBR) 49.0
1972	John Akii-bua (UGA) 47.82*	Ralph V. Mann (USA) 48.51	David P. Hemery (GBR) 48.52
1976	Edwin Moses (USA) 47.64*	Michael Shine (USA) 48.69	Evgeniy Gavrilenko (URS) 49.45
1980	Volker Beck (GDR) 48.70	Vasily Arkhipenko (URS) 48.86	Gary Oakes (GBR) 49.11

The performances listed below were Olympic records set additionally in preliminaries.

57.0	Bacon	1908	52.8	Tisdall	1932	50.1	Southern	1956
56.4	Hillman	1908	51.9	Larsson	1948	49.0	Ronald Whitney	
53.4	Taylor	1928	51.9	Cochran	1948		(USA)	1968
52.8	Hardin	1932	50.8	Moore	1952			

---

[1] Hurdles only 2 ft. 6 in. *75,9 cm* high instead of more usual 3 ft. 0 in. *91,1 cm.*
[2] Record not allowed because a hurdle was knocked down.

LEFT: Amos Biwott (KEN), the 1968 steeplechase champion, was born at a high altitude, as were most of the victors in endurance events at Mexico City. RIGHT: Ed Moses (USA) broke the Olympic and world records in winning the 400 meters hurdles event in 1976.

3,000 METERS (1 mile 1,520 yd. 1 ft.) STEEPLECHASE

Steeplechases were held in 1900 (two races), 1904 and 1908 but none were over obstacles or at distances comparable with the existing event. No steeplechase event was held in 1896, 1906 or 1912.

	GOLD	SILVER	BRONZE
1920	Percy Hodge (GBR) 10:00.4*	Patrick J. Flynn (USA) 100 yd.	Ernesto Ambrosini (ITA) 40 yd.
1924	Ville Ritola (FIN) 9:33.6*	Elias Katz (FIN) 9:44.0	Paul Bontemps (FRA) 9:45.2
1928	Toivo A. Loukola (FIN) 9:21.8*	Paavo J. Nurmi (FIN) 9:31.2	Ove Andersen (FIN) 9:35.6
1932[1]	Volmari Iso-Hollo (FIN) 10:33.4	Thomas Evenson (GBR) 10:46.0	Joseph P. McCluskey (USA) 10:46.2
1936	Volmari Iso-Hollo (FIN) 9:03.8*	Kaarlo Tuominen (FIN) 9:06.8	Alfred Dompert (GER) 9:07.2
1948	Tore Sjöstrand (SWE) 9:04.6	Erik Elmsäter (SWE) 9:08.2	Göte Hagström (SWE) 9:11.8
1952	Horace Ashenfelter (USA) 8:45.4*	Vladimir V. Kazantsev (URS) 8:51.6	John I. Disley (GBR) 8:51.8
1956	Christopher W. Brasher (GBR) 8:41.2*	Sándor Rozsnyói (HUN) 8:43.6	Ernst Larsen (NOR) 8:44.0
1960	Zdzislaw Krzyszkowiak (POL) 8:34.2*	Nikolay Sokolov (URS) 8:36.4	Semyon Rzhishchin (URS) 8:42.2
1964	Gaston Roelants (BEL) 8:30.8*	Maurice Herriott (GBR) 8:32.4	Ivan Belyayev (URS) 8:33.8
1968	Amos Biwott (KEN) 8:51.0	Benjamin Kogo (KEN) 8:51.6	George Young (USA) 8:51.8
1972	H. Kipchoge Keino (KEN) 8:23.6*	Benjamin W. Jipcho (KEN) 8:24.6	Tapio Kantanen (FIN) 8:24.8
1976	Anders Garderud (SWE) 8:08.0*	Bronislaw Malinowski (POL) 8:09.1	Frank Baumgartl (GDR) 8:10.4
1980	Bronislaw Malinowski (POL) 8:09.7	Filbert Bayi (TAN) 8:12.5	Eshetu Tura (ETH) 8:13.6

[1] Distance in final was 3,460 meters due to error on part of lap-scoring official.

Horace Ashenfelter (USA), number 998, won the gold medal in the 3,000 meters steeplechase in 1952 at Helsinki, beating Vladimir Kazantsev (URS), number 436, by about 6 seconds. The leader here is the Finn Olavi Rinteenpää.

Italy's Maurizio Damilano won the 20 kilometer road walk in Olympic record time in 1980.

The performances listed below were Olympic records set additionally in preliminaries.

10:17.4	Hodge	1920	8:51.0	Ashenfelter		8:24.8	Kantanen 1972
9:43.8	Katz	1924			1952	8:23.8	Biwott 1972
9:18.8	Evenson	1932	8:33.0	Herriott	1964	8:18.6	Bronislaw
9:14.6	Iso-Hollo	1932	8:31.8	Adolfas			Malinowski
8:58.0	Kazantsev			Aleksiejunas			1976
		1952		(URS)	1964		

20,000 METERS (12 miles 752 yd.) ROAD WALK

	GOLD	SILVER	BRONZE
1896–1952	Event not held		
1956	Leonid Spirin (URS) 1h 31:27.4*	Antonas Mikenas (URS) 1h 32:03.0	Bruno Junk (URS) 1 h 32.12.0
1960	Vladimir Golubnichiy (URS) 1h 34:07.2	Noel F. Freeman (AUS) 1h 34:16.4	Stanley F. Vickers (GBR) 1h 34:56.4
1964	Kenneth J. Matthews (GBR) 1h 29:34.0*	Dieter Lindner (GER) 1h 31:13.2	Vladimir Golubnichiy (URS) 1h 31:59.4
1968	Vladimir Golubnichiy (URS) 1h 33:58.4	José Pedraza (MEX) 1h 34:0.0	Nickolay Smaga (URS) 1h 34:03.4
1972	Peter Frenkel (GDR) 1h 26:42.4*	Vladimir Golubnichiy (URS) 1h 26:55.2	Hans Reimann (GDR) 1h 27:16.6
1976	Daniel Bautista (MEX) 1h 24:40.6*	Hans Reimann (GDR) 1h 25:13.8	Peter Frenkel (GDR) 1h 25:29.4
1980	Maurizio Damilano (ITA) 1h 23:35.5*	Pyotr Pochinchuk (URS) 1h 24:45.4	Roland Wieser (GDR) 1h 25:58.2

50,000 METERS (31 miles 120 yd.) ROAD WALK

1896–1928	Event not held		
1932	Thomas Green (GBR) 4h 50:10.0*	Janis Dalinsh (LAT) 4h 47:20.0	Ugo Frigerio (ITA) 4h 59:06.0
1936	Harold Whitlock (GBR) 4h 30:41.1*	Arthur Schwab (SUI) 4h 32:09.2	Adalberts Bubenko (LAT) 4h 32:42.2
1948	John Ljunggren (SWE) 4h 41:52.0	Gaston Godel (SUI) 4h 48:17.0	Tebbs Lloyd Johnson (GBR) 4h 48:31.0
1952	Guiseppe Dordoni (ITA) 4h 28:07.8*	Josef Dolezal (TCH) 4h 30:17.8	Antal Roka (HUN) 4h 31:27.2
1956	Norman Read (NZL) 4h 30:42.8	Yevgeniy Maskinskov (URS) 4h 32:57.0	John Ljunggren (SWE) 4h 35:02.0
1960	Don Thompson (GBR) 4h 25:30.0*	John Ljunggren (SWE) 4h 25:47.0	Abdon Pamich (ITA) 4h 27:55.4
1964	Abdon Pamich (ITA) 4h 11:12.4*	Paul Nihill (GBR) 4h 11:31.2	Ingvar Pettersson (SWE) 4h 14:17.4
1968	Christoph Höhne (GDR) 4h 20:13.6	Antal Kiss (HUN) 4h 30:17.0	Larry Young (USA) 4h 31:55.4
1972	Bernd Kannenberg (GER) 3h 56:11.6*	Veniamin Soldatenko (URS) 3h 58:24.0	Larry Young (USA) 4h 00:46.0
1976	Event not held		
1980	Hartwig Gauder (GDR) 3h 49:24.0*	Jorge Liopart (ESP) 3h 51:25.0	Yevgeny Ivchenko (URS) 3h 56:32.0

HIGH JUMP

	GOLD	SILVER	BRONZE
1896	Ellery H. Clark (USA) 5'11" *1,81 m**	[1]	[1]
1900	Irving K. Baxter (USA) 6'2¾" *1,90 m**	Patrick J. Leahy (GBR) 5' 10" *1,78 m*	Lajos Gönczy (HUN) 5' 8¾" *1,75 m*
1904	Samuel S. Jones (USA) 5' 11" *1,80 m*	Garrett P. Serviss (USA) 5' 10" *1,77 m*	Paul Weinstein (GER) 5' 10" *1,77 m*
1906	Con Leahy (GBR/IRL) 5' 9¾" *1,77 m*	Lajos Gönczy (HUN) 5'8¾" *1,75 m*	[2]
1908	Harry F. Porter (USA) 6' 3" *1,905 m**	[3]	[3]
1912	Alma W. Richards (USA) 6' 4" *1,93 m**	Hans Liesche (GER) 6' 3¼" *1,91 m*	George L. Horine (USA) 6' 2½" *1,89 m*
1920	Richmond W. Landon (USA) 6' 4¼" *1,94 m**	Harold P. Muller (USA) 6' 2¾" *1,90 m*	Bo Ekelund (SWE) 6' 2¾" *1,90 m*
1924	Harold M. Osborn (USA) 6' 6" *1,98 m**	Leroy T. Brown (USA) 6' 4¾" *1,95 m*	Pierre Lewden (FRA) 6' 3¼" *1,92 m*
1928	Robert W. King (USA) 6' 4¼" *1,94 m*	Ben Van D. Hedges (USA) 6' 3¼" *1,91 m*	Claude Ménard (FRA) 6' 3¼" *1,91 m*
1932	Duncan McNaughton (CAN) 6' 5½" *1,97 m*	Robert L. Van Osdel (USA) 6' 5½" *1,97 m*	Simeon G. Toribio (PHI) 6' 5½" *1,97 m*

[1] Tie for second place between James B. Connolly (USA) and Robert S. Garrett (USA) at 5' 4¾" *1,65 m.*
[2] Tie for third place between Herbert Kerrigan (USA) and Themistoklis Diakidis (GRE) at 5' 7½" *1,72 m.*
[3] Con Leahy (GBR/IRL), István Somodi (HUN) and Geo André (FRA) tied for second place at 6' 2" *1,88 m.*

Dick Fosbury (USA), whose back flop style in winning the high jump in 1968 at 7 feet 4¼ inches caught the imagination of the stadium and television viewers all over the world.

	GOLD	SILVER	BRONZE
1936	Cornelius C. Johnson (USA) 6′ 7¾″ *2,03 m**	David D. Albritton (USA) 6′ 6¾″ *2,00 m*	Delos P. Thurber (USA) 6′ 6¾″ 2,00 m
1948	John A. Winter (AUS) 6′ 6″ *1,98 m*	Björn Paulsen (NOR) 6′ 4¾″ *1,95 m*	George A. Stanich (USA) 6′ 4¾″ *1,95 m*
1952	Walter F. Davis (USA) 6′ 8¼″ *2,04 m**	Kenneth G. Wiesner (USA) 6′ 7″ *2,01 m*	Jose Telles da Conceicao (BRA) 6′ 6″ *1,98 m*
1956	Charles E. Dumas (USA) 6′ 11½″ *2,12 m**	Charles Porter (AUS) 6′ 10½″ *2,10 m*	Igor Kashkarov (URS) 6′ 9¾″ *2,08 m*
1960	Robert Shavlakadze (URS) 7′ 1″ *2,16 m**	Valeriy N. Brumel (URS) 7′ 1″ *2,16 m**	John C. Thomas (USA) 7′ 0¼″ *2,14 m*
1964	Valeriy N. Brumel (URS) 7′ 1¾″ *2,18 m**	John C. Thomas (USA) 7′ 1¾″ *2,18 m**	John Rambo (USA) 7′ 1″ *2,16 m*
1968	Richard Fosbury (USA) 7′ 4¼″ *2,24 m**	Edward J. Caruthers (USA) 7′ 3½″ *2,22 m*	Valentin Gavrilov (URS) 7′ 2½″ *2,20 m*
1972	Yuri Tarmak (URS) 7′ 3¾″ *2,23 m*	Stefan Junge (GDR) 7′ 3″ *2,21 m*	Dwight E. Stones (USA) 7′ 3″ *2,21 m*
1976	Jacek Wszola (POL) 7′ 4½″ *2,25 m**	Greg Joy (CAN) 7′ 3¾″ *2,23 m*	Dwight E. Stones (USA) 7′ 3″ *2,21 m*
1980	Gerd Wessig (GDR) 7′ 9″ *2,36 m**	Jacek Wszola (POL) 7′ 7″ *2,31 m*	Jorg Freimuth (GDR) 7′ 7″ *2,31 m*

POLE VAULT

1896	William W. Hoyt (USA) 10′ 9¾″ *3,30 m**	Albert C. Tyler (USA) 10′ 7¾″ *3,25 m*	Evangelos Damaskos (GRE) 9′ 4″ *2,85 m*
1900	Irving K. Baxter (USA) 10′ 9¾″ *3,30 m**	M. B. Colkett (USA) 10′ 7¾″ *3,25 m*	Carl-Albert Andersen (NOR) 10′ 5¾″ *3,20 m*
1904	Charles E. Dvorak (USA) 11′ 6″ *3,50 m**	Leroy Samse (USA) 11′ 3″ *3,43 m*	L. Wilkins (USA) 11′ 3″ *3,43 m*
1906	Fernand Gonder (FRA) 11′ 1¾″ *3,40 m*	Bruno Söderström (SWE) 11′ 1¾″ *3,40 m*	Ernest C. Glover (USA) 10′ 11¾″ *3,35 m*
1908	Edward T. Cooke (USA) 12′ 2″ *3,70 m**	Alfred C. Gilbert[1] (USA) 12′ 2″ *3,70 m**	[2]
1912	Harry S. Babcock (USA) 12′ 11½″ *3,95 m**	[3]	
1920	Frank K. Foss (USA) 13′ 5″ *4,09 m**	Henry Petersen (DEN) 12′ 1½″ *3,70 m*	Edwin E. Meyers (USA) 11′ 9½″ *3,60 m*
1924	Lee S. Barnes (USA) 12′ 11½″ *3,95 m*	Glenn Graham (USA) 12′ 11½″ *3,95 m*	James K. Brooker (USA) 12′ 9½″ *3,90 m*
1928	Sabin W. Carr (USA) 13′ 9¼″ *4,20 m**	William Droegemuller (USA) 13′ 5¼″ *4,10 m*	Charles E. McGinnis (USA) 12′ 11½″ *3,95 m*
1932	William W. Miller (USA) 14′ 1¾″ *4,31 m**	Shuhei Nishida (JPN) 14′0″ *4,26 m*	George G. Jefferson (USA) 13′ 9″ *4,19 m*
1936	Earle Meadows (USA) 14′ 3¼″ *4,35 m**	Shuhei Nishida (JPN) 13′ 11¼″ *4,25 m*	Sueo Oe (JPN) 13′ 11¼″ *4,25 m*
1948	O. Guinn Smith (USA) 14′ 1¼″ *4,30 m*	Erkki O. Kataja (FIN) 13′ 9¼″ *4,20 m*	Robert E. Richards (USA) 13′ 9¼″ *4,20 m*
1952	Robert E. Richards (USA) 14′ 11″ *4,55 m**	Donald D. R. Laz (USA) 14′ 9″ *4,50 m*	Ragnar T. Lundberg (SWE) 14′ 5″ *4,40 m*
1956	Robert E. Richards (USA) 14′ 11½″ *4,56 m**	Robert A. Gutowski (USA) 14′ 10¼″ *4,53 m*	Georgios Roubanis (GRE) 14′ 9″ *4,50 m*
1960	Donald G. Bragg (USA) 15′ 5″ *4,70 m**	Ronald H. Morris (USA) 15′ 1″ *4,60 m*	Eeles Landström (FIN) 14′ 11″ *4,55 m*
1964	Frederick M. Hansen (USA) 16′ 8¾″ *5,10 m**	Wolfgang Reinhardt (GER) 16′ 6¾″ *5,05 m*	Klaus Lehnertz (GER) 16′ 4¾″ *5,00 m*
1968	Robert L. Seagren (USA) 17′ 8½″ *5,40 m**	Claus Schiprowski (GER) 17′ 8½″ *5,40 m**	Wolfgant Nordwig (GDR) 17′ 8½″ *5,40 m**

[1] Tied for gold medal.
[2] Tie for bronze medal between Edward B. Archibald (CAN), Charles S. Jacobs (USA) and Bruno Söderström (SWE) at 11′ 9″ *3,58 m*.
[3] Tie for silver medal between Frank T. Nelson (USA) and Marcus S. Wright (USA) at 12′ 7½″ *3,85 m*.

GOLD	SILVER	BRONZE
1972 Wolfgang Nordwig (GDR) 18' 0½" 5,50 m*	Robert L. Seagren (USA) 17' 8½" 5,40 m	Jan E. Johnson (USA) 17' 6½" 5,35 m
1976 Tadeusz Slusarski (POL) 18' 0½" 5,50 m*	Antti Kalliomaki (FIN) 18' 0½" 5,50 m*	David Roberts (USA) 18' 0½" 5,50 m*
1980 Wladyslaw Kozakiewicz (POL) 18' 11½" 5,78 m*	Konstantin Volkov (URS) 18' 6½" 5,65 m	Tadeusz Slusarski (POL) 18' 6½" 5,65 m

Bob Seagren retained the USA unbeaten gold medal run in the pole vault, but only on the "count back" from two Germans who also cleared 17 feet 8½ inches in 1968.

BROAD JUMP (LONG JUMP)

	GOLD	SILVER	BRONZE
1896	Ellery H. Clark (USA) 20' 10" 6,35 m*	Robert S. Garrett (USA) 20' 3¼" 6,18 m	James B. Connolly (USA) 20' 0½" 6,11 m
1900	Alvin C. Kraenzlein (USA) 23' 6¾" 7,18 m*	Myer Prinstein (USA) 23' 6¼" 7,17 m	Patrick J. Leahy (GBR) 22' 9½" 6,95 m
1904	Myer Prinstein (USA) 24' 1" 7,34 m*	Daniel Frank (USA) 22' 7¼" 6,89 m	Robert S. Stangland (USA) 22' 7" 6,88 m
1906	Myer Prinstein (USA) 23' 7¼" 7,20 m	Peter O'Connor (GBR/IRL) 23' 0½" 7,02 m	Hugo Friend (USA) 22' 10" 6,96 m
1908	Francis C. Irons (USA) 24' 6½" 7,48 m*	Daniel J. Kelly (USA) 23' 3¼" 7,09 m	Calvin D. Bricker (CAN) 23' 3" 7,08 m
1912	Albert L. Gutterson (USA) 24' 11" 7,60 m*	Calvin D. Bricker (CAN) 23' 7¾" 7,21 m	Georg Åberg (SWE) 23' 6½" 7,18 m
1920	William Petterson (SWE) 23' 5¼" 7,15 m	Carl E. Johnson (USA) 23' 3¼" 7,09 m	Erik Abrahamsson (SWE) 23' 2½" 7,08 m
1924[1]	William De Hart Hubbard (USA) 24' 5" 7,44 m	Edward O. Gourdin (USA) 23' 10¼" 7,27 m	Sverre Hansen (NOR) 23' 9¾" 7,26 m
1928	Edward B. Hamm (USA) 25' 4¼" 7,73 m*	Silvio Cator (HAI) 24' 10¼" 7,58 m	Alfred H. Bates (USA) 24' 3¼" 7,40 m

[1] In the 1924 Pentathlon Robert LeGendre (US) had jumped 25' 5¾" 7,76 m but this was not classed as the Olympic broad jump record.

LEFT: Francis Irons (USA) handily won the 1908 long jump with an Olympic record leap of 24 feet 6½ inches.

RIGHT: Bob Beamon (USA) achieving the star performance of the 1968 Olympics with a world-record-shattering long jump of 29 feet 2½ inches. This record is confidently predicted as one that will last into the 21st century.

LEFT: In an incredible display of athletic longevity, Viktor Saneyev (URS) won the gold medal in the Olympic triple jump event in 1968, 1972 and again in 1976.

	GOLD	SILVER	BRONZE

1932	Edward L. Gordon (USA) 25' 0¾" 7,63 m	C. Lambert Redd (USA) 24' 11¼" 7,60 m	Chuhei Nambu (JPN) 24' 5¼" 7,44 m
1936	Jesse Owens (USA) 26' 5¼" 8,06 m*	Luz Long (GER) 25' 9¾" 7,87 m	Naoto Tajima (JPN) 25' 4½" 7,74 m
1948	William S. Steele (USA) 25' 7¾" 7,82 m	Thomas Bruce (AUS) 24' 9" 7,55 m	Herbert P. Douglas (USA) 24' 8¾" 7,54 m
1952	Jerome C. Biffle (USA) 24' 10" 7,57 m	Meredith C. Gourdine (USA) 24' 8¼" 7,53 m	Ödön Földessy (HUN) 23' 11¼" 7,30 m
1956	Gregory C. Bell (USA) 25' 8¼" 7,83 m	John D. Bennett (USA) 25' 2¼" 7,68 m	Jorma Valkama (FIN) 24' 6¼" 7,48 m
1960	Ralph H. Boston (USA) 26' 7½" 8,12 m*	Irvin Roberson (USA) 26' 7¼" 8,11 m	Igor A. Ter-Ovanesyan (URS) 26' 4½" 8,04 m
1964	Lynn Davies (GBR) 26' 5½" 8,07 m	Ralph H. Boston (USA) 26' 4" 8,03 m	Igor A. Ter-Ovanesyan (URS) 26' 2½" 7,99 m
1968	Robert Beamon (USA) 29' 2½" 8,90 m*	Klaus Beer (GDR) 26' 10¼" 8,19 m	Ralph H. Boston[2] (USA) 26' 9¼" 8,16 m
1972	Randy L. Williams (USA) 27' 0¼" 8,24 m	Hans Baumgartner (GER) 26' 10" 8,18 m	Arnie Robinson (USA) 26' 4" 8,03 m
1976	Arnie Robinson (USA) 27' 4¾" 8,35 m	Randy L. Williams (USA) 26' 7¼" 8,11 m	Frank Wartenberg (GDR) 26' 3¾" 8,02 m
1980	Lutz Dombrowski (GDR) 28' 0¼" 8,54 m	Frank Paschek (GDR) 26' 11¼" 8,21 m	Valery Podluzhnyi (URS) 26' 10" 8,18 m

[2] Set Olympic record of 27' 1¼" 8,27 m in qualifying round.

TRIPLE JUMP[1]

1896[2]	James B. Connolly (USA) 44' 11¾" 13,71 m*	Alexandre Tuffere (FRA) 41' 8" 12,70 m	Joannis Persakis (GRE) 41' 0¾" 12,52 m
1900	Myer Prinstein (USA) 47' 5½" 14,47 m*	James B. Connolly (USA) 45' 10" 13,97 m	Lewis P. Sheldon (USA) 44' 9" 13,64 m
1904	Myer Prinstein (USA) 47' 1" 14,35 m	Frederick Englehardt (USA) 45' 7¼" 13,90 m	Robert S. Stangland (USA) 43' 10¼" 13,36 m
1906	Peter O'Connor (GBR/IRL) 46' 2" 14,07 m	Con Leahy (GBR/IRL) 45' 10¼" 13,98 m	Thomas Cronan (USA) 44' 11¼" 13,70 m
1908	Timothy J. Ahearne (GBR) 48' 11¼" 14,91 m*	J. Garfield McDonald (CAN) 48' 5¼" 14,76 m	Edvard Larsen (NOR) 47' 2¾" 14,39 m
1912	Gustaf Lindblom (SWE) 48' 5" 14,76 m	Georg Åberg (SWE) 47' 7¼" 14,51 m	Erik Almlöf (SWE) 46' 5¾" 14,17 m
1920	Vilho Tuulos (FIN) 47' 7" 14,50 m	Folke Jansson (SWE) 47' 6" 14,48 m	Erik Almlöf (SWE) 46' 9¾" 14,27 m
1924	Anthony W. Winter (AUS) 50' 11¼" 15,52 m*	Luis Brunetto (ARG) 50' 7¼" 15,42 m	Vilho Tuulos (FIN) 50' 5" 15,37 m
1928	Mikio Oda (JPN) 49' 10¾" 15,21 m	Levi Casey (USA) 49' 9" 15,17 m	Vilho Tuulos (FIN) 49' 6¾" 15,11 m
1932	Chuhei Nambu (JPN) 51' 7" 15,72 m*	Erik Svensson (SWE) 50' 3¼" 15,32 m	Kenkichi Oshima (JPN) 49' 7¼" 15,12 m
1936	Naoto Tajima (JPN) 52' 5¾" 16,00 m*	Masao Harada (JPN) 51' 4½" 15,66 m	John P. Metcalfe (AUS) 50' 10" 15,50 m
1948	Arne Åhman (SWE) 50' 6¼" 15,40 m	George G. Avery (AUS) 50' 4¾" 15,36 m	Ruhi Sarialp (TUR) 49' 3½" 15,02 m
1952	Adhemar Ferreira da Silva (BRA) 53' 2½" 16,22 m*	Leonid Shcherbakov (URS) 52' 5" 15,98 m	Arnoldo Devonish (VEN) 50' 11" 15,52 m
1956	Adhemar Ferreira da Silva (BRA) 53' 7½" 16,35 m*	Vilhjálmur Einarsson (ISL) 53' 4" 16,26 m	Vitold Kreyer (URS) 52' 6½" 16,02 m
1960	Józef Schmidt (POL) 55' 1¾" 16,81 m*	Vladimir Goryayev (URS) 54' 6½" 16,63 m	Vitold Kreyer (URS) 53' 10¾" 16,43 m

[1] Formerly known as the Hop, Step and Jump.
[2] Winner took two hops with his right foot, contrary to present rule.

Leo Sexton (USA), the 1932 gold medal winner in the shot put, is one of a long line of American champions in this event.

	GOLD	SILVER	BRONZE
1964	Józef Schmidt (POL) 55′ 3¼″ *16,85 m**	Olyeg Fyedoseyev (URS) 54′ 4¾″ *16,58 m*	Viktor Kravchenko (URS) 54′ 4¼″ *16,57 m*
1968	Viktor Saneyev (URS) 57′ 0¾″ *17,39 m**	Nelson Prudencio (BRA) 56′ 7¾″ *17,27 m*	Giuseppe Gentile (ITA) 56′ 5¾″ *17,22 m*
1972	Viktor Saneyev (URS) 56′ 11″ *17,35 m*	Joerg Drehmel (GDR) 56′ 9¼″ *17,31 m*	Nelson Prudencio (BRA) 55′ 11¼″ *17,05 m*
1976	Viktor Saneyev (URS) 56′ 8¾″ *17,29 m*	James Butts (USA) 56′ 8½″ *17,18 m*	Joao de Oliveira (BRA) 55′ 5½″ *16,90 m*
1980	Jaak Uudmae (URS) 56′ 11″ *17,35 m*	Viktor Saneyev (URS) 56′ 6¾″ *17,24 m*	Joao de Oliveira (BRA) 56′ 6″ *17,22 m*

SHOT PUT

1896[1]	Robert S. Garrett (USA) 36′ 9½″ *11,22 m**	Miltiades Gouskos (GRE) 36′ 6¾″ *11,15 m*	Georgios Papasideris (GRE) 33′ 11¾″ *10,36 m*
1900[1]	Richard Sheldon (USA) 46′ 3″ *14,10 m**	Josiah C. McCracken (USA) 42′ 1¾″ *12,85 m*	Robert S. Garrett (USA) 40′ 7″ *12,37 m*
1904[1]	Ralph W. Rose (USA) 48′ 7″ *14,80 m**	W. Wesley Coe (USA) 47′ 3″ *14,40 m*	Leon E. J. Feuerbach (USA) 43′ 10½″ *13,37 m*
1906	Martin Sheridan (USA) 40′ 5″ *12,32 m*	Mihály Dávid (HUN) 38′ 9½″ *11,83 m*	Erik V. Lemming (SWE) 36′ 11¼″ *11,26 m*
1908	Ralph W. Rose (USA) 46′ 7½″ *14,21 m*	Dennis Horgan (GBR) 44′ 8¼″ *13,61 m*	John C. Garrels (USA) 43′ 3″ *13,18 m*
1912	Patrick J. McDonald (USA) 50′ 4″ *15,34 m**	Ralph W. Rose (USA) 50′ 0¼″ *15,25 m*	Lawrence A. Whitney (USA) 46′ 5″ *14,15 m*
1920	Ville Pörhölä (FIN) 48′ 7″ *14,81 m*	Elmer Niklander (FIN) 46′ 5¼″ *14,155 m*	Harry B. Liversedge (USA) 46′ 5″ *14,15 m*
1924	Clarence L. Houser (USA) 49′ 2″ *14,99 m*	Glenn Hartranft (USA) 49′ 1¾″ *14,98 m*	Ralph G. Hills (USA) 48′ 0¼″ *14,64 m*
1928	John Kuck (USA) 52′ 0¾″ *15,87 m**	Herman H. Brix (USA) 51′ 8″ *15,75 m*	Emil Hirschfeld (GER) 51′ 6¾″ *15,72 m*
1932	Leo J. Sexton (USA) 52′ 5¾″ *16,00 m**	Harlow P. Rothert (USA) 51′ 5″ *15,67 m*	František Douda (TCH) 51′ 2½″ *15,60 m*
1936	Hans Woelke (GER) 53′ 1¾″ *16,20 m**	Sulo Bärlund (FIN) 52′ 10½″ *16,12 m*	Gerhard Stöck (GER) 51′ 4½″ *15,66 m*
1948	Wilbur M. Thompson (USA) 56′ 2″ *17,12 m**	F. James Delaney (USA) 54′ 8½″ *16,68 m*	James E. Fuchs (USA) 53′ 10¼″ *16,42 m*
1952	W. Parry O'Brien (USA) 57′ 1¼″ *17,41 m**	C. Darrow Hooper (USA) 57′ 0½″ *17,39 m*	James E. Fuchs (USA) 55′ 11½″ *17,06 m*
1956	W. Parry O'Brien (USA) 60′ 11″ *18,57 m**	William H. Nieder (USA) 59′ 7½″ *18,18 m*	Jiři Skobla (TCH) 57′ 10¾″ *17,65 m*

[1] The shot was put from a 7 foot *2,13 m* square.

GOLD	SILVER	BRONZE
1960 William H. Nieder (USA) 64' 6¾" 19,68 m*	W. Parry O'Brien (USA) 62' 8¼" 19,11 m	Dallas C. Long (USA) 62' 4¼" 19,01 m
1964 Dallas C. Long (USA) 66' 8¼" 20,33 m*	J. Randel Matson (USA) 66' 3¼" 20,20 m	Vilmos Varju (HUN) 63' 7¼" 19,39 m
1968 J. Randel Matson[2] (USA) 67' 4½" 20,54 m	George R. Woods (USA) 66' 0" 20,12 m	Eduard Gushchin (URS) 65' 10¾" 20,09 m
1972 Wladyslaw Komar (POL) 69' 6" 21,18 m*	George R. Woods (USA) 69' 5½" 21,17 m	Hartmut Briesenick (GDR) 69' 4¼" 21,14 m
1976 Udo Beyer (GDR) 69' 0¾" 21,05 m	Evgeniy Mironov (URS) 69' 0" 21,03 m	Alexandr Baryshnikov[3] (URS) 68' 10¾" 21,00 m
1980 Vladimir Kiselyov (URS) 70' 0½" 21, 35 m*	Alexandr Baryshnikov (URS) 69' 2" 21,08 m	Udo Beyer (GDR) 69' 1¼" 21,06 m

[2] Set Olympic record of 67' 10¼" 20,68 m in qualifying round.
[3] Set Olympic record of 69' 11½" 21,32 m in qualifying round.

DISCUS THROW

GOLD	SILVER	BRONZE
1896 Robert S. Garrett (USA) 95' 7½" 29,15 m*	Panagiotis Paraskeyopoulos (GRE) 94' 11½" 28,95 m	Sotirios Versis (GRE) 94' 5" 28,78 m
1900 Rudolf Bauer (HUN) 118' 2½" 36,04 m*	František Janda-Suk (BOH) 115' 7½" 35,25 m	Richard Sheldon (USA) 113' 6" 34,60 m
1904 Martin J. Sheridan[1] (USA) 128' 10½" 39,28 m*	Ralph W. Rose (USA) 128' 10½" 39,28 m*	Nicolaos Georgantas (GRE) 123' 7½" 37,68 m
1906 Martin J. Sheridan (USA) 136' 0" 41,46 m*	Nicolaos Georgantas (GRE) 124' 10" 38,06 m	Werner Järvinen (FIN) 120' 9½" 36,82 m
1908 Martin J. Sheridan (USA) 134' 2" 40,89 m	Merritt H. Giffin (USA) 133' 6½" 40,70 m	Marquis F. Horr (USA) 129' 5" 39,44 m
1912 Armas R. Taipale (FIN) 148' 3½" 45,21 m*	Richard L. Byrd (USA) 138' 10" 42,32 m	James H. Duncan (USA) 138' 8½" 42,28 m
1920 Elmer Niklander (FIN) 146' 7" 44,68 m	Armas R. Taipale (FIN) 144' 11½" 44,19 m	Augustus R. Pope (USA) 138' 2½" 42,13 m
1924 Clarence L. Houser (USA) 151' 5" 46,15 m*	Vilho A. Niittymaa (FIN) 147' 5½" 44,95 m	Thomas J. Lieb (USA) 147' 0½" 44,83 m
1928 Clarence L. Houser (USA) 155' 2½" 47,32 m*	Antero Kivi (FIN) 154' 11" 47,23 m	James Corson (USA) 154' 6" 47,10 m
1932 John F. Anderson (USA) 162' 4½" 49,49 m*	Henri J. Laborde (FRA) 159' 0½" 48,47 m	Paul Winter (FRA) 157' 0" 47,85 m
1936 Kenneth K. Carpenter (USA) 165' 7" 50,48 m*	Gordon G. Dunn (USA) 161' 11" 49,36 m	Giorgio Oberweger (ITA) 161' 6" 49,23 m
1948 Adolfo Consolini (ITA) 173' 1½" 52,78 m*	Giuseppe Tosi (ITA) 169' 10½" 51,78 m	Fortune E. Gordien (USA) 166' 6½" 50,77 m
1952 Sim G. Iness (USA) 180' 6½" 55,03 m*	Adolfo Consolini (ITA) 176' 5" 53,78 m	James L. Dillion (USA) 174' 9½" 53,28 m
1956 Alfred A. Oerter (USA) 184' 10½" 56,36 m*	Fortune E. Gordien (USA) 179' 9½" 54,81 m	Desmond Koch (USA) 178' 5½" 54,40 m
1960 Alfred A. Oerter (USA) 194' 1½" 59,18 m*	Richard A. Babka (USA) 190' 4" 58,02 m	Richard L. Cochran (USA) 187' 6" 57,16 m
1964 Alfred A. Oerter (USA) 200' 1½" 61,00 m*	Ludvik Danek (TCH) 198' 6½" 60,52 m	David Weill (USA) 195' 2" 59,49 m
1968 Alfred A. Oerter (USA) 212' 6" 64,78 m*	Lothar Milde (GDR) 206' 11" 63,08 m	Ludvik Danek (TCH) 206' 5" 62,92 m
1972 Ludvik Danek (TCH) 211' 3" 64,40 m	L. Jay Silvester (USA) 208' 4" 63,50 m	Rickard Bruch (SWE) 208' 0" 63,40 m
1972 Ludvik Danek (TCH) 211' 3" 64.40 m	L. Jay Silvester (USA) 208' 4" 63.50 m	Rickard Bruch (SWE) 208' 0" 63,40 m
1976 Maurice MacWilkins (USA) 221' 5" 67,50 m[2]	Wolfgang Schmidt (GDR) 217' 3" 66,22 m	John Powell (USA) 215' 7" 65,70 m
1980 Viktor Rasshchupkin (URS) 218' 7" 66,64 m	Imrich Bugar (TCH) 217' 9" 66,38 m	Luis Delis (CUB) 217' 7" 66,32 m

[1] First place decided by a throw-off.
[2] Set Olympic record of 224' 0" 68,28 m in qualifying round.

ABOVE: Al Oerter (USA) dominated the discus competition for 4 consecutive meetings (1956 to 1968), a unique achievement in Olympic track and field.

RIGHT: The first Olympian to put the shot farther than 70 meters, Vladimir Kiselyov (URS) earned the gold medal at the 1980 Games.

LEFT: Hal Connolly (USA) won the hammer throw in Melbourne in 1956 with a throw of 207 feet 3½ inches.

HAMMER THROW

	GOLD	SILVER	BRONZE
1896	Event not held		
1900[1]	John J. Flanagan (USA) 163' 1½" *49,73 m*	Truxton T. Hare (USA) 161' 2" *49,13 m*	Josiah C. McCracken (USA) 139' 3½" *42,46 m*
1904	John J. Flanagan (USA) 168' 0½" *51,23 m**	John R. DeWitt (USA) 164' 10½" *50,26 m*	Ralph W. Rose (USA) 150' 0" *45,73 m*
1906	Event not held		
1908	John J. Flanagan (USA) 170' 4" *51,92 m**	Matthew J. McGrath (USA) 167' 11" *51,18 m*	Cornelius Walsh (CAN) 159' 1½" *48,50 m*
1912	Matthew J. McGrath (USA) 179' 7" *54,74 m**	Duncan Gillis (CAN) 158' 9" *48,39 m*	Clarence C. Childs (USA) 158' 0" *48,17 m*
1920	Patrick J. Ryan (USA) 173' 5½" *52,87 m*	Carl Johan Lind (SWE) 158' 10½" *48,43 m*	Basil Bennet (USA) 158' 3½" *48,25 m*
1924	Frederick D. Tootell (USA) 174' 10" *53,29 m*	Matthew J. McGrath (USA) 166' 9½" *50,84 m*	Malcolm C. Nokes (GBR) 160' 4" *48,87 m*
1928	Patrick O'Callaghan (IRL) 168' 7" *51,39 m*	Ossian Skiöld (SWE) 168' 3" *51,29 m*	Edmund F. Black (USA) 160' 10" *49,03 m*
1932	Patrick O'Callaghan (IRL) 176' 11" *53,92 m*	Ville Pörhölä (FIN) 171' 6" *52,27 m*	Peter E. Zaremba (USA) 165' 1½" *50,33 m*
1936	Karl Hein (GER) 185' 4" *56,49 m**	Erwin Blask (GER) 180' 6½" *55,04 m*	Fred Warngård (SWE) 179' 10½" *54,83 m*
1948	Imre Németh (HUN) 183' 11" *56,07 m*	Ivan Gubijan (YUG) 178' 0½" *54,27 m*	Robert H. Bennett (USA) 176' 3" *53,73 m*
1952	József Csermák (HUN) 197' 11½" *60,34 m**	Karl Storch (GER) 193' 1" *58,86 m*	Imre Németh (HUN) 189' 5" *57,74 m*
1956	Harold V. Connolly (USA) 207' 3½" *63,19 m**	Mikhail P. Krivonosov (URS) 206' 9" *63,03 m*	Anatoliy Samotsvetov (URS) 205' 2½" *62,56 m*
1960	Vasiliy Rudenkov (URS) 220' 1½" *67,10 m**	Gyula Zsivótzky (HUN) 215' 10" *65,79 m*	Tadeusz Rut (POL) 215' 4" *65,64 m*
1964	Romuald Klim (URS) 228' 9½" *69,74 m**	Gyula Zsivótzky (HUN) 226' 8" *69,09 m*	Uwe Beyer (GER) 223' 4½" *68,09 m*
1968	Gyula Zsivótzky (HUN) 240' 8" *73,36 m**	Romuald Klim (URS) 240' 5" *73,28 m*	Lázár Lovász (HUN) 228' 11" *69,78 m*
1972	Anatoli Bondarchuk (URS) 247' 8" *75,50 m**	Jochen Sachse (GDR) 245' 11" *74,96 m**	Vasili Khmelevski (URS) 242' 10½" *74,04 m*
1976	Yuri Sedykh (URS) 254' 4" *77,52 m**	Alexei Spiridonov (URS) 249' 7" *76,08 m*	Anatoli Bondarchuk (URS) 247' 8" *75,48 m*
1980	Yuri Sedykh (URS) 268' 4" *81,80 m**	Sergei Litvinov (URS) 264' 6" *80,64 m*	Yuri Tamm 259' 0" *78,96 m*

[1] Thrown from a 9 foot *2,74 m* instead of the now regular 7 foot *2,135 m* circle.

JAVELIN THROW

	GOLD	SILVER	BRONZE
1896–1904	Event not held		
1906	Erik V. Lemming (SWE) 176' 10" *53,90 m**	Knut Lindberg (SWE) 148' 2" *45,17 m*	Bruno Söerström (SWE) 147' 10½" *44,92 m*
1908	Erik V. Lemming (SWE) 179' 10½" *54,82 m**	Arne Halse (NOR) 165' 11" *50,57 m*	Otto Nilsson (SWE) 154' 6" *47,09 m*
1912	Erik V. Lemming (SWE) 198' 11" *60,64 m**	Juho Saaristo (FIN) 192' 5" *58,66 m*	Mór Kóczán (HUN) 182' 1" *55,50 m*
1920	Jonni Myyrä (FIN) 215' 9½" *65,78 m**	Urho Peltonen (FIN) 208' 4" *63,50 m*	Pekka Johansson (FIN) 207' 0" *63,09 m*
1924	Jonni Myyrä (FIN) 206' 6½" *62,96 m*	Gunnar Lindström (SWE) 199' 10" *60,92 m*	Eugene G. Oberst (USA) 191' 5" *58,35 m*
1928	Erik Lundkvist (SWE) 218' 6" *66,60 m**	Béla Szepes (HUN) 214' 1" *65,26 m*	Olav Sunde (NOR) 209' 10½" *63,97 m*
1932	Matti Järvinen (FIN) 238' 6½" *72,71 m**	Matti Sippala (FIN) 229' 0" *69,79 m*	Eino Penttila (FIN) 225' 4½" *68,69 m*
1936	Gerhard Stöck (GER) 235' 8" *71,84 m*	Yrjö Nikkanen (FIN) 232' 2" *70,77 m*	Kalervo Toivonen (FIN) 232' 0" *70,72 m*

Track and Field Athletics ■ 181

GOLD	SILVER	BRONZE
1948 K. Tapio Rautavaara (FIN) 228' 10½" 69,77 m	Steve A. Seymour (USA) 221' 7½" 67,56 m	József Várszegi (HUN) 219' 10½" 67,03 m
1952 Cyrus C. Young (USA) 242' 0½" 73,78 m*	William Miller (USA) 237' 8½" 72,46 m	Toivo Hyytiäinen (FIN) 235' 10" 71,89 m
1956 Egil Danielsen (NOR) 281' 2" 85,71 m*	Janusz Sidlo (POL) 262' 4½" 79,98 m	Viktor Tsibulenko (URS) 260' 9½" 79,50 m
1960 Viktor Tsibulenko (URS) 277' 8" 84,64 m	Walter Krüger (GER) 260' 4" 79,36 m	Gergely Kulcsár (HUN) 257' 9" 78,57 m
1964 Pauli Nevala (FIN) 271' 2" 82,66 m	Gergely Kulcsár (HUN) 270' 0½" 82,32 m	Janis Lusis (URS) 264' 2" 80,57 m

Bruce Jenner (USA) acknowledges the cheers of the crowd after shattering Olympic and world records in the 1976 decathlon.

GOLD	SILVER	BRONZE
1968 Janis Lusis	Jorma V. P. Kinnunen	Gergely Kulcsár
(URS) 295' 7" 90,10 m*	(FIN) 290' 7" 88,58 m	(HUN) 285' 7½" 87,06 m
1972 Klaus Wolfermann	Janis Lusis	William Schmidt
(GER) 296' 10" 90.48 m*	(URS) 296' 9" 90,46 m	(USA) 276' 11½" 84,42 m
1976 Miklos Nemeth	Hannu Siitonen	Gheorghe Megelea
(HUN) 310' 4" 94,58 m*	(FIN) 288' 5" 87,92 m	(ROM) 285' 11" 87,16 m
1980 Dainis Kula	Aleksandr Makarov	Wolfgang Hanisch
(URS) 299' 2" 91,20 m	(URS) 294' 1" 89,64 m	(GDR) 284' 6" 86,72 m

DECATHLON[1]

(Figures refer to points scored)

1896–1908   Event not held

GOLD	SILVER	BRONZE
1912 Hugo Wieslander[2]	Charles Lomberg	Gösta Holmér
(SWE) 6,162	(SWE) 5,943	(SWE) 5,956
1920 Helge Løvland	Brutus Hamilton	Bertil Ohlson
(NOR) 5,970	(USA) 5,912	(SWE) 5,825
1924 Harold M. Osborn	Emerson Norton	Aleksander Klumberg
(USA) 6,668	(USA) 6,360	(EST) 6,260
1928 Paavo Yrjölä	Akilles Järvinen	J. Kenneth Doherty
(FIN) 6,774	(FIN) 6,815	(USA) 6,593
1932 James A. B. Bausch	Akilles Järvinen	Wolrad Eberle
(USA) 6,986	(FIN) 7,038	(GER) 6,830
1936 Glenn E. Morris	Robert H. Clark	Jack Parker
(USA) 7,421	(USA) 7,226	(USA) 6,918
1948 Robert B. Mathias	Ignace Heinrich	Floyd M. Simmons
(USA) 6,826	(FRA) 6,740	(USA) 6,711
1952 Robert B. Mathias	Milton G. Campbell	Floyd M. Simmons
(USA) 7,731	(USA) 7,132	(USA) 7,069
1956 Milton G. Campbell	Rafer L. Johnson	Vasiliy Kuznetsov
(USA) 7,708	(USA) 7,568	(URS) 7,461
1960 Rafer L. Johnson	Yang Chuan-kwang	Vasiliy Kuznetsov
(USA) 8,001	(TAI) 7,930	(URS) 7,624
1964 Willi Holdorf	Rein Aun	Hans-Joachim Walde
(GER) 7,887	(URS) 7,842	(GER) 7,809
1968 William A. Toomey	Hans-Joachim Walde	Kurt Bendlin
(USA) 8,193*	(FRG) 8,111	(FRG) 8,064
1972 Nikolai Avilov	Leonid Litvinenko	Ryszard Katus
(URS) 8,454*	(URS) 8,035	(POL) 7,984
1976 Bruce Jenner	Guido Kratschmer	Nikolai Avilov
(USA) 8,618*	(FRG) 8,411	(URS) 8,369
1980 Daley Thompson	Yuri Kutsenko	Sergei Zhelanov
(GBR) 8,495	(URS) 8,331	(URS) 8,135

---

[1] The decathlon consists of 100 m, long jump, shot put, high jump, 400 m, 110 m hurdles, discus, pole vault, javelin and 1500 m. The competition occupies 2 days (but 3 days in 1912). Scores given above are all recalculated on the 1962 tables. 1912 scores were based on the then Olympic record; the 1920–1932 scores on the Olympic records standing after the 1912 Games; the 1936 and 1948 Games were scored on the tables published in 1934; 1952–1960 Games on tables published in 1952, since then on tables published in 1962. It is noted that in 3 years (1912, 1928 and 1932) the original medal order would have been different had the 1962 values then prevailed.
[2] Jim Thorpe (USA) finished first with 6,845 pts but was later disqualified for a breach of the then amateur rules. He was reinstated posthumously by the IOC in 1982, but only as joint first.

Track and Field Athletics (Women)

MARRIED NAMES
The following won medals under both their maiden and their married names:

Becker—Mickler	Kohler—Birkemeyer	Schaller—Klier
Brehmer—Lathan	Manning—Jackson	Schlaak—Jahl
Eckert—Wockel	Odam—Tyler	Strickland—Delahunty
Foulds—Paul	Oelsner—Gohr	Vergova—Petkova
Khnykina—Dvalishvili	Richter—Górecka	Wieczorek—Ciepla
Kirszenstein—Szewinska	Romashkova—Ponomaryeva	Zharkova—Maslakova

100 METERS (109 yd. 1 ft.)

	GOLD	SILVER	BRONZE
1928	Elizabeth Robinson (USA) 12.2*	Fanny Rosenfeld (CAN) inches	Ethel Smith (CAN) inches
1932	Stanislawa Walasiewicz (POL) 11.9*	Hilda Strike (CAN) 11.9*	Wilhelmina von Bremen (USA) 12.0
1936	Helen H. Stephens (USA) 11.5	Stanislawa Walasiewicz (POL) 11.7	Kathe Krauss (GER) 11.9
1948	Francina E. Blankers-Koen (HOL) 11.9	Dorothy G. Manley (GBR) 12.2	Shirley B. Strickland (AUS) 12.2
1952	Marjorie Jackson (AUS) 11.5	Daphne L. E. Hasenjager (SAF) 11.8	Shirley B. Strickland (AUS) 11.9
1956	Betty Cuthbert (AUS) 11.5	Christa Stubnick (GER) 11.7	Marlene J. Mathews (AUS) 11.7

Wyomia Tyus (USA) successfully defends her 100 meters title in 1968 in the world record of 11.0 seconds.

Renate Stecher (No. 147) edges Raelene Boyle of Australia to become the fifth woman ever to win the 100 meters/200 meters double.

	GOLD	SILVER	BRONZE
1960	Wilma G. Rudolph (USA) 11.0*	Dorothy Hyman (GBR) 11.3	Giuseppina Leone (ITA) 11.3
1964	Wyomia Tyus (USA) 11.4	Edith Maguire (USA) 11.6	Ewa Kobukowska (POL) 11.6
1968	Wyomia Tyus (USA) 11.0*	Barbara A. Ferrell (USA) 11.1	Irena Szewinska (POL) 11.1
1972	Renate Stecher (GDR) 11.07	Raelene A. Boyle (AUS) 11.23	Silvia Chivas (CUB) 11.24
1976	Annegret Richter (GER) 11.08	Renate Stecher (GDR) 11.13	Inge Helten (GER) 11.17
1980	Ludmila Kondrateva (URS) 11.06	Marlies Gohr (GDR) 11.07	Ingrid Auerswald (GDR) 11.14

The performances listed below were Olympic records set additionally in preliminaries.

(Nine records were established prior to the 1928 final.)

12.2	Marie Dollinger (GER)	1932	11.4	Cuthbert	1956
11.9	Walasiewicz (twice)	1932	11.3	Rudolph	1960
			11.01	Richter	1976

Performances of 11.4 and 11.5 (final) by Stephens in 1936; 11.5 (final) by Cuthbert 1956; 11.0 (final) by Rudolph 1960; 11.3 by Tyus in 1964; 11.1 by Ferrell and 11.0 by Tyus in 1968 were wind assisted.

200 METERS (218 yd. 2 ft.)

	GOLD	SILVER	BRONZE
1928–1936	Event not held		
1948	Francina E. Blankers-Koen (HOL) 24.4	Audrey D. Williamson (GBR) 25.1	Audrey Patterson[1] (USA) 25.2
1952	Marjorie Jackson (AUS) 23.7	Bertha Brouwer (HOL) 24.2	Nadyezhda Khnykina (URS) 24.2
1956	Betty Cuthbert (AUS) 23.4*	Christa Stubnick (GER) 23.7	Marlene J. Mathews (AUS) 23.8
1960	Wilma G. Rudolph (USA) 24.0	Jutta Heine (GER) 24.4	Dorothy Hyman (GBR) 24.7
1964	Edith Maguire (USA) 23.0*	Irena Kirszenstein (POL) 23.1	Marilyn M. Black (AUS) 23.1
1968	Irena Szewinska (POL) 22.5*	Raelene A. Boyle (AUS) 22.7	Jennifer Lamy (AUS) 22.8
1972	Renate Stecher (GDR) 22.40*	Raelene A. Boyle (AUS) 22.45	Irena Szewinska (POL) 22.74
1976	Barbel Eckert (GDR) 22.37*	Annegret Richter (GER) 22.39	Renate Stecher (GDR) 22.47
1980	Barbel Wockel (GDR) 22.03*	Natalya Bochina (URS) 22.19	Merlene Ottey (JAM) 22.20

[1] A recently discovered photo-finish indicates that Shirley Strickland (AUS) was third.

The performances listed below were Olympic records set additionally in preliminaries.

25.7	Blankers-Koen	1948	24.3	Blankers-Koen	1948	22.9	Barbara A. Ferrell (USA) 1968
25.6	Cynthia A. Thompson (JAM) 1948		24.3	Khnykina	1952	22.9	Boyle 1968
			23.6	Jackson	1952	22.8	Ferrell 1968
			23.4	Jackson	1952		
25.3	Daphne L. E. Robb (SAF) 1948		23.2	Rudolph	1960		
			23.0	Boyle	1968		

400 METERS (437 yd. 1 ft.)

	GOLD	SILVER	BRONZE
1928–1960	Event not held		
1964	Betty Cuthbert (AUS) 52.0*	Ann E. Packer (GBR) 52.2	Judith F. Amoore (AUS) 53.4
1968	Colette Besson (FRA) 52.0*	Lillian B. Board (GBR) 52.1	Natalya Pyechenkina (URS) 52.2
1972	Monika Zehrt (GDR) 51.08*	Rita Wilden (GER) 51.21	Kathy Hammond (USA) 51.64
1976	Irena Szewinska (POL) 49.29*	Christina Brehmer (GDR) 50.51	Ellen Streidt (GDR) 50.55
1980	Marita Koch (GDR) 48.88*	Jarmila Kratochvilova (TCH) 49.46	Christina Lathan (GDR) 49.66

The performances listed below were Olympic records set additionally in preliminaries.

54.4	Antonia Munkácsi (HUN) 1964		51.94	Charlene Rendina (AUS) 1972		51.68	Helga Seidler (GDR) 1972
						51.47	Zehrt 1972
53.1	Packer	1964	51.71	Györgyi Balogh (HUN) 1972		50.48	Szewinska 1976
52.7	Packer	1964					

The 200 meters final in 1960 with Wilma Rudolph (USA) (far right), the gold medal winner of the 100 meters dash as well, wearing No. 117; Jutta Heine (GER), the silver medal winner wearing No. 77; and Dorothy Hyman (GBR), the bronze medal winner wearing No. 100. Also in the photo is Giuseppina Leone (ITA), No. 181, bronze medal winner in the 100 meters dash.

At the 1980 Games, Barbel Wockel (née Eckert) (GDR) successfully defended her Olympic titles at 200 meters and the 4 × 100 meters relay, thus becoming only the third woman athlete to win 4 gold medals in track and field.

800 METERS (874 yd. 2 ft.)

	GOLD	SILVER	BRONZE
1928	Lina Radke (GER) 2:16.8*	Kinuye Hitomi (JPN) 2:17.6	Inga Gentzel (SWE) 2:17.8
1932–1956	Event not held		
1960	Ludmila I. Shevtsova (URS) 2:04.3*	Brenda Jones (AUS) 2:04.4	Ursula Donath (GER) 2:05.6
1964	Ann E. Packer (GBR) 2:01.1*	Maryvonne Dupureur (FRA) 2:01.9	M. Ann M. Chamberlain (NZL) 2:02.8
1968	Madeline Manning (USA) 2:00.9*	Ilona Silai (ROM) 2:02.5	Maria F. Gommers (HOL) 2:02.6

LEFT: At Montreal in 1976, Irena Szewinska (POL), 30 years old, won the 400 meters event in world record time, giving her 7 Olympic medals since 1964. She is the only woman to win a medal in 4 successive Games. RIGHT: Lyudmila Bragina (URS) won the 1,500 meters in 1972 in a time faster than 6 past men's champions.

Tatyana Kazankina (URS) here wins the 800 meters event in 1976 in world record time. In the same Games she also won the gold medal at 1,500 meters and then successfully defended that title in 1980.

	GOLD	SILVER	BRONZE
1972	Hildegard Falck (GER) 1:58.6*	Niole Sabaite (URS) 1:58.7	Gunhild Hoffmeister (GDR) 1:59.2
1976	Tatyana Kazankina (URS) 1:54.9*	Nikolina Chtereva (BUL) 1:55.4	Elfi Zinn (GDR) 1:55.6
1980	Nadezhda Olizarenko (URS) 1:53.5*	Olga Mineyeva (URS) 1:54.9	Tatyana Providokhina (URS) 1:55.5

The performances listed below were Olympic records set additionally in preliminaries.

2:10.9	Antje Gleichfeid (GER) 1960	2:07.8 2:05.9	Donath 1960 Dixie I. Willis (AUS) 1960	2:04.1 1:58.9 1:56.5	Dupureur 1964 Svetla Zlateva (BUL) 1972 Anita Weiss (GDR) 1976

1,500 METERS (1640 yd. 1 ft.)

1928–68 Event not held

	GOLD	SILVER	BRONZE
1972	Lyudmila Bragina[1] (URS) 4:01.4*	Gunhild Hoffmeister (GDR) 4:02.8	Paola Cacchi-Pigni (ITA) 4:02.9
1976	Tatyana Kazankina (URS) 4:05.5	Gunhild Hoffmeister (GDR) 4:06.0	Ulrike Klapezynski (GDR) 4:06.1
1980	Tatyana Kazankina (URS) 3:56.6*	Christiane Wartenberg (GDR) 3:57.8	Nadezhda Olizarenko (URS) 3:59.6

[1]Set Olympic Records of 4:06.5 and 4:05.1 in preliminaries.

4 × 100 METERS (109 yd. 1 ft.) RELAY

1928	CANADA 48.4*	UNITED STATES 48.8	GERMANY 49.2
	Fanny Rosenfeld	Mary Washburn	Rosa Kellner
	Ethel Smith	Jessie Gross	Leni Schmidt
	Florence Bell	Loretta McNeil	Anni Holdmann
	Myrtle Cook	Elizabeth Robinson	Leni Junker
1932	UNITED STATES 47.0*	CANADA 47.0*	GREAT BRITAIN 47.6
	Mary L. Carew	Mildred Frizell	Eileen M. Hiscock
	Evelyn Furtsch	Lilian Palmer	Gwendoline A. Porter
	Annette J. Rogers	Mary Frizell	Violet R. Webb
	Wilhelmina Von Bremen	Hilda Strike	Nellie Halstead
1936	UNITED STATES 46.9	GREAT BRITAIN 47.6	CANADA 47.8
	Harriet C. Bland	Eileen M. Hiscock	Dorothy E. Brookshaw
	Annette J. Rogers	Violet Olney	Mildred J. Dolson
	Elizabeth Robinson	Audrey K. Brown	Hilda M. Cameron
	Helen H. Stephens	Barbara H. A. Burke	Aileen A. Meagher
1948	NETHERLANDS 47.5	AUSTRALIA 47.6	CANADA 47.8
	Xenia Stad-de-Jong	Shirley B. Strickland	Viola Myers
	Jeanette J. M. Witziers-Timmers	Joy E. Maston	Nancy Mackay
	Gerda J. M. Van der Kade Koudijs	Betty L. McKinnon	Doris P. Foster
	Francina E. Blankers-Koen	Joyce A. King	Patricia Jones
1952	UNITED STATES 45.9*	GERMANY 45.9*	GREAT BRITAIN 46.2
	Mae Faggs	Ursula Knab	Sylvia Cheeseman
	Barbara P. Jones	Maria Sander	June F. Foulds
	Janet T. Moreau	Helga Klein	Jean C. Desforges
	Catherine Hardy	Marga Peterson	Heather J. Armitage
1956	AUSTRALIA 44.5*	GREAT BRITAIN 44.7	UNITED STATES 44.9
	Shirley B. Delahunty	Anne Pashley	Mae Faggs
	Norma Crocker	Jean E. Scrivens	Margaret Matthews
	Fleur Mellor	June F. Paul	Wilma G. Rudolph
	Betty Cuthbert	Heather J. Armitage	Isabelle Daniels

	GOLD	SILVER	BRONZE
1960	**UNITED STATES** 44.5	GERMANY 44.8	POLAND 45.0
	Martha Hudson	Martha Langbein	Tereza B. Wieczorek
	Lucinda Williams	Anni Biechl	Barabara Janiszewska
	Barbara P. Jones	Brunhilde Hendrix	Celina Jesionowska
	Wilma G. Rudolph	Jutta Heine	Halina Richter
1964	**POLAND** 43.6*	UNITED STATES 43.9	GREAT BRITAIN 44.0
	Tereza B. Ciepla	Willye D. White	Janet M. Simpson
	Irena Kirzsenstein	Wyomia Tyus	Mary D. Rand
	Halina Górecka	Marilyn White	Daphne Arden
	Ewa Klobukowska	Edith Maguire	Dorothy Hyman
1968	**UNITED STATES** 42.8*	CUBA 43.3	U.S.S.R. 43.4
	Barbara A. Ferrell	Marlene Elejarde	Ludmila Zharkova
	Margaret A. Bailes	Fulgencia Romay	Galina Bukharina
	Mildrette Netter	Violeta Quesada	Vyera Popkova
	Wyomia Tyus	Miguelina Cobián	Ludmila Samotyesova
1972	**WEST GERMANY** 42.81*	EAST GERMANY 42.95	CUBA 43.36
	Christine Krause	Evelyn Kaufer	Marlene Elejarde
	Ingrid Mickler	Christina Heinich	Carmen Valdes
	Annegret Richter	Barbel Struppert	Fulgencia Romay
	Heidemarie Rosendahl	Renate Stecher	Silvia Chivas
1976	**EAST GERMANY** 42.55*	WEST GERMANY 42.59	U.S.S.R. 43.09
	Marlies Oelsner	Elvira Possekel	Tatyana Prorochenko
	Renate Stecher	Inge Helten	Ludmila Maslakova
	Carla Bodendorf	Annegret Richter	Nadezda Besfamilnaya
	Barbel Eckert	Annegret Kroniger	Vera Anisimova
1980	**EAST GERMANY** 41.60*	U.S.S.R. 42.10	GREAT BRITAIN 42.43
	Romy Muller	Vera Komissova	Heather Hunte
	Barbel Wockel	Ludmila Maslakova	Kathryn Smallwood
	Ingrid Auerswald	Vera Anissimova	Beverley Goddard
	Marlies Gohr	Natalya Bochina	Sonia Lannaman

Soviet women pass the baton enroute to their gold medal in the 4 × 400 meters relay in Moscow in 1980.

Close finish in the 4 × 100 meters relay in 1956, which produced a world record and gold medals for Australia, with Betty Cuthbert (middle) the winner over Great Britain's anchor runner Heather Armitage.

The performances listed below were Olympic records set additionally in preliminaries.

49.4	Canada	1928	44.9	Australia	1956	43.4	United States	1968
46.4	Germany	1936	44.9	Germany	1956	43.4	Netherlands	1968
46.1	Australia	1952	44.4	United States	1960	42.61	West Germany	1976

4 × 400 METERS (437 yd. 1 ft.) RELAY

GOLD	SILVER	BRONZE
1928–68 Event not held		
1972 **EAST GERMANY** 3:23.0*	**UNITED STATES** 3:25.2	**WEST GERMANY** 3:26.5
Dagmar Kasling	Mable Fergerson	Annette Ruckes
Rita Kuhne	Madeline Jackson	Inge Bödding
Helga Seidler	Cheryl Toussaint	Hildegard Falck
Monika Zehrt	Kathy Hammond	Rita Wilden
1976 **EAST GERMANY** 3:19.2*	**UNITED STATES** 3:22.8	U.S.S.R. 3:24.2
Doris Maletzki	Debra Sapenter	Inta Klimovicha
Brigitte Rohde	Sheila Ingram	Ludmila Aksenova
Ellen Streidt	Pam Jiles	Natalia Sokolova
Christina Brehmer	Rosalyn Bryant	Nadezda Ilina
1980 U.S.S.R. 3:20.2	**EAST GERMANY** 3:20.4	**GREAT BRITAIN** 3:27.5
Tatyana Prorochenko	Gabriele Lowe	Linsey MacDonald
Tatyana Goichik	Barbara Krug	Michelle Probert
Nina Zuskova	Christina Lathan	Joslyn Hoyte-Smith
Irina Nazarova	Marita Koch	Janine MacGregor

The following record times were set in the preliminaries of the 1972 Games: 3:29.3 West Germany, 3:28.5 East Germany.

Annelie Ehrhardt of East Germany took the gold medal at the first running of the women's 100 meters hurdles in 1972.

East German Rosemarie Ackermann used the "old fashioned" straddle style jump to win the gold medal in the high jump at Montreal in 1976.

100 METERS (109 yd.1 ft.) HURDLES

	GOLD	SILVER	BRONZE
1928–68	Event not held		
1972	Annelie Ehrhardt (GDR) 12.59*	Valeria Bufanu (ROM) 12.84	Karin Balzer (GDR) 12.90
1976	Johanna Schaller (GDR) 12.77	Tatyana Anisimova (URS) 12.78	Natalia Lebedeva (URS) 12.80
1980	Vera Komisova (URS) 12.56*	Johanna Klier (GDR) 12.63	Lucyna Langer (POL) 12.65

The following record times were set in the preliminaries of the 1972 Games: 12.0 and 12.73 by Ehrhardt.

HIGH JUMP

	GOLD	SILVER	BRONZE
1928	Ethel Catherwood (CAN) 5' 2½" 1,59 m*	Carolina A. Gisolf (HOL) 5' 1¼" 1,56 m	Mildred Wiley (USA) 5' 1¼" 1,56 m
1932	Jean M. Shiley (USA) 5' 5" 1,65 m*	Mildred Didrikson (USA) 5' 5" 1,65 m*	Eva Dawes (CAN) 5' 3" 1,60 m
1936	Ibolya Csák (HUN) 5' 3" 1,60 m	Dorothy J.B. Odam (GBR) 5' 3" 1,60 m	Elfriede Kaun (GER) 5' 3" 1,60 m
1948	Alice Coachman (USA) 5' 6" 1,68 m*	Dorothy J.B. Tyler (GBR) 5' 6" 1,68 m*	Micheline O. M. Ostermeyer (FRA) 5'3¼" 1,61 m
1952	Esther C. Brand (SAF) 5' 5½" 1,67 m	Sheila W. Lerwill (GBR) 5' 5" 1,65 m	Alexandra G. Chudina (URS) 5' 4" 1,63m
1956	Mildred McDaniel (USA) 5' 9¼" 1,76 m*		
1960	Iolanda Balas (ROM) 6' 0¾" 1,85 m*	[2]	[2]
1964	Iolanda Balas (ROM) 6' 2¾" 1,90 m*	Michele Brown (AUS) 5' 10¾" 1,80 m	Taisia Chenchik (URS) 5' 10" 1,78 m
1968	Miloslava Rezkova (TCH) 5' 11½" 1,82 m	Antonina Okorokova (URS) 5' 10¾" 1,80 m	Valentina Kozyr (URS) 5' 10¾" 1,80 m
1972	Ulrike Meyfarth (GER) 6' 3½" 1,92 m*	Yordanka Blagoyeva (BUL) 6' 2" 1,88 m	Ilona Gusenbauer (AUT) 6' 2" 1,88 m
1976	Rosemarie Ackermann (GDR) 6' 4" 1,93 m*	Sara Simeoni (ITA) 6' 3¼" 1,91 m	Yordanka Blagoyeva (BUL) 6' 3¼" 1,91 m
1980	Sara Simeoni (ITA) 6' 5½" 1,97 m*	Urszula Kielan (POL) 6' 4½" 1,94 m	Jutta Kirst (GDR) 6' 4½" 1,94 m

[1] Tie for second place by Thelma E. Hopkins (GBR) and Maria Pissrayeva (URS) at 5' 5½" 1,67 m.
[2] Tie for second place by Jaroslawa Józwiakowska (POL) and Dorothy A. Shirley (GBR) at 5' 7¼" 1,71 m.

LONG JUMP

	GOLD	SILVER	BRONZE
1928–1936	Event not held		
1948	V. Olga Gyarmati (HUN) 18' 8" 5,69 m*	Noemi Simonetto de Portela (ARG) 18' 4¼" 5,60 m	B. Ann-Britt Leyman (SWE) 18' 3¼" 5,57 m
1952	Yvette W. Williams (NZL) 20' 5½" 6,24 m*	Alexandra G. Chudina (URS) 20' 1½" 6,14 m	Shirley Cawley (GBR) 19' 5" 5,92 m
1956	Elzbieta Krzesinska (POL) 20' 10" 6,35 m*	Willye D. White (USA) 19' 11¾" 6,09 m	Nadyezhda Dvalishvili (URS) 19' 10¾" 6,07 m
1960	Vyera Krepkina (URS) 20' 10¾" 6,37 m*	Elzbieta Krzesinska (POL) 20' 6¾" 6,27 m	Hildrun Claus (GER) 20' 4¼" 6,21 m

	GOLD	SILVER	BRONZE
1964	Mary D. Rand (GBR) 22′ 2¼″ 6,76 m*	Irena Kirszenstein (POL) 21′ 7¾″ 6,60 m	Tatyana S. Schelkanova (URS) 21′ 0¾″ 6,42 m
1968	Viorica Viscopoleanu (ROM) 22′ 4½″ 6,82 m*	Sheila Sherwood (GBR) 21′ 10¾″ 6,68 m	Tatyana Talysheva (URS) 21′ 10″ 6,66 m
1972	Heidemarie Rosendahl[1] (GER) 22′ 3″ 6,78 m	Diana Yorgova (BUL) 22′ 2½″ 6,77 m	Eva Suranova (TCH) 21′ 10¾″ 6,67 m
1976	Angela Voigt (GDR) 22′ 0¾″ 6,72 m	Kathy McMillan (USA) 21′ 10¼″ 6,66 m	Lidia Alfeyeva (URS) 21′ 8″ 6,60 m
1980	Tatiana Kolpakova (URS) 23′ 2″ 7,06 m*	Brigitte Wujak (GDR) 23′ 1¼″ 7,04 m	Tatiana Skachko (URS) 23′ 0″ 7,01 m

[1]Set Olympic record of 22′ 5″ 6,83 m in Pentathlon.

SHOT PUT

	GOLD	SILVER	BRONZE
1928–1936	Event not held		
1948	Micheline O. M. Ostermeyer (FRA) 45′ 1¼″ 13,75 m*	Amelia Piccinini (ITA) 42′ 11½″ 13,09 m	Ina Schäffer (AUT) 42′ 10¾″ 13,08 m
1952	Galina I. Zybina (URS) 50′ 1½″ 15,28 m*	Marianne Werner (GER) 47′ 9½″ 14,57 m	Klavdia Tochenova (URS) 47′ 6¾″ 14,50 m
1956	Tamara Tyshkyevich (URS) 54′ 5″ 16,59 m*	Galina I. Zybina (URS) 54′ 2¾″ 16,53 m	Marianne Werner (GER) 51′ 2½″ 15,61 m
1960	Tamara N. Press (URS) 56′ 9¾″ 17,32 m*	Johanna Lüttge (GER) 54′ 5¾″ 16,61 m	Earlene I. Brown (USA) 53′ 10¼″ 16,42 m
1964	Tamara N. Press (URS) 59′ 6″ 18,14 m*	Renate Garisch (GER) 57′ 9¼″ 17,61 m	Galina I. Zybina (URS) 57′ 3″ 17,45 m
1968	Margitta Gummel (GDR) 64′ 4″ 19,61 m*	Marita Lange (GDR) 61′ 7¼″ 18,78 m	Nadyezhda Chizhova (URS) 59′ 8″ 18,19 m
1972	Nadyezhda Chizhova (URS) 69′ 0″ 21,03 m*	Margitta Gummel (GDR) 66′ 4¼″ 20,22 m	Ivanka Khristova (BUL) 63′ 6″ 19,35 m
1976	Ivanka Khristova (BUL) 69′ 5¼″ 21,16 m*	Nadyezhda Chizhova (URS) 68′ 9¼″ 20,96 m	Helena Fibingerova (TCH) 67′ 9¾″ 20,67 m
1980	Ilona Slupianek (GDR) 73′ 6¼″ 22,41m*	Svetlana Krachevskaya (URS) 70′ 3¼″ 21,42 m	Margitta Pufe (GDR) 69′ 6¾″ 21,20 m

Tamara Andreyevna Tyschkyevich, the Russians' 244-lb. gold medal winner in the shot put in 1956.

DISCUS THROW

	GOLD	SILVER	BRONZE
1928	Helena Konopacka (POL) 129' 11½" 39,62m*	Lillian Copeland (USA) 121' 7½" 37,08 m	Ruth Svedberg (SWE) 117' 10" 35,92 m
1932	Lillian Copeland (USA) 133' 1½" 40,58 m*	Ruth Osburn (USA) 131' 7½" 40,11 m	Jadwiga Wajsówna (POL) 127' 1" 38,73 m
1936	Gisela Mauermayer (GER) 156' 3" 47,63 m*	Jadwiga Wajsówna (POL) 151' 7½" 46,22 m	Paula Mollenhauer (GER) 130' 6½" 39,80 m
1948	Micheline O. M. Ostermeyer (FRA) 137' 6" 41,92 m	Edera C. Gentile (ITA) 135' 0½" 41,17 m	Jacqueline Mazeas (FRA) 132' 9" 40,47 m
1952	Nina Romashkova (URS) 168' 8" 51,42 m*	Yelizaveta Bagryantseva (URS) 154' 5½" 47,08 m	Nina Dumbadze (URS) 151' 10" 46,29 m
1956	Olga Fikotová (TCH) 176' 1½" 53,69 m*	Irina Beglyakova (URS) 172' 4½" 52,54 m	Nina Ponomaryeva (URS) 170' 8" 52,02 m
1960	Nina Ponomaryeva (URS) 180' 9" 55,10 m*	Tamara N. Press (URS) 172' 6" 52,59 m	Lia Manoliu (ROM) 171' 9" 52,36 m
1964	Tamara N. Press (URS) 187' 10½" 57,27 m*	Ingrid Lotz (GER) 187' 8" 57,21 m	Lia Manoliu (ROM) 186' 10½" 56,97 m
1968	Lia Manoliu (ROM) 191' 2" 58,28 m*	Liesel Westermann (GER) 189' 6" 57,76 m	Jolán Kleiber (HUN) 180' 1" 54,90 m
1972	Faina Melnik (URS) 218' 7" 66,62 m*	Argentina Menis (ROM) 213' 5" 65,06 m	Vassilka Stoyeva (BUL) 211' 1" 64,34 m
1976	Evelin Schlaak (GDR) 226' 4" 69,00 m*	Maria Vergova (BUL) 220' 9" 67,30 m	Gabriele Hinzmann (GDR) 219' 3" 66,84 m
1980	Evelin Jahl (GDR) 229' 6" 69,96 m*	Maria Petkova (BUL) 222' 9" 67,90 m	Tatyana Lesovaya (URS) 221' 1" 67,40 m

JAVELIN THROW

	GOLD	SILVER	BRONZE
1928	Event not held		
1932	Mildred Didrikson (USA) 143' 4" 43,68 m*	Ellen Braumüller (GER) 142' 8½" 43,49 m	Tilly Fleischer (GER) 142' 1¼" 43,40 m
1936	Tilly Fleischer (GER) 148' 2½" 45,18 m*	Luise Krüger (GER) 142' 0" 43,29 m	Marja Kwasniewska (POL) 137' 1½" 41,80 m
1948	Herma Bauma (AUT) 149' 6" 45,57 m*	Kaisa V. Parviainen (FIN) 143' 8" 43,79 m	Lily M. L. Carlstedt (DEN) 140' 6½" 42,08 m
1952	Dana Zátopková (TCH) 165' 7" 50,47 m*	Alexandra G. Chudina (URS) 164' 0½" 50,01 m	Yelena Y. Gorchakova (URS) 163' 3" 49,76 m
1956	Inese Jaunzeme (URS) 176' 8" 53,86 m*	Marlene Ahrens (CHI) 165' 3" 50,38 m	Nadyezhda E. Konyayeva (URS) 164' 11½" 50,28 m
1960	Elvira A. Ozolina (URS) 183' 7½" 55,98 m*	Dana Zátopková (TCH) 176' 5" 53,78 m	Birute Kalediene (URS) 175' 4" 53,45 m
1964	Mihaela Penes (ROM) 198' 7" 60,54 m	Martá Rudase (HUN) 191' 2" 58,27 m	Yelena Y. Gorchakova (URS) 187' 2" 57,06 m[1]
1968	Angéla Németh (HUN) 198' 0" 60,36 m	Mihaela Penes (ROM) 196' 7" 59,92 m	Eva Janko (AUT) 190' 5" 58,04 m
1972	Ruth Fuchs (GDR) 209' 7" 63,88m*	Jacqueline Todten (GDR) 205' 2" 62,54 m	Kathy Schmidt (USA) 196' 8" 59,94 m
1976	Ruth Fuchs (GDR) 216' 4" 65,94 m*	Marion Becker (GDR) 212' 3" 64,70 m[2]	Kathy Schmidt (USA) 209' 10" 63,96 m
1980[3]	Maria Colon (CUB) 224' 5" 68,40 m*	Saida Gunba (URS) 222' 2" 67,76 m	Ute Hommola (GDR) 218' 4" 66,56 m

---

[1] Set Olympic record of 204' 8½" 62,40 m in qualifying round.
[2] Set Olympic record of 213' 8" 65,14 m in qualifying round.
[3] Ute Richter (GDR) set Olympic record of 218' 8" 66,67 m in qualifying round.

ABOVE: Ruth Fuchs (GDR) was a convincing winner in the 1972 javelin throw, beating the previous Olympic record by nearly 5 feet.

ABOVE: Dana Zatopkova (Czechoslovakia), whose husband won 4 gold medals, won a gold medal in the javelin throw herself in the 1952 Olympics.

RIGHT: Powerful Nadezhda Tkachenko (URS) turned in a world record performance in capturing the women's pentathlon gold medal in 1980.

PENTATHLON[1]
(Figures refer to points scored)

	GOLD	SILVER	BRONZE
1928–1960	Event not held		
1964	Trina R. Press (URS) 5,246*	Mary D. Rand (GBR) 5,035	Galina Bystrova (URS) 4,956
1968	Ingrid Becker (GER) 5,098	Liese Prokop (AUT) 4,966	Annamária Tóth (HUN) 4,959
1972	Mary E. Peters (GBR) 4,801*[2]	Heidemarie Rosendahl (GER) 4,791	Burglinde Pollak (GDR) 4,768
1976	Sigrun Siegl (GDR) 4,745[3]	Christine Laser (GDR) 4,745	Burglinde Pollak (GDR) 4,740
1980	Nadezhda Tkachenko (URS) 5,083*	Olga Rukavishnikova (URS) 4,937	Olga Kuragina (URS) 4,875

[1] The Pentathlon consisted of 100 m hurdles, shot put, high jump, long jump and 200 m from 1964 to 1976. In 1980 the 200 m was replaced by 800 m.
[2] New scoring tables introduced in May 1971.
[3] Siegl finished ahead of Laser in three events.

18. Volleyball (Men)

1896–1960	Event not held		
1964	**U.S.S.R.**	**CZECHOSLOVAKIA**	**JAPAN**
	Yury Chesnokov	Václav Šmidl	Yataka Demachi
	Yury Vengerovsky	Josef Labuda	Tsutomu Koyama
	Eduard Sibiryakov	Josef Musil	Sadatoshi Sugahara
	Dmitry Voskoboynikov	Petr Kop	Naohiro Ikeda
	Vazha Kacharava	Milan Čuda	Yasutaka Sato
	Stanislaw Ljugailo	Karel Paulus	Toshiaki Kosedo
	Vitaly Kovalenko	Bohumil Golián	Tokihiko Higuchi
	Yury Poyarkov	Boris Perušič	Masayuki Minami
	Ivan Bugaenkov	Pavel Schenk	Takeshi Tokutomi
	Nikolay Burobin	Ladislav Toman	Teruhisa Moriyama
	Valery Kalachikhin	Zdenek Humhal	Yuzo Nakamura
	Georgy Mondzolevsky	Josef Šorim	Katsutoshi Nekoda
1968	**U.S.S.R.**	**JAPAN**	**CZECHOSLOVAKIA**
	Eduard Sibiryakov	Naohiro Ikeda	Antonin Procházka
	Valery Kravchenko	Masayuki Minami	Jiri Svoboda
	Vladimir Belyaev	Katsutoshi Nekoda	Lubomir Zajíček
	Evgeny Lapinsky	Mamoru Shiragami	Josef Musil
	Oleg Antropov	Isao Koizumi	Josef Smolka
	Vasilijus Matushevas	Kenji Kimura	Vladimir Petlak
	Victor Mikhalchuk	Yasuaki Mitsumori	Petr Kop
	Yury Poyarkov	Jungo Morita	František Sokol
	Boris Tereshuk	Tadayoshi Yokota	Bohumil Golián
	Vladimir Ivanov	Seiji Oko	Zdenek Groessl
	Ivan Bugaenkov	Tetsuo Sato	Pavel Schenk
	Georgy Mondzolevsky	Kenji Shimaoka	Drahomir Koudelka
1972	**JAPAN**	**EAST GERMANY**	**U.S.S.R.**
	Katsutoshi Nekoda	Arnold Schulz	Valery Kravchenko
	Kenji Kimura	Wolfgang Webner	Efim Tchulak
	Yoshihide Fukao	Siegfried Schneider	Vladimir Poutiatov
	Jungo Morita	Wolfgang Weise	Vladimir Patkin
	Tadayoshi Yokota	Rudi Schumann	Leonid Zaiko
	Seiji Oko	Eckehard Pietzsch	Yuri Starunski
	Kenji Shimaoka	Wolfgang Löwe	Vladimir Kondra
	Yuzo Nakamura	Wolfgang Maibohm	Viatcheslav Domani
	Masayuki Minami	Rainer Tscharke	Victor Borsch
	Tetsuo Sato	Jürgen Maune	Alexandre Saprykine
	Yasuhiro Noguchi	Horse Peter	Evgeny Lapinsky
	Tetsuo Nishimoto	Horse Hagen	Yury Poyarkov

	GOLD	SILVER	BRONZE
1976	**POLAND**	**U.S.S.R.**	**CUBA**
	Wlodzimierz Stefanski	Anatoli Polishuk	Leonel Marshall
	Bronislaw Bebel	Viacheslav Zaitsev	Victoriano Sarmientos
	Lech Lasko	Efim Tchulak	Ernesto Martinez
	Tomasz Wojtowicz	Vladimir Dorohov	Victor Garcia
	Edward Skorek	Aleksandr Ermilov	Carlos Salas
	Wieslaw Gawlowski	Pavel Selivanov	Raul Vilches
	Miroslaw Rybaczewski	Oleg Moliboga	Jesus Savigne
	Zbigniew Lubiejewski	Vladimir Kondra	Lorenzo Martinez
	Ryszard Bosek	Yuri Starunski	Diego Lapera
	Wlodzimierz Sadalski	Vladimir Chernyshov	Antonio Rodriguez
	Zbigniew Zarzycki	Vladimir Ulanov	Alfredo Figueredo
	Marek Karbarz	Aleksandr Savin	Jorge Perez

The gold medal winning Polish team is seen here beating the Japanese by a 3–2 score in a semi-final match in 1976.

GOLD	SILVER	BRONZE
1980 U.S.S.R.	**BULGARIA**	**RUMANIA**
Yuriy Panchenko	Stoyan Guntchev	Corneliu Oros
Viacheslav Zaitsev	Kristo Stoyanov	Laurentiu Dumanoiu
Aleksandr Savin	Dimitar Zlatanov	Dan Girleanu
Vladimir Dorohov	Stefan Dimitrov	Nicu Stoian
Aleksandr Ermilov	Tzano Tzanov	Sorin Macavei
Pavel Selivanov	Petko Petkov	Constantin Sterea
Oleg Moliboga	Mitko Todorov	Neculae Vasile Pop
Vladimir Kondra	Emil Valchev	Gunter Enescu
Vladimir Chernyshov	Kristo Iliyev	Valter-Corneliu Chifu
Feodor Lashchenov	Yordan Ánghelov	Marius Cata-Chitiga
Vilyar Loor	Dimitar Dimitrov	Florin Mina
Valeriy Krivov	Kaspar Simeonov	Viorel Manole

Volleyball (Women)

GOLD	SILVER	BRONZE
1896–1960 Event not held		
1964 JAPAN	**U.S.S.R.**	**POLAND**
Masae Kasai	Antonina Ryzhova	Krystyna Czajkowska
Emiko Miyamoto	Astra Biltauer	Jozefa Ledwigowa
Kinuko Tanida	Ninel Lukanina	Maria Golimowska
Yuriko Handa	Ljudmila Buldakova	Jadwiga Rutkowska
Yoshiko Matsumara	Nelly Abramova	Danuta Kordaczuk
Sata Isobe	Tamara Tikhonina	Krystyna Jakobowska
Masako Kondo	Valentina Kamenek	Jadwiga Marko
Ayano Shibuki	Inna Ryskal	Maria Sliwkowa
Katsumi Matsumara	Marita Katusheva	Zofia Szczesniewska
Yoko Shinozaki	Tatyana Roschina	Krystyna Krupowa
Yuko Fujimoto	Valentina Mishak	
Setsuko Sasaki	Ludmila Gureeva	
1968 U.S.S.R.	**JAPAN**	**POLAND**
Ljudmila Buldakova	Setsuko Yoshika	Krystyna Czajkowska
Ljudmila Mikhailovskaya	Suzue Takayama	Jozefa Ledwigowa
Vera Lantratova	Toyoko Iwahara	Elzbieta Porzec
Vera Galushka	Yukiyo Kojima	Wanda Wiecha
Tatyana Sarycheva	Sachiko Fukunaka	Zofia Szczesniewska
Tatyana Ponyaeva	Kunie Shiskikura	Krystyna Jakobowska
Nina Smoleeva	Setsuko Inoue	Lidia Chmielnicka
Inna Ryskal	Sumie Oinuma	Barbara Niemczyk
Galina Leantieva	Keiko Hama	Krystyna Krupowa
Roza Salikhova		Halina Aszkielowicz
Valentina Vinogradova		Jadwiga Ksiazek
		Krystyna Ostromecka
1972 U.S.S.R.	**JAPAN**	**N. KOREA**
Inna Ryskal	Sumie Oinuma	Chun Ok Ri
Vera Douiounova	Noriko Yamashita	Myong Suk Kim
Tatyana Tretiakova	Seiko Shimakage	Zung Bok Kim
Nina Smoleeva	Makiko Furukawa	Ok Sun Kang
Roza Salikhova	Takako Iida	Yeun Ja Kim
Ljudmila Buldakova	Katsumi Matsumura	He Suk Hwang
Tatyana Gonobobleva	Michiko Shiokawa	Ok Rim Jang
Lubov Turina	Takako Shirai	Myong Suk Paek
Galina Leontieva	Mariko Okamoto	Chun Ja Ryom
Tatyana Sarycheva	Keiko Hama	Su Dae Kim
Ludmila Borozna	Yaeko Yamazaki	Ok Jin Jong
Natalia Koudreva	Toyoko Iwahara	
1976 JAPAN	**U.S.S.R.**	**KOREA**
Takako Iida	Anna Rostova	Soonbok Lee
Mariko Okamoto	Ludmila Shetinina	Junghye Yu
Echiko Maeda	Lilia Osadchaya	Kyungja Byon
Noriko Matsuda	Natalia Kushnir	Soonok Lee
Takako Shirai	Olga Kozakova	Myungsun Baik
Kiyomi Kato	Nina Smoleeva	Heesook Chang

GOLD	SILVER	BRONZE
Yuko Arakida	Lubov Rudovskaya	Kumja Ma
Katsuko Kanesaka	Larisa Bergen	Youngnae Yun
Mariko Yoshida	Inna Ryskal	Kyunghwa Yu
Shoko Takayanagi	Ludmila Chernysheva	Mikum Park
Hiromi Yano	Zoya Iusova	Soonok Jung
Juri Yokoyamma	Nina Muradian	Heajung Jo
1980 U.S.S.R.	EAST GERMANY	BULGARIA
Nadyezda Radzevich	Ute Kostrzeva	Tania Dimitrova
Natalya Razumova	Andrea Heim	Silva Petrunova
Olga Solovova	Annette Schultz	Anka Khristolova
Yelena Akhaminova	Christine Mummhardt	Verka Borissova
Irina Makagonova	Heike Lehmann	Roumiana Kaicheva
Lubov Kozyreva	Barbara Czekalla	Maya Gheorghieva
Svetlana Nikishina	Karla Roffeis	Tania Gogova
Ludmila Chernysheva	Martina Schmidt	Tzevetana Bojourina
Svetlana Badulina	Anke Westendorf	Valentina Iliyeva
Lidiya Loginova	Karin Puschel	Galina Stantcheva
Larisa Pavlova	Brigitte Fetzer	Margarita Gerasimova
Yelena Andreyuk	Katharina Bullin	Rossitza Dimitrova

19. Weightlifting

This sport became standardized in 1928 with the result depending on the aggregate weight of three two-handed overhead lifts: the Press, the Snatch and Jerk. But from 1976 the competition is decided by the aggregate of the Snatch and the Jerk only. The present Middleweight, Light-Heavyweight and Middle Heavyweight were previously called Welterweight, Middleweight, and Light-Heavyweight respectively.

FLYWEIGHT

(Weight up to *52 kg* 114½ lb)

	GOLD	SILVER	BRONZE
1928–1968	Event not held		
1972	Zygmunt Smalcerz (POL) 744 lb *337,5 kg**	Lajos Szuecs (HUN) 727½ lb *330 kg*	Sandor Holczreiter (HUN) 722 lb *327,5 kg*
1976	Alexandr Voronin (URS) 534½ lb *242,5 kg*	Gyorgy Koszegi (HUN) 523½ lb *237,5 kg*	Mohammad Nassiri (IRN) 518 lb *235,0 kg*
1980	Kanybek Osmanoliev (URS) 540 lb *245 kg*	Bong Chol Ho (PRK) 540 lb *245 kg*	Gyong Si Han (PRK) 540 lb *245 kg*

BANTAMWEIGHT

(Weight up to *56 kg* 123½ lb)

	GOLD	SILVER	BRONZE
1928–1936	Event not held		
1948	Joseph de Pietro (USA) 678 lb *307,5 kg*	Julian Creus (GBR) 655¾ lb *297,5 kg*	Richard Tom (USA) 650¼ lb *295 kg*
1952	Ivan Udodov (URS) 694¼ lb *315 kg*	Mahmoud Namdjou (IRN) 678 lb *307,5 kg*	Ali Mirzai (IRN) 661¼ lb *300 kg*
1956	Charles Vinci (USA) 755 lb *342,5 kg*	Vladimir Stogov (URS) 744 lb *337,5 kg*	Mahmoud Namdjou (IRN) 733 lb *332,5 kg*
1960	Charles Vinci (USA) 760½ lb *345 kg*	Yoshinobu Miyake (JPN) 744 lb *337,5 kg*	Esmail E. Khan (IRN) 727½ lb *330 kg*
1964	Alexey Vakhonin (URS) 788 lb *357,5 kg*	Imre Földi (HUN) 782½ lb *355 kg*	Shiro Ichinoseki (JPN) 766 lb *347,5 kg*
1968	Mohammad Nassiri (IRN) 810 lb *367,5 kg*	Imre Földi (HUN) 810 lb *367,5 kg*	Henryk Trebicki (POL) 788 lb *357,5 kg*
1972	Imre Földi (HUN) 832 lb *377,5 kg*	Mohammad Nassiri (IRN) 815½ lb *370 kg*	Gennadi Chetin (URS) 810 lb *367,5 kg*

René Duverger (FRA) won the gold medal in the lightweight division in 1932.

	GOLD	SILVER	BRONZE
1976	Norair Nurikyan (BUL) 578½ lb *262,5 kg*	Grzegorz Cziura (POL) 556½ lb *252,5 kg*	Kenkichi Ando (JPN) 551 lb *250 kg*
1980	Daniel Nunez (CUB) 606¼ lb *275 kg*	Yurik Sarkisian (URS) 595 lb *270 kg*	Tadeusz Dembonczyk (POL) 584 lb *265 kg*

FEATHERWEIGHT
(Weight up to *60 kg* 132 lb)

	GOLD	SILVER	BRONZE
1928	Franz Andrysek (AUT) 633¾ lb *287,5 kg*	Pierino Gabetti (ITA) 622¾ lb *282,5 kg*	Hans Wölpert (GER) 622¾ lb *282,5 kg*
1932	Raymond Suvigny (FRA) 633¾ lb *287,5 kg*	Hans Wölpert (GER) 622¾ lb *282,5 kg*	Anthony Terlazzo
1936	Anthony Terlazzo (USA) 688¾ lb *312,5 kg*	Saleh Moh Soliman (EGY) 672¼ lb *305 kg*	Ibrahim H. Shams (EGY) 661¼ lb *300 kg*
1948	Mahmoud Fayad (EGY) 733 lb *332,5 kg*	Rodney Wilkes (TRI) 699¾ lb *317,5 kg*	Jaffar Salmassi (IRN) 688¾ lb *312,5 kg*
1952	Rafael Chimishkyan (URS) 774 lb *337,5 kg*	Nikolay Saksonov (URS) 733 lb *332,5 kg*	Rodney Wilkes (TRI) 711 lb *322,5 kg*
1956	Isaac Berger (USA) 777 lb *352,5 kg*	Evgeniy Minayev (URS) 755 lb *342,5 kg*	Marian Zielinski (POL) 738½ lb *355 kg*
1960	Evgeniy Minayev (URS) 821 lb *372,5 kg*	Isaac Berger (USA) 799 lb *362,5 kg*	Sebastiano Mannironi (ITA) 777 lb *352,5 kg*
1964	Yoshinobu Miyake (JPN) 876¼ lb *397,5 kg*	Isaac Berger (USA) 843¼ lb *382,5 kg*	Mieczyslaw Nowak (POL) 832 lb *377,5 kg*
1968	Yoshinobu Miyake (JPN) 865¼ lb *392,5 kg*	Dito Shanidze (URS) 854¼ lb *387,5 kg*	Yoshiyuki Miyake (JPN) 848¾ lb *385 kg*
1972	Norair Nurikyan (BUL) 887¼ lb *402,5 kg*	Dito Shanidze (URS) 881¾ lb *400 kg*	Janos Benedek (HUN) 859¾ lb *390 kg*
1976	Nikolai Kolesnikov (URS) 628¼ lb *285 kg*	Georgi Todorov (BUL) 617¼ lb *280 kg*	Kuzumasa Hirai (JPN) 606¼ lb *275 kg*
1980	Viktor Mazin (URS) 639¼ lb *290 kg*	Stefan Dimitrov (BUL) 633¾ lb *287,5 kg*	Marek Seweryn (POL) 622¾ lb *282,5 kg*

LIGHTWEIGHT
(Weight up to 67,5 kg 149 lb)

	GOLD	SILVER	BRONZE
1928[1]	Kurt Helbig (GER) 711 lb *322,5 kg* Hans Haas (AUT) 711 lb *322,5 kg*	—	Fernand Arnout (FRA) 666¾ lb *302,5 kg*
1932	René Duverger (FRA) 716½ lb *325 kg*	Hans Haas (AUT) 678 lb *307,5 kg*	Gastone Pierini (ITA) 666¾ lb *302,5 kg*
1936[1]	Anwar Mohammed Mesbah (EGY) 755 lb *342,5 kg* Robert Fein (AUT) 755 lb *342,5 kg*		Karl Jansen (GER) 722 lb *327,5 kg*
1948	Ibrahim H. Shams (EGY) 793½ lb *360 kg*	Attia Hamouda (EGY) 793½ lb *360 kg*	James Halliday (GBR) 749½ lb *340 kg*
1952	Thomas Kono (USA) 799 lb *365,5 kg*	Yevgeniy Lopatin (URS) 771½ lb *350 kg*	Verne Barberis (AUS) 771½ lb *350 kg*
1956	*Igor Rybak (URS) 837¾ lb 380 kg*	*Ravil Khabutdinov (URS) 821 lb 372,5 kg*	*Chang-Hee Kim (KOR) 815½ lb 370 kg*
1960	Viktor Bushuyev (URS) 876¼ lb *397,5 kg*	Howe-Liang Tan (SIN) 837¾ lb *380 kg*	Abdul Wahid Aziz (IRQ) 837¾ lb *380 kg*
1964	Waldemar Baszanowski (POL) 953¼ lb *432,5 kg*	Vladimir Kaplunov (URS) 953¼ lb *432,5 kg*	Marian Zielinski (POL) 925¾ lb *420 kg*
1968	Waldemar Baszanowski (POL) 964½ lb *437,5 kg*	Parviz Jalayer (IRN) 931¼ lb *422,5 kg*	Marian Zielinski (POL) 925¾ lb *420 kg*
1972	Mukharbi Kirzhinov (URS) 1,014 lb *460 kg*	Mladen Koutchev (BUL) 992 lb *450 kg*	Zbigniew Kaczmarek (POL) 964½ lb *437,5 kg*
1976[2]	Piotr Korol (URS) 672¼ lb *305 kg*	Daniel Senet (FRA) 661¼ lb *300 kg*	Kazimierz Czarnecki (POL) 650¼ lb *295 kg*
1980	Yanko Roussev (URS) 755 lb *342,5 kg*	Joachim Kunz (GDR) 738½ lb *335 kg*	Mintcho Pachov (BUL) 716 lb *325 kg*

[1] Results and bodyweights being equal both were declared champions.
[2] Zbigniew Kaczmarek (POL) finished in first place with 677¾ lb *307,5 kg* but was subsequently disqualified.

MIDDLEWEIGHT
(Weight up to 75 kg 165¼ lb)

1928	Roger François (FRA) 738½ lb *335 kg*	Carlo Galimberti (ITA) 733 lb *332,5 kg*	August Scheffer (HOL) 712 lb *327,5 kg*
1932	Rudolf Ismayr (GER) 760½ lb *345 kg*	Carlo Galimberti (ITA) 749½ lb *340 kg*	Karl Hipfinger (AUT) 744 lb *337,5 kg*
1936	Khadr S. El Touni (EGY) 854¼ lb *387,5 kg*	Rudolf Ismayr (GER) 777 lb *352,5 kg*	Adolf Wagner (GER) 777 lb *352,5 kg*
1948	Frank Spellman (USA) 859¾ lb *390 kg*	Peter George (USA) 843¾ lb *382,5 kg*	Sung-Jip Kim (KOR) 837¾ lb *380 kg*
1952	Peter George (USA) 881¾ lb *400 kg*	Gérard Gratton (CAN) 859¾ lb *390 kg*	Sung-Jip Kim (KOR) 843¼ lb *382,5 kg*
1956	Fyodor Bogdanovskiy (URS) 925¾ lb *420 kg*	Peter George (USA) 909¼ lb *412,5 kg*	Ermanno Pignatti (ITA) 843¼ lb *382,5 kg*
1960	Aleksandr Kurynov (URS) 964½ lb *437,5 kg*	Thomas Kono (USA) 942¼ lb *427,5 kg*	Győző Veres (HUN) 892¾ lb *405 kg*
1964	Hans Zdražila (TCH) 981 lb *445 kg*	Viktor Kurentsov (URS) 970 lb *440 kg*	Masashi Ouchi (JPN) 964½ lb *437,5 kg*
1968	Viktor Kurentsov (URS) 1,047 lb *475 kg*	Masashi Ouchi (JPN) 1,003 lb *455 kg*	Károly Bakos (HUN) 970 lb *440 kg*
1972	Yordan Bikov (BUL) 1,069 lb *485 kg*	Mohamed Trabulsi (LIB) 1,041½ lb *472,5 kg*	Anselmo Silvino (ITA) 1,036 lb *470 kg*
1976	Yordan Mitkov (BUL) 738½ lb *335 kg*	Vartan Militosyan (URS) 727½ lb *330 kg*	Peter Wenzel (GDR) 722 lb *327,5 kg*
1980	Assen Zlatev (BUL) 793½ lb *360 kg*	Alexandr Pervy (URS) 788 lb *357,5 kg*	Nedeltcho Kolev (BUL) 760½ lb *345 kg*

LIGHT-HEAVYWEIGHT
(Weight up to *82,5 kg* 182 lb)

	GOLD	SILVER	BRONZE
1928	Said Nosseir (EGY) 782½ lb *355 kg*	Louis Hostin (FRA) 777 lb *352,5 kg*	Johannes Verheijen (HOL) 744 lb *337,5 kg*
1932	Louis Hostin (FRA) 804½ lb *365 kg*	Svend Olsen (DEN) 793½ lb *360 kg*	Henry Duey (USA) 727½ lb *330 kg*
1936	Louis Hostin (FRA) 821 lb *372,5 kg*	Eugen Deutsch (GER) 804½ lb *365 kg*	Ibrahim Wasif (EGY) 793½ lb *360 kg*
1948	Stanley Stanczyk (USA) 920¼ lb *417,5 kg*	Harold Sakata (USA) 837¾ lb *380 kg*	Gösta Magnusson (SWE) 826½ lb *375 kg*
1952	Trofim Lomakin (URS) 920¼ lb *417,5 kg*	Stanley Stanczyk (USA) 914¾ lb *415 kg*	Arkhadiy Vorobyov (URS) 898¼ lb *407,5 kg*
1956	Thomas Kono (USA) 986½ lb *447,5 kg*	Vasiliy Stepanov (URS) 942¼ lb *427,5 kg*	James George (USA) 920¼ lb *417,5 kg*
1960	Ireneusz Palinski (POL) 975½ lb *442,5 kg*	James George (USA) 947¾ lb *430 kg*	Jan Bochenek (POL) 925¾ lb *420 kg*
1964	Rudolf Plukfelder (URS) 1,047 lb *475 kg*	Géza Tóth (HUN) 1,030½ lb *467;5 kg*	Győző Veres (HUN) 1,030½ lb *467;5 kg*
1968	Boris Selitsky (URS) 1,069 lb *485 kg*	Vladimir Belyaev (URS) 1,069 lb *485 kg*	Norbert Ozimek (POL) 1,041½ lb *472,5 kg*
1972	Leif Jenssen (NOR) 1,118¾ lb *507,5 kg*	Norbert Ozimek (POL) 1,096¾ lb *497,5 kg*	György Horvath (HUN) 1,091¼ lb *495 kg*
1976[1]	Valeri Schary (URS) 804½ lb *365 kg*	Trendachil Stoichev (BUL) 793½ lb *360 kg*	Peter Baczako (HUN) 760½ lb *345 kg*
1980	Yurik Vardanyan (URS) 881¾ lb *400 kg*	Blagoi Blagoev (BUL) 821 lb *372,5 kg*	Dusan Poliacik (TCH) 810 lb *367,5 kg*

[1] Blagoi Blagoev (BUL) finished in second place with 799 lb *362,5 kg* but was subsequently disqualified.

Valeri Schary of the Soviet Union won the gold medal in the light-heavyweight division in 1976.

MIDDLE-HEAVYWEIGHT

(Weight up to *90 kg* 198¼ lb)

	GOLD	SILVER	BRONZE
1928–1948	Event not held		
1952	Norbert Shemansky (USA) 981 lb *445 kg*	Grigoriy Novak (URS) 903¾ lb *410 kg*	Lennox Kilgour (TRI) 887¼ lb *402,5 kg*
1956	Arkhadiy Vorobyov (URS) 1,019½ lb *462,5 kg*	David Sheppard (USA) 975½ lb *442,5 kg*	Jean Debuf (FRA) 936¾ lb *425 kg*
1960	Arkhadiy Vorobyov (URS) 1,041½ lb *472,5 kg*	Trofim Lomakin (URS) 1,008½ lb *457,5 kg*	Louis Martin (GBR) 981 lb *445 kg*
1964	Vladimir Golovanov (URS) 1,074¾ lb *487,5 kg*	Louis Martin (GBR) 1,047 lb *475 kg*	Ireneusz Palinski (POL) 1,030½ lb *467,5 kg*
1968	Kaarlo Kangasniemi (FIN) 1,140¾ lb *517,5 kg*	Jan Talts (URS) 1,118¾ lb *507,5 kg*	Marek Golab (POL) 1,091¼ lb *495 kg*
1972	Andon Nikolav (BUL) 1,157¼ lb *525 kg*	Atanas Shopov (BUL) 1,140¾ lb *517,5 kg*	Hans Bettembourg (SWE) 1,129¾ lb *512,5 kg*
1976	David Rigert (URS) 843¼ lb *382,5 kg*	Lee James (USA) 799 lb *362,5 kg*	Atanas Shopov (BUL) 793½ lb *360 kg*
1980	Peter Baczako (URS) 832 lb *377,5 kg*	Roumen Alexandrov (BUL) 826½ lb *375 kg*	Frank Mantek (GDR) 815½ lb *370 kg*

100 kg.

(Weight up to *100 kg* 220½ lb)

1928–1976	Event not held		
1980	Ota Zaremba (TCH) 870¾ lb *395 kg*	Igor Nikitin (URS) 865¼ lb *392,5 kg*	Alberto Blanco (CUB) 848¾ lb *385 kg*

HEAVYWEIGHT

From 1928 to 1952 Heavyweight had to be over *82,5 kg* 182 lb. From 1956 to 1968 the limit was *90,0 kg* 198¼ lb. Since 1972 the top weight has been *110 kg* 242 lb.

1928	Josef Strassberger (GER) 821 lb *372,5 kg*	Arnold Luhaäär (EST) 793½ lb *360 kg*	Jaroslav Skobla (TCH) 788 lb *357,5 kg*
1932	Jaroslav Skobla (TCH) 837¾ lb *380 kg*	Václav Pšenička (TCH) 832 lb *377,5 kg*	Josef Strassberger (GER) 832 lb *377,5 kg*
1936	Josef Manger (AUT) 903¾ lb *410 kg*	Václav Pšenička (TCH) 887¼ lb *402,5 kg*	Arnold Luhaäär (EST) 881¾ lb *400 kg*
1948	John Davis (USA) 997½ lb *452,5 kg*	Norbert Schemansky (USA) 936¾ lb *425 kg*	Abraham Charité (HOL) 909¼ lb *412,5 kg*
1952	John Davis (USA) 1,014 lb *460 kg*	James Bradford (USA) 964½ lb *437,5 kg*	Humberto Selvetti (ARG) 953¼ lb *432,5 kg*
1956	Paul Anderson (USA) 1,102 lb *500 kg*	Humberto Selvetti (ARG) 1,102 lb *500 kg*	Alberto Pigaiani (ITA) 997½ lb *452,5 kg*
1960	Yuriy Vlassov (URS) 1,184¾ lb *537,5 kg*	James Bradford (USA) 1,129¾ lb *512,5 kg*	Norbert Schemansky (USA) 1,102 lb *500 kg*
1964	Leonid Zhabotinsky (URS) 1,262 lb *572,5 kg*	Yuriy Vlassov (URS) 1,256½ lb *570 kg*	Norbert Schemansky (USA) 1,184¾ lb *537,5 kg*
1968	Leonid Zhabotinsky (URS) 1,262 lb *572,5 kg*	Serge Reding (BEL) 1,223½ lb *555 kg*	Joseph Dube (USA) 1,223½ lb *555 kg*
1972	Jan Talts (URS) 1,278½ lb *580 kg*	Alexandre Kraitchev (BUL) 1,240 lb *562,5 kg*	Stefan Gruetzner (GDR) 1,223½ lb *555 kg*
1976[1]	Yuri Zaitsev (URS) 848¾ lb *385 kg*	Krastio Semerdjiev (BUL) 848¾ lb *385 kg*	Tadeusz Rutkowski (POL) 832 lb *377,5 kg*
1980	Leonid Taranenko (URS) 931¼ lb *422,5 kg*	Valentin Khristov (BUL) 892¾ lb *405 kg*	Gyorgy Szlai (HUN) 859 ¾ lb *390 kg*

[1] Valentin Khristov (BUL) finished in first place with 881¾ lb *400 kg*, but was subsequently disqualified.

SUPER-HEAVYWEIGHT
(Weight limit over *110 kg* 242½ lb)

GOLD	SILVER	BRONZE
1928–1968	Event not held	
1972 Vassili Alexeev	Rudolf Mang	Gerd Bonk
(URS) 1,410¾ lb *640 kg*	(GER) 1,344¾ lb *610 kg*	(GDR) 1,262 lb *572,5 kg*
1976 Vassili Alexeev	Gerd Bonk	Helmut Losch
(URS) 970 lb *440 kg*	(GDR) 892¾ lb *405 kg*	(GDR) 854¼ lb *387,5 kg*
1980 Sultan Rakhmanov	Jurgen Heuser	Tadeusz Rutkowski
(URS) 970 lb *440 kg*	(GDR) 903¾ lb *410 kg*	(POL) 898¼ lb *407,5 kg*

ABOVE: Paul Anderson (USA) set an Olympic record in winning the heavyweight class gold medal in 1956. A year later he raised 6,270 lb. on his back.

LEFT: In 1980, Sultan Rakhmanov (URS) earned the super-heavyweight gold medal, succeeding the famous former two-time champion, Vassili Alexeev.

20. Wrestling

The contemporary descriptions of some bodyweight classes have varied during the history of the Games. Current descriptions are used in the lists below.

FREE-STYLE—LIGHT FLYWEIGHT
(Weight up to *48 kg* 105¾ lb.)

	GOLD	SILVER	BRONZE
1896–1900	Event not held		
1904	Robert Curry (USA)	John Heim (USA)	Gustav Thiefenthaler (USA)
1906–1968	Event not held		
1972	Roman Dmitriev (URS)	Ognian Nikolov (BUL)	Ebrahim Javadpour (IRN)
1976	Khassan Issaev (BUL)	Roman Dmitriev (URS)	Akira Kudo (JPN)
1980	Claudio Pollio (ITA)	Se Hong Jang (PRK)	Sergei Kornilaev (URS)

FREE-STYLE—FLYWEIGHT

Note: 1904 weight up to 115 lb *52,16 kg*. From 1948 weight up to *52 kg* 114½ lb.

	GOLD	SILVER	BRONZE
1896–1900	Event not held		
1904	George Mehnert (USA)	Gustave Bauers (USA)	William Nelson (USA)
1906–1936	Event not held		
1948	Lennart Viitala (FIN)	Halit Balamir (TUR)	Thure Johansson (SWE)
1952	Hasan Gemici (TUR)	Yushu Kitano-Ali (JPN)	Mahmoud Mollaghassemi (IRN)
1956	Mirian Tsalkalamanidze (URS)	Mohamad-Ali Khojastehpour (IRN)	Hüseyin Akbas (TUR)
1960	Ahmet Bilek (TUR)	Masayuki Matsubara (JPN)	Mohamad Saifpour Saidabadi (IRN)
1964	Yoshikatsu Yoshida (JPN)	Chang-sun Chang (KOR)	Said Aliaakbar Haydari (IRN)
1968	Shigeo Nakata (JPN)	Richard Sanders (USA)	Surenjav Sukhbaatar (MGL)
1972	Kiyomi Kato (JPN)	Arsen Alakhverdiev (URS)	Hyong Kim Gwong (PRK)
1976	Yuji Takada (JPN)	Alexandr Ivanov (URS)	Hae-Sup Jeon (KOR)
1980	Anatoly Beloglazov (URS)	Wladyslaw Stecyk (POL)	Nermedin Selimov (BUL)

FREE-STYLE—BANTAMWEIGHT

Note: The weight limit for this event has been: 1908, 125 lb *56,70 kg*; 1980, 119 lb *54 kg*; 1924–1936, *56 kg* 123½ lb and from 1948, *57 kg* 125¾ lb.

	GOLD	SILVER	BRONZE
1896–1900	Event not held		
1904	Isaac Niflot (USA)	August Wester (USA)	Z. B. Strebler (USA)
1906	Event not held		
1908	George Mehnert (USA)	William Press (GBR)	Aubert Côté (CAN)

GOLD	SILVER	BRONZE
1912–1920 Event not held		
1924 Kustaa Pihlajamäki (FIN)	Kaarlo Mäkinen (FIN)	Bryant Hines (USA)
1928 Kaarlo Mäkinen (FIN)	Edmond Spapen (BEL)	James Trifunov (CAN)
1932 Robert Pearce (USA)	Ödön Zombori (HUN)	Aatos Jaskari (FIN)
1936 Ödön Zombori (HUN)	Ross Flood (USA)	Johannes Herbert (GER)
1948 Nasuk Akar (TUR)	Gerald Leeman (USA)	Charles Kouyos (FRA)
1952 Shohachi Ishii (JPN)	Rashid Mamedbekov (URS)	Kha-Shaba Jadav (IND)
1956 Mustafa Dagistanli (TUR)	Mohamad Yaghoubi (IRN)	Mikhail Chakhov (URS)
1960 Terrence McCann (USA)	Nejdet Zalev (BUL)	Tadeusz Trojanowski (POL)
1964 Yojiro Uetake (JPN)	Hüseyin Akbas (TUR)	Aidyn Ibragimov (URS)
1968 Yojiro Uetake (JPN)	Donald Behm (USA)	Abutaleb Gorgori (IRN)
1972 Hideaki Yanagide (JPN)	Richard Sanders (USA)	László Klinga (HUN)
1976 Vladimir Umin (URS)	Hans-Dieter Bruchert (GDR)	Masao Arai (JPN)
1980 Sergei Beloglazov (URS)	Ho Pyong Li (PRK)	Dugarsuren Quinbold (MGL)

A free-style bout between bantamweights at Empress Hall, Earls Court, London in the 1948 Olympics. Nasuk Akar (TUR), the eventual gold medal winner, is on top of Charles Kouyos (FRA), who won the bronze medal.

FREE-STYLE—FEATHERWEIGHT

Note: The weight limit for this event has been: 1904, 135 lb *61,24 kg*; 1908, 133 lb *60,30 kg*; 1920, 132¼ lb *60 kg*; 1924–1936, 134½ lb *61 kg*; 1948–1960, and 1972, *62 kg* 136½ lb; 1964–1968, *63 kg* 138¾ lb.

	GOLD	SILVER	BRONZE
1896–1900	Event not held		
1904	Benjamin Bradshaw (USA)	Theodore McLear (USA)	Charles Clapper (USA)
1906	Event not held		
1908	George Dole (USA)	James P. Slim (GBR)	William McKie (GBR)
1912	Event not held		
1920	Charles E. Ackerly (USA)	Samuel Gerson (USA)	P. W. Bernard (GBR)
1924	Robin Reed (USA)	Chester Newton (USA)	Katsutoshi Naito (JPN)
1928	Allie Morrison (USA)	Kustaa Pihlajamäki (FIN)	Hans Minder (SUI)
1932	Hermanni Pihlajamäki (FIN)	Edgar Nemir (USA)	Einar Karlsson (SWE)
1936	Kustaa Pihlajamäki (FIN)	Francis Millard (USA)	Gösta Jönsson (SWE)
1948	Gazanfer Bilge (TUR)	Ivar Sjölin (SWE)	Adolf Müller (SUI)
1952	Bayram Sit (TUR)	Nasser Guivehtchi (IRN)	Josiah Henson (USA)
1956	Shozo Sasahara (JPN)	Joseph Mewis (BEL)	Erkki Penttilä (FIN)
1960	Mustafa Dagistanli (TUR)	Stantcho Ivanov (BUL)	Vladimir Rubashvili (URS)
1964	Osamu Watanabe (JPN)	Stantcho Ivanov (BUL)	Nodar Khokhashvili (URS)
1968	Masaaki Kaneko (JPN)	Enyu Todorov (BUL)	Shamseddin Seyed-Abbassi (IRN)
1972	Zagalav Abdulbekov (URS)	Vehbi Akdag (TUR)	Ivan Krastev (BUL)
1976	Jung-Mo Yang (KOR)	Zeveg Oidov (MGL)	Gene Davis (USA)
1980	Magomedgasan Abushev (URS)	Mikho Doukov (BUL)	Georges Hadjioannidis (GRE)

FREE-STYLE—LIGHTWEIGHT

Note: The weight limit for this event has been: 1904, 145 lb *65,77 kg*; 1908, 146¾ lb *66,60 kg*; 1920, 148¾ lb *67,50 kg*; 1924 to 1936, 145½ lb *66 kg*; 1948 to 1960, *67 kg* 147½ lb; 1964 and 1968, *70 kg* 154 lb; and from 1972, *68 kg* 149¾ lb.

	GOLD	SILVER	BRONZE
1896–1900	Event not held		
1904	Otto Roehm (USA)	R. Tesing (USA)	Albert Zirkel (USA)
1906	Event not held		
1908	G. de Relwyskow (GBR)	William Wood (GBR)	Albert Gingell (GBR)
1912	Event not held		
1920	Kalle Anttila (FIN)	Gottfrid Svensson (SWE)	Peter Wright (GBR)
1924	Russell Vis (USA)	Volmart Wickström (FIN)	Arvo Haavisto (FIN)
1928	Osvald Käpp (EST)	Charles Pacôme (FRA)	Eino Leino (FIN)

GOLD	SILVER	BRONZE
1932 Charles Pacôme (FRA)	Károly Kárpáti (HUN)	Gustaf Klarén (SWE)
1936 Károly Kárpáti (HUN)	Wolfgang Ehrl (GER)	Hermanni Pihlajamäki (FIN)
1948 Celal Atik (TUR)	Gösta Frändfors (SWE)	Hermann Baumann (SUI)
1952 Olle Anderberg (SWE)	J. Thomas Evans (USA)	Djahanbakte Tovfighe (IRN)
1956 Emamali Habibi (IRN)	Shigeru Kasahara (JPN)	Alimberg Bestayev (URS)
1960 Shelby Wilson (USA)	Viktor Sinyavskiy (URS)	Enyu Dimov (BUL)
1964 Enyu Valtschev[1] (BUL)	Klaus-Jürgen Rost (GER)	Iwao Horiuchi (JPN)
1968 Abdollah Movahed Ardabili (IRN)	Enyu Valtschev[1] (BUL)	Sereeter Danzandarjaa (MGL)
1972 Dan Gable (USA)	Kikuo Wada (JPN)	Ruslan Ashuraliev (URS)
1976 Pavel Pinigin (URS)	Lloyd Keaser (USA)	Yasaburo Sagawara (JPN)
1980 Saipulla Absaidov (URS)	Ivan Yankov (BUL)	Saban Sejdi (YUG)

[1] Valtschev competed as Dimov in 1960.

FREE-STYLE—WELTERWEIGHT

Note: The weight limit for this event has been: 1904, 158 lb *71,67 kg*; 1924 to 1936, 158½ lb *72 kg*; 1948 to 1960, *73 kg* 160¾ lb; from 1972, *74 kg* 163 lb.

GOLD	SILVER	BRONZE
1896–1900 Event not held		
1904 Charles Erickson (USA)	William Beckmann (USA)	Jerry Winholtz (USA)
1906–1920 Event not held		
1924 Hermann Gehri (SUI)	Eino Leino (FIN)	Otto Müller (SUI)
1928 Arvo Haavisto (FIN)	Lloyd Appleton (USA)	Maurice Letchford (CAN)
1932 Jack van Bebber (USA)	Daniel MacDonald (CAN)	Eino Leino (FIN)
1936 Frank Lewis (USA)	Ture Andersson (SWE)	Joseph Schleimer (CAN)
1948 Yasar Dogu (TUR)	Richard Garrard (AUS)	Leland Merrill (USA)
1952 William Smith (USA)	Per Berlin (SWE)	Abdullah Modjtabavi (IRN)
1956 Mitsuo Ikeda (JPN)	Ibrahim Zengin (TUR)	Vakhtang Balavadze (URS)
1960 Douglas Blubaugh (USA)	Ismail Ogan (TUR)	Mohammad Bashir (PAK)
1964 Ismail Ogan (TUR)	Guliko Sagaradze (URS)	Mohamad-Ali (IRN) Sanatkaran
1968 Mahmut Atalay (TUR)	Daniel Robin (FRA)	Dagvasuren Purev (MGL)
1972 Wayne Wells (USA)	Jan Karlsson (SWE)	Adolf Seger (GER)
1976 Jiichiro Date (JPN)	Mansour Barzegar (IRN)	Stanley Dziedzic (USA)
1980 Valentin Raitchev (BUL)	Jamtsying Davaajav (MGL)	Dan Karabin (TCH)

FREE-STYLE—MIDDLEWEIGHT

Note: The weight limit for this event has been: 1908, 161 lb *73 kg*; 1920, 165¼ lb *75 kg*; 1924 to 1960, 174 lb *79 kg*; 1964 and 1968, *87 kg* 191¾ lb; from 1972, *82 kg* 180¾ lb.

	GOLD	SILVER	BRONZE
1896–1906	Event not held		
1908	Stanley Bacon (GBR)	George de Relwyskow (GBR)	Frederick Beck (GBR)
1912	Event not held		
1920	Eino Leino (FIN)	Väinö Penttala (FIN)	Charles Johnson (USA)
1924	Fritz Hagmann (SUI)	Pierre Ollivier (BEL)	Vilho Pekkala (FIN)
1928	Ernst Kyburz (SUI)	Donald P. Stockton (CAN)	Samuel Rabin (GBR)
1932	Ivar Johansson (SWE)	Kyösti Luukko (FIN)	József Tunyogi (HUN)
1936	Emile Poilvé (FRA)	Richard Voliva (USA)	Ahmet Kireiçci (TUR)
1948	Glen Brand (USA)	Adil Candemir (TUR)	Erik Lindén (SWE)
1952	David Tsimakuridze (URS)	Gholamheza Takhti (IRN)	György Gurics (HUN)
1956	Nikola Stautscher (BUL)	Daniel Hodge (USA)	Georgiy Skhirtladze (URS)
1960	Hasan Güngör (TUR)	Georgiy Skhirtladze (URS)	Hans Y. Antonsson (SWE)
1964	Prodan Gardschev (BUL)	Hasan Güngör (TUR)	Daniel Brand (USA)
1968	Boris Gurevitch (URS)	Munkbat Jigjid (MGL)	Prodan Gardschev (BUL)
1972	Levan Tediashvili (URS)	John Peterson (USA)	Vasile Jorga (ROM)
1976	John Peterson (USA)	Viktor Novojilov (URS)	Adolf Seger (GER)
1980	Ismail Abilov (BUL)	Magomedhan Aratsilov (URS)	Istvan Kovacs (HUN)

FREE-STYLE—LIGHT-HEAVYWEIGHT

Note: The weight limit for this event has been: 1920, 181¾ lb *82,5 kg*; 1924 to 1960, *87 kg* 191¾ lb; 1964 and 1968, *97 kg* 213¾ lb; from 1972, *90 kg* 198¼ lb.

1896–1912	Event not held		
1920	Anders Larsson (SWE)	Charles Courant (SUI)	Walter Maurer (USA)
1924	John Spellman (USA)	Rudolf Svensson (SWE)	Charles Courant (SUI)
1928	Thure Sjöstedt (SWE)	Anton Bögli (SUI)	Henri Lefèbre (FRA)
1932	Peter Mehringer (USA)	Thure Sjöstedt (SWE)	Eddie Scarf (AUS)
1936	Knut Fridell (SWE)	August Neo (EST)	Erich Siebert (GER)
1948	Henry Wittenberg (USA)	Fritz Stöckli (SUI)	Bengt Fahlkvist (SWE)
1952	Wiking Palm (SWE)	Henry Wittenberg (USA)	Adil Atan (TUR)
1956	Gholam Reza Tahkti (IRN)	Boris Kulayev (URS)	Peter S. Blair (USA)
1960	Ismet Atli (TUR)	Gholam Reza Tahkti (IRN)	Anatoliy Albul (URS)

John Peterson (right side up), the only American wrestler to win a gold medal at the 1976 Games, here defeats Mehmet Uzun (TUR) in a semi-final bout.

	GOLD	SILVER	BRONZE
1964	Alexander Medved (URS)	Ahmet Ayik (TUR)	Said Mustafafov (BUL)
1968	Ahmet Ayik (TUR)	Shota Lomidze (URS)	József Csatári (HUN)
1972	Ben Peterson (USA)	Gennadi Strakhov (URS)	Karoly Bajko (HUN)
1976	Levan Tediashvili (URS)	Ben Peterson (USA)	Stelica Morcov (ROM)
1980	Sanasar Oganesyan (URS)	Uwe Neupert (GDR)	Aleksander Cichon (POL)

FREE-STYLE—HEAVYWEIGHT

Note: The weight limit for this event has been: 1904, over 158 lb *71,6 kg*; 1908, over 161 lb *73 kg*; 1920, over 181¾ lb *82,5 kg*; 1924 to 1960, over 87 *kg* 191¾ lb; 1964 and 1968, over 97 *kg* 213¾ lb; from 1972, up to *100 kg* 220¼ lb.

1896–1900	Event not held		
1904	B. Hansen (USA)	Frank Kungler (USA)	F. C. Warmbold (USA)
1906	Event not held		
1908	George C. O'Kelly (GBR/IRL)	Jacob Gundersen (NOR)	Edmond Barrett (GBR/IRL)
1912	Event not held		
1920	Robert Roth (SUI)	Nathan Pendleton (USA)	Ernst Nilsson (SWE) Frederick Meyer (USA)

GOLD	SILVER	BRONZE
1924 Harry Steele (USA)	Henry Wernli (SUI)	Andrew McDonald (GBR)
1928 Johan Richthoff (SWE)	Aukusti Sihvola (FIN)	Edmond Dame (FRA)
1932 Johan Richthoff (SWE)	John Riley (USA)	Nikolaus Hirschl (AUT)
1936 Kristjan Palusalu (EST)	Josef Klapuch (TCH)	Hjalmar Nyström (FIN)
1948 Gyula Bóbis (HUN)	Bertil Antonsson (SWE)	Joseph Armstrong (AUS)
1952 Arsen Mekokishvili (URS)	Bertil Antonsson (SWE)	Kenneth Richmond (GBR)
1956 Hamit Kaplan (TUR)	Hussein Mekhmedov (BUL)	Taisto Kangasniemi (FIN)
1960 Wilfried Dietrich (GER)	Hamit Kaplan (TUR)	Savkus Dzarassov (URS)
1964 Alexandr Ivanitsky (URS)	Liutvi Djiber (BUL)	Hamit Kaplan (TUR)
1968 Alexander Medved (URS)	Osman Duraliev (BUL)	Wilfried Dietrich (GER)
1972 Ivan Yarygin (URS)	Khorloo Baianmunkh (MGL)	József Csatáti (HUN)
1976 Ivan Yarygin (URS)	Russell Hellickson (USA)	Dimo Kostov (BUL)
1980 Ilya Mate (URS)	Slavtcho Tchervenkov (BUL)	Julius Strnisko (TCH)

FREE-STYLE—SUPER-HEAVYWEIGHT
(Weight over 220¼ lb *100 kg*)

1896–1968 Event not held		
1972 Alexander Medved (URS)	Osman Duraliev (BUL)	Chris Taylor (USA)
1976 Soslan Andiev (URS)	Jozsef Balla (HUN)	Ladislau Simon (ROM)
1980 Soslan Andiev (URS)	Jozsef Balla (HUN)	Adam Sandruski (POL)

GRECO-ROMAN—LIGHT-FLYWEIGHT
(Weight up to *48 kg* 105¾ lb)

1896–1968 Event not held		
1972 Gheorghe Berceanu (ROM)	Rahim Ahabadi (IRN)	Stefan Anghelov (BUL)
1976 Alexei Shumakov (URS)	Gheorghe Berceanu (ROM)	Stefan Anghelov (BUL)
1980 Zaksylik Ushkempirov (URS)	Constantin Alexandru (ROM)	Ferenc Seres (HUN)

GRECO-ROMAN—FLYWEIGHT
(Weight up to 114½ lb *52 kg*)

1896–1936 Event not held		
1948 Pietro Lombardi (ITA)	Kenan Olcay (TUR)	Reino Kangasmäki (FIN)
1952 Boris Gurevich (URS)	Ignazio Fabra (ITA)	Leo Honkala (FIN)
1956 Nikolay Solovyov (URS)	Ignazio Fabra (ITA)	Durum Ali Egribas (TUR)

	GOLD	SILVER	BRONZE
1960	Dumitru Pirvulescu (ROM)	Osman Sayed (UAR)	Mohamad Paziraye (IRAN)
1964	Tsutomu Hanahara (JPN)	Angel Kerezov (BUL)	Dumitru Pirvulescu (ROM)
1968	Petar Kirov (BUL)	Vladimir Bakulin (URS)	Miroslav Zeman (TCH)
1972	Petar Kirov (BUL)	Koichiro Hirayama (JPN)	Giuseppe Bognanni (ITA)
1976	Vitali Konstantinov (URS)	Nicu Ginga (ROM)	Koichiro Hirayama (JPN)
1980	Vakhtang Blagidze (URS)	Lajos Racz (HUN)	Mladen Mladenov (BUL)

GRECO-ROMAN—BANTAMWEIGHT

Note: The weight limit for this event has been: 1924 to 1928, 127¾ lb. *58 kg.;* 1932 to 1936, 123¼ lb. *56 kg.;* since 1948, 125½ lb. *57 kg.*

1896–1920 Event not held

	GOLD	SILVER	BRONZE
1924	Eduard Pütsep (EST)	Anselm Ahlfors (FIN)	Väinö Ikonen (FIN)
1928	Kurt Leucht (GER)	Jindrich Maudr (TCH)	Giovanni Gozzi (ITA)
1932	Jakob Brendel (GER)	Marcello Nizzola (ITA)	Louis François (FRA)
1936	Márton Lörincz (HUN)	Egon Svensson (SWE)	Jakob Brendel (GER)
1948	Kurt Pettersén (SWE)	Aly Mahmoud Hassan (EGY)	Habil Kaya (TUR)
1952	Imre Hódos (HUN)	Zakaria Chihab (LIB)	Artem Teryan (URS)
1956	Konstantin Vyrupayev (URS)	Evdin Veseterby (SWE)	Francisc Horvat (ROM)
1960	Olyeg Karavayev (URS)	Ion Cernea (ROM)	Petrov Dinko (BUL)
1964	Masamitsu Ichiguchi (JPN)	Vladlen Trostiansky (URS)	Ion Cernea (ROM)
1968	János Varga (HUN)	Ion Baciu (ROM)	Ivan Kochergin (URS)
1972	Rustem Kazakov (URS)	Hans-Jürgen Veil (GER)	Risto Björlin (FIN)
1976	Pertti Ukkola (FIN)	Ivan Frgic (YUG)	Farhat Mustafin (URS)
1980	Shamil Serikov (URS)	Josef Lipien (POL)	Benni Ljungbeck (SWE)

GRECO-ROMAN—FEATHERWEIGHT

Note: The weight limit for this event has been: 1912 to 1920, 132¼ lb. *60 kg.;* 1924 to 1928, 1948 to 1960 and since 1972, *62 kg.* 136½ lb.; 1932 to 1936, *61 kg.* 134¼ lb.; 1964 to 1968, *63 kg.* 138¾ lb.

1896–1908 Event not held

	GOLD	SILVER	BRONZE
1912	Kaarlo Koskelo (FIN)	Georg Gerstacker (GER)	Otto Lasanen (FIN)
1920	Oskari Friman (FIN)	Hekki Kähkönen (FIN)	Fridtjof Svensson (SWE)
1924	Kalle Antila (FIN)	Aleksanteri Toivola (FIN)	Erik Malmberg (SWE)
1928	Voldemar Väli (EST)	Erik Malmberg (SWE)	Giacomo Quaglia (ITA)

GOLD	SILVER	BRONZE
1932	Giovanni Gozzi (ITA)	Wolfgang Ehrl (GER)	Lauri Koskela (FIN)
1936	Yasar Erkan (TUR)	Aarne Reini (FIN)	Einar Karlsson (SWE)
1948	Mehmet Oktav (TUR)	Olle Anderberg (SWE)	Ferenc Tóth (HUN)
1952	Yakov Punkin (URS)	Imre Polyák (HUN)	Abdel Rashed (EGY)
1956	Rauno Mäkinen (FIN)	Imre Polyák (HUN)	Roman Dzneladze (URS)
1960	Müzahir Sille (TUR)	Imre Polyák (HUN)	Konstantin Vyrupayev (URS)
1964	Imre Polyák (HUN)	Roman Rurua (URS)	Branko Martinovič (YUG)
1968	Roman Rurua (URS)	Hideo Fujimoto (JPN)	Simeon Popescu (ROM)
1972	Gheorghi Markov (BUL)	Heinz-Helmut Wehling (GDR)	Kazimierz Lipien (POL)
1976	Kazimierz Lipien (POL)	Nelson Davidian (URS)	Laszlo Reczi (HUN)
1980	Stilianos Migiakis (GRE)	Istvan Toth (HUN)	Boris Kramorenko (URS)

GRECO-ROMAN—LIGHTWEIGHT

Note: The weight limit for this event has been: 1906, 165¼ lb, *75 kg.;* 1908, 146¾ lb. *66,6 kg.;* 1912 to 1928, 148¾ lb. *67.5 kg.;* 1932 to 1936, 145½ lb. *66 kg.;* 1948 to 1960, 147½ lb. *67 kg.;* 1964 to 1968, 154¼ lb. *70 kg.;* since 1972, 149¾ lb. *68 kg.*

1896–1904	Event not held		
1906	Rudolf Watzl (AUT)	Karl Karlsen (DEN)	Ferenc Holuban (HUN)
1908	Enrico Porro (ITA)	Nikolay Orlov (URS)	Avid Lindén-Linko (FIN)
1912	Eemil Wäre (FIN)	Gustaf Malmström (SWE)	Edvin Matiasson (SWE)
1920	Eemil Wäre (FIN)	Taavi Tamminen (FIN)	Fritjof Andersen (NOR)
1924	Oskari Friman (FIN)	Lajos Keresztes (HUN)	Kalle Westerlund (FIN)
1928	Lajos Keresztes (HUN)	Eduard Sperling (GER)	Eduard Westerlund (FIN)
1932	Erik Malmberg (SWE)	Abraham Kurland (DEN)	Eduard Sperling (GER)
1936	Lauri Koskela (FIN)	Josef Herda (TCH)	Voldemar Väli (EST)
1948	Gustaf Freij (SWE)	Aage Eriksen (NOR)	Károly Ferencz (HUN)
1952	Shazam Safin (URS)	Gustaf Freij (SWE)	Mikuláš Athanasov (TCH)
1956	Kyösti Lehtonen (FIN)	Riza Dogan (TUR)	Gyul Tóth (HUN)
1960	Avtandil Koridze (URS)	Branislav Martinovič (YUG)	Gustaf Freij (SWE)
1964	Kazim Ayvaz (TUR)	Valeriu Bularca (ROM)	David Gvantseladze (URS)
1968	Munji Mumemura (JPN)	Stevan Horvat (YUG)	Petros Galaktopoulos (GRE)
1972	Shamil Khisamutdinov (URS)	Stoyan Apostolov (BUL)	Gian Matteo Ranzi (ITA)
1976	Suren Nalbandyan (URS)	Stefan Rusu (ROM)	Heinz-Helmut Wehling (GDR)
1980	Stefan Rusu (ROM)	Andrzej Supron (POL)	Lars-Erik Skiold (SWE)

GRECO-ROMAN—WELTERWEIGHT

Note: The weight limit for this event has been: 1932 to 1936, 158½ lb. *72 kg.;* 1948 to 1960, 160¾ lb. *73 kg.;* 1964 to 1968, 171¾ lb. *78 kg.;* since 1972, 163 lb. *74 kg.*

	GOLD	SILVER	BRONZE
1896–1928	Event not held		
1932	Ivar Johansson (SWE)	Väinö Kajander (FIN)	Ercole Gallegatti (ITA)
1936	Rudolf Svedberg (SWE)	Frit Schäfer (GER)	Eino Virtanen (FIN)
1948	Gösta Andersson (SWE)	Miklós Szilvási (HUN)	Henrik Hansen (DEN)
1952	Miklós Szilvási (HUN)	Gösta Andersson (SWE)	Khalil Taha (LIB)
1956	Mithat Bayrak (TUR)	Vladimir Maneyev (URS)	Per Berlin (SWE)
1960	Mithat Bayrak (TUR)	Günther Maritschnigg (GER)	René Schiermeyer (FRA)
1964	Anatoly Kolesov (URS)	Cyril Todorov (BUL)	Bertil Nyström (SWE)
1968	Rudolf Vesper (GDR)	Daniel Robin (FRA)	Károly Bajkó (HUN)
1972	Vitezslav Mache (TCH)	Petros Galaktopoulos (GRE)	Jan Karlsson (SWE)
1976	Alexandr Bykov (URS)	Vitezslav Macha (TCH)	Karlheinz Helbing (GER)
1980	Ferenc Kocsis (HUN)	Anatoly Bykov (URS)	Mikko Huntala (FIN)

GRECO-ROMAN—MIDDLEWEIGHT

Note: The weight limit for this event has been: 1906, 187¼ lb. *85 kg.;* 1908, 160¾ lb. *73 kg.;* 1912 to 1928, 165¼ lb. *75 kg.;* 1932 to 1960, 174 lb. *79 kg.;* 1964 to 1968, 191¾ lb. *87 kg.;* since 1972, 180¾ lb. *82 kg.*

	GOLD	SILVER	BRONZE
1896–1904	Event not held		
1906	Verner Weckman (FIN)	Rudolf Lindmayer (AUT)	Robert Bebrens (DEN)
1908	Frithiof Mårtensson (SWE)	Mauritz Andersson (SWE)	Anders Andersen (DEN)
1912	Claes Johansson (SWE)	Martin Klein[1] (URS)	Alfred Asikainen (FIN)
1920	Carl Westergren (SWE)	Artur Lindfors (FIN)	Matti Perttila (FIN)
1924	Eduard Westerlund (FIN)	Artur Lindfors (FIN)	Roman Steinberg (EST)
1928	Väinö Kokkinen (FIN)	László Papp (HUN)	Albert Kusnetz (EST)
1932	Väinö Kokkinen (FIN)	Jean Földeák (GER)	Axel Cadier (SWE)
1936	Ivar Johansson (SWE)	Ludwig Schweikert (GER)	József Palotás (HUN)
1948	Axel Grönberg (SWE)	Muhlis Tayfur (TUR)	Ercole Gallegatti (ITA)
1952	Axel Grönberg (SWE)	Kalervo Rauhala (FIN)	Nikolay Byelov (URS)
1956	Guivi Kartozia (URS)	Dimiter Dobrev (BUL)	Rune Jansson (SWE)
1960	Dimiter Dobrev (BUL)	Lothar Metz (GER)	Ion Taranu (ROM)
1964	Branislav Simic (YUG)	Jiri Kormanik (TCH)	Lothar Metz (GER)

[1] In fact an Estonian.

GOLD	SILVER	BRONZE
1968 Lothar Metz (GDR)	Valentin Olenik (URS)	Branislav Simič (YUG)
1972 Csaba Hegedus (HUN)	Anatoli Nazarenko (URS)	Milan Nenadic (YUG)
1976 Momir Petkovic (YUG)	Vladimir Cheboksarov (URS)	Ivan Kolev (BUL)
1980 Gennady Korban (URS)	Jan Dolgowicz (POL)	Pavel Pavlov (BUL)

Verner Weckman and Yrjo Saarela, both of Finland, battled out the final match of the 1908 light-heavyweight Greco-Roman competition.

GRECO-ROMAN—LIGHT-HEAVYWEIGHT

Note: The weight limit in this event has been: 1908, 205 lb. *93 kg.;* 1912 to 1928, 181¾ lb. *82.5 kg.;* 1932 to 1960, 191¾ lb. *87 kg.;* 1964 to 1968, 213¾ lb. *97 kg.;* since 1972, 198¼ lb. *90 kg.*

1896–1906 Event not held		
1908 Verner Weckman (FIN)	Yrjö Saarela (FIN)	Carl Jensen (DEN)
1912 —	Anders Ahlgren† (SWE) Ivar Böhling (FIN)	Béla Varga (HUN)
1920 Claes Johansson (SWE)	Edil Rosenqvist (FIN)	Johannes Eriksen (DEN)
1924 Carl Westergren (SWE)	Rudolf Svensson (SWE)	Onni Pellinen (FIN)
1928 Ibrahim Moustafa (EGY)	Adolf Rieger (GER)	Onni Pellinen (FIN)
1932 Rudolf Svensson (SWE)	Onni Pellinen (FIN)	Mario Gruppioni (ITA)
1936 Axel Cadier (SWE)	Edwins Bietags (LITH)	August Néo (EST)

† Declared equal second after 9 hours of wrestling—no gold medal awarded.

GOLD	SILVER	BRONZE
1948 Karl-Erik Nilsson (SWE)	Kaelpo Gröndahl (FIN)	Ibrahim Orabi (EGY)
1952 Kaelpo Gröndahl (FIN)	Shalva Shikhladze (URS)	Karl-Erik Nilsson (SWE)
1956 Valentin Nikolayev (URS)	Petko Sirakov (BUL)	Karl-Erik Nilsson (SWE)
1960 Tevfik Kis (TUR)	Krali Bimbalov (BUL)	Givy Kartozlya (URS)
1964 Boyan Radev (BÚL)	Pev Sfensson (SWE)	Heinz Kiehl (GER)
1968 Boyan Radev (BÚL)	Nikolai Yakovenko (URS)	Nicolae Martinescu (ROM)
1972 Valeri Rezantsev (URS)	Josip Corak (YUG)	Czeslaw Kwiecinski (POL)
1976 Valeri Rezantsev (URS)	Stoyan Ivanov (BÚL)	Czeslaw Kwiecinski (POL)
1980 Norbert Nottny (HUN)	Igor Kanygin (URS)	Petre Dicu (ROM)

GRECO-ROMAN—HEAVYWEIGHT

Note: The weight limit for this event has been: 1896, open: 1906, over 187¼ lb. *85 kg;* 1908, over 205 lb. *93 kg.;* 1912 to 1928, over 181¾ lb. *82.5 kg.;* 1932 to 1960, over 191¾ lb. *87 kg.;* 1964 to 1968, over 213¾ lb. *97 kg.;* since 1972, up to 202¼ lb. *100 kg.*

1896 Carl Schuhmann (GER)	Georgios Tsitas (GRE)	Stephanos Christopoulos (GRE)
1900–1904 Event not held		
1906 Sören M. Jensen (DEN)	Heari Baur (AUT)	Marcel Dubois (BEL)
1908 Richard Weisz (HUN)	Aliksandr Petrov (URS)	Sören M. Jensen (DEN)
1912 Yrjö Saarela (FIN)	Johan Olin (FIN)	Sören M. Jensen (DEN)
1920 Adolf Lindfors (FIN)	Poul Hansen (DEN)	Martti Nieminen (FIN)
1924 Henri Deglane (FRA)	Edil Rosenqvist (FIN)	Raymund Badó (HÚN)
1928 Rudolf Svensson (SWE)	Hjalmar E. Nyström (FIN)	Georg Gehring (GER)
1932 Carl Westergren (SWE)	Josef Urban (TCH)	Nikolaus Hirschl (AUT)
1936 Kirstjan Palusalu (EST)	John Nyman (SWE)	Kurt Hornfischer (GER)
1948 Ahmet Kireçci (TUR)	Tor Nilsson (SWE)	Guido Fantoni (ITA)
1952 Johannes Kotkas (URS)	Josef Ružička (TCH)	Tauno Kovanen (FIN)
1956 Anatoliy Parfenov (URS)	Wilfried Dietrich (GER)	Adelmo Bulgarelli (ITA)
1960 Ivan Bogdan (URS)	Wilfried Dietrich (GER)	Bohumil Kubat (TCH)
1964 István Kozma (HUN)	Anatoly Roshin (URS)	Wilfried Dietrich (GER)
1968 István Kozma (HUN)	Anatoly Roshin (URS)	Petr Kment (TCH)
1972 Nicolae Martinescu (ROM)	Nikolai Yakovenko (URS)	Ferenc Kiss (HUN)
1976 Nikolai Bolboshin (URS)	Kamen Goranov (BUL)	Andrzej Skrzylewski (POL)
1980 Gheorgi Raikov (BUL)	Roman Bierla (POL)	Vasile Andrei (ROM)

GRECO-ROMAN—SUPER-HEAVYWEIGHT
(Weight over *100 kg.* 202¼ lb.)

	GOLD	SILVER	BRONZE
1896–1968	Event not held		
1972	Anatoly Roshin (URS)	Alexandre Tomov (BUL)	Victor Dolipschi (ROM)
1976	Alexandr Kolchinski (URS)	Alexandre Tomov (BUL)	Roman Codreanu (ROM)
1980	Alexandr Kolchinski (URS)	Alexandre Tomov (BUL)	Hassan Bchara (LIB)

21. Yachting

INTERNATIONAL SOLING CLASS

	GOLD	SILVER	BRONZE
1896–1968	Event not held		
1972	UNITED STATES Harry Melges, Jr. William Bentsen William Allen	SWEDEN Stig Wennerstroem Bo Knape Stefan Krook	CANADA David Miller John Ekels Paul Cote
1976	DENMARK Paul Jensen Vald Bandolowski Erik Hansen	UNITED STATES John Kolius Walter Glasgow Richard Hoepfner	EAST GERMANY Dieter Below Michael Zachries Olaf Engelhardt
1980	DENMARK Paul Jensen Vald Bandolowski Erik Hansen	U.S.S.R Boris Budnikov Aleksandr Budnikov Nikolai Polyakov	GREECE Anastassios Boudouris Anastassios Gavrilis Aristidis Rapanakis

INTERNATIONAL STAR CLASS

	GOLD	SILVER	BRONZE
1896–1928	Event not held		
1932	UNITED STATES Gilbert Gray Andrew Libano, Jr.	GREAT BRITAIN Colin Ratsey Peter Jaffe	SWEDEN Gunnar Asther Daniel Sunden-Cullberg
1936	GERMANY Peter Bischoff Hans-Joachim Weise	SWEDEN Arved Laurin Uno Wallentin	NETHERLANDS Adriaan Maas Willem de Vries Lentsch
1948	UNITED STATES Hilary Smart Paul Smart	CUBA Carlos de Cardenas Carlos de Cardenas, Jr.	NETHERLANDS Adriaan Maas Edward Stutterheim
1952	ITALY Agostino Straulino Nicolo Rode	UNITED STATES John Reid John Price	PORTUGAL Francisco de Andrade Joaquim Fiuza
1956	UNITED STATES Herbert Williams Lawrence Low	ITALY Agostino Straulino Nicolo Rode	BAHAMAS Durward Knowles Sloan Farrington
1960	U.S.S.R. Timir Pinegin Fyedor Shutkov	PORTUGAL Mario Quina José Quina	UNITED STATES William Parks Robert Halperin
1964	BAHAMAS Durward Knowles Cecil Cooke	UNITED STATES Richard Stearns Lynn Williams	SWEDEN Pelle Pettersson Holger Sundstrom
1968	UNITED STATES Lowell North Peter Barrett	NORWAY Peder Lunde Per Olav Wiken	ITALY Franco Cavallo Camillo Gargano
1972	AUSTRALIA David Forbes John Anderson	SWEDEN Pelle Pettersson Stellan Westerdahl	WEST GERMANY Willi Kuhweide Karsten Meyer
1976	Event not held		
1980	U.S.S.R. Valentin Mankin Aleksandr Muzychenko	AUSTRIA Hubert Raudaschl Karl Ferstl	ITALY Giorgio Gorla Alfio Peraboni

INTERNATIONAL FLYING DUTCHMAN CLASS

	GOLD	SILVER	BRONZE

1896–1956   Event not held

	GOLD	SILVER	BRONZE
1960	**NORWAY** Peder Lunde Jr. Björn Bergvall	**DENMARK** Hans Fogh Ole Erik Petersen	**GERMANY** Rolf Mulka Ingo von Bredow
1964	**NEW ZEALAND** Helmer Pedersen Earle Wells	**GREAT BRITAIN** Franklyn Musto Jr. Arthur Morgan	**UNITED STATES** Harry Melges Jr. William Bentsen
1968	**GREAT BRITAIN** Rodney Pattisson Iain Macdonald-Smith	**WEST GERMANY** Ullrich Libor Peter Naumann	**BRAZIL** Reinaldo Conrad Burkhard Cordes
1972	**GREAT BRITAIN** Rodney Pattisson Christopher Davies	**FRANCE** Yves Pajot Marc Pajot	**WEST GERMANY** Ullrich Libor Peter Naumann
1976	**WEST GERMANY** Jorg Diesch Eckart Diesch	**GREAT BRITAIN** Rodney Pattisson Julian Brooke Houghton	**BRAZIL** Reinaldo Conrad Peter Ficker
1980	**SPAIN** Alejandro Abascal Miguel Noguer	**IRELAND** David Wilkins James Wilkinson	**HUNGARY** Szabolcs Detre Zsolt Detre

INTERNATIONAL 470 CLASS

1896–1972   Event not held

	GOLD	SILVER	BRONZE
1976	**WEST GERMANY** Frank Huebner Harro Bode	**SPAIN** Antonio Gorostegui Pedro Millet	**AUSTRALIA** Ian Brown Ian Ruff
1980	**BRAZIL** Marcos Soares Eduardo Penido	**EAST GERMANY** Jorn Borowski Egbert Swensson	**FINLAND** Jouko Lindgren Georg Tallberg

INTERNATIONAL FINN CLASS

1896–1948   Event not held

	GOLD	SILVER	BRONZE
1952	Paul Elvström (DEN)	Charles Currey (GBR)	Rickard Sarby (SWE)
1956	Paul Elvström (DEN)	André Nelis (BEL)	John Marvin (USA)
1960	Paul Elvström (DEN)	Aleksandr Chuchelov (URS)	André Nelis (BEL)
1964	Willi Kuhweide (GER)	Peter Barrett (USA)	Henning Wind (DEN)
1968	Valentin Mankin (URS)	Hubert Raudaschl (AUT)	Fabio Albarelli (ITA)
1972	Serge Maury (FRA)	Ilias Hatzipavlis (GRE)	Victor Potapov (URS)
1976	Jochen Schumann (GDR)	Andrei Balashov (URS)	John Bertrand (AUS)
1980	Esko Rechardt (FIN)	Wolfgang Mayrhofer (AUT)	Andrei Balashov (URS)

INTERNATIONAL TORNADO CLASS

1896–1972   Event not held

	GOLD	SILVER	BRONZE
1976	**GREAT BRITAIN** Reginald White John Osborn	**UNITED STATES** David McFaull Michael Rothwell	**WEST GERMANY** Jorg Spengler Jorg Schmall
1980	**BRAZIL** Alexandre Welter Lars Bjorkstrom	**DENMARK** Peter Due Per Kjergard	**SWEDEN** Goran Marstrom Jorgen Ragnarsson

WINTER OLYMPIC GAMES
TABLE OF MEDAL WINNERS
BY NATIONS 1908–1980

(including ice events in 1908 and 1920)

Note: These totals include all first, second and third places including those in events no longer on the current schedule. Results of demonstration events are not included.

		GOLD	SILVER	BRONZE	TOTAL
1.	U.S.S.R	62	38	41	108
2.	Norway	51	55	48	154
3.	U.S.A	36	42	31	109
4.	Sweden	28	23	27	78
5.	Finland	25	39	26	90
6.	Austria	25	33	29	87
7.	Germany[1]	22	21	20	63
8.	East Germany[2]	21	17	23	61
9.	Switzerland	16	18	19	53
10.	Canada	12	9	14	35
11.	France	12	9	13	34
12.	Netherlands	10	15	10	35
13.	Italy	10	9	7	26
14.	Great Britain	6	4	10	20
15.	Czechoslovakia	2	5	7	14

[1] Germany 1908–1964, West Germany from 1968
[2] East Germany (GDR) from 1968

DEVELOPMENT OF THE
WINTER OLYMPIC GAMES

These figures relate to the Winter Games, and Ice Events in 1908 and 1920.

GAMES	NO. OF COUNTRIES	NO. OF SPORTS	NO. OF COMPETITORS	
			Male	Female
London (IVth Summer)	6	1	14	7
Antwerp (VIIth Summer)	10	2	73	12
I Chamonix	16	5	281	13
II St. Moritz	25	6	468	27
III Lake Placid	17	5	274	32
IV Garmisch	28	6	675	80
V St. Moritz	28	7	636	77
VI Oslo	30	6	623	109
VII Cortina	32	6	687	132
VIII Squaw Valley	27	5	521	144
IX Innsbruck	36	7	986	200
X Grenoble	37	7	1,065	228
XI Sapporo	35	7	1,128	217
XII Innsbruck	36	7	1,092	276
XIII Lake Placid	37	7	1,012	271

THE WINTER OLYMPICS

Although the Winter Games were not inaugurated until 1924—28 years after the Modern Olympics were first held in Athens in 1896—there were ice rink events held in both the IVth Games in 1908 and the VIIth Games in 1920. Indeed ice skating was on the draft program for the IInd 1900 Games at Paris.

In London in 1908 there were four ice skating events to which six nations—Argentina, Germany, Great Britain, Russia, Sweden and the United States—sent competitors. The Swedes dominated the men's competition with the great Ulrich Salchow showing why he was 10 times world champion. Britain's Madge Syers won the ladies championships. In a special figure contest Nikolai Panin of Russia won the gold medal.

In 1920 at Antwerp there were individual figure skating events won by Sweden and the pairs by Finland. An ice hockey tournament was won by Canada. Ten countries sent competitors.

Nikolai Panin, winner of a special figure skating title of 1908, was the only Russian to win an Olympic gold medal prior to the 1952 Games.

1924—Ist Winter Games, Chamonix-Mont Blanc, France

The success of the 1920 events assisted the advocates of a separate Winter Games against Nordic opposition. Sixteen nations sent teams to the Games which were only retrospectively recognized as the Ist Winter Olympics. The heroes were the Finnish speed skater Clas Thunberg who won 3 gold, 1 silver and 1 bronze medal and Thorleif Haug (Norway) who won 3 gold and a bronze medal for Nordic skiing. Little noticed was a tiny 11-year-old Norwegian figure skater who came last—Sonja Henie. The Canadians trounced all ice hockey opposition, scoring 85 goals in three games.

1928—IInd Winter Games, St. Mortiz, Switzerland

All real opposition to a series of Winter Olympics was subdued by the success of the Chamonix celebration. This time 25 countries including, for example, Japan and Mexico, appeared. The unwelcome warm weather nearly spoiled the Games—one speed skating event was cancelled and the bobsleigh program curtailed. The top skiier proved to be the Norwegian Johan Gröttumsbraaten while Thunberg collected two more speed skating golds. In figure skating the Swede Grafström won his third gold medal and the 15-year-old Sonja Henie opened her massive account.

North America dominated the bobsleigh with two USA crews and the ice hockey with the Canadians harvesting 38 goals to nil in three games.

1932—IIIrd Winter Games, Lake Placid, New York, USA

The world economic recession coupled with the long trans-Atlantic travelling time that would be necessary for Europeans, who have always numerically predominated, depleted the competitors from 495 to 306.

Again the weather spoiled some events: snow had to be transported to repair the cross-country skiing courses. The Nordic skiiers maintained their Olympic monopoly as the inevitable introduction of Alpine skiing was still four years away but Norway's stranglehold was broken by the Swedes and Finns. In the speed skating North Americans predominated because of their successful insistence on imposing their bunched start rules which invited bodily contact instead of the more clinical European pair starts. The figure skating saw the eclipse of Grafström by Austria's Karl Schäfer and the high noon of Sonja Henie's talent.

1936—IVth Winter Games, Garmisch-Partenkirchen, Germany

The Winter Olympics hit the "big time" in 1936 with half a million paying spectators, which was more than the first three Games in aggregate. Twenty-eight countries, now including, for example, Australia and Turkey, sent 755 competitors. The weather smiled on this prestige exercise by the Nazi State and the level of competition hit new heights. The introduction of Alpine skiing events was sensational as two Nordics, the Norwegians Birger Ruud, the great ski jumper, and Laila Schou Nilsen, a sixteen-year-old girl who held all five speed skating records, won the downhill races. These remarkable performances only earned them a fourth place and a bronze medal respectively because the only Alpine championship was a combined event with a slalom section (watched by a record 70,000 people) in which the Central Europeans recovered their lost ground. The Norwegian speed skater Ivan Ballangrud dominated the rink with 3 golds; in figure skating Schäfer (Austria) and Sonja Henie (Norway) gained their final Olympic laurels; and a British team sensationally won the ice hockey tournament largely thanks to recruiting a number of Anglo-Canadians.

ABOVE: Canada, in white, won the 1932 ice hockey gold medal.

LEFT: Sonja Henie, a Norwegian who later became wealthy from professional ice shows, won the second of her 3 gold medals at Lake Placid in 1932

1948—Vth Winter Games, St. Mortiz, Switzerland

The Games in 1940 were originally intended for Sapporo, Japan, but the Sino-Japanese war put an end to that. The situtation then became highly confused because of the open hostilities between the International Skiing Federation (F.I.S.), who wanted to allow ski instructors to appear in the Games, and the International Olympic Committee (I.O.C.), who regarded them as professionals. In the context of this battle, Oslo, Helsinki, St. Mortiz and Garmisch all in turn offered to host the Games. The war clouds overshadowed this conflict and also eclipsed thoughts as to the best site for 1944. On a postal vote the I.O.C. granted the Vth Winter Games of 1948 to St. Mortiz and twenty-eight countries sent 713 competitors.

The ice hockey tournament of 1948 was fought in the shadow of the Olympic flame.

Alpine skiing with six championships now attracted a far wider entry than the five Nordic skiing titles.

The most successful Alpine skier was Henri Oreiller (France) with two golds and a bronze. Gretchen Fraser (USA) by winning the slalom achieved the first ever non-European skiing success. North America grabbed both individual figure skating titles through Richard Button (USA) and the glamorous Barbara Ann Scott (Canada). The Norwegians dominated the speed skating as did the Americans and Swiss the bob races. The ice hockey tournament was marred by a blazing row over which of two US teams should represent their country. The Canadians won very narrowly over the Czechs.

1952—VIth Winter Games, Oslo, Norway

It is perhaps extraordinary that the Games of 1952 are the only ones to be held in a Nordic country. Norway is the top medal-winning nation and Finland and Sweden are also in the top six countries as regards successes in these Games.

There was a record number of 30 countries present—with Germany and Japan being allowed back into the fold—and a new attendance record of 541,407 paying spectators.

The Norwegians excelled on their home ground with Stein Erikson even winning the less familiar Alpine skiing event, the giant slalom. Hjalmar Andersen with 3 golds was the most successful speed skater in the packed Bislet Stadium. Figure skating saw the master, Richard Button (USA), retain his crown while Britain's Jeanette Altwegg's impeccable compulsory figures survived the onslaught of several more dramatic free skaters.

The two winning German bob teams were so grotesquely heavy (they averaged over 260 lb. a man) that the International Federation legislated for a maximum weight limit in future contests. The Canadians again won the ice hockey but the quality of their opposition was rising steadily.

1956—VIIth Winter Games, Cortina d'Ampezzo, Italy

These Games were paradoxically largely financed by Italian soccer, via pools. New ground was broken·in the first appearance since 1908 of Russians who promptly won the men's 4 × 10 km relay and took three out of the first four places in the women's 10 km race, harvested many speed skating successes and sensationally won the ice hockey tournament. The hero of the Games was Toni Sailer (Austria), who won a grand slam in the three Alpine skiing events—all by an imperious margin.

The USA triumphed in both the men's and the women's individual figure skating. These Winter Games were the first to be televised and so enjoyed by record numbers of people, but the price for spreading the interest in this way was some loss in the gate money from spectators actually attending the Games.

1960—VIIIth Winter Games, Squaw Valley, California, USA

In 1955 these Games were awarded by two votes to this then virtually non-existent ski resort in preference to the famous established center of Innsbrück. In the end, despite furious objections from the bobsleighers who were not provided for any by the Nordic skiers, because they disliked the great altitude of their courses (2,000 meters or over 6,500 ft.), the Games were a remarkable success. One strong feature was the compactness of the sites, which made it possible for spectators to see a large variety of the competitions.

The program was extended by the addition of speed skating for women and the Winter Biathlon (cross-country skiing and shooting). The Swedish iron man Sixten Jernberg added to his Cortina successes by winning the tough 30 km Nordic race. The Russian women's four entrants in the 10 km event took the first four places. For the first time ever a non-Scandinavian, Georg Thoma (Germany), won the combined event, while another German, Helmut Recknagel, decisively won the special ski jump.

No one skier established personal ascendancy in the very tightly contested Alpine events. The speed skating times were sensational especially in the 10,000 meters in which Knut Johannesen (Norway) beat the world's record by some 46 seconds.

David Jenkins (USA), extracting a rare six points (the maximum possible) from one judge, won the gold medal for figure skating. The USA and Canada shunted the USSR, the winners at Cortina, to third place in the ice hockey tournament.

Jean-Claude Killy (FRA) achieved the triple in Alpine skiing of downhill, slalom, and giant slalom before a home crowd at Grenoble in 1968.

1964—IXth Winter Games, Innsbrück, Austria

These Games hit new high water marks regarding the number of competitors present, the number of nations represented and the number of paying spectators—nearly a million.

The USSR collected 25 medals, the USA, with the largest team, only 6, and neighboring Switzerland an embarrassing nil.

The heroine of the Games was a Russian lady, Lydia Skoblikova, who won a Winter Games record of four golds. She was a speed skater with a superb style, who had already won two previous golds in 1960.

To the French contingent the Goitschel sisters Christine, 19 (slalom gold) and Marielle, 18 (giant slalom gold) were goddesses, especially as each was a runner-up to the other in these events. Austria and France were 3-all over the six Alpine titles. The Scandinavians allowed not one trespasser in the men's Nordic events but the Russians monopolized the women's cross-country program and the Russian men recaptured the ice hockey title which they had won in 1956 and lost in 1960.

Two lowland nations, the Netherlands and Britain, each had a popular success. Sjoukje Dijkstra, in front of her Queen, won the women's figure skating and so Netherlands' first gold. Britain's Tony Nash and the Hon. Robin Dixon won the boblet gold.

1968—Xth Winter Games, Grenoble, France

These Games were Jean-Claude Killy's. The handsome hotelier's rather disputatious Alpine skiing grand slam was hard fought with winning margins for the downhill, slalom and giant slalom being 8/100th, 9/100th and 2.3 seconds respectively. The outstanding Nordic skiier was a Swedish lady—Toini Gustafsson—who collected two individual golds and a relay silver. The East German ladies were disqualified from the Luge event for secretly heating their runners.

The speed skating, despite pessimistic forecasts, produced fast times and three golds for the Netherlands, but only one out of eight for the Russians. The Soviets, however, retained their ice hockey title despite losing a very tense match 4-5 to the Czechs.

1972—XIth Winter Games, Sapporo, Japan

These Games, which cost the Japanese $61 million to stage, reflected the mounting strain that international sport suffers as the competitive screw turns. The magic of the Japanese-style opening ceremony seemed however to quell the endless behind-the-scenes rows about the alleged professionalism of full-time skiiers who are inevitably regarded as commercial models by equipment and clothing manufacturers. Austria's hero, Karl Schranz, was sent home by the Committee before the Games opened.

The Alpine nations were stunned when the slalom title went to a Spaniard—"Paquito" Fernandez Ochoa. There was an unexpected but popular double gold by a seventeen-year-old Swiss miss—Marie-Therese Nadig—leaving the slalom for Barbara Cochran, the United States' first skiing gold medalist for twenty years.

The Russians won 4 out of the 6 Nordic cross-country titles includ-

Ard Schenk (HOL) was the hero of the Sapporo Games in 1972, winning 3 out of the 4 speed-skating events.

ing an individual double by Galina Kulakova, who won a third gold in the relay. The Japanese by dint of endless practice were able to achieve a grand slam in the 70 meter hill ski jumping. Individual star of Asia's first Winter Games was Ard Schenk, the Dutch speed skater, who outclassed the world and won three gold medals.

1976—XIIth Winter Games, Innsbrück, Austria

The citizens of Colorado, USA, by referendum, forced the Denver organizing committee to withdraw its application for the allocation of the XIIth Games to that city. Innsbrück, host for the second time, kept it "simple." An influenza epidemic could not stop Germany's Rosi Mittermaier becoming the personality of these Games, with only 13/100ths of a second in the giant slalom between her and an unprecedented Alpine skiing grand slam by a woman.

1980—XIIIth Winter Games, Lake Placid, New York, U.S.A.

Lake Placid had been applying for the Games unsuccessfully since 1962 and finally was rewarded in 1974. With remarkable foresight speed skater Eric Heiden was selected to take the oath. Mainland China and Cyprus made their Winter Games debuts. There were many complaints about the organization of the Games, the prime one being in the field of transportation. Spectators in particular found it very difficult to get to sites.

Eric Heiden (USA) won the most medals at the Games with an unprecedented sweep of all five speed skating gold medals, all in Olympic record times. His sister Beth also won a bronze in the women's events.

Galina Kulakova (URS) won a silver in the Nordic relay to bring her total to a women's Winter Games record of eight medals, comprising four golds, two silvers and two bronze, in the four Games since 1968.

At the end of the Lake Placid Games only Great Britain, Sweden and the United States could claim to have been represented in all Winter events of the Modern Olympics, including those of 1908 and 1920.

1984—XIVth Winter Games, Sarajevo, Yugoslavia

Sarajevo, with a population of about 500,000, is the second largest city to host the Winter Games (only Sapporo was larger). Construction of facilities is ahead of schedule and plans for ensuring adequate transportation for the expected 2,300 competitors, over 4,000 media representatives, and thousands of visitors are well advanced. An unusual feature will be the accommodation of most of those visitors in private homes instead of hotels. All competition sites are within 27 km of the city. The I.O.C. has sanctioned one new event, a 20 km Nordic race for women, and is considering the inclusion of an Alpine Combination event, which has not been contested since 1948.

ROLL OF OLYMPIC MEDAL WINNERS IN THE WINTER EVENTS SINCE 1908

1. Nordic Skiing (Men)

15 KM. (9.3 miles) CROSS-COUNTRY

	GOLD	SILVER	BRONZE
1908–1920	Event not held		
1924[1]	Thorleif Haug (NOR) 1h 14:31.0	Johan Gröttumsbraaten (NOR) 1h 15:51.0	Tipani Niku (FIN) 1h 26:26.0
1928[2]	Johan Gröttumsbraaten (NOR) 1h 37:01.0	Ole Hegge (NOR) 1h 39:01.0	Reidar Ödegaard (NOR) 1h 40:11.0
1932[3]	Sven Utterström (SWE) 1h 23:07.0	Axel T. Wikström (SWE) 1h 25:07.0	Veli Saarinen (FIN) 1h 25:24.0
1936[1]	Erik-August Larsson (SWE) 1h 14:38.0	Oddbjörn Hagen (NOR) 1h 15:33.0	Pekka Niemi (FIN) 1h 16:59.0
1948[1]	Martin Lundström (SWE) 1h 13:50.0	Nils Östensson (SWE) 1h 14:22.0	Gunnar Eriksson (SWE) 1h 16:06.0
1952[1]	Hallgeir Brenden (NOR) 1h 1:34.0	Tapio Mäkelä (FIN) 1h 2:09.0	Paavo Lonkila (FIN) 1h 2:20.0
1956	Hallgeir Brenden (NOR) 49:39.0	Sixten Jernberg (SWE) 50:14.0	Pavel Koltschin (URS) 50:17.0
1960	Haakon Brusveen (NOR) 51:55.5	Sixten Jernberg (SWE) 51:58.6	Veikko Hakulinen (FIN) 52:03.0
1964	Eero Mäntyranta (FIN) 50:54.1	Harald Grönningen (NOR) 51:34.8	Sixten Jernberg (SWE) 51:42.2
1968	Harald Grönningen (NOR) 47:54.2	Eero Mäntyranta (FIN) 47:56.1	Gunnar Larsson (SWE) 48:33.7
1972	Sven-Ake Lundback (SWE) 45:28.24	Fedor Simaschov (URS) 46:00.84	Ivar Formo (NOR) 46:02.86
1976	Nikolay Bajukov (URS) 43:58.47	Evgeniy Beliayev (URS) 44:01.10	Arto Koivisto (FIN) 44:19.25
1980	Thomas Wassberg (SWE) 41:57.63	Juha Mieto (FIN) 41:57.64	Ove Aunli (NOR) 42:28.62

[1] The distance was 18 km.
[2] The distance was 19.7 km.
[3] The distance was 18.2 km.

30 KM. (18.6 miles) CROSS-COUNTRY

	GOLD	SILVER	BRONZE
1908–1952	Event not held		
1956	Veikko Hakulinen (FIN) 1h 44:06.0	Sixten Jernberg (SWE) 1h 44:30.0	Pavel Koltschin (URS) 1h 45:45.0
1960	Sixten Jernberg (SWE) 1h 51:03.9	Rolf Rämgård (SWE) 1h 51:61.9	Nikolay Anikin (URS) 1h 52:28.2
1964	Eero Mäntyranta (FIN) 1h 30:50.7	Harald Grönningen (NOR) 1h 32:02.3	Igor Voronchikin (URS) 1h 32:15.8
1968	Franco Nones (ITA) 1h 35:39.2	Odd Martinsen (NOR) 1h 36:28.9	Eero Mäntyranta (FIN) 1h 36:55.3

GOLD	SILVER	BRONZE
1972 Viaceslav Vedenine (URS) 1h 36:31.2	Paal Tyldum (NOR) 1h 37:25.3	Johs Harviken (NOR) 1h 37:32.4
1976 Sergei Savelyev (URS) 1h 30:29.38	William Koch (USA) 1h 30:57.84	Ivan Garanin (URS) 1h 31:09.29
1980 Nikolai Simyatov (URS) 1h 27:02.80	Vasiliy Rochev (URS) 1h 27:34.22	Ivan Lebanov (BUL) 1h 28:03.87

50 KM. (31 miles) CROSS-COUNTRY

1908–1920   Event not held

1924 Thorleif Haug (NOR) 3h 44:32.0	Thoralf Strömstad (NOR) 3h 46:23.0	Johan Gröttumsbraaten (NOR) 3h 47:46.0
1928 Per Erik Hedlund (SWE) 4h 52:03.0	Gustaf Jonsson (SWE) 5h 05:30.0	Volger Andersson (SWE) 5h 05:46.0
1932 Veli Saarinen (FIN) 4h 28:00.0	Väinö Likkanen (FIN) 4h 28:20.0	Arne Rustadstuen (NOR) 4h 31:53.0
1936 Elis Wiklund (SWE) 3h 30:11.0	Axel Wikström (SWE) 3h 33:20.0	Nils-Joel Englund (SWE) 3h 34:10.0
1948 Nils Karlsson (SWE) 3h 47:48.0	Harald Eriksson (SWE) 3h 52:20.0	Benjamin Vanninen (FIN) 3h 57:28.0
1952 Veikko Hakulinen (FIN) 3h 33:33.0	Eero Kolehmainen (FIN) 3h 38:11.0	Magnar Estenstad (NOR) 3h 38:28.0
1956 Sixten Jernberg (SWE) 2h 50:27.0	Veikko Hakulinen (FIN) 2h 51:45.0	Fyedor Terentyeve (URS) 2h 53:32.0
1960 Kalevi Hämäläinen (FIN) 2h 59:06.3	Veikko Hakulinen (FIN) 2h 59:26.7	Rolf Rämgård (SWE) 3h 02:46.7
1964 Sixten Jernberg (SWE) 2h 43:52.6	Assar Roennlund (SWE) 2h 44:58.2	Arto Tiainen (FIN) 2h 45:30.4
1968 Olle Ellefsaeter (NOR) 2h 28:45.8	Viaceslav Vedenine (URS) 2h 29:02.5	Josef Haas (SUI) 2h 29:14.8
1972 Paal Tyldrum (NOR) 2h 43:14.75	Magne Myrmo (NOR) 2h 43:29.45	Viaceslav Vedenine (URS) 2h 44:00.19
1976 Ivar Formo (NOR) 2h 37:30.50	Gert-Dietmar Klause (GDR) 2h 38:13.21	Benny Soedergren (SWE) 2h 39:39.21
1980 Nikolai Simyatov (URS) 2h 27:24.60	Juha Mieto (FIN) 2h 30:20.52	Aleksandr Savyalov (URS) 2h 30:51.52

RELAY RACE 4 x 10 KM. (6 miles 376 yd.)

1908–1932   Event not held

1936 FINLAND 2h 41:33.0 Sulo Nurmela Klaes Karppinen Matti Lahde Kalle Jalkanen	NORWAY 2h 41:39.0 Oddbjörn Hagen Olaf Hoffsbakken Sverre Brodahl Bjarne Iversen	SWEDEN 2h 43:03.0 John Berger Erik-August Larsson Artur Häggblad Martin J. Matsbo
1948 SWEDEN 2h 32:08.0 Nils Ostensson Nils Täpp Gunnar Eriksson Martin Lundström	FINLAND 2h 41:06.6 Lauri Silvennoinen Teuvo Laukkanen Sauli Rytky August Kiuru	NORWAY 2h 44:33.0 Erling Evensen Olav Okern Reidar Nyborg Olav Hagen
1952 FINLAND 2h 20:16.0 Heikki Hasu Paavon Lonkila Urho Korhonen Tapio Mäkelä	NORWAY 2h 23:13.0 Magnar Estenstad Mikal Kirkholt Martin Stokken Hallgeir Brenden	SWEDEN 2h 24:13.0 Nils Täpp Sigurd Andersson Enar Josefsson Martin Lundström
1956 U.S.S.R. 2h 15:30.0 Fhedor Terentyev Pavel Koltschin Nikolay Anikin Vladimir Kusin	FINLAND 2h 16:31.0 August Kiuru Jorma Kortelainen Arvo Viitanen Veikko Hakulinen	SWEDEN 2h 17:42.0 Lennart Larsson Gunnar Samuelsson Per-Erik Larsson Sixten Jernberg

	GOLD	SILVER	BRONZE
1960	**FINLAND** 2h 18:45.6 Toimi Alatalo Eero Mäntyranta Vaino Huhtala Veikko Hakulinen	**NORWAY** 2h 18:46.4 Harald Grönningen Hallgeir Brenden Einar Ostby Haakon Brusveen	**U.S.S.R.** 2h 21:21.6 Anatoliy Schelyuchin Gennadiy Vaganov Aleksey Kusnetsov Nikolay Anikin
1964	**SWEDEN** 2h 18:34.6 Karl-Ake Asph Sixten Jernberg Janne Stefansson Assar Roennlund	**FINLAND** 2h 18:42.4 Vaino Huhtala Arto Tiainen Kalevi Laurila Eero Mäntyranta	**U.S.S.R.** 2h 18:46.9 Ivan Utrobin Gennadiy Vaganov Igor Voronchikin Pavel Koltschin
1968	**NORWAY** 2h 08:33.5 Odd Martinsen Paal Tyldrum Harald Grönningen Olle Ellefsaeter	**SWEDEN** 2h 10:13.2 Jan Halvarsson Bjarne Andersson Gunnar Larsson Assar Roennlund	**FINLAND** 2h 10:56.7 Kalevi Oikarainen Hannu Taipale Kalevi Laurila Eero Mäntyranta
1972	**U.S.S.R.** 2h 04:47.94 Vladimir Voronkov Yuri Skobov Fedor Simaschov Viaceslav Vedenine	**NORWAY** 2h 04:57.06 Oddvar Braa Paal Tyldrum Ivor Formo Johs Harviken	**SWITZERLAND** 2h 07:00.06 Alfred Kaflin Albert Giger Alois Kaelin Edi Hauser
1976	**FINLAND** 2h 07:59.72 Matti Pitkaenen Juha Mieto Pertti Teurajaervi Arto Koivisto	**NORWAY** 2h 09:58.36 Paal Tyldum Einar Sagstuen Ivar Formo Odd Martinsen	**U.S.S.R.** 2h 10:51.46 Eveniy Beliayev Nikolay Bajukov Sergei Savelyev Ivan Garanin
1980	**U.S.S.R.** 1h 57:03.46 Vasiliy Rochev Nikolai Bajukov Eveniy Beliayev Nikolai Simyatov	**NORWAY** 1h 58:45.77 Lars Erik Eriksen Per Knut Aalund Ove Aunli Oddvar Bra	**FINLAND** 2h 00:00.18 Harri Kirvesniemi Pertti Teurajaervi Matti Pitkaenen Juha Mieto

Sixten Jernberg of Sweden has won more medals in winter Olympic competition than any other athlete—4 gold, 3 silver, and 2 bronze.

Ski Jumping

1924–1960   Held on one hill only

BIG HILL (90 meters)

	GOLD	SILVER	BRONZE
1964	Toralf Engan (NOR) 230.70	Veikko Kankkonen (FIN) 228.90	Torgeir Brandtzaeg (NOR) 227.20
1968	Vladimir Beloussov (URS) 231.3	Jiri Raska (TCH) 229.4	Lars Grini (NOR) 214.3
1972	Wojciech Fortuna (POL) 219.9	Walter Steiner (SUI) 219.8	Rainer Schmidt (GDR) 219.3
1976	Karl Schnabl (AUT) 234.8	Anton Innauer (AUT) 232.9	Henry Glass (GDR) 221.7
1980	Jouko Tormanen (FIN) 271.0	Hubert Neuper (AUT) 262.4	Jari Puikkonen (FIN) 248.5

SMALL HILL (70 meters)

1964	Veikko Kankkonen (FIN) 229.90	Toralf Engan (NOR) 226.30	Torgeil Brandtzaeg (NOR) 222.90
1968	Jiri Raska (TCH) 216.5	Reinhold Bachler (AUT) 214.2	Baldur Preiml (AUT) 212.6
1972	Yukio Kasaya (JPN) 244.2	Akitsugo Konno (JPN) 234.8	Seiji Aochi (JPN) 229.5
1976	Hans-Georg Aschenbach (GDR) 252.0	Jochen Danneberg (GDR) 246.2	Karl Schnabl (AUT) 242.0
1980	Toni Innauer (AUT) 266.3	Manfred Deckert (GDR) 249.2 Hirokazu Yagi (JPN) 249.2	—

Karl Schnabl of Austria won a gold medal on the 90 meter hill at Innsbruck in 1976, and a bronze medal on the 70 meter hill.

NORDIC COMBINED (15 km.[2] and jumping)

	GOLD	SILVER	BRONZE
1908–1920	Event not held		
1924[1]	Thorleif Haug (NOR)	Thoralf Strömstad (NOR)	Johan Gröttumsbraaten (NOR)
1928[1]	Johan Gröttumsbraaten (NOR)	Hans Vinjarengen (NOR)	John Snersrud (NOR)
1932	Johan Gröttumsbraaten (NOR) 446.0	Ole Stenen (NOR) 436.05	Hans Vinjarengen (NOR) 434.60
1936	Oddbjörn Hagen (NOR) 430.30	Olaf Hoffsbakken (NOR) 419.80	Sverre Brodahl (NOR) 408.10
1948	Heikki Hasu (FIN) 448.80	Martti Huhtala (FIN) 433.65	Sfen Israelsson (SWE) 433.40
1952	Simon Slåttvik (NOR) 451.621	Heikki Hasu (FIN) 447.5	Sverre Stenersen (NOR) 436.335
1956	Sverre Stenersen (NOR) 455.0	Bengt Eriksson (SWE) 473.4	Franciszek Gron-Gasienica (POL) 436.8
1960	Georg Thoma (GER) 457.952	Tormod Knutsen (NOR) 453.0	Nikolay Gusakow (URS) 452.0
1964	Tormod Knutsen (NOR) 469.28	Nikolai Kiselev (URS) 453.04	Georg Thoma (GER) 452.88
1968	Frantz Keller (GER) 449.04	Alois Kaelin (SUI) 447.94	Andreas Kunz (GDR) 444.10
1972	Ulrich Wehling (GDR) 413.34	Rauno Mittinen (FIN) 405.55	Karl-Heinz Luck (GDR) 398.80
1976	Ulrich Wehling (GDR) 423.39	Urban Hettich (GR) 418.90	Konrad Winkler (GDR) 417.47
1980	Ulrich Wehling (GDR) 432.20	Jouko Karjalainen (FIN) 429.50	Konrad Winkler (GDR) 425.32

[1] In 1924 and 1928, the scoring was decided upon a different basis from that used from 1932 onwards.
[2] From 1924–1952 distance was 18 km.

Biathlon

10 KM.

1908–1976	Event not held		
1980	Frank Ullrich (GDR) 32:10.69	Vladimir Alikin (URS) 32:53.10	Anatoliy Alyabiev (URS) 33:09.16

20 KM.

1908–1956	Event not held		
1960	Klas Lestander (SWE) 1h 33:21.6	Antti Tyrväinen (FIN) 1h 33:57.7	Aleksandr Privalov (URS) 1h 34:54.2
1964	Vladimir Melyanin (URS) 1h 20:26.8	Aleksandr Privalov (URS) 1h 23:42.5	Olav Jordet (NOR) 1h 24:38.8
1968	Magnar Solberg (NOR) 1h 13:45.9	Alexander Tikhonov (URS) 1h 14:40.4	Vladimir Goundartsev (URS) 1h 18:27.4
1972	Magnar Solberg (NOR) 1h 15:55.5	Hans-Jürg Knauthe (GDR) 1h 16:07.6	Lars Arvidson (SWE) 1h 16:27.03
1976	Nikolay Kruglov (URS) 1h 14:12.26	Heikki Ikola (FIN) 1h 15:54.10	Alexander Elizarov (URS) 1h 16:05.57
1980	Anatoliy Alyabiev (URS) 1h 08:16.31	Frank Ullrich (GDR) 1h 08:27.79	Eberhard Rosch (GDR) 1h 11:11.73

BIATHLON RELAY (4 × 7.5 km.)

GOLD	SILVER	BRONZE
1908–1964 Event not held		
1968 **U.S.S.R.**	**NORWAY**	**SWEDEN**
Alexander Tikhonov	Ola Waerhaug	Lars Arvidson
Nikolai Pousanov	Olav Jordet	Tore Eriksson
Victor Mamatov	Magnar Solberg	Olle Petrusson
Vladimir Groundartsev	Jon Istad	Holmfrid Olsson
2h 13:02.4	2h 14:50.2	2h 17:26.3
1972 **U.S.S.R.**	**FINLAND**	**EAST GERMANY**
Rinnat Safine	Esko Saira	Hans-Jürg Knauthe
Ivan Biakov	Juhani Suutarinen	Joachim Mischner
Victor Mamatov	Heikki Ikola	Heinz Dieter Speer
Alexander Tikhonov	Mauri Röppänen	Horst Koschla
1h 51:44.92	1h 54:37.22	1h 54:57.67
1976 **U.S.S.R.**	**FINLAND**	**EAST GERMANY**
Alexander Elizarov	Henrik Floejt	Karl-Heinz Menz
Ivan Biakov	Esko Saira	Frank Ullrich
Nikolay Kruglov	Juhani Suutarinen	Manfred Beer
Alexander Tikhonov	Heikki Ikola	Manfred Geyer
1h 57:55.64	2h 01:45.58	2h 04:08.61
1980 **U.S.S.R.**	**EAST GERMANY**	**GERMANY**
Vladimir Alikin	Mathias Jung	Franz Bernreiter
Alexandr Tikhonov	Klaus Siebert	Hans Estner
Vladimir Barnashov	Frank Ullrich	Peter Angerer
Anatoliy Alyabiev	Eberhard Rosch	Gerhard Winkler
1h 34:03.27	1h 34:56.99	1h 37:30.26

The 4 × 7.5 kilometer biathlon relay has been contested four times since its insertion in the 1968 program, and Soviet biathlete Alexander Tikhinov has been on the gold medal team at each Celebration.

Galina Kulakova (URS) set a women's Winter Games record with 8 total medals (4 gold, 2 silver and 2 bronze) in the 4 Games since 1968.

Nordic Skiing (Women)

5 KM. CROSS-COUNTRY (3 miles 188 yd.)

GOLD	SILVER	BRONZE
1908–1960 Event not held		
1964 Klaudia Boyarskikh (URS) 17:50.5	Mirja Lehtonen (FIN) 17:52.9	Alevtina Koltschina (URS) 18:08.4
1968 Toini Gustafsson (SWE) 16:45.2	Galina Kulakova (URS) 16:48.4	Alevtina Koltschina (URS) 16:51.6
1972 Galina Kulakova (URS) 17:00.50	Marjatta Kajosmaa (FIN) 17:05.50	Helena Sikolova (TCH) 17:07.32
1976 Helena Takalo (FIN) 15:48.69	Raisa Smetanina (URS) 15:49.73	Nina Baldicheva[1] (URS) 16:12.82
1980 Raisa Smetanina (URS) 15:06.92	Hilkka Riihivuori (FIN) 15:11.96	Kvetslava Jeriova (TCH) 15:23.44

[1] Third finisher Galina Kulakova (URS) disqualified.

10 KM. CROSS-COUNTRY (6.2 miles)

1908–1948 Event not held		
1952 Lydia Widemen (FIN) 41:40.0	Mirja Hietamies (FIN) 42:39.0	Siiri Rantanen (FIN) 42:50.0
1956 Lyubov Kosyryeva (URS) 38:11.0	Radya Yeroschina (URS) 38:16.0	Sonja Edström (SWE) 38:23.0
1960 Maria Gusakova (URS) 39:46.6	Lyubov Baranova-Kosyryeva (URS) 40:04.2	Radya Yeroschina (URS) 40:06.0

	GOLD	SILVER	BRONZE
1964	Klaudia Boyarskikh (URS) 40:24.3	Eudokia Mekshilo (URS) 40:26.6	Maria Gusakova (URS) 40:46.6
1968	Toini Gustafsson (SWE) 36:46.5	Berit Moerdre (NOR) 37:54.6	Inger Aufles (NOR) 37:59.9
1972	Galina Kulakova (URS) 34:17.8	Alevtina Olunina (URS) 34:54.1	Marjatta Kajosmaa (FIN) 34:56.5
1976	Raisa Smetanina (URS) 30:13.41	Helena Takalo (FIN) 30:14.28	Galina Kulakova (URS) 30:38.61
1980	Barbara Petzold (GDR) 30:31.54	Hilkka Riihivuori (FIN) 30:35.05	Helena Takalo (FIN) 30:45.25

4 × 5 KM. RELAY[1]

1908–1952	Event not held		
1956	FINLAND 1:9:01.0	U.S.S.R. 1h 9:28.0	SWEDEN 1h 9:48.0
	Sirkka Polkunen	Lyubov Kosyryeva	Irma Johansson
	Mirja Hietamies	Alevtina Koltschina	Anna-Lisa Eriksson
	Siiri Rantanen	Radya Yeroschina	Sonja Edström
1960	SWEDEN 1h 4:21.4	U.S.S.R. 1h 5:2.6	FINLAND 1h 6:27.5
	Irma Johansson	Radya Yeroschina	Siiri Rantanen
	Britt Strandberg	Maria Gusakova	Eeva Ruoppa
	Sonja Ruthström-Edström	Lyubov Baranova-Kosyryeva	Toini Pöysti
1964	U.S.S.R. 59:20.2	SWEDEN 1h 1:27.0	FINLAND 1h 2:45.1
	Alevtina Koltschina	Barbo Martinsson	Senja Pusula
	Eudokia Mekshilo	Britt Strandberg	Toini Pöysti
	Klaudia Boyarskikh	Toini Gustafsson	Mirja Lehtonen
1968	NORWAY 57:30.0	SWEDEN 57:51.0	U.S.S.R. 58:13.6
	Inger Aufles	Britt Strandberg	Alevtina Koltschina
	Babben Enger Damon	Toini Gustafsson	Rita Achkina
	Berit Moerdre	Barbo Martinsson	Galina Kulakova
1972	U.S.S.R. 48:46.15	FINLAND 49:19.37	NORWAY 49:51.49
	Lyubov Moukhateva	Helena Takalo	Inger Aufles
	Alevtina Olunina	Hilkka Kuntola	Aslaug Dahl
	Galina Kulakova	Marjatta Kajosmaa	Berit Lammedal
1976	U.S.S.R. 1h 07:49.75	FINLAND 1h 08:36.57	EAST GERMANY 1h 09:57.95
	Nina Baldicheva	Liisa Suihkonen	Monika Debertshaeuser
	Zinaida Amosova	Marjatta Kajosmaa	Sigrun Krause
	Raisa Smetanina	Hilkka Kuntola	Barbara Petzold
	Galina Kulakova	Helena Takalo	Veronika Schmid
1980	EAST GERMANY 1h 02:11.10	U.S.S.R. 1h 03:18.30	NORWAY 1h 04:13.50
	Marlies Rostock	Nina Baldicheva	Brit Pettersen
	Carola Anding	Nina Rocheva	Anette Boe
	Veronika Hesse	Galina Kulakova	Marit Myrmael
	Barbara Petzold	Raisa Smetanina	Berit Aunli

---

[1] Race over three stages before 1976.

---

2. Alpine Skiing (Men)

GIANT SLALOM

1908–1948	Event not held		
1952	Stein Erikson (NOR) 2:25.0	Christian Pravda (AUT) 2:26.9	Toni Spiss (AUT) 2:28.8

	GOLD	SILVER	BRONZE
1956	Anton Sailer (AUT) 3:00.1	Andreas Molterer (AUT) 3:06.3	Walter Schuster (AUT) 3:07.2
1960	Roger Staub (SUI) 1:48.3	Josef Stiegler (AUT) 1:48.7	Ernst Hinterseer (AUT) 1:49.1
1964	Francois Boulieu (FRA) 1:46.71	Karl Schranz (AUT) 1:47.09	Josef Stiegler (AUT) 1:48.05
1968	Jean-Claude Killy (FRA) 3:29.28	Willy Favre (SUI) 3:31.50	Heinrich Messner (AUT) 3:31.83
1972	Gustavo Thoeni (ITA) 3:09.62	Edmund Bruggmann (SUI) 3:10.75	Werner Mattle (SUI) 3:10.99
1976	Heini Hemmi (SUI) 3:26.97	Ernst Good (SUI) 3:27.17	Ingemar Stenmark (SWE) 3:27.41
1980	Ingemar Stenmark (SWE) 2:40.74	Andreas Wenzel (LIE) 2:41.49	Hans Enn (AUT) 2:42.51

SLALOM

1908–1936	Event not held		
1948	Edi Reinalter (SUI) 2:10.3	James Couttet (FRA) 2:10.8	Henri Oreiller (FRA) 2:12.8
1952	Othmar Schneider (AUT) 2:00.0	Stein Eriksen (NOR) 2:01.2	Guttorm Berge (NOR) 2:01.7
1956	Anton Sailer (AUT) 3:14.7	Chiharu Igaya (JPN) 3:18.7	Stig Sollander (SWE) 3:20.2
1960	Ernst Hinterseer (AUT) 2:08.9	Matthias Lietner (AUT) 2:10.3	Charles Bozon (FRA) 2:10.4
1964	Josef Stiegler (AUT) 2:21.13	William Kidd (USA) 2:21.27	James Heuga (USA) 2:21.52
1968	Jean-Claude Killy (FRA) 1:39.73	Herbert Huber (AUT) 1:39.82	Alfred Matt (AUT) 1:40.09
1972	Francisco Fernandez Ochoa (ESP) 1:49.27	Gustavo Thoeni (ITA) 1:50.28	Rolando Thoeni (ITA) 1:50.30
1976	Piero Gros (ITA) 2:03.29	Gustavo Thoeni (ITA) 2:03.73	Willy Frommelt (LIE) 2:04.28
1980	Ingemar Stenmark (SWE) 1:44.26	Phil Mahre (USA) 1:44.76	Jacques Luethy (SUI) 1:45.06

DOWNHILL

1908–1936	Event not held		
1948	Henri Oreiller (FRA) 2:55.0	Franz Gabl (AUT) 2:59.1	Karl Molitor (SUI) 3:00.3 Rolf Olinger (SUI) 3:00.3
1952	Zeno Colo (ITA) 2:30.8	Othmar Schneider (AUT) 2:32.0	Christian Pravda (AUT) 2:32.4
1956	Anton Sailer (AUT) 2:52.2	Raymond Fellay (SUI) 2:55.7	Andreas Molterer (AUT) 2:56.2
1960	Jean Vuarnet (FRA) 2:06.0	Hans-Peter Lanig (GER) 2:06.5	Guy Perillat (FRA) 2:06.9
1964	Egon Zimmermann (AUT) 2:18.16	Leo Lacroix (FRA) 2:18.90	Wolfgang Bartels (GER) 2:19.48
1968	Jean-Claude Killy (FRA) 1:59.85	Guy Périllat (FRA) 1:59.93	J. Daniel Daetwyler (SUI) 2:00.32
1972	Bernhard Russi (SUI) 1:51.43	Roland Collombin (SUI) 1:52.07	Heinrich Messner (AUT) 1:52.40
1976	Franz Klammer (AUT) 1:45.73	Bernhard Russi (SUI) 1:46.06	Herbert Plank (ITA) 1:46.59
1980	Leonhard Stock (AUT) 1:45.50	Peter Wirnsberger (AUT) 1:46.12	Stephen Podborski (CAN) 1:46.62

Toni Sailer (AUT) dominated the Alpine skiing in the 1956 Games at Cortina, winning all 3 gold medals.

Although he regularly dominated the Alpine World Cup competition, Ingemar Stenmark (SWE) was frustrated in his desire for an Olympic gold medal until he swept the slalom and giant slalom events at Lake Placid in 1980.

Franz Klammer (AUT) won the 1976 gold medal in the downhill at an average speed of 63 m.p.h.

Alpine Skiing (Women)

GIANT SLALOM

GOLD	SILVER	BRONZE
1908–1948 Event not held		
1952 Andrea Lawrence-Mead (USA) 2:06.8	Dagmar Rom (AUT) 2:09.0	Annemarie Buchner (GER) 2:10.0
1956 Ossi Reichert (GER) 1:56.5	Josefine Frandl (AUT) 1:57.8	Dorothea Hochleitner (AUT) 1:58.2
1960 Yvonne Rüegg (SUI) 1:39.9	Penelope Pitou (USA) 1:40.0	Giuliana Chenal-Minuzzo (ITA) 1:40.2
1964 Marielle Goitschel (FRA) 1:52.24	Christine Goitschel (FRA) 1:53.11	Jean Saubert (USA) 1:53.11
1968 Nancy Greene (CAN) 1:51.97	Annie Famose (FRA) 1:54.61	Fernande Bochatay (SUI) 1:54.74
1972 Marie-Therese Nadig (SUI) 1:29.90	Annemarie Pröll (AUT) 1:30.75	Wiltrud Drexel (AUT) 1:32.35
1976 Kathy Kreiner (CAN) 1:29.13	Rosi Mittermaier (GER) 1:29.25	Danielle Debernard (FRA) 1:29.95
1980 Hanni Wenzel (LIE) 2:41.66	Irene Epple (GER) 2.42.12	Perrine Pelen (FRA) 2:42.41

SLALOM

1908–1936 Event not held		
1948 Gretchen Fraser (USA) 1:57.2	Antoinette Meyer (SUI) 1:57.7	Erika Mahringer (AUT) 1:58.0
1952 Andrea Lawrence-Mead (USA) 2:10.6	Ossi Reichert (GER) 2:11.4	Annemarie Buchner (GER) 2:13.3
1956 Renée Colliard (SUI) 1:52.3	Regina Schöpf (AUT) 1:55.4	Jevginija Sidorova (URS) 1:56.7
1960 Anne Heggtveit (CAN) 1:49.6	Betsy Snite (USA) 1:52.9	Barbi Henneberger (GER) 1:56.6
1964 Christine Goitschel (FRA) 1:29.86	Marielle Goitschel (FRA) 1:30.77	Jean Saubert (USA) 1:31.36

	GOLD	SILVER	BRONZE
1968	Marielle Goitschel (FRA) 1:25.86	Nancy Greene (CAN) 1:26.15	Annie Famose (FRA) 1:27.89
1972	Barbara Cochran (USA) 1:31.24	Danielle Debernard (FRA) 1:31.26	Florence Steurer (FRA) 1:32.69
1976	Rosi Mittermaier (GER) 1:30.54	Claudia Giordani (ITA) 1:30.87	Hanny Wenzel (LIE) 1:32.20
1980	Hanni Wenzel (LIE) 1:25.09	Christa Kinshofer (GER) 1:26.50	Erika Hess (SUI) 1:27.89

DOWNHILL

	GOLD	SILVER	BRONZE
1908–1936	Event not held		
1948	Hedy Schlunegger (SUI) 2:28.3	Trude Beiser (AUT) 2:29.1	Resi Hammerer (AUT) 2:30.2
1952	Trude Jochum-Beiser (AUT) 1:47.1	Annemarie Buchner (GER) 1:48.0	Giuliana Minuzzo (ITA) 1:49.0
1956	Madeleine Berthod (SUI) 1:40.7	Frieda Dänzer (SUI) 1:45.4	Lucile Wheeler (CAN) 1:45.9
1960	Heidi Biebl (GER) 1:37.6	Penelope Pitou (USA) 1:38.6	Traudl Hecher (AUT) 1:38.9
1964	Christl Haas (AUT) 1:55.39	Edith Zimmerman (AUT) 1:56.42	Traudl Hecher (AUT) 1:56.66
1968	Olga Pall (AUT) 1:40.87	Isabelle Mir (FRA) 1:41.33	Christl Haas (AUT) 1:41.41
1972	Marie-Therese Nadig (SUI) 1:36.68	Annemarie Pröll (AUT) 1:37.00	Susan Corrock (USA) 1:37.68
1976	Rosi Mittermaier (GER) 1:46.16	Brigitte Totschnig (AUT) 1:46.68	Cindy Nelson (USA) 1:47.50
1980	Annemarie Moser-Pröll (AUT) 1:37.52	Hanni Wenzel (LIE) 1:38.22	Marie-Therese Nadig (SUI) 1:38.36

Gretchen Fraser (USA) won the women's slalom race the first time it was contested, in 1948 at St. Mortiz.

RIGHT: Hanni Wenzel, from the tiny Principality of Liechtenstein (66 sq. miles), won gold medals in the slalom and giant slalom, as well as the silver medal in the downhill, at the 1980 Winter Games.

Rosi Mittermaier of West Germany won 2 golds and one silver in women's Alpine skiing events at Innsbruck in 1976.

3. Figure Skating (Men)

	GOLD	SILVER	BRONZE
1908	Ulrich Salchow (SWE) 1,886.5 pts.	Richard Johansson (SWE) 1,826.0 pts.	Per Thorén (SWE) 1,787.0 pts.
1920	Gillis Grafström (SWE) 2,838.5 pts.	Andreas Krogh (NOR) 2,634 pts.	Martin Stixrud (NOR) 2,561.5 pts.
1924	Gillis Grafström (SWE) 2,575.25 pts.	Willy Böckl (AUT) 2,518.75 pts.	Georges Gautschi (SUI) 2,233.5 pts.
1928	Gillis Grafström (SWE) 2,698.25 pts.	Willy Böckl (AUT) 2,682.50 pts.	Robert v. Zeebroeck (BEL) 2,578.75 pts.
1932	Karl Schäfer (AUT) 2,602.0 pts.	Gillis Grafström (SWE) 2,514.5 pts.	Montgomery Wilson (CAN) 2,448.3 pts.
1936	Karl Schäfer (AUT) 2,959.0 pts.	Ernst Baier (GER) 2,805.3 pts.	Felix Kaspar (AUT) 2,801.0 pts.
1948	(Richard Button (USA) 1,720.6 pts.	Hans Gerschwiler (SUI) 1,630.1 pts.	Edi Rada (AUT) 1,603.2 pts.
1952	Richard Button (USA) 1,730.3 pts.	Helmut Seibt (AUT) 1,621.3 pts.	James Grogan (USA) 1,627.4 pts.
1956	Hayes Alan Jenkins (USA) 1,497.95 pts.	Ronald Robertson (USA) 1,492.15 pts.	David Jenkins (USA) 1,465.41 pts.
1960	David Jenkins (USA) 1,440.2 pts.	Jarol Divin (TCH) 1,414.3 pts.	Donald Jackson (CAN) 1,401.0 pts.
1964	Manfred Schnelldorfer (GER) 1,916.9 pts.	Alain Calmat (FRA) 1,876.5 pts.	Scott Allen (USA) 1,873.6 pts.
1968	Wolfgang Schwartz (AUT) 1,094.1 pts.	Timothy Wood (USA) 1,891.6 pts.	Patrick Péra (FRA) 1,864.5 pts.
1972	Ondrej Nepela (TCH) 2,739.1 pts.	Sergei Chetverukhin (URS) 2,672.4 pts.	Patrick Péra (FRA) 2,653.1 pts.
1976	John Curry (GBR) 192.74 pts.	Vladimir Kovalev (URS) 187.64 pts.	Toller Cranston (CAN) 187.38 pts.
1980	Robin Cousins (GBR) 189.48 pts.	Jan Hoffmann (GDR) 189.72 pts.	Charles Tickner (USA) 187.06 pts.

Figure Skating (Women)

	GOLD	SILVER	BRONZE
1908	E. Madge Syers (GBR) 1,262.5 pts.	Elsa Rendschmidt (GER) 1,055.0 pts.	Dorothy Greenough-Smith (GBR) 960.5 pts.
1920	Magda Julin-Mauroy (SWE) 913.5 pts.	Svea Norén (SWE) 887.75 pts.	Theresa Weld (USA) 898.0 pts.
1924	Herma Planck-Szabo (AUT) 2,094.25 pts.	Beatrix Loughran (USA) 1,959.0 pts.	Ethel Muckelt (GBR) 1,750.50 pts.
1928	Sonja Henie (NOR) 2,452.25 pts.	Fritzi Burger (AUT) 2,248.50 pts.	Beatrix Loughran (USA) 2,254.50 pts.
1932	Sonja Henie (NOR) 2,302.5 pts.	Fritzi Burger (AUT) 2,167.1 pts.	Maribel Vinson (USA) 2,158.5 pts.
1936	Sonja Henie (NOR) 2,971.4 pts.	Cecilia Colledge (GBR) 2,926.8 pts.	Vivi-Anne Hultén (SWE) 2,763.2 pts.
1948	Barbara Scott (CAN) 1,467.7 pts.	Efa Pawlik (AUT) 1,418.3 pts.	Jeanette Altweg (GBR) 1,405.5 pts.
1952	Jeanette Altwegg (GBR) 1,455.8 pts.	Tenley Albright (USA) 1,432.2 pts.	Jacqueline du Bief (FRA) 1,422.0 pts.
1956	Tenley Albright (USA) 1,866.39 pts.	Carol Heiss (USA) 1,848.24 pts.	Ingrid Wendl (AUT) 1,753.91 pts.
1960	Carol Heiss (USA) 1,490.1 pts.	Sjoukje Dijkstra (HOL) 1,424.8 pts.	Barbara Roles (USA) 1,414.8 pts.
1964	Sjoukje Dijkstra (HOL) 2,018.5 pts.	Regine Heitzer (AUT) 1,945.5 pts.	Petra Burka (CAN) 1,940.0 pts.
1968	Peggy Fleming (USA) 1,970.5 pts.	Gabrielle Seyfert (GDR) 1,882.3 pts.	Hana Maskova (TCH) 1,828.8 pts.

GOLD	SILVER	BRONZE
1972 Beatrix Schuba (AUT) 2,751.5 pts.	Karen Magnussen (CAN) 2,673.2 pts.	Janet Lynn (USA) 2,663.1 pts.
1976 Dorothy Hamill (USA) 193.80 pts.	Dianne De Leeuw (HOL) 190.24 pts.	Christine Errath (GDR) 188.16 pts.
1980 Anett Poetzsch (GDR) 189.00 pts.	Linda Fratianne (USA) 188.30 pts.	Dagmar Lurz (GER) 183.04 pts.

PAIRS

GOLD	SILVER	BRONZE
1908 Anna Hübler Heinrich Burger (GER) 56.0 pts.	Phyllis W. Johnson James H. Johnson (GBR) 51.5 pts.	Madge Syers Edgar Syers (GBR) 48.0 pts.
1920 Ludovika Jakobsson Walter Jakobsson (FIN) 80.75 pts.	Alexia Bryn Yngvar Bryn (NOR) 72.75 pts.	Phyllis W. Johnson Basi Williams (GBR) 66.25 pts.
1924 Helene Engelmann Alfred Berger (AUT) 74.50 pts.	Ludovika Jakobsson Walter Jakobsson (FIN) 71.75 pts.	Andrée Joly Pierre Brunet (FRA) 69.25 pts.
1928 Andrée Joly Pierre Brunet (FRA) 100.50 pts.	Lilly Scholz Otto Kaiser (AUT) 99.25 pts.	Melitta Brunner Ludwig Wrede (AUT) 93.25 pts.
1932 Andrée Brunet Pierre Brunet (FRA) 76.7 pts.	Beatrix Loughran Sherwin Badger (USA) 77.5 pts.	Emilia Rotter László Szollás (HUN) 76.4 pts.
1936 Maxi Herber Ernst Baier (GER) 103.3 pts.	Ilse Pausin Erik Pausin (AUT) 102.7 pts.	Emilia Rotter László Szollás (HUN) 97.6 pts.
1948 Micheline Lannoy Pierre Baugniet (BEL) 123.5 pts.	Andrea Kékessy Ede Király (HUN) 122.2 pts.	Suzanne Morrow Wallace Diestelmeyer (CAN) 121.0 pts.
1952 Ria Falk Paul Falk (GER) 102.6 pts.	Karol Estelle Kennedy Michael Kennedy (USA) 100.6 pts.	Marianna Nagy László Nagy (HUN) 97.4 pts.
1956 Elisabeth Schwarz Kurt Oppelt (AUT) 101.8 pts.	Frances Dafoe Norris Bowden (CAN) 101.9 pts	Marianna Nagy László Nagy (HUN) 99.3 pts.
1960 Barbara Wagner Robert Paul (CAN) 80.4 pts.	Marika Kilius Hansjürgen Bäumler (GER) 76.8 pts.	Nancy Ludington Ronald Ludington (USA) 76.2 pts.
1964[1] Ludmilla Belousova Oleg Protopopov (URS) 104.4 pts.	Debbie Wilkes Guy Revell (CAN) 98.5 pts.	Vivian Joseph Ronald Joseph (USA) 98.2 pts.
1968 Ludmilla Belousova Oleg Protopopov (URS) 315.2 pts.	Tatiána Chesternyava Alexander Gorelík (URS) 312.3 pts.	Margo Glockshuber Wolfgang Danne (GER) 304.4 pts.
1972 Irina Rodnina Alexei Ulanov (URS) 420.4 pts.	Ludmila Smirnova Andrei Suraikin (URS) 419.4 pts.	Manuela Gross Uwe Kagelmann (GDR) 411.8 pts.
1976 Irina Rodnina Aleksander Zaitsev (URS) 140.54 pts.	Romy Kermer Rolf Oesterreich (GDR) 136.35 pts.	Manuela Grosse Uwe Kagelmann (GDR) 134.57 pts.
1980 Irina Rodnina Aleksander Zaitsev (URS) 147.26 pts.	Marina Tcherkosova Sergey Shakrai (URS) 143.80 pts.	Manuela Mager Uwe Bewersdorff (GDR) 140.52 pts.

[1] Marika Kilius and Hansjürgen Bäumler (GER) finished second but were subsequently disqualified.

ICE DANCE

GOLD	SILVER	BRONZE
1908–1972 Event not held		
1976 Ludmila Pakhomova Aleksander Gorshkov (URS) 209.92 pts.	Irina Moiseyeva Andrei Minenkov (URS) 204.88 pts.	Colleen O'Connor James Millns (USA) 202.64 pts.
1980 Natalya Linichuk Gennadiy Karponosov (URS) 205.48 pts.	Krisztina Regoczy Andras Sallay (HUN) 204.52 pts.	Irina Moiseyeva Andrei Minenkov (URS) 201.86 pts.

4. Speed Skating (Men)

500 METERS

GOLD	SILVER	BRONZE
1908–1920 Event not held		
1924 Charles Jewtraw (USA) 44.0*	Oskar Olsen (NOR) 44.2	Roald Larsen (NOR) 44.8 Clas Thunberg (FIN) 44.8
1928 Clas Thunberg (FIN) 43.4* Bernt Evensen (NOR) 43.4*		John O'Neil Farrell (USA) 43.6 Roald Larsen (NOR 43.6 Jaako Friman (FIN) 43.6
1932 John Amos Shea (USA) 43.4*	Bernt Evensen (NOR) d.n.a.	Alexander Hurd (CAN) d.n.a.
1936 Ivar Ballangrud (NOR) 43.4*	Georg Krog (NOR) 43.5	Leo Freisinger (USA) 44.0
1948 Finn Helgesen (NOR) 43.1*	Kenneth Bartholomew (USA) 43.2 Thomas Byberg (NOR) 43.2 Robert Fitzgerald (USA) 43.2	
1952 Kenneth Henry (USA) 43.2	Donald McDermott (USA) 43.9	Arne Johansen (NOR) 44.0 Gordon Audley (CAN) 44.0
1956 Yevgeniy Grischin (URS) 40.2*	Rafael Gratsch (URS) 40.8	Alv Gjestvang (NOR) 41.0
1960 Yevgeniy Grischin (URS) 40.2*	William Disney (USA) 40.3	Rafael Gratsch (URS) 40.4
1964 Richard McDermott (USA) 40.1*	Yevgeniy Grischin (URS) 40.6 Vladimir Orlov (URS) 40.6 Alv Gjestvang (NOR) 40.6	
1968 Erhard Keller (GER) 40.3	Richard McDermott (USA) 40.5 Magne Thomassen (NOR) 40.5	
1972 Erhard Keller (GER) 39.44*	Hasse Borjes (SWE) 39.69	Valeriy Muratov (URS) 39.80
1976 Evgeniy Kulikov (URS) 39.17*	Valeriy Muratov (URS) 39.25	Daniel Immerfall (USA) 39.54
1980 Eric Heiden (USA) 38.03*	Yevgeniy Kulikov (URS) 38.37	Lieuwe de Boer (HOL) 38.48

1,000 METERS

GOLD	SILVER	BRONZE
1909–1972 Event not held		
1976 Peter Mueller (USA) 1:19.32*	Jorn Didriksen (NOR) 1:20.45	Valeriy Muratov (URS) 1:20.57
1980 Eric Heiden (USA) 1:15.18*	Gaetan Boucher (CAN) 1:16.68	Frode Ronning (NOR) 1:16.91 Vladimir Lobanov (URS) 1:16.91

1,500 METERS

GOLD	SILVER	BRONZE
1908–1920 Event not held		
1924 Clas Thunberg (FIN) 2:20.8*	Roald Larsen (NOR) 2:22.0	Sigurd Moen (NOR) 2:25.6
1928 Clas Thunberg (FIN) 2:21.1	Bernt Evensen (NOR) 2:21.9	Ivar Ballangrud (NOR) 2:22.6
1932 John Amos Shea (USA) 2:57.5	Alexander Hurd (CAN) d.n.a.	William F. Logan (CAN) d.n.a.
1936 Charles Mathiesen (NOR) 2:19.2*	Ivar Ballangrud (NOR) 2:20.2	Birger Wasenius (FIN) 2:20.9
1948 Sverre Farstad (NOR) 2:17.6*	Ake Seyffarth (SWE) 2:18.1	Odd Lundberg (NOR) 2:18.9
1952 Hjalmar Andersen (NOR) 2:20.4	Willem van der Voort (HOL) 2:20.6	Roald Aas (NOR) 2:21.6
1956 Yevgeniy Grischin (URS) 2:08.6 Yuriy Michailov (URS) 2:08.6		Toivo Salonen (FIN) 2:09.4
1960 Roald Aas (NOR) 2:10.4 Yevgeniy Grischin (URS) 2:10.4		Boris Stenin (URS) 2:11.5
1964 Ants Antson (URS) 2:10.3	Cornelis Verkerk (HOL) 2:10.6	Villy Haugen (NOR) 2:11.25
1968 Cornelis Verkerk (HOL) 2:03.4*	Ard Schenk (HOL) 2:05.0 Ivar Eriksen (NOR) 2:05.0	
1972 Ard Schenk (HOL) 2:02.96*	Roar Gronvold (NOR) 2:04.26	Goran Classon (SWE) 2:05.89
1976 Jan Egil Storholt (NOR) 1:59.38*	Yuriy Kondakov (URS) 1:59.97	Hans Van Helden (HOL) 2:00.87
1980 Eric Heiden (USA) 1:53.44*	Kai Stenshjemmet (NOR) 1:56.81	Terje Andersen (NOR) 1:56.92

5,000 METERS

GOLD	SILVER	BRONZE
1908–1920 Event not held		
1924 Clas Thunberg (FIN) 8:39.0*	Julius Skutnabb (FIN) 8:48.4	Roald Larsen (NOR) 8:50.2
1928 Ivar Ballangrud (NOR) 8:50.5	Julius Skutnabb (FIN) 8:59.1	Bernt Evensen (NOR) 9:01.1
1932 Irving Jaffee (USA) 9:40.8	Edward S. Murphy (USA) d.n.a.	William F. Logan (CAN) d.n.a.
1936 Ivar Ballangrud (NOR) 8:19.6*	Birger Wasenius (FIN) 8:23.3	Antero Ojala (FIN) 8:30.1
1948 Reidar Liaklev (NOR) 8:29.4	Odd Lundberg (NOR) 8:32.7	Göthe Hedlund (SWE) 8:34.8
1952 Hjalmar Andersen (NOR) 8:10.6*	Kees Broekman (HOL) 8:21.6	Sverre Haugli (NOR) 8:22.4
1956 Boris Schilkow (URS) 7:48.7*	Sigvard Ericsson (SWE) 7:56.7	Oleg Gontscharenko (URS) 7:57.5

	GOLD	SILVER	BRONZE
1960	Viktor Kositschkin (URS) 7:51.3	Knut Johannesen (NOR) 8:00.8	Jan Pesman (HOL) 8:05.1
1964	Knut Johannesen (NOR) 7:38.4*	P. Moe (NOR) 7:38.6	F. Anton Maier (NOR) 7:42.0
1968	F. Anton Maier (NOR) 7:22.4*	Cornelis Verkerk (HOL) 7:23.2	Petrus Nottet (HOL) 7:25.5
1972	Ard Schenk (HOL) 7:23.6	Roar Gronvold (NOR) 7:28.18	Sten Stensen (NOR) 7:33.39
1976	Sten Stensen (NOR) 7:24.48	Piet Kleine (HOL) 7:26.47	Hans Van Helden (HOL) 7:26.54
1980	Eric Heiden (USA) 7:02.29*	Kai Stenshjemmet (NOR) 7:03.28	Tom Oxholm (NOR) 7:05.59

10,000 METERS

	GOLD	SILVER	BRONZE
1908–1920	Event not held		
1924	Julius Skutnabb (FIN) 18:04.8*	Clas Thunberg (FIN) 18:07.8	Roald Larsen (NOR) 18:12.2
1928	Event abandoned		
1932	Irving Jaffee (USA) 19:13.6	Ivar Ballangrud (NOR) d.n.a.	Frank Stack (CAN) d.n.a.
1936	Ivar Ballangrud (NOR) 17:24.3*	Birger Wasenius (FIN) 17:28.2	Max Stiepl (AUT) 17:30.0
1948	Ake Seyffarth (SWE) 17:26.3	Lauri Parkkinen (FIN) 17:36.0	Pentti Lammio (FIN) 17:42.7
1952	Hjalmar Andersen (NOR) 16:45.8*	Kees Broekman (HOL) 17:10.6	Carl-Erik Asplund (SWE) 17:16.6
1956	Sigvard Ericsson (SWE) 16:35.9*	Knut Johannesen (NOR) 16:36.9	Oleg Gontscharenko (URS) 16:42.3
1960	Knut Johannesen (NOR) 15:46.6*	Viktor Kositschkin (URS) 15:49.2	Kjell Bäckman (SWE) 16:14.2
1964	Johnny Nilsson (SWE) 15:50.1	F. Anton Maier (NOR) 16:06.0	Knut Johannesen (Nor) 16:06.3
1968	Johnny Hoeglin (SWE) 15:23.6*	F. Anton Maier (NOR) 15:23.9	Orejan Sandler (SWE) 15:31.8
1972	Ard Schenk (HOL) 15:01.35*	Cornelis Verkerk (HOL) 15:04.70	Sten Stensen (NOR) 15:07.08
1976	Piet Kleine (HOL) 14:50.59*	Sten Stensen (NOR) 14:53.30	Hans Van Helden (HOL) 15:02.02
1980	Eric Heiden (USA) 14:28.13*	Piet Kleine (HOL) 14:36.03	Tom Oxholm (NOR) 14:36.60

Speed Skating (Women)

1908–1956 Events not held, but in 1932 there were three demonstration events for women speed skaters.

500 METERS

	GOLD	SILVER	BRONZE
1960	Helga Hasse (GER) 45.9*	Natalie Dontschenko (URS) 46.0	Jeanne Ashworth (USA) 46.1
1964	Lydia Skoblikova (URS) 45.0*	Irina Yegorova (URS) 45.4	Tatyana Sidorova (URS) 45.5
1968	Ludmila Titova (URS) 46.1	Mary Meyers (USA) 46.3 Dianne Holum (USA) 46.3 Jennifer Fish (USA) 46.3	No bronze award

The Russian speed skater
Lydia Skoblikova won a
record 6 Olympic gold
medals in the 1960 and
1964 Games.

	GOLD	SILVER	BRONZE
1972	Anne Henning (USA) 43.33*	Vera Krasnova (URS) 44.01	Ludmila Titova (URS) 44.45
1976	Sheila Young (USA) 42.76*	Catherine Priestner (CAN) 43.12	Tatyana Averina (URS) 43.17
1980	Karin Enke (GDR) 41.78*	Leah Mueller (USA) 42.26	Natalya Petruseva (URS) 42.42

1,000 METERS

1960	Klala Guseva (URS) 1:34.1*	Helga Haase (GER) 1:34.3	Tamara Rylova (URS) 1:34.8
1964	Lydia Skoblikova (URS) 1:33.2*	Irina Yegorova (URS) 1:34.3	Kaija Mustonen (FIN) 1:34.8
1968	Carolina Geijssen (HOL) 1:32.6	Ludmila Titova (URS) 1:32.9	Dianne Holum (USA) 1:33.4
1972	Monika Pflug (GER) 1:31.40*	Atje Keulen-Deelstra (HOL) 1:31.61	Anne Henning (USA) 1:31.62
1976	Tatyana Averina (URS) 1:28.43*	Leah Poulos (USA) 1:28.57	Sheila Young (USA) 1:29.14
1980	Natalya Petruseva (URS) 1:24.10*	Leah Mueller (USA) 1:25.41	Sylvia Albrecht (GDR) 1:26.46

1,500 METERS

1960	Lydia Skoblikova (URS) 2:25.2*	Elvira Seroczynska (POL) 2:25.7	Helena Pilejeyk (POL) 2:27.1
1964	Lydia Skoblikova (URS) 2:22.6*	Kaija Mustonen (FIN) 2:25.5	Berta Kolokoltseva (URS) 2:27.1
1968	Kaija Mustonen (FIN) 2:22.4*	Carolina Geijssen (HOL) 2:22.7	Christina Kaiser (HOL) 2:24.5
1972	Dianne Holum (USA) 2:20.85*	Christina Baas-Kaiser (HOL) 2:21.05	Atje Keulen-Deelstra (HOL) 2:22.05
1976	Galina Stepanskaya (URS) 2:16.58*	Sheila Young (USA) 2:17.06	Tatyana Averina (URS) 2:17.96
1980	Annie Borckink (HOL) 2:10.95*	Ria Visser (HOL) 2:12.35	Sabine Becker (GDR) 2:12.38

3,000 METERS

	GOLD	SILVER	BRONZE
1960	Lydia Skoblikova (URS) 5:14.3*	Valentina Stenina (URS) 5:16.9	Eevi Huttunen (FIN) 5:21.0
1964	Lydia Skoblikova (URS) 5:14.9	Valentina Stenina (URS) 5:18.5 Pil-Hwa Han (PRK) 5:18.5	
1968	Johanna Schut (HOL) 4:56.2*	Kaija Mustonen (FIN) 5:01.0	Christina Kaiser (HOL) 5:01.3
1972	Christina Baas-Kaiser (HOL) 4:52.14*	Dianne Holum (USA) 4:58.67	Atje Keulen-Deelstra (HOL) 4:59.91
1976	Tatyana Averina (URS) 4:45.19*	Andrea Mitscherlich (GDR) 4:45.23	Lisbeth Korsmo (NOR) 4:45.24
1980	Bjorg Eva Jensen (NOR) 4:32.13*	Sabine Becker (GDR) 4:32.79	Beth Heiden (USA) 4:33.77

5. Bobsleigh

2-MAN BOB

1908–1928 Event not held

	GOLD	SILVER	BRONZE
1932	UNITED STATES I 8:14.74	SWITZERLAND II 8:16.28	UNITED STATES II 8:29.15
	J. Hubert Stevens Curtis P. Stevens	R. Capadrutt O. Geier	J. R. Heaton R. Minton
1936	UNITED STATES I 5:29.29	SWITZERLAND II 5:30.64	UNITED STATES II 5:33.96
	Ivan Brown Alan Washbond	F. Feierabend J. Beerli	G. Colgate R. Lawrence
1948	SWITZERLAND II 5:29.2	SWITZERLAND I 5:30.4	UNITED STATES II 5:35.3
	Felix Endrich Friedrich Waller	F. Feierabend P. Eberhard	F. Fortune S. Carron
1952	GERMANY I 5:24.54	UNITED STATES I 5:26.89	SWITZERLAND I 5:27.71
	Andreas Ostler Lorenz Nieberl	S. Benham P. Martin	F. Feierabend S. Waser
1956	ITALY I 5:30.14	ITALY II 5:31.45	SWITZERLAND I 5:37.46
	Lamberto Dall Costa Giacomo Conti	Eugenio Monti R. Alvera	M. Angst H. Warburton
1960	Event not held		
1964	GREAT BRITAIN 4:21.90	ITALY II 4:22.02	ITALY I 4:22.63
	Anthony J. D. Nash The Hon. Robin Dixon	S. Zardini R. Bonagura	Eugenio Monti S. Siorpaes
1968	ITALY I 4:41.54	WEST GERMANY I 4:41.54	RUMANIA I 4:44.46
	Eugenio Monti Luciano de Paolis	Horst Floth Pepi Bader	Ion Panturu Nicolae Neagoe
1972	WEST GERMANY II 4:57.07	WEST GERMANY I 4:58.84	SWITZERLAND I 4:59.33
	Wolfgang Zimmerer Peter Utzschneider	Horst Floth Pepi Bader	Jean Wicki Egy Hubacher
1976	EAST GERMANY II 3:44.42	GERMANY I 3:44.99	SWITZERLAND I 3:45.70
	Meinhard Nehmer Bernard Germeshausen	Wolfgang Zimmerer Manfred Schumann	Erich Schaerer Josef Benz

GOLD	SILVER	BRONZE
1980 SWITZERLAND II 4:09.36	**EAST GERMANY II** 4:10.93	**EAST GERMANY I** 4:11.08
Erich Shaerer Josef Benz	Bernhard Germeshausen Hans-Jurgen Gerhardt	Meinhard Nehmer Bogdan Musiol

4-MAN BOB

1908–1920 Event not held

GOLD	SILVER	BRONZE
1924 SWITZERLAND I 5:45.54	**GREAT BRITAIN II** 5:48.83	**BELGIUM I** 6:02.29
Eduard Scherrer Alfred Neveu Alfred Schläppi Heinrich Schläppi	R. H. Broome T. A. Arnold H. A. W. Richardson R. E. Soher	C. Mulder R. Mortiaux P. v. d. Broeck V. A. Verschueren or H. P. Willems
1928 UNITED STATES II 3:20.5 (5-man event)	**UNITED STATES I** 3:21.0	**GERMANY II** 3:21.9
William Fiske Nion Tocker Charles Mason Clifford Gray Richard Parke	J. Heaton D. Granger L. Hine T. Doe J. O'Brien	H. Kilian V. Krempl H. Hess S. Huber H. Nägle
1932 UNITED STATES I 7:53.68	**UNITED STATES II** 7:55.70	**GERMANY I** 8:00.04
William Fiske Edward Eagen Clifford Gray Jay O'Brien	H. Homburger P. Bryant F. P. Stevens E. Horton	H. Kilian M. Ludwig Dr. H. Mehlhorn S. Huber
1936 SWITZERLAND II 5:19.85	**SWITZERLAND II** 5:22.73	**GREAT BRITAIN** 5:23.41
Pierre Mussy Arnold Gartmann Charles Bouvier Joseph Beerli	R. Capadrutt H. Aichele F. Feierabend H. Bütikofer	F. McEvoy J. Cardno G. Dugdale C. Green
1948 UNITED STATES II 5:20.1	**BELGIUM** 5:21.3	**UNITED STATES I** 5:21.5
Francis Tyler Patrick Martin Edward Rimkus William D'Amico	M. Houben F. Mansveld G. Niels J. Mouvet	J. Bickford T. Hicks D. Dupree W. Dupree
1952 GERMANY 5:07.84	**UNITED STATES I** 5:10.48	**SWITZERLAND I** 5:11.70
Andreas Ostler Friedrich Kuhn Lorenz Nieberl Franz Kemser	S. Benham P. Martin H. Crossett J. Atkinson	F. Feierabend A. Madörin A. Filippini S. Waser
1956 SWITZERLAND I 5:10.44	**ITALY II** 5:12.10	**UNITED STATES** 5:12.39
Franz Kapus Gottfried Diener Robert Alt Heinrich Angst	Eugenio Monti U. Girardi R. Alvera R. Mocellini	A. Tyler W. Dodge C. Butler J. Lamy
1960 Event not held		
1964 CANADA I 4:14.46	**AUSTRIA I** 4:15.48	**ITALY II** 4:15.60
Victor Emery Peter Kirby Douglas Anakin John Emery	Erwin Thaler A. Knoxeder J. Nairz Reinhold Durnthaler	Eugenio Monti S. Siorpaes B. Rigoni G. Siorpaes
1968 ITALY I 2:17.39	**AUSTRAIA I** 2:17.48	**SWITZERLAND** 2:18.04
Eugenio Monti Luciano De Paolis Roberto Zandonella Mario Armano	Erwin Thaler Reinhold Durnthaler Herbert Gruber Josef Eder	Jean Wicki Hans Candrian Willi Hofmann Walter Graf

GOLD	SILVER	BRONZE
1972 SWITZERLAND I 4:43.07	ITALY I 4:43.83	WEST GERMANY I 4:43.92
Jean Wicki	Nevio de Zordo	Wolfgang Zimmerer
Edy Hubacher	G. Bonichon	Peter Utzschneider
Hans Leutenegger	Adriano Frassinelli	Stefan Gaisreister
Werner Camichel	C. dal Fabbo	Walter Steinbauer
1976 EAST GERMANY I 3:40.43	SWITZERLAND II 3:40.89	GERMANY I 3:41.37
Meinhard Nehmer	Erich Schaerer	Wolfgang Zimmerer
Jochen Babok	Ulrich Baechli	Peter Utzschneider
Bernhard Germeshausen	Rudolf Marti	Bodo Bittner
Bernhard Lehmann	Josef Benz	Manfred Schumann
1980 EAST GERMANY I 3:59.92	SWITZERLAND I 4:00.87	EAST GERMANY II 4:00.97
Meinhard Nehmer	Erich Shaerer	Horst Schonau
Bogdan Musiol	Ulrich Baechli	Roland Wetzig
Bernhard Germeshausen	Rudolf Marti	Detlef Richter
Hans-Jurgen Gerhardt	Josef Benz	Andreas Kirchner

---

6. Tobogganing (Lugeing)

SINGLE SEATER—MEN

1908–1960 Event not held

Year	GOLD	SILVER	BRONZE
1964	Thomas Koehler (GER) 3:26.77	Klaus Bonsack (GER) 3:27.04	Hans Plenk (GER) 3:30.15
1968	Manfred Schmid (AUT) 2:52.48	Thomas Koehler (GDR) 2:52.66	Klaus Bonsack (GDR) 2:53.33
1972	Wolfgang Scheidel (GDR) 3:27.58	Harald Ehrig (GDR) 3:28.39	Wolfram Fiedler (GDR) 3:28.73
1976	Detlef Guenther (GDR) 3:27.688	Josef Fendt (GER) 3:28.196	Hans Rinn (GER) 3:28.574
1980	Bernhard Glass (GDR) 2:54.796	Paul Hildgartner (ITA) 2:55.372	Anton Winkler (GER) 2:56.545

TWO-SEATER—MEN

1908–1960 Event not held

Year	GOLD	SILVER	BRONZE
1964	AUSTRIA 1:41.62	AUSTRIA 1:41.91	ITALY 1:42.87
	Josef Feistmantl	Reinhold Senn	W. Aussendorfer
	Manfred Stengl	H. Thaler	S. Mair
1968	EAST GERMANY 1:35.85	AUSTRIA 1:36.34	GERMANY 1:37.29
	Klaus Bonsack	Manfred Schmid	Wolfgang Winkler
	Thomas Koehler	Ewald Walch	Fritz Nachmann
1972	ITALY 1:28.35		EAST GERMANY 1:29.16
	Paul Hildgartner		Klaus Bonsack
	Walter Plaikner		Wolfram Fiedler
	EAST GERMANY 1:28.35		
	Horst Hornlein		
	Reinhard Bredow		
1976	EAST GERMANY 1:25.604	GERMANY 1:25.889	AUSTRIA 1:25.919
	Hans Rinn	Hans Brandner	Rudolf Schmid
	Norbert Hahn	Balthasar Schwarm	Franz Schachner

GOLD	SILVER	BRONZE
1980 **EAST GERMANY** 1:19.331	**ITALY** 1:19.606	**AUSTRIA** 1:19.795
Hans Rinn	Peter Gschitzer	Georg Fluckinger
Norbert Hahn	Karl Brunner	Karl Schrott

SINGLE-SEATER—WOMEN

1908–1960 Event not held		
1964 Otrun Enderlein (GER) 3:24.67	Ilse Geisler (GER) 3:27.42	Helene Thurner (AUT) 3:29.06
1968 Erica Lechner (ITA) 2:28.66	Christa Schmuck (GER) 2:29.37	Angelika Duenhaupt (GER) 2:29.56
1972 Anna-Maria Muller (GDR) 2:59.18	Ute Ruchrold (GDR) 2:59.49	Margit Schumann (GDR) 2:59.54
1976 Margit Schumann (GDR) 2:50.621	Ute Ruchrold (GDR) 2:50.846	Elisabeth Demleitner (GER) 2:51.056
1980 Vera Sosulya (URS) 2:36.537	Melitta Sollmann (GDR) 2:37.657	Ingrida Amantova (URS) 2:37.817

7. Ice Hockey

1908 Event not held		
1920 **CANADA**	**UNITED STATES**	**CZECHOSLOVAKIA**
Robert J. Benson	Raymond L. Bonney	Dr. Adolf Dusek
Wally Byron	Anthony J. Conroy	Dr. Karel Hartmann
Frank Frederickson	Herbert L. Drury	Vilém Loos
Chris Fridfinnson	J. Edward Fitzgerald	Jan Pallausch
Mike Goodman	George P. Geran	Jan Peka
Haldor Halderson	Frank X. Goheen	Dr. Karel Pesek
Konrad Johannesson	Joseph McCormick	Josef Sroubek
A. "Huck" Woodman	Lawrence J. McCormick	Otakar Vindyš
	Frank A. Synott	
	Leon P. Tuck	
	Cyril Weidenborner	
1924 **CANADA**	**UNITED STATES**	**GREAT BRITAIN**
Jack A. Cameron	Clarence J. Abel	W. H. Anderson
Ernest J. Collett	Herbert L. Drury	Lorne H. Carr-Harris
Albert J. McCaffery	Alphonse A. Lacroix	Colin G. Carruthers
Harold E. McMunn	John A. Langley	Eric D. Carruthers
Duncan B. Munro	John J. Lyons	Guy E. Clarkson
W. Beattie Ramsay	Justin J. McCarthy	Ross Cuthbert
Cyril S. Slater	Willard W. Rice	George Holmes
Reginald J. Smith	Irving W. Small	Hamilton D. Jukes
Harry E. Watson	Frank A. Synott	Edward B. Pitblado
		Blane N. Sexton
1928 **CANADA**	**SWEDEN**	**SWITZERLAND**
Charles Delahay	Carl Abrahamsson	Giannin Andreossi
Frank Fisher	Emil Bergman	Mezzi Andreossi
Dr. Louis Hudson	Birger Holmqvist	Robert Breiter
Norbert Mueller	Gustaf Johansson	Louis Dufour
Herbert Plaxton	Henry Johansson	Charles Fasel
Hugh Plaxton	Nils Johansson	Albert Geromini
Roger Plaxton	Ernst Karlberg	Fritz Kraatz
John G. Porter	Erik Larsson	Arnold Martignoni
Frank Sullivan	Bertil Linde	Heini Meng
Dr. Joseph Sullivan	Sigurd Oberg	Anton Morosani
Ross Taylor	Vilhelm Petersen	Dr. Luzius Rüedi
David Trottier	Kurt Sucksdorff	Richard Torriani

	GOLD	SILVER	BRONZE
1932	**CANADA**	**UNITED STATES**	**GERMANY**
	William H. Cockburn	Osborn Anderson	Rudi Ball
	Clifford T. Crowley	John B. Bent	Alfred Heinrich
	Albert G. Duncanson	John Chase	Erich Herker
	George F. Garbutt	John E. Cookman	Gustav Jaenecke
	Roy Hinkel	Douglas N. Everett	Werner Korff
	C. Victor Lindquist	Franklin Farrell	Walter Leinwever
	Norman J. Malloy	Joseph F. Fitzgerald	Erich Römer
	Walter Monson	Edward M. Frazier	F. Marquardt Slevogt
	Kenneth S. Moore	John B. Garrison	Martin Schröttle
	N. Romeo Rivers	Gerard Hallock III	Georg Strobl
	Harold A. Simpson	Robert C. Livingston	
	Hugh R. Sutherland	Francis A. Nelson	
	W. Stanley Wagner	Winthrop H. Palmer	
	J. Aliston Wise	Gordon Smith	
1936	**GREAT BRITAIN**	**CANADA**	**UNITED STATES**
	Alexander Archer	Maxwell Deacon	John B. Garrison
	James Borland	Hugh Farquharson	August F. Kammer
	Edgar Brenchley	Kenneth Farmer	Philip W. LaBatte
	James Chappell	James Haggarty	John C. Lax
	John Coward	Walter Kitchen	Thomas H. Moone
	Gordon Dailley	Raymond Milton	Eldridge B. Ross
	John Davey	Francis W. Moore	Paul E. Rowe
	Carl Erhardt	Herman Murray	Francis J. Shaugnessy
	James Foster	Arthur Nash	Gordon Smith
	John Kilpatrick	David Neville	Francis J. Spain
	Archibald Stinchcombe	Ralph St. Germain	Frank R. Stubbs
	Robert Wyman	Alexander Sinclair	
		William Thomson	
1948	**CANADA**	**CZECHOSLOVAKIA**	**SWITZERLAND**
	Murray-Alb Dowey	Vladimir Bouzek	Hans Bänninger
	Bernard Dunster	Augustin Bubnik	Alfred Bieler
	Orval Gravelle	Jaroslav Drobny	Heinrich Boller
	Patrick Guzzo	Premsyl Hajny	Ferdinand Cattini
	Walter Halder	Zdenek Jarkovsky	Hans Cattini
	Thomas Hibbert	Stanislav Konopásek	Hans Dürst
	Ross King	Bohumil Modry	Walter Dürst
	Henri-André Laperrire	Miloslav Pokorny	Emil Handschin
	John Lecompte	Vaclay Rozinak	Heini Lohrer
	George A. Mara	Dr. Miroslav Sláma	Werner Lohrer
	Albert Renaud	Karel Stibor	Reto Perl
	Reginald Schroeter	Vilém Stovik	Gebhard Poltera
		Ladislav Troják	Ulrich Poltera
		Josef Trousilek	Beat Ruedi
		Oldrich Zábrodsky	Otto Schubinger
		Vladimir Zábrodsky	Richard Torriani
			Hans Trepp
1952	**CANADA**	**UNITED STATES**	**SWEDEN**
	George G. Able	Ruben E. Bjorkman	Gote Almqvist
	John F. Davies	Leonard S. Ceglarski	Hans Andersson
	William Dawe	Joseph J. Czarnota	S. "Tvilling" Andersson
	Robert B. Dickson	Richard J. Desmond	Ake Andersson
	Donald V. Gauf	Andre P. Gambucci	Lars Bjorn
	William J. Gibson	Clifford N. Harrison	Gote Blomqvist
	Ralph L. Hansch	Gerald W. Kilmartin	Thord Flodqvist
	Robert R. Meyers	John F. Mulhern	Erik Johansson
	David E. Miller	Joyn M. Noah	Gosta Johansson
	Eric E. Paterson	Arnold C. Oss, Jr.	Rune Johansson
	Thomas A. Pollock	Robert E. Rompre	Sven Johansson
	Allan R. Purvis	James W. Sedin	Ake Lassas
	Gordon Robertson	Allen A. Van	Holger Nurmela
	Louis J. Secco	Donald F. Whiston	Hans Oberg
	Francis C. Sullivan	Kenneth J. Yackel	Lars Pettersson
	Robert Watt		Lars Svensson
			Sven Thunman

GOLD	SILVER	BRONZE
1956 U.S.S.R.	**UNITED STATES**	**CANADA**
Yevgeniy Babitsch	Wendell Anderson	Denis Brodeur
Usevold Bobrov	Wellington Burnett	Charles Brooker
Nikolay Chlystov	Eugene Campbell	William Colvin
Aleksey Guryschev	Gordon Christian	Alfred J. Horne
Juriy Krylov	William Cleary	Arthur Hurst
Alfred Kutschewskiy	Richard Dougherty	Byrle Klinck
Vlanetin Kusin	Willard Ikola	Paul Knox
Grigoriy Mkrttschan	John Matchefts	Kenneth Laufman
Viktor Nikiforov	John Mayasich	Howard Lee
Juriy Pantjuchov	Daniel McKinnon	James Logan
Nikolay Putschkov	Richard Meredith	Floyd Martin
Viktor Schuwalov	Weldon Olson	Jack McKenzie
Genrich Sidorenkov	John E. Petroske	Donald Rope
Nikolay Sologubov	Kenneth Purpur	Georges Scholes
Ivan Tregubov	Ronald Rigazio	Gerald Theberge
Dmitriy Ukolov	Richard Rodenhiser	Robert White
Aleksandr Uwarov	Edward Sampson	Keith Woodall
1960 UNITED STATES	**CANADA**	**U.S.S.R.**
Roger A. Christian	Bob Attersley	Veniamin Aleksandrov
William Christian	Moe Benoit	Aleksandr Aljimetov
Robert B. Cleary	Jim Connelly	Juriy Baulin
William J. Cleary	Jack Douglas	Michail Bytschkov
Eygene Grazia	Fred Etcher	Vladimir Grebennikov
Paul Johnson	Bob Forhan	Yevgeniy Groschev
John Kirrane	Don Head	Viktor Jakuschev
John Mayasich	Harold Hurley	Yevgeniy Jerkin
Jack McCartan	Kenneth Laufman	Nikolay Karpov
Robert McVey	Floyd Martin	Alfred Kutschewskiy
Richard Meredith	Bob McKnight	Konstantin Loktev
Weldon Olson	Clifford Pennington	Stanislav Petuchov
Edwyn Owen	Donald Rope	V. Prjaschtschnikov
Rodney Paavola	Bob Rousseau	Nikolay Putschkov
Lawrence Palmer	George Samolenko	Genrich Sidorenkov
Richard Rodenhiser	Harry Sinden	Nikolay Sologybov
Thomas Williams	Darryl Sly	Juriy Tsitsinov
1964 U.S.S.R.	**SWEDEN**	**CZECHOSLOVAKIA**
Viktor Konovalenko	K. Svensson	Vlado Dzurila
Boris Zaitsev	L. Haeggroth	Vlado Nadrchal
Viktor Kuzkin	G. Blome	F. Gregor
Eduard Ivanov	R. Stoltz	R. Potsch
Vitaliy Davidov	N. Johansson	F. Tikal
Aleksandr Ragulin	B. Nordlander	S. Sventek
Olyeg Zatisev	N. Nilsson	L. Smid
Aleksandr Almetov	U. Sterner	J. Walter
Viktor Yakushev	T. Johansson	Josef Golonka
Vyacheslav Starchinov	R. Pettersson	Jiri Holik
Konstantin Loktev	E. Maeaettae	V. Bubnik
Boris Mayorov	L. Johansson	Jan Klapac
Anatoliy Firsov	L. Lundvall	J. Dolana
Stanislav Petuchov	C. Oeberg	S. Pryl
Veniamin Aleksandrov	A. Andersson	M. Vlach
Evgeniy Maiorov	U. Oehrlund	Jaroslav Jirik
Leonid Volkov	H. Mild	Josef Cerny

	GOLD	SILVER	BRONZE
1968	**U.S.S.R.**	**CZECHOSLOVAKIA**	**CANADA**
	Viktor Zinger	Vladimir Nadrchal	Wayne Stephenson
	Viktor Konovalenko	Vlado Dzurila	Kenneth Broderick
	Vitaliy Davidov	Oldrich Machac	Marshall Johnston
	Viktor Blinov	Jan Suchy	Brian Glennie
	Igor Romishevskiy	Josef Horesovsky	Barry Mckenzie
	Olyeg Zaitsev	Frantisek Pospisil	Paul Conlin
	Aleksandr Ragulin	Karel Masopust	Edward Hargreaves
	Viktor Kuzkin	Frantisek Sevcik	Terence O'Malley
	Boris Mayorov	Jan Havel	Raymond Cadieux
	Anatoliy Firsov	Jan Hrbaty	Stephen Monteith
	Evgeniy Zymin	Vaclav Nedomansky	William Macmillan
	Viktor Polupanov	Josef Golonka	Francis Huck
	Anatoliy Ionov	Petr Hejma	Garry Dineen
	Vyacheslav Starchinov	Jiri Kochta	Danny O'Shea
	Evgeniy Michakov	Jaroslav Jirik	Morris Mott
	Vladimir Vikulov	Jiri Holik	Herbert Pinder
	Yuriy Moiseyev	Josef Cerny	Rogert Bourbonnais
	Venyamin Aleksandrov	Jan Klapac	Gerry Pinder
1972	**U.S.S.R.**	**UNITED STATES**	**CZECHOSLOVAKIA**
	Vladislav Tretiak	Michael Curran	Vado Dzurila
	Aleksandr Pachkov	Peter Sears	Jiri Holocek
	Viktor Kuzkin	James McElmury	Rudolf Tajcnar
	Vitaliy Davidov	Thomas Mellor	Jaroslav Holik
	Yevgeniy Michalkov	Frank Sanders	Vaclav Nedomansky
	Aleksandr Maltsev	Charles Brown	Vladimir Bednar
	Aleksandr Iakuchev	Richard McGlynn	Frantisek Pospisil
	Vladimir Lutchenko	Walter Old	Jiri Holik
	Aleksandr Ragulin	Kenneth Ahearn	Karal Vohralik
	Igor Romichevskiy	Stuart Irving	Josef Horesovsky
	Gennadiy Tsygankov	Mark Howe	Oldrich Machac
	Valeri Kharlamov	Henry Bucha	Josef Cerny
	Yuriy Blinov	Keith Christiansen	Bohuslav Stastny
	Vladimir Petrov	Robbie Ftorek	Richard Farda
	Anatoliy Firsov	Ronald Marsland	Ivan Hlinka
	Boris Mikhailov	Craig Farmer	Jiri Kochta
	Vladimir Vikulov	Timothy Sheehy	Vladimir Martinec
1976	**U.S.S.R.**	**CZECHOSLOVAKIA**	**GERMANY**[1]
	Alexandr Sidelnikov	Jiri Holecek	Erich Weishaupt
	Vladislav Tretiak	Pavel Svitana	Anton Kehle
	Alexiandr Gusev	Oldrich Machac	Rudolf Thanner
	Vladimir Lutchenko	Milan Chalupa	Josef Voelk
	Sergei Babinov	Frantisek Pospisil	Udo Kiessling
	Yuriy Liapkin	Miroslav Dvorak	Stefan Metz
	Valeriy Vasilyev	Milan Kajkl	Klans Auhuber
	Gennadiy Tsygankov	Jiri Bubla	Ignaz Berndaner
	Sergei Kapustin	Milan Novy	Rainer Philipp
	Victor Shalimov	Vladimir Martinec	Lorenz Funk
	Alexandr Maltsev	Jiri Novak'	Wolfgang Boos
	Boris Alexandrov	Bohuslav Stastny	Ernst Koepf
	Boris Mikhailov	Jiri Holik	Ferenc Vozar
	Alexandr Iakuchev	Ivan Hlinka	Walter Koeberle
	Vladimir Petrov	Eduard Novak	Erich Kuehnhackl
	Valeriy Kharlamov	Jaroslav Pouzar	Alois Schloder
	Vladimir Shadrin	Bohuslav Ebermann	Martin Hinterstocker
	Victor Jlutkov	Josef Augusta	Franz Reindl

---

[1] Three-way tie for bronze with USA and Finland decided on goal average.

GOLD	SILVER	BRONZE
1980 **UNITED STATES**	**U.S.S.R.**	**SWEDEN**
Steven Janaszak	Vladimir Mischkin	Pelle Lindbergh
James Craig	Vladislav Tretiak	William Lofqvist
Kenneth Morrow	Vyacheslav Fetissov	Tomas Jonsson
Michael Ramsey	Vasiliy Pervuchin	Sture Andersson
William Baker	Valeriy Vassilyev	Ulf Weinstock
John O'Callahan	Aleksey Kasanotov	Jan Eriksson
Bob Suter	Sergey Starikov	Tommy Samuelsson
David Silk	Zinetula Bilyaletdinov	Mats Waltin
Neal Broten	Vladimir Krutov	Thomas Eriksson
Mark Johnson	Alexandr Maltsev	Per Lundqvist
Steven Christoff	Yuriy Lebedyev	Mats Ahlberg
Mark Wells	Boris Mikhaïlov	Hakan Eriksson
Mark Pavelich	Vladimir Petrov	Mats Naslund
Eric Strobel	Valeriy Kharlamov	Lennart Norberg
Michael Eruzione	Helmut Balderis	Bengt Lundholm
David Christain	Victor Jlutkov	Leif Holmgren
Robert McLanahan	Aleksandr Golikov	Bo Berglund
William Schneider	Sergey Makarov	Harald Luckner
Philip Verchota	Vladimir Golikov	Dan Soderstrom
John Harrington	Aleksandr Skvortzov	Lars Molin

The U.S.A. hockey team celebrated wildly after its 4-3 upset victory in the semi-finals against the heavily favored Soviet team in 1980. A 4-2 victory over Finland in the final game secured the gold medal for the American skaters.

OLYMPIC RECORDS

ARCHERY

EVENT	POINTS	NAME & COUNTRY	YEAR
Men's Double FITA	2571	Darrell Pace (USA)	1976
Women's Double FITA	2499	Luann Ryon (USA)	1976

CYCLING

EVENT	MIN/SEC	NAME & COUNTRY	YEAR
1000 meters time trial	1 02.955	Lothar Thoms (GDR)	1980
4000 meters individual pursuit	4 34.92	Robert Dill-Bundi (SWI)	1980
4000 meters team pursuit	4 14.64	U.S.S.R.	1980

SHOOTING

EVENT	POINTS	NAME & COUNTRY	YEAR
Small bore rifle (3 pos)	1173	Viktor Vlasov (URS)	1980
Small bore rifle(prone)	599	Ho Jun Li (PRK)	1972
	599	Karl-Heinz Smieszek (GER)	1976
	599	Karoly Varga (HUN)	1980
	599	Hellfried Heilfort (GDR)	1980
Free pistol	581	Aleksandr Melentev (URS)	1980
Rapid fire pistol	597	Norbert Klaar (GDR)	1976
Running game	589	Igor Sokolov (URS)	1980
	589	Thomas Pfeffer (GDR)	1980
Trap	199	Angelo Scalzone (ITA)	1972
Skeet	198	Evgeny Petrov (URS)	1968
	198	Romano Garagnani (ITA)	1968
	198	Konrad Wirnhier (GER)	1968
	198	Josef Panacek (TCH)	1976
	198	Eric Swinkels (HOL)	1976
	198	Luciano Giovannetti (ITA)	1980

SWIMMING

MEN

EVENT	MIN./SEC.	NAME & COUNTRY	YEAR
100 meters freestyle	49.99	James Montgomery (USA)	1976
200 meters freestyle	1 49.81	Sergey Kopliakov (URS)	1980
400 meters freestyle	3 51.31	Vladimir Salnikov (URS)	1980
1500 meters freestyle	14 58.27	Vladimir Salnikov (URS)	1980
4 × 100 meters freestyle relay	3 26.42	U.S.A	1972
4 × 200 meters freestyle relay	7 23.22	U.S.A.	1976
100 meters breaststroke	1 03.11	John Hencken (USA)	1976
200 meters breaststroke	2 15.11	David Wilkie (GBR)	1976
100 meters butterfly	54.27	Mark Spitz (USA)	1972
200 meters butterfly	1 59.23	Michael Bruner (USA)	1976
100 meters backstroke	55.49	John Naber (USA)	1976
200 meters backstroke	1 59.19	John Naber (USA)	1976
200 meters medley	2 07.17	Gunnar Larsson (SWE)	1972
400 meters medley	4 22.89	Aleksandr Sidorenko (URS)	1980
4 × 100 meters medley relay	3 42.22	U.S.A.	1976

WOMEN

100 meters freestyle			54.79	Barbara Krause (GDR)	1980
200 meters freestyle		1	58.33	Barbara Krause (GDR)	1980
400 meters freestyle		4	08.76	Ines Diers (GDR)	1980
800 meters freestyle		8	28.90	Michelle Ford (AUS)	1980
4 × 100 meters freestyle relay		3	42.71	East Germany	1980
100 meters breaststroke		1	10.11	Ute Geweniger (GDR)	1980
200 meters breaststroke		2	29.54	Lina Kachushite (URS)	1980
100 meters butterfly		1	00.13	Kornelia Ender (GDR)	1976
200 meters butterfly		2	10.44	Ines Geissler (GDR)	1980
100 meters backstroke		1	00.86	Rica Reinisch (GDR)	1980
200 meters backstroke		2	11.77	Rica Reinisch (GDR)	1980
200 meters medley		2	23.07	Shane Gould (AUS)	1972
400 meters medley		4	36.29	Petra Schneider (GDR)	1980
4 × 100 meters medley relay		4	06.67	East Germany	1980

TRACK & FIELD ATHLETICS

MEN

EVENT	HR	MIN	SEC	NAME & COUNTRY	YEAR
100 meters			9.95	Jim Hines (USA)	1968
200 meters			19.83	Tommie Smith (USA)	1968
400 meters			43.86	Lee Evans (USA)	1968
800 meters		1	43.50	Alberto Juantorena (CUB)	1976
1500 meters		3	34.91	Kipchoge Keino (KEN)	1968
5000 meters		13	20.34	Brendan Foster (GBR)	1976
10000 meters		27	38.35	Lasse Viren (FIN)	1972
Marathon	2	09	55.0	Waldemar Cierpinski (GDR)	1976
20 km walk	1	23	36.0	Maurizio Damilano (ITA)	1980
50 km walk	3	49	24.0	Hartwig Gauder (GDR)	1980
110 meters hurdles			13.24	Rod Milburn (USA)	1972
400 meters hurdles			47.64	Ed Moses (USA)	1976
3000 meters steeplechase		8	08.02	Anders Garderud (SWE)	1976
4 × 100 meters relay			38.19	U.S.A.	1968
			38.19	U.S.A.	1972
4 × 400 meters relay		2	56.16	U.S.A.	1968

	meters		
High jump	2.36	Gerd Wessig (GDR)	1980
Pole vault	5.78	Wladyslaw Kozakiewics (POL)	1980
Long jump	8.90	Bob Beamon (USA)	1968
Triple jump	17.39	Viktor Saneyev (URS)	1968
Shot put	21.35	Vladimir Kiselyev (URS)	1980
Discus throw	68.28	Mac Wilkins (USA)	1976
Hammer throw	81.80	Yuriy Sedykh (URS)	1980
Javelin throw	94.58	Miklos Nemeth (HUN)	1976
Decathlon	8618 points	Bruce Jenner (USA)	1976

WOMEN

	MIN	SEC		
100 meters		11.01	Annegret Richter (GER)	1976
200 meters		22.03	Barbel Wöckel (GDR)	1980
400 meters		48.88	Marita Koch (GDR)	1980
800 meters	1	53.43	Nadezda Olizarenko (URS)	1980
1500 meters	3	56.56	Tatyana Kazankina (URS)	1980
3000 meters	Not previously held			
Marathon	Not previously held			
100 meters hurdles		12.56	Vera Komissova (URS)	1980
400 meters hurdles	Not previously held			
4 × 100 meters relay		41.60	East Germany	1980
4 × 400 meters relay	3	19.23	East Germany	1976

	meters		
High jump	1.97	Sara Simeoni (ITA)	1980
Long jump	7.06	Tatyana Kolpakova (URS)	1980

Shot put	22.41	Ilona Slupianek (GDR)	1980
Discus throw	69.96	Evelin Jahl (GDR)	1980
Javelin throw	68.40	Maria Colon (CUB)	1980
Heptathlon	Not previously held		

WEIGHTLIFTING

EVENT	TOTAL WEIGHT (KG)	NAME & COUNTRY	YEAR
52 kg class	245.0	Kanykek Osmonoliev (URS)	1980
	245.0	Ho Bong Chol (PRK)	1980
	245.0	Han Gyong Si (PRK)	1980
	245.0	Bela Olah (HUN)	1980
56 kg class	275.0	Daniel Nunez (CUB)	1980
60 kg class	290.0	Viktor Mazin (URS)	1980
67.5 kg class	342.5	Yanko Rusev (BUL)	1980
75 kg class	360.0	Asen Zlatev (BUL)	1980
82.5 kg class	400.0	Yurik Vardanyan (URS)	1980
90 kg class	382.5	David Rigert (URS)	1976
100 kg class	395.0	Ota Zaremba (TCH)	1980
110 kg class	422.5	Leonid Taranenko (URS)	1980
100 + kg class	440.0	Vasiliy Alexeyev (URS)	1976
	440.0	Sultan Rachmanov (URS)	1980

SPEED SKATING

MEN EVENT	MIN	SEC	NAME & COUNTRY	YEAR
500 meters		38.03	Eric Heiden (USA)	1980
1000 meters	1	15.18	Eric Heiden (USA)	1980
1500 meters	1	55.44	Eric Heiden (USA)	1980
3000 meters	7	02.29	Eric Heiden (USA)	1980
5000 meters	14	28.13	Eric Heiden (USA)	1980

WOMEN	MIN	SEC	NAME & COUNTRY	YEAR
500 meters		41.78	Karin Enke (GDR)	1980
1000 meters	1	24.10	Natalya Petruseva (URS)	1980
1500 meters	2	10.95	Annie Borcvink (HOL)	1980
3000 meters	4	32.13	Bjorg-Eva Jenssen (NOR)	1980

ANOTHER IMPRESSIVE RECORD HOLDER

In the U.S., Slow-K has the following clinical record for 1975-1982:*
- 9.4 million patients treated[†]
- 51.8 million new and refill prescriptions
- 4.3 billion tablets dispensed

In 1982 alone:*
- 2,043,000 patients treated[†]
- 10,951,000 new and refill prescriptions
- 939,595,800 tablets dispensed

In 1983 alone:*
- Still the most widely prescribed K supplement[‡]
- Averaging over 800,000 total (new and refill) prescriptions per month
- Over 500,000 more total (new and refill) prescriptions per month ahead of the second most prescribed K supplement

It delivers.

Slow-K®
potassium chloride
slow-release tablets 8 mEq (600 mg)

References
1. Tarpley EL: Controlled-release potassium supplementation. *Curr Ther Res* 1974 (July); 16 (4): 734-741.
2. Hutchison JC: Clinical evaluation of a new sugar-coated potassium chloride supplement. *J Clin Pharmacol* 1974 (Nov-Dec); 14 (11 & 12): 624-629.
3. Data on file, CIBA Pharmaceutical Company.

Slow-K®
potassium chloride
slow-release tablets

DESCRIPTION
Slow-K is a sugar-coated (not enteric-coated) tablet containing 600 mg potassium chloride (equivalent to 8 mEq) in a wax matrix. This formulation is intended to provide a controlled release of potassium from the matrix to minimize the likelihood of producing high localized concentrations of potassium within the gastrointestinal tract.

ACTIONS
Potassium ion is the principal intracellular cation of most body tissues. Potassium ions participate in a number of essential physiological processes, including the maintenance of intracellular tonicity, the transmission of nerve impulses, the contraction of cardiac, skeletal, and smooth muscle and the maintenance of normal renal function.

Potassium depletion may occur whenever the rate of potassium loss through renal excretion and/or loss from the gastrointestinal tract exceeds the rate of potassium intake. Such depletion usually develops slowly as a consequence of prolonged therapy with oral diuretics, primary or secondary hyperaldosteronism, diabetic ketoacidosis, severe diarrhea, or inadequate replacement of potassium in patients on prolonged parenteral nutrition. Potassium depletion due to these causes is usually accompanied by a concomitant deficiency of chloride and is manifested by hypokalemia and metabolic alkalosis. Potassium depletion may produce weakness, fatigue, disturbances of cardiac rhythm (primarily ectopic beats), prominent U-waves in the electrocardiogram, and in advanced cases flaccid paralysis and/or impaired ability to concentrate urine.

Potassium depletion associated with metabolic alkalosis is managed by correcting the fundamental causes of the deficiency whenever possible and administering supplemental potassium chloride, in the form of high potassium food or potassium chloride solution or tablets.

In rare circumstances (*eg*, patients with renal tubular acidosis) potassium depletion may be associated with metabolic acidosis and hyperchloremia. In such patients potassium replacement should be accomplished with potassium salts other than the chloride, such as potassium bicarbonate, potassium citrate, or potassium acetate.

INDICATIONS
BECAUSE OF REPORTS OF INTESTINAL AND GASTRIC ULCERATION AND BLEEDING WITH SLOW-RELEASE POTASSIUM CHLORIDE PREPARATIONS, THESE DRUGS SHOULD BE RESERVED FOR THOSE PATIENTS WHO CANNOT TOLERATE OR REFUSE TO TAKE LIQUID OR EFFERVESCENT POTASSIUM PREPARATIONS OR FOR PATIENTS IN WHOM THERE IS A PROBLEM OF COMPLIANCE WITH THESE PREPARATIONS.

1. For therapeutic use in patients with hypokalemia with or without metabolic alkalosis; in digitalis intoxication and in patients with hypokalemic familial periodic paralysis.
2. For prevention of potassium depletion when the dietary intake of potassium is inadequate in the following conditions: Patients receiving digitalis and diuretics for congestive heart failure; hepatic cirrhosis with ascites; states of aldosterone excess with normal renal function; potassium-losing nephropathy, and certain diarrheal states.

Slow-K® (potassium chloride)

3. The use of potassium salts in patients receiving diuretics for uncomplicated essential hypertension is often unnecessary when such patients have a normal dietary pattern. Serum potassium should be checked periodically, however, and, if hypokalemia occurs, dietary supplementation with potassium-containing foods may be adequate to control milder cases. In more severe cases supplementation with potassium salts may be indicated.

CONTRAINDICATIONS

Potassium supplements are contraindicated in patients with hyperkalemia since a further increase in serum potassium concentration in such patients can produce cardiac arrest. Hyperkalemia may complicate any of the following conditions: chronic renal failure, systemic acidosis such as diabetic acidosis, acute dehydration, extensive tissue breakdown as in severe burns, adrenal insufficiency, or the administration of a potassium-sparing diuretic (eg, spironolactone, triamterene).

Wax-matrix potassium chloride preparations have produced esophageal ulceration in certain cardiac patients with esophageal compression due to an enlarged left atrium.

All solid dosage forms of potassium supplements are contraindicated in any patient in whom there is cause for arrest or delay in tablet passage through the gastrointestinal tract. In these instances, potassium supplementation should be with a liquid preparation.

WARNINGS

Hyperkalemia

In patients with impaired mechanisms for excreting potassium, the administration of potassium salts can produce hyperkalemia and cardiac arrest. This occurs most commonly in patients given potassium by the intravenous route but may also occur in patients given potassium orally. Potentially fatal hyperkalemia can develop rapidly and be asymptomatic.

The use of potassium salts in patients with chronic renal disease, or any other condition which impairs potassium excretion, requires particularly careful monitoring of the serum potassium concentration and appropriate dosage adjustment.

Interaction with Potassium-Sparing Diuretics

Hypokalemia should not be treated by the concomitant administration of potassium salts and a potassium-sparing diuretic (eg, spironolactone or triamterene), since the simultaneous administration of these agents can produce severe hyperkalemia.

Gastrointestinal lesions

Potassium chloride tablets have produced stenotic and/or ulcerative lesions of the small bowel and deaths. These lesions are caused by a high localized concentration of potassium ion in the region of a rapidly dissolving tablet, which injures the bowel wall and thereby produces obstruction, hemorrhage, or perforation. Slow-K is a wax-matrix tablet formulated to provide a controlled rate of release of potassium chloride and thus to minimize the possibility of a high local concentration of potassium ion near the bowel wall. While the reported frequency of small-bowel lesions is much less with wax-matrix tablets (less than one per 100,000 patient-years) than with enteric-coated potassium chloride tablets (40-50 per 100,000 patient-years), cases associated with wax-matrix tablets have been reported both in foreign countries and in the United States. In addition, perhaps because the wax-matrix preparations are not enteric-coated and release potassium in the stomach, there have been reports of upper gastrointestinal bleeding associated with these products. The total number of gastrointestinal lesions remains approximately one per 100,000 patient-years. Slow-K should be discontinued immediately and the possibility of bowel obstruction or perforation considered if severe vomiting, abdominal pain, distention, or gastrointestinal bleeding occurs.

Metabolic acidosis

Hypokalemia in patients with metabolic *acidosis* should be treated with an alkalinizing potassium salt such as potassium bicarbonate, potassium citrate, or potassium acetate.

PRECAUTIONS

The diagnosis of potassium depletion is ordinarily made by demonstrating hypokalemia in a patient with a clinical history suggesting some cause for potassium depletion. In interpreting the serum potassium level, the physician should bear in mind that acute alkalosis *per se* can produce hypokalemia in the absence of a deficit in total body potassium, while acute acidosis *per se* can increase the serum potassium concentration into the normal range even in the presence of a reduced total body potassium. The treatment of potassium depletion, particularly in the presence of cardiac disease, renal disease, or acidosis, requires careful

Prescribing Information continued on next page.

Slow-K®(potassium chloride)

Continuation of Prescribing Information

attention to acid-base balance and appropriate monitoring of serum electrolytes, the electrocardiogram, and the clinical status of the patient.

ADVERSE REACTIONS

The most common adverse reactions to oral potassium salts are nausea, vomiting, abdominal discomfort, and diarrhea. These symptoms are due to irritation of the gastrointestinal tract and are best managed by diluting the preparation further, taking the dose with meals, or reducing the dose.

One of the most severe adverse effects is hyperkalemia (see Contraindications, Warnings and Overdosage). There also have been reports of upper and lower gastrointestinal conditions including obstruction, bleeding, ulceration and perforation (see Contraindications and Warnings); other factors known to be associated with such conditions were present in many of these patients. Skin rash has been reported rarely.

OVERDOSAGE

The administration of oral potassium salts to persons with normal excretory mechanisms for potassium rarely causes serious hyperkalemia. However, if excretory mechanisms are impaired or if potassium is administered too rapidly intravenously, potentially fatal hyperkalemia can result (see Contraindications and Warnings). It is important to recognize that hyperkalemia is usually asymptomatic and may be manifested only by an increased serum potassium concentration and characteristic electrocardiographic changes (peaking of T-waves, loss of P-wave, depression of S-T segment, and prolongation of the QT interval). Late manifestations include muscle paralysis and cardiovascular collapse from cardiac arrest.

Treatment measures for hyperkalemia include the following: (1) elimination of foods and medications containing potassium and of potassium-sparing diuretics; (2) intravenous administration of 300 to 500 ml/hr of 10% dextrose solution containing 10-20 units of insulin per 1,000 ml; (3) correction of acidosis, if present, with intravenous sodium bicarbonate; (4) use of exchange resins, hemodialysis, or peritoneal dialysis.

In treating hyperkalemia, it should be recalled that in patients who have been stabilized on digitalis, too rapid a lowering of the serum potassium concentration can produce digitalis toxicity.

DOSAGE AND ADMINISTRATION

The usual dietary intake of potassium by the average adult is 40 to 80 mEq per day. Potassium depletion sufficient to cause hypokalemia usually requires the loss of 200 or more mEq of potassium from the total body store. Dosage must be adjusted to the individual needs of each patient but is typically in the range of 20 mEq per day for the prevention of hypokalemia to 40-100 mEq per day or more for the treatment of potassium depletion.

Note: Slow-K slow-release tablets must be swallowed whole and never crushed or chewed.

HOW SUPPLIED

Tablets 600 mg potassium chloride (equiv. to 8 mEq)—round, buff colored, sugar-coated (imprinted CIBA 165)

Bottles of 100 . . . . NDC 0083-0165-30
Bottles of 1000 . . . . NDC 0083-0165-40
Consumer Pack–One Unit
  (12 Bottles–100 tablets each) . . . . NDC 0083-0165-65
Accu-Pak® Unit Dose (blister pack)
  Box of 100 (strips of 10) . . . . NDC 0083-0165-32
Protect from moisture. Protect from light.
Do not store above 86°F (30°C).
Dispense in tight, light-resistant container (USP)   C82-58 (Rev. 1/83)

Consult complete product information before prescribing.

Dist. by:
CIBA Pharmaceutical Company
Division of CIBA-GEIGY Corporation
Summit, New Jersey 07901

C I B A